M I L L E R

NOT-FOR-PROFIT
REPORTING

A/C   TA

100   200

INC TAX REF   30   60   Δ = 30
     42   30   0

    AR 60

41   INC TAX REF   30
            DEO TAX LIAB 30
_____

42   DEO TAX LIAB 30
          INC TAX REF 30

NOT-FOR-PROFIT REPORTING

GAAP
Tax, Financial, and Regulatory Requirements

Mary F. Foster • Howard Becker
DELOITTE & TOUCHE LLP

Richard J. Terrano
ROSENBERG, NEUWIRTH & KUCHNER, CPAs PC

Harcourt
Professional Publishing

SAN DIEGO   NEW YORK   CHICAGO   LONDON

The publisher has not sought nor obtained approval of this publication from any other organization, profit or nonprofit, and is solely responsible for its contents.

Copyright © 2000 by Harcourt, Inc.

IMPRESS and logo is a trademark of Harcourt, Inc.

Printed in the United States of America

ISBN: 0-15-607011-1

99 00 01 02 MG 5 4 3 2 1

Contents

PART I: INTRODUCTION AND BACKGROUND

PART II: ACCOUNTING FOR NOT-FOR-PROFIT ORGANIZATIONS

PART III: EXTERNAL FINANCIAL REPORTING

PART IV: REGULATORY FINANCIAL REPORTING

Preface

Each year around this time, we review what has taken place in the accounting profession, to see how we can improve *Miller Not-for-Profit Reporting: GAAP, Tax, Financial, and Regulatory Requirements*. We improve by addition and subtraction. This year's edition adds to its already generous coverage to clarify the most important materials affecting not-for-profit organizations right now, including:

- FASB Statement No. 136 (Transfer of Assets to a Not-for-Profit Organization or Charitable Trust That Raises or Holds Contributions for Others)
- SAS-87 (Restricting the Use of an Auditor's Report)
- SAS-86 (Amendment to SAS No. 72, Letters for Underwriters and Certain Other Requesting Parties)

Subtraction occurs when we simplify and clarify the language contained in the original pronouncements. We are actively involved in not-for-profit engagements as auditors and advisors, and we work closely with other practitioners in our offices to make sure that we impart information in a user-friendly fashion. We trust that *Miller Not-for-Profit Reporting* is a useful tool for you.

Year 2000 issues have attracted the attention of entities of every stripe. GASB, FASB, and the AICPA have each spoken out about the accounting, auditing, and business attributes of the potential millennium bug. We really do not know what will happen on January 1, 2000, but in this edition of *Miller Not-for-Profit Reporting* we summarize the related activities and requirements of these standard-setters.

As we go to press, we are expecting a final Consolidated Financial Statements pronouncement from FASB, and the Board has just issued Statement No. 136, Transfers of Assets Involving a Not-for-Profit Organization That Raises or Holds Contributions for Others. The Governmental Accounting Standards Board (GASB) has finally issued its Reporting Model for state and local governments. (At the time of this writing, GASB's final version of a College and University Reporting Model is not expected imminently.) OMB has issued its new *Compliance Supplement* and has proposed revisions to its Circular A-110, *Uniform Administrative Requirements for Grants and Agreements with Institutions of Higher Education, Hospitals and Non-Profit Organizations*. The IRS has issued new regulations regarding Intermediate Sanctions. The IRS has also issued Proposed Regulations on Hope and Lifetime Learning Credits. The Clinton Administration has included in its budget proposal that net investment income of §501(c)(6) trade associations be subject to tax.

The AICPA's Not-for-Profit Organizations Committee has a busy agenda, including clarification of the accounting for HUD advances to not-for-profit organizations and reporting on comparative financial information if the prior-year information is less than a full GAAP presentation.

Finally, the General Accounting Office (GAO) has several Exposure Drafts outstanding that may result in changes and/or clarifications related to conducting Yellow Book audits. These are *Government Auditing Standards: Auditor Communication; Government Auditing Standards: Additional Documentation Requirements When Assessing Control Risk at Maximum for Computer-Related Controls; and Government Auditing Standards: Meaning of "Present Fairly in Conformity with Generally Accepted Accounting Principles" in Reports on Financial Statements of the Federal Government and Its Component Entities.*

Miller Not-for-Profit Reporting is organized to focus first on existing pronouncements and proposed pronouncements that are expected to be issued in the near future. Those pronouncements apply directly to not-for-profit organizations and are covered in Part I, "Introduction and Background." Part II, "Accounting for Not-for-Profit Organizations," addresses accounting for individual account types and transactions recorded in the books of a not-for-profit organization. Part III, "External Financial Reporting," deals with external financial reporting, and Part IV, "Regulatory Financial Reporting," deals with regulatory reporting in the government arena, including requirements of the OMB Circulars and federal and state tax rules.

This volume analyzes all FASB Statements to the extent that they relate to reporting by not-for-profit organizations. Accordingly, not all of the recent pronouncements will be reported on in depth. As we did last year, we encourage you to use the *Miller Complete Library for Business*—consisting of the *Miller GAAP Guide*, the *Miller GAAP Implementation Manual*, and the monthly *Miller GAAP Update Service*—also published by Harcourt—to keep current on accounting and reporting matters that pertain to all entities.

This edition of *Miller Not-for-Profit Reporting* continues to include sample financial statements for different types of not-for-profit organizations. Appendixes A and B present a net asset class model and a fund accounting model, respectively. In sample format in Appendix C are financial statements that the authors have gathered from their own practices. We have disguised them as much as possible to prevent identification of specific organizations.

IMPRESS™ Cross References

IMPRESS™ stands for the Integrated Miller Professional Reference and Engagement Series System. It is the system by which all Miller publications are thoroughly cross-referenced to one another on a chapter-by-chapter basis. The system is designed to facilitate comprehensive research and to assure that you will always find the complete answers you need. The IMPRESS™ Comprehensive Table of Contents shows the system in its entirety across all Miller reference guides. The IMPRESS™ Cross-References at the beginning of each chapter refer you to corresponding chapters in our reference and engagement publications as well as to related chapters in 2000 *Miller Not-for-Profit Reporting.* The foundation of the IMPRESS™ system is the GAAP hierarchy of authoritative accounting pronouncements, established by Statement on Auditing Standards (SAS) No. 69 (The Meaning of "Present Fairly in Conformity with Generally Accepted Accounting Principles" in the Independent Auditor's Report).

Mary Foster
Howard Becker
Richard Terrano

About the Authors

Mary F. Foster, CPA

Mary F. Foster, CPA, is a partner in the New York Tri-State office of Deloitte & Touche LLP, and serves as the firm's National Director for the Nonprofit Industry Group. She has more than twenty years of service in public accounting and for the past seventeen years has served not-for-profit organizations.

Ms. Foster is contributing author of Deloitte & Touche's national newsletter, *Not-for-Profit Review*; serves on the editorial board of the *CPA Government & Nonprofit Report*, a Harcourt professional publication; and is co-author of "Implementation Issues of FASB Statements No. 116 'Accounting for Contributions' and No. 117 'Financial Statement Display for Nonprofit Organizations,'" in *Journal of Corporate and Accounting Finance*. Ms. Foster previously has served as the chairperson for the American Institute of Certified Public Accountants Not-for-Profit Organizations Committee. She is a frequent speaker at not-for-profit conferences.

Howard Becker, CPA

Howard Becker, CPA, Director in the New York Tri-State office of Deloitte & Touche LLP, has more than thirty years of service in public accounting, the past twelve with Deloitte & Touche LLP. He has served clients in all segments of the economy. For the past eight years, he has concentrated in the area of not-for-profit organizations and the related field of compliance auditing. At Deloitte & Touche LLP, Mr. Becker is a member of the Tri-State Region's Professional Practices Group and is the independent reviewer for substantially all not-for-profit audits.

For the past six years, Mr. Becker has been the editor of Deloitte & Touche's national newsletter, *Not-for-Profit Review*. For four years with Main Hurdman and Co. (prior to its merger with KPMG Peat Marwick), Mr. Becker was the coordinator for its accounting newsletter, the *MainView*. He has presented numerous seminars to clients and others on a wide variety of subjects, most recently concentrating on the changes to OMB Circular A-133.

Mr. Becker is a member of the American Institute of Certified Public Accountants, NACUBO, and a member of the New York State Society of Certified Public Accountants, for which he is currently serving on the Not-for-Profit Organizations and Government Accounting and Auditing Committees.

Richard J. Terrano, CPA

Richard J. Terrano, CPA, is a partner and the Director of Not-for-Profit Services at Rosenberg, Neuwirth and Kuchner, CPAs PC (RNK). Before joining RNK, he was a Senior Manager in the Deloitte & Touche Middle Market Services Group. While he has significant expertise in not-for-profit accounting and taxation, Mr. Terrano also has substantial experience serving closely held companies in the areas of manufacturing, service, distribution, and other industries. He is a member of the American Institute of Certified Public Accountants and the New York and New Jersey State Societies of Certified Public Accountants.

Abbreviations

The following abbreviations are used throughout the book to represent common accounting and auditing publications, principles, and terms:

ACNO	AICPA Audit and Accounting Guide *Audits of Certain Nonprofit Organizations*
ACU	AICPA Audit and Accounting Guide *Audits of Colleges and Universities*
AICPA	American Institute of Certified Public Accountants
APB	Accounting Principles Board
ARB	Accounting Research Bulletin
AVHWO	AICPA Audit and Accounting Guide *Audits of Voluntary Health and Welfare Organizations*
CAS	Cost Accounting Standard
CASB	Cost Accounting Standards Board
FAS-#	FASB Statement
FASB	Financial Accounting Standards Board
FASB:CON	FASB Concepts Statement
GAAP	Generally accepted accounting principles
GAAS	Generally accepted auditing standards
GAS	*Government Auditing Standards* (Yellow Book)
GASB	Governmental Accounting Standards Board
GASB-#	GASB Statements
HCO	AICPA Audit and Accounting Guide *Health Care Organizations*
IRC	Internal Revenue Code
IRS	Internal Revenue Service
NPO	AICPA Audit and Accounting Guide *Not-for-Profit Organizations*
OMB	Office of Management and Budget
SAS	AICPA Statement on Auditing Standards
SEC	Securities and Exchange Commission
SOP	AICPA Statement of Position

Accounting Resources on the Web

The following World Wide Web addresses are just a few of the resources on the Internet that are available to practitioners. Because of the evolving nature of the Internet, some addresses may change. In such a case, refer to one of the many Internet search engines, such as Yahoo! (http://www.yahoo.com).

AICPA   http://www.aicpa.org/

American Accounting Association   http://www.rutgers.edu/accounting/raw/aaa/

FASB   http://www.rutgers.edu:80//Accounting/raw/fasb/

Federal Tax Code Search   http://www.tns.lcs.mit.edu:80/uscode/

Fedworld   http://www.fedworld.gov

GASB   http://www.rutgers.edu/Accounting/raw/gasb/

General Accounting Office   http://www.gao.gov/

Harcourt Professional Publishing   http://www.hbpp.com

House of Representatives   http://www.house.gov/

IRS Digital Daily   http://www.irs.ustreas.gov/prod/cover.html

Library of Congress   http://lcweb.loc.gov/homepage/

Office of Management and Budget   http://www.gpo.gov/omb/omb001.html

Securities and Exchange Commission   http://www.sec.gov/

Thomas Legislative Research   http://thomas.loc.gov/

IMPRESS™

INTEGRATED MILLER PROFESSIONAL REFERENCE AND ENGAGEMENT SERIES SYSTEM

IMPRESS™ stands for the Integrated Miller Professional Reference and Engagement Series System. It is the system by which all Miller publications are thoroughly cross-referenced to one another on a chapter-by-chapter basis. The system is designed to facilitate comprehensive research and to assure that you will always find the complete answers you need.

Comprehensive Table of Contents
GENERALLY ACCEPTED ACCOUNTING PRINCIPLES

MILLER GUIDE CHAPTER*

IMPRESS™ Topic	2000 MILLER GAAP GUIDE	2000 MILLER GAAP IMPLEMENTATION MANUAL	2000 MILLER GOVERNMENTAL GAAP GUIDE	2000 MILLER GAAS GUIDE	2000 MILLER NOT-FOR-PROFIT REPORTING
Accounting Changes	1	1	—	342, 420	—
Accounting Policies and Standards	2	2	2, 3	411, 420, 431, 544	9

*Section for *GAAS Guide*

CROSS-REFERENCE

ORIGINAL PRONOUNCEMENTS TO
MILLER NOT-FOR-PROFIT REPORTING

This locator provides instant cross-reference between an original pronouncement and the chapter(s) in this publication in which a pronouncement is covered. Original pronouncements are listed chronologically on the left and the chapter(s) in which they appear in the *1999 Miller Not-for-Profit Reporting* on the right.

ACCOUNTING RESEARCH BULLETINS

ORIGINAL PRONOUNCEMENT	*NOT-FOR-PROFIT REPORTING* REFERENCE
ARB No. 51 Consolidated Financial Statements	
	Overview of Current Pronouncements, ch. **2** Organizational Issues, ch. **7**

ACCOUNTING PRINCIPLES BOARD OPINIONS

ORIGINAL PRONOUNCEMENT	*NOT-FOR-PROFIT REPORTING* REFERENCE
APB Opinion No. 9 Reporting the Results of Operations	
	Overview of Current Pronouncements, ch. **2**
APB Opinion No. 12 Omnibus Opinion—1967	
	Overview of Current Pronouncements, ch. **2**
APB Opinion No. 16 Business Combinations	
	Overview of Current Pronouncements, ch. **2** Organizational Issues, ch. **7**

APB Opinion No. 18

The Equity Method of Accounting for Investments in Common Stock

APB Opinion No. 21

Interest on Receivables and Payables

APB Opinion No. 26

Early Extinguishment of Debt

APB Opinion No. 29

Accounting for Nonmonetary Transactions

APB Opinion No. 30

Reporting the Results of Operations—Reporting the Effects of Disposal of a Segment of a Business, and Extraordinary, Unusual and Infrequently Occurring Events and Transactions

FINANCIAL ACCOUNTING STANDARDS BOARD STATEMENTS

ORIGINAL PRONOUNCEMENT

NOT-FOR-PROFIT REPORTING
REFERENCE

Original Pronouncements

FASB Statement No. 4

Reporting Gains and Losses from Extinguishment of Debt

FASB Statement No. 5

Accounting for Contingencies

FASB Statement No. 14

Financial Reporting for Segments of a Business Enterprise

FASB Statement No. 136
Transfer of Assets to a Not-for-Profit Organiza-
tion or Charitable Trust That Raises or Holds
Contributions for Others

Liabilities, ch. **6**

FINANCIAL ACCOUNTING STANDARDS BOARD INTERPRETATIONS

ORIGINAL PRONOUNCEMENT	*NOT-FOR-PROFIT REPORTING* REFERENCE

FASB Interpretation No. 14
Reasonable Estimation of the Amount of a Loss

Overview of Current Pronouncements, ch. **2**

FASB Interpretation No. 40
Applicability of Generally Accepted Account-
ing Principles to Mutual Life Insurance and
Other Enterprises

Overview of Current Pronouncements, ch. **2**

FASB Interpretation No. 42
Accounting for Transfers of Assets in Which a
Not-for-Profit Organization Is Granted Vari-
ance Power

Overview of Current Pronouncements, ch. **2**

FINANCIAL ACCOUNTING STANDARDS BOARD TECHNICAL BULLETINS

ORIGINAL PRONOUNCEMENT	*NOT-FOR-PROFIT REPORTING* REFERENCE

FASB Technical Bulletin 79-5
Meaning of the Term "Customer" as It Applies
to Health Care Facilities under FASB Statement
No. 14

Organizational Issues, ch. **7**

FINANCIAL ACCOUNTING STANDARDS BOARD CONCEPTS STATEMENTS

ORIGINAL PRONOUNCEMENT	*NOT-FOR-PROFIT REPORTING* REFERENCE

FASB Concepts Statement No. 4
Objectives of Financial Reporting by Nonbusiness Organizations

Service Efforts and Accomplishments, ch. **12**

FASB Concepts Statement No. 6
Elements of Financial Statements

Expenses, ch. **4**

AICPA STATEMENTS OF POSITION

ORIGINAL PRONOUNCEMENT	*NOT-FOR-PROFIT REPORTING* REFERENCE

SOP 78-10 (10,250)

Accounting Principles and Reporting Practices for Certain Nonprofit Organizations (a)

Overview of Current Pronouncements, ch. **2**

Revenues, ch. **3**

Assets, ch. **5**

SOP 87-2 (10,420)

Accounting for Joint Costs of Informational Materials and Activities of Not-for-Profit Organizations That Include a Fund-Raising Appeal (a)

Overview of Current Pronouncements, ch. **2**

Expenses, ch. **4**

SOP 92-9 (11,260)

Audits of Not-for-Profit Organizations Receiving Federal Awards

Office of Management and Budget, ch. **15**

SOP 93-7

Reporting on Advertising Costs

Overview of Current Pronouncements, ch. **2**

SOP 94-2 (10,600)

The Application of the Requirements of Accounting Research Bulletins, Opinions of the Accounting Principles Board, and Statements and Interpretations of the Financial Accounting Standards Board to Not-for-Profit Organizations (a)

Overview of Current Pronouncements, ch. **2**

SOP 94-3 (10,610)

Reporting of Related Entities by Not-for-Profit Organizations

Overview of Current Pronouncements, ch. **2**

Revenues, ch. **3**

Organizational Issues, ch. **7**

SOP 94-6 (10,640)

Disclosure of Certain Significant Risks and Uncertainties

Overview of Current Pronouncements, ch. **2**

Expenses, ch. **4**

(a) Superseded by AICPA Audit and Accounting Guide *Not-for-Profit Organizations.*

SOP 98-1

Disclosure for the Costs of Computer Software
Developed or Obtained for Internal Use

Overview of Current Pronouncements, ch. **2**

SOP 98-2

Accounting for Costs of Activities of Not-for-
Profit Organizations and State and Local Governmental Entities that Include Fund-Raising

Overview of Current Pronouncements, ch. **2**
Expenses, ch. **4**

SOP 98-3

Audits of States, Local Governments, and Not-
for-Profit Organizations Receiving Federal
Awards

Overview of Current Pronouncements, ch. **2**
Office of Management and Budget, ch. **15**

SOP 98-5

Reporting on the Costs of Start-up Activities

Overview of Current Pronouncements, ch. **2**

AICPA AUDIT AND ACCOUNTING GUIDES

ORIGINAL PRONOUNCEMENT	NOT-FOR-PROFIT REPORTING REFERENCE
Audits of Certain Nonprofit Organizations (a)	Overview of Current Pronouncements, ch. **2**
Audits of Colleges and Universities (a)	Overview of Current Pronouncements, ch. **2**
Audits of Providers of Health Care Services (a)	Overview of Current Pronouncements, ch. **2**
Audits of Voluntary Health and Welfare Organizations (a)	Overview of Current Pronouncements, ch. **2**
Health Care Organizations	Overview of Current Pronouncements, ch. **2**
Not-for-Profit Organizations	Overview of Current Pronouncements, ch. **2** Service Efforts and Accomplishments, ch. **12**

(a) Superseded by AICPA Audit and Accounting Guide *Not-for-Profit Organizations*.

AICPA STATEMENTS ON AUDITING STANDARDS

SAS-83
Establishing an Understanding With the Client

Overview of Current Pronouncements, ch. **2**

SAS-84
Communications Between Predecessor and Successor Auditors

Overview of Current Pronouncements, ch. **2**

SAS-85
Management Representations

Overview of Current Pronouncements, ch. **2**

SAS-86
Amendment to SAS No. 72, Letters for Underwriters and Certain Other Requesting Parties

Overview of Current Pronouncements, ch. **2**

SAS-87
Restricting the Use of an Auditor's Report

Overview of Current Pronouncements, ch. **2**

GENERAL ACCOUNTING OFFICE STANDARDS

ORIGINAL PRONOUNCEMENT	*NOT-FOR-PROFIT REPORTING* REFERENCE
Government Auditing Standards (Yellow Book)	Office of Management and Budget, ch. **15**

OFFICE OF MANAGEMENT AND BUDGET CIRCULARS

ORIGINAL PRONOUNCEMENT	GAAP FOR NOT-FOR-PROFITS REFERENCE
OMB Circular A-21 Cost Principles for Educational Institutions	Office of Management and Budget, ch. **15** Cost Accounting Standards, ch. **16**
OMB Circular A-110 Uniform Administrative Requirements for Grants and Agreements with Institutions of Higher Education, Hospitals, and Other Nonprofit Organizations	Office of Management and Budget, ch. **15**

OMB Circular A-122
Cost Principles for Nonprofit Organizations

Expenses, ch. **4**
Office of Management and Budget, ch. **15**
Cost Accounting Standards, ch. **16**

OMB Circular A-133
Audits of States, Local Governments, and Non-Profit Organizations

Office of Management and Budget, ch. **15**

OMB Circular A-133
Compliance Supplement

Office of Management and Budget, ch. **15**

COST ACCOUNTING STANDARDS

ORIGINAL PRONOUNCEMENT	NOT-FOR-PROFIT REPORTING REFERENCE

Cost Accounting Standard 401
Consistency in Estimating, Accumulating and Reporting Costs

Cost Accounting Standards, ch. **16**

Cost Accounting Standard 402
Consistency in Allocating Costs Incurred for the Same Purpose

Cost Accounting Standards, ch. **16**

Cost Accounting Standard 403
Allocation of Home Office Expenses to Segments

Cost Accounting Standards, ch. **16**

Cost Accounting Standard 404
Capitalization of Tangible Assets

Cost Accounting Standards, ch. **16**

Cost Accounting Standard 405
Accounting for Unallowable Costs

Cost Accounting Standards, ch. **16**

Cost Accounting Standard 406
Cost Accounting Period

Cost Accounting Standards, ch. **16**

Cost Accounting Standard 407
Use of Standard Costs for Direct Material and Direct Labor

Cost Accounting Standards, ch. **16**

PART I
INTRODUCTION AND BACKGROUND

Chapter 1
INTRODUCTION

CONTENTS

CHAPTER 1
INTRODUCTION

CROSS-REFERENCES

2000 MILLER GAAP GUIDE: Chapter 2, "Accounting Policies and Standards"

2000 MILLER GAAP IMPLEMENTATION MANUAL: Chapter 1, "Accounting Changes"

Description of a Not-for-Profit Organization

A not-for-profit entity is one that:

- Receives significant contributions from resource providers who do not expect a matching return;
- Does not expect to receive a profit from the goods and services it provides in fulfilling its mission; and
- Has no ownership interest as a for-profit entity would.

This description would preclude from classification as a "not-for-profit organization" those entities that provide proportionate benefits to owners or investors, e.g., employee benefit plans, credit unions, and farm cooperatives. FAS-116 (Accounting for Contributions Received and Contributions Made) provides the basis for the description.

Not-for-profit organizations serve a variety of purposes and constituencies. They educate the public through institutions of higher education, museums, and zoological and botanical societies; provide essential services to the indigent and those not able to care for themselves through social service and health care institutions; conduct research that will lead to a better quality of life; gather information for and represent special interests through membership organizations such as labor unions and trade and professional associations; and provide entertainment through public broadcasting stations, performing arts, and other cultural institutions. Nearly every activity in our daily lives is touched in some fashion by not-for-profit organizations. The introduction to American Institute of Certified Public Accountants (AICPA) Statement of Position (SOP) 78-10 (Accounting Principles and Reporting Practices for Certain Nonprofit Organizations) lists, in addition to the organizations noted in FAS-116, organizations that are considered not-for-profits:

- Cemetery organizations
- Civic organizations
- Fraternal organizations
- Libraries
- Political parties
- Private and community foundations
- Private elementary and secondary schools
- Religious organizations
- Research and scientific organizations
- Social and country clubs

associations
churches

Changing Not-for-Profit Accounting

In the last few years, the Financial Accounting Standards Board (FASB) and the AICPA have focused a great deal of attention on the not-for-profit arena. The FASB has issued a number of Statements, and the AICPA Accounting Standards Executive Committee (AcSEC) and Not-for-Profit Organizations and Health Care Committees have presented guidance through Industry Audit and Accounting Guides and Statements of Position, resulting in the rescission of several of the guides and the issuance of two new guides for not-for-profits and for health-care entities.

Specifically, two FASB Statements—FAS-116 and FAS-117 (Financial Statements of Not-for-Profit Organizations)—have established dramatic new accounting and reporting rules for not-for-profit organizations. Also, the AICPA has issued new Audit and Accounting Guides for not-for-profit organizations and health care entities. In addition, FAS-124 (Accounting for Certain Investments Held by Not-for-Profit Organizations) has introduced mark-to-market accounting for most securities owned by not-for-profit organizations. In concept, this is very similar to the accounting for investments of for-profit entities mandated by FAS-115 (Accounting for Certain

Investments in Debt and Equity Securities). Together, the FASB and the AICPA seem to be moving toward greater comparability and similarity between the financial statements of not-for-profit organizations and those of for-profit organizations.

The AICPA recognizes that most not-for-profit organizations have common characteristics. Through the issuance of its Guide *Not-for-Profit Organizations*, the AICPA expects to eliminate the separate guidance previously provided in its separate Guides for voluntary health and welfare organizations, certain nonprofit organizations, and colleges and universities.

> **OBSERVATION:** A task force of the AICPA Not-for-Profit Organizations committee is currently collecting and assembling samples of financial statements issued after the adoption of FAS-117. This task force will publish samples from the financial statements to display the flexibility allowed by the FASB and to allow organizations from similar organizations to develop "best practices" in the presentation of meaningful financial information for users of their financial statements.

In addition to FASB and AICPA actions, the federal government, through the Office of Management and Budget (OMB) has increased its activities relating to the administration of federal awards, costs charged to these programs, and audit requirements. Most notably, the OMB has revamped the single audit process. Final revisions to OMB Circular A-133 (Audits of States, Local Governments and Non-Profit Organizations) were issued in June 1996. Higher thresholds for triggering A-133's audit requirements may result in thousands of not-for-profit organizations no longer being subject to its provisions. The independent-auditor-driven, risk-based approach to selecting programs to test in accordance with A-133 may further reduce the number of audited federally funded programs.

> **OBSERVATION:** At the same time that OMB may be reducing the need for audits of assistance to not-for-profit organizations, states and funders within state governments may not relax their audit requirements. Auditees need to understand the audit requirements of programs from which they receive funding. Auditors must be aware of audit requirements in the localities in which they practice and aware of the requirements of local funders, because these requirements may not follow OMB Circular A-133.

Also, the Internal Revenue Service (IRS) has increased its scrutiny of not-for-profit organizations and their compliance with regulations relating to independent contractors, reporting of unrelated business income, private inurement, and other factors that affect a not-for-profit organization's ability to maintain its tax-exempt status. Regulations relating to intermediate sanctions for those who enter into excess benefit transactions with organizations will cause many to look at relationships with trustees and members of management.

Fund Accounting versus the Net Asset Class Model

Many not-for-profit organizations maintain their books of account using "fund accounting." Fund accounting provides the organization with a vehicle to observe limitations on resources received for particular purposes. Resources of the organization are classified for accounting purposes into funds associated with specific activities or objectives. A review of a chart of accounts for a college, for example, would provide a myriad of different funds related to fixed assets, loan funds, debt, funds restricted by the board of trustees, operating funds, and endowment funds. When preparing the financial statements, not-for-profit organizations group funds that have similar characteristics.

Until the issuance of FAS-117, significant differences existed between the financial statements of not-for-profit organizations and the financial statements of for-profit entities. The former provided more detail about the funds and the components of the assets and liabilities that related to the particular fund groupings. As a result, the financial statements could be quite cumbersome and difficult to understand. In fact, for colleges and universities, the financial statement that most resembled an income statement of a for-profit entity—the statement of current funds revenues, expenditures, and other changes—was always explained in the notes to the financial statements as not purporting to present the results of operations or the net income or loss for the period as would a statement of income or a statement of revenues and expenses. It merely reported on the activities of one of the funds maintained in the accounts of the institution.

FAS-117's goal was to have a not-for-profit organization's financial statements reflect the financial position, activities, and cash flows of the organization as a whole. This results in financial presentations that more closely resemble the financial statements of for-profit entities. In fact, FAS-117 permits preparers of financial statements of not-for-profit organizations the same flexibility in presenting information as is currently afforded preparers of financial statements of for-profit entities.

Future Developments

Not-for-profit organizations continue to face severe budget restrictions as governments and individuals tighten their belts. There is more stringent review of programs and the benefits yielded in relation to their costs. As funding decreases, organizations will have to make difficult decisions affecting survival, growth, and downsizing. Many organizations in the health care community are combining; this is also happening with social service organizations as they strive to maintain their programs.

The requirements of SOP 98-2 (Accounting for Costs of Activities of Not-for-Profit Organizations and State and Local Governmental Entities That Include Fund-Raising) will cause organizations to review how they present "joint costs." A presentation that shifts more cost to the fund-raising classification may cause a perception by funders that the not-for-profit is not well managed and, accordingly, is not worthy of contributions or grants for programs.

In addition to providing fewer funds, governments are looking more carefully at how their assistance is being spent, which means tighter reviews of internal controls at organizations. In addition to confronting expanded governmental scrutiny, not-for-profit organizations also must face increased media scrutiny. Recently, several highly visible not-for-profits have found their programs and costs scrutinized by the media. Waste and abuse at several not-for-profit organizations have come to the attention of the contributing public, and losses of funds through risky investing in derivative securities have raised questions about stewardship of contributed assets.

Chapter 2
OVERVIEW OF
CURRENT PRONOUNCEMENTS

CONTENTS

CHAPTER 2
OVERVIEW OF
CURRENT PRONOUNCEMENTS

CROSS-REFERENCES

2000 MILLER NOT-FOR-PROFIT REPORTING: Chapter 3, "Revenues"; Chapter 5, "Assets"; Chapter 6, "Liabilities"; Chapter 7, "Organizational Issues"; Chapter 9, "Note Disclosures"; Chapter 10, "Cash Flows"; Chapter 11, "Display of Certain GAAP Transactions"; Chapter 14, "Payroll and Miscellaneous Requirements"

2000 MILLER GAAP GUIDE: Chapter 4, "Business Combinations"; Chapter 8, "Consolidated Financial Statements"; Chapter 9, "Contingencies, Risks, and Uncertainties"; Chapter 16, "Extinguishment of Debt"; Chapter 17, "Financial Instruments"; Chapter 18, "Foreign Operations and Exchange"; Chapter 21, "Income Taxes"; Chapter 23, "Intangible Assets"; Chapter 25, "Interest on Receivables and Payables"; Chapter 28, "Investments in Debt and Equity Securities"; Chapter 31, "Long-Term Obligations"; Chapter 32, "Nonmonetary Transactions"; Chapter 39, "Related Party Disclosures"; Chapter 41, "Results of Operations"; Chapter 42, "Revenue Recognition"; Chapter 47, "Troubled Debt Restructuring"

2000 MILLER GAAP IMPLEMENTATION MANUAL: Chapter 3, "Advertising"; Chapter 4, "Balance Sheet Classification"; Chapter 6, "Business Combinations"; Chapter 12, "Contingencies, Risks and Uncertainties"; Chapter 16, "Extinguishment of Debt"; Chapter 17, "Financial Instruments"; Chapter 18, "Foreign Operations and Exchange"; Chapter 20, "Income Taxes"; Chapter 21, "Intangible Assets"; Chapter 22, "Interest on Receivables and Payables"; Chapter 25, "Investments in Debt and Equity Securities"; Chapter 28, "Nonmonetary Transactions"; Chapter 35, "Results of Operations"; Chapter 36, "Revenue Recognition"; Chapter 41, "Troubled Debt Restructuring"

2000 MILLER GOVERNMENTAL GAAP GUIDE: Chapter 5, "Governmental Financial Reporting"; Chapter 9, "Revenues"; Chapter 14, "Assets"; Chapter 17, "Liabilities"; Chapter 21, "Risk Financing and

Related Insurance Issues"; Chapter 30, "General Long-Term Debt Account Group"

2000 Miller GAAS Guide: Sections 310, 315, 316, 319, 325, 326, 332, 333, 341, 380, 411, 431, 504, 508, 532, 543, 634

2000 Miller Not-for-Profit Organization Audits: Chapter 1, "Introduction and Background"

Background

Not-for-profit organizations must follow the accounting standards set forth by the Financial Accounting Standards Board (FASB) unless they are defined as part of a governmental entity. Governmental not-for-profit organizations must follow the standards set forth by the Governmental Accounting Standards Board (GASB).

Not-for-profit organizations must follow all FASB pronouncements, unless the pronouncement specifically excludes them from its scope. In other words, not-for-profit organizations use the same accounting methods as commercial enterprises.

Not-for-profit organizations also must follow certain standards established by the American Institute of Certified Public Accountants (AICPA), including Statements of Position (SOP) and Industry and Audit and Accounting Guides.

Accounting principles specifically for not-for-profit organizations were first established in certain Audit Guides, which included the following:

NFP Guides:

1. • *Hospital Audit Guide,* originally issued in 1972

2. • *Audits of Voluntary Health and Welfare Organizations*

3. • *Audits of Certain Nonprofit Organizations*

In 1978, the AICPA issued SOP 78-10 (Accounting Principles and Reporting Practices for Certain Nonprofit Organizations) to establish accounting principles for those not-for-profit organizations that were not covered by one of the existing Audit Guides. Since that time, several AICPA and FASB pronouncements have superseded portions of SOP 78-10, including FASB Statement (FAS) No. 116, FAS-117, FAS-124, and SOP 94-3. Finally, in 1996, the AICPA issued a new Audit and Accounting Guide, *Not-for-Profit Organizations,* to supersede SOP 78-10 and the three aforementioned Audit and Accounting Guides in their entirety.

The pronouncements in this chapter have special significance to not-for-profit organizations. They are as follows:

- AICPA Audit and Accounting Guides
- SOP 78-10 (Accounting Principles and Reporting Practices for Certain Nonprofit Organizations) [superseded]
- SOP 87-2 (Accounting for Joint Costs of Informational Materials and Activities of Not-for-Profit Organizations That Include a Fund-Raising Appeal) [superseded by SOP 98-2 for years beginning on or after December 15, 1998]
- SOP 94-2 (The Application of the Requirements of Accounting Research Bulletins, Opinions of the Accounting Principles Board, and Statements and Interpretations of the Financial Accounting Standards Board to Not-for-Profit Organizations)
- SOP 94-3 (Reporting of Related Entities by Not-for-Profit Organizations)
- SOP 94-6 (Disclosure of Certain Significant Risks and Uncertainties)
- SOP 98-2 (Accounting for Costs of Activities of Not-for-Profit Organizations and State and Local Governmental Entities That Include Fund Raising) [effective for years beginning on or after December 15, 1998]
- SOP 98-3 (Audits of States, Local Governments, and Not-for-Profit Organizations Receiving Federal Awards)
- SOP 98-5 (Reporting on the Costs of Start-Up Activities)
- SAS-59 (The Auditor's Consideration of an Entity's Ability to Continue as a Going-Concern)
- SAS-64 (Omnibus Statement on Auditing Standards—1990)
- SAS-69 (The Meaning of "Present Fairly" in Conformity with Generally Accepted Accounting Principles" in the Independent Auditor's Report)
- SAS-72 (Letters for Underwriters and Certain Other Requesting Parties) [amended by SAS-86]
- SAS-78 (Consideration of Internal Control in a Financial Statement Audit: An Amendment to SAS No. 55)
- SAS-80 (An Amendment to Statement on Auditing Standards No. 31, Evidential Matter)
- SAS-81 (Auditing Investments)
- SAS-82 (Consideration of Fraud in a Financial Statement Audit)
- SAS-83 (Establishing an Understanding with the Client)
- SAS-84 (Communications Between Predecessor and Successor Auditors)
- SAS-85 (Management Representations)
- SAS-86 (Amendment to SAS No. 12, Letters for Underwriters and Certain Other Requesting Parties)
- SAS-87 (Restricting the Use of an Auditor's Report)

- FAS-63 (Financial Reporting by Broadcasters)
- FAS-93 (Recognition of Depreciation by Not-for-Profit Organizations)
- FAS-105 (Disclosure of Information About Financial Instruments with Off-Balance-Sheet Risk and Financial Instruments with Concentrations of Credit Risk)
- FAS-107 (Disclosures About Fair Value of Financial Instruments)
- FAS-116 (Accounting for Contributions Received and Contributions Made)
- FAS-117 (Financial Statements of Not-for-Profit Organizations)
- FAS-121 (Accounting for the Impairment of Long-Lived Assets and for Long-Lived Assets to Be Disposed Of)
- FAS-124 (Accounting for Certain Investments Held by Not-for-Profit Organizations)
- FAS-125 (Accounting for Transfers and Servicing of Financial Assets and Extinguishments of Liabilities)
- FAS-126 (Exemption from Certain Required Disclosures about Financial Instruments for Certain Nonpublic Entities)
- FAS-129 (Disclosure of Information about Capital Structure)
- FAS-132 (Employer's Disclosures about Pensions and Other Post Retirement Benefits)
- FAS-133 (Accounting for Derivative Instruments and Hedging Activities on Hedge Accounting)
- FAS-136 (Transfers of Assets to a Not-for-Profit Organization or Charitable Trust That Raises or Holds Contributions for Others)

Not-for-profit organizations that receive grants or other awards from the federal governmental also must follow cost and administrative requirements created by the Office of Management and Budget, the Cost Accounting Standards Board, and the federal agencies from which the not-for-profit organization receives its funds. These requirements are covered in detail in Part IV, "Regulatory Financial Reporting," of this Guide. OMB CASB

AICPA AUDIT AND ACCOUNTING GUIDES

As discussed in the section on "Statement on Auditing Standards No. 69," SAS-69 establishes a hierarchy for the sources of generally accepted accounting principles. It classifies sources of accounting principles into four categories, with Category A having the highest level of authority. Category B includes the following (SAS-69, par. 5):

Pronouncements of bodies, composed of expert accountants, that deliberate accounting issues in public forums for the purpose of establishing accounting principles or describing existing accounting practices that are generally accepted, provided those pronouncements have been exposed for public comment and have been cleared by a body referred to in category (a).

AICPA Audit and Accounting Guides are included in Category B and, accordingly, must be adhered to when recording and presenting transactions that are not specifically covered by FASB Statements, FASB Interpretations, Accounting Principles Board (APB) Opinions, and Accounting Research Bulletins (ARBs). AICPA members should be prepared to justify departures from the material in the Guides. The AICPA Guides currently applicable to not-for-profit organizations are:

/ / ①
- *Not-for-Profit Organizations* / /   ⊃uper cedes
②
- *Health Care Organizations*

In 1996, the AICPA Not-for-Profit Organizations Committee published an Audit and Accounting Guide titled *Not-for-Profit Organizations*. This Guide superseded the following documents:

- *Audits of Voluntary Health and Welfare Organizations*
- *Audits of Colleges and Universities*
- *Audits of Certain Nonprofit Organizations*
- SOP 74-8 (Financial Accounting and Reporting by Colleges and Universities)
- SOP 78-10 (Accounting Principles and Reporting Practices for Certain Nonprofit Organizations)

Simultaneously, the AICPA Health Care Committee and Health Care Audit Guide Task Force issued a Guide titled *Health Care Organizations*. This Guide superseded *Audits of Providers of Health Care Services*, SOP 89-5 (Financial Accounting and Reporting by Providers of Prepaid Health Care Service), and SOP 90-8 (Financial Accounting and Reporting by Continuing Care Retirement Communities).

Audits of Voluntary Health and Welfare Organizations

Audits of Voluntary Health and Welfare Organizations was originally issued in 1974 and had been revised periodically until, finally, in 1996 it was superseded by the issuance of the new Guide, *Not-for-Profit Organizations*.

The older Guide presented "recommendations of the AICPA Committee on Voluntary Health and Welfare Organizations on the application of generally accepted auditing standards to audits of financial statements of voluntary health and welfare organizations." It also presented recommendations and descriptions of financial accounting and reporting principles for these organizations. Voluntary health and welfare organizations are a class of not-for-profit organizations that derive their revenue "primarily from voluntary contributions from the general public to be used for general or specific purposes connected with health, welfare, or community services" (AVHWO, preface).

Audits of Colleges and Universities

Audits of Colleges and Universities was originally issued in 1973 and reissued each year. The most recent version, prior to the issuance of *Not-for-Profit Organizations*, included changes the AICPA staff felt were necessitated by the issuance of authoritative pronouncements since the Guide was originally issued.

The Guide presented "recommendations of the AICPA Committee on College and University Accounting and Auditing on the application of generally accepted auditing standards to audits of financial statements of colleges and universities," and included "the committee's recommendations on and descriptions of financial accounting and reporting principles and practices for colleges and universities."

This Guide does not relate to audits of private or independent schools. The preface to the Guide instructs auditors of financial statements of these institutions to refer to the guidance in *Audits of Certain Nonprofit Organizations*. The preface also notes:

> Governmental colleges and universities that follow the AICPA College Guide Model (as described in GASB Statement No. 15, *Governmental College and University Accounting and Financial Reporting Models*) should continue to apply the accounting provisions of this guide as modified by subsequent GASB pronouncements.

Therefore, governmental colleges and universities will not be adopting FAS-116 and FAS-117, which will reduce the comparability of financial statements of governmental colleges and universities and nongovernmental institutions of higher education.

Audits of Certain Nonprofit Organizations

Audits of Certain Nonprofit Organizations was originally issued in 1981 and reissued each year. The most current version includes changes the AICPA staff felt were necessitated by the issuance of authoritative pronouncements since the Guide was originally issued. This original pronouncement was superseded by the 1996 release titled *Not-for-Profit Organizations*. The Guide presented "recommendations of the AICPA Not-for-Profit Organizations Subcommittee on the application of generally accepted auditing standards to audits of financial statements of certain nonprofit organizations."

Chapter 1 of the Guide provides a lengthy, but not all-inclusive, list of organizations covered by the Guide. This listing is carried forward to, and expanded in, the new Guide on *Not-for-Profit Organizations*. The changes can be seen in Table 2-1.

Some of the differences between the 1981 Guide and the 1996 Guide reflect changes in our society (e.g., the inclusion of political action committees in the 1996 Guide). Others reflect the consolidation of three previously issued Guides into one Guide (i.e., the inclusion of certain educational institutions and voluntary health and welfare organizations in the Guide).

Audits of Providers of Health Care Services

Because many health care institutions have operating aspects that are similar to those of for-profit organizations, and because of the nature of their revenue streams (i.e., third-party reimbursements), these institutions were not included in either the older *Audits of Certain Nonprofit Organizations* or the 1996 *Not-for-Profit Organizations*. Instead, health care entities were required to follow the guidance in *Audits of Providers of Health Care Services*, an Industry Audit Guide. The AICPA has issued a revised version of this Guide, titled *Health Care Organizations*, which incorporates the provisions of FAS-116 and FAS-117 as they apply to health care institutions.

The drafters of the health care Guide were particularly interested in two issues:

1. Expirations of donor-imposed restrictions on long-lived assets
2. Accounting for investments

Expirations of donor-imposed restrictions on long-lived assets   The health care Guide eliminates the choice allowed by FAS-116 to recognize the expiration of donor-imposed restrictions on long-lived assets either (1) when the asset is placed into service or (2) over the useful life of the asset. The drafters of the Guide selected Option 1 "to achieve consistency of reporting for not-for-profit health care organizations, especially with respect to the operating measure."

> **OBSERVATION:** Although the AICPA is moving away from separate guidance for each type of not-for-profit organization, health care organizations will continue to use a specific Industry

Table 2-1: Organizations Covered by *Not-for-Profit Organizations* (partial list)

Audits of Certain Nonprofit Organizations	Not-for-Profit Organizations
Cemetery organizations	Cemetery organizations
Civic organizations	Civic and community organizations
*****	Colleges and universities
*****	Elementary and secondary schools
*****	Federated fund-raising organizations
Fraternal organizations	Fraternal organizations
Labor unions	Labor unions
Libraries	Libraries
Museums	Museums
Other cultural organizations	Other cultural organizations
Performing arts organizations	Performing arts organizations
Political parties	Political parties
*****	Political action committees
Private and community foundations	Private and community foundations
Private elementary and secondary schools	*****
Professional associations	Professional associations
Public broadcasting stations	Public broadcasting stations
Religious organizations	Religious organizations
Research and scientific organizations	Research and scientific organizations
Social and country clubs	Social and country clubs
Trade associations	Trade associations
*****	Voluntary health and welfare organizations
Zoological and botanical societies	Zoological and botanical societies

Audit Guide. This specialized guidance is not analyzed in detail in this publication. However, specific topics relevant to the health care industry are discussed. For example, Chapter 3 discusses third-party reimbursements, a funding mechanism that is essential to the resources provided to health care institutions.

STATEMENT OF POSITION 78-10

In December 1978, the Accounting Standards Division of the AICPA issued SOP 78-10 (Accounting Principles and Reporting Practices for Certain Nonprofit Organizations) to set standards for the many not-for-profit organizations not covered by the existing Industry Audit Guides: *Hospital Audit Guide* (1972), *Audits of Colleges and Universities* (1973), *Audits of Voluntary Health and Welfare Organizations* (1974), and *Audits of State and Local Governmental Units* (1974). Not-for-profit organizations following existing Industry Guides, employee benefit and pension plans, mutual insurance companies, mutual banks, trusts, and farm cooperatives were excluded from the provisions of SOP 78-10.

SOP 78-10's goal was to create uniformity in the reporting of not-for-profit organizations' financial statements and to set standards for the reporting of the organizations' available resources, the use of these resources, and the changes in the various fund balances. SOP 78-10 also set standards meant to improve the usability of financial information to the readers of the financial statements.

Although it was superseded by the 1996 Guide, *Not-for-Profit Organizations*, SOP 78-10 provided the basis for not-for-profit GAAP and so is discussed here.

Accrual Basis of Accounting

SOP 78-10 required not-for-profit organizations to use the accrual basis of accounting when preparing their financial statements. The use of the cash basis or other comprehensive basis of accounting (OCBOA) does not result in a financial statement presentation in accordance with generally accepted accounting principles. Statements prepared on the cash basis or OCBOA would be considered special-purpose statements, and auditor's reports must state that the statements are not in conformity with generally accepted accounting principles. SOP 78-10 also recommended that not-for-profit organizations disclose significant commitments that are not accrued in the notes to the financial statements or designate on the balance sheet the portion of fund balances that are committed.

Fund Accounting

SOP 78-10 recognized that many organizations receive restricted contributions and that organizations' boards may designate funds for specific programs. Fund accounting was seen as a way to provide information on restricted funds, as each fund would be a separate accounting entity. Common practice was to group the like-kind funds on the financial statements. The SOP supported the use of fund accounting to segregate unrestricted funds from restricted funds. Organizations choosing not to segregate these funds were required to disclose all significant restricted resources. (Note that FAS-117 allows the use of fund accounting but does not consider its use necessary.) Under the provisions of FAS-117, however, financial statement display is moving away from the disaggregated presentation as attention focuses on the organization as a whole and on donor intent—not on individual funds.

Basic Financial Statements

SOP 78-10 identified the following as the basic financial statements of a not-for-profit organization:

- Balance sheet
- Statement of activity
- Statement of changes in financial position

Much of the guidance provided by the SOP for the above statements has been superseded by FAS-116 and FAS-117. Some of the significant differences are as follows:

- SOP 78-10 required restricted revenues, whose restrictions were not met, to be reported as deferred income on the balance sheet. FAS-116 requires the recognition of restricted revenue when an unconditional contribution is received.

- SOP 78-10 did not require financial statements to present the totals of all funds of the organization. FAS-117 requires these totals and focuses the financial statements on the organization as a whole.

- SOP 78-10 recommended that not-for-profit organizations present a statement of changes in financial position. FAS-117 amended FAS-95 to require not-for-profits to present a statement of cash flows.

Comparative Financial Statements

SOP 78-10 and FAS-117 recommend the use of comparative financial statements. However, under both pronouncements, summarized prior years' information may *not* be a fair presentation in accordance with generally accepted accounting principles.

Carrying Amounts of Investments

Under SOP 78-10, organizations were allowed to report their investments on the following basis:

- When there existed both the ability and the intention to hold the securities to maturity, marketable debt securities could be reported at amortized cost, market value, or the lower of amortized cost or market value.

- Marketable equity securities and marketable debt securities that were not expected to be held to maturity could be reported at either market value or the lower of cost or market value.

- Other types of investments (e.g., real estate or oil and gas interests) could be reported at either fair value or the lower of cost or fair value.

In December 1995, the FASB issued FAS-124, which establishes new standards for the reporting of certain investments. FAS-124 is discussed later in this chapter.

Subscription and Membership Income

Program service income or subscription income received by an organization is recognized as income in the period in which the goods or services are provided or earned. Membership income would be recognized as income on an allocated basis over the period of the membership. Those dues or nonrefundable fees (that are in substance really contributions and benefits that are not provided) are recognized as income in the period in which the organization is entitled to receive those amounts. Nonrefundable initiation fees or lifetime membership fees are recognized as revenue in the period in which they become receivable, provided that the fees charged in future periods are expected to cover the future costs of memberships. If not, then these fees would be recorded as revenue over the estimated life of the membership.

Functional Classification of Expenses

Expenses reported on a functional basis should be charged to one of the following categories:

1. • Program services
2. • Management and general costs   (G+A)
3. • Fund-raising and other supporting services

Program services   A not-for-profit organization will conduct one or more programs to achieve its mission. Each program should be reported by service or function type and should be described in the disclosures.

Not-for-profit organizations that are local agents for related national or statewide organizations, and that are required to remit all or a fixed part of their contributions to this other organization, should report these payments as a reduction of contribution revenues. All other types of remittances to other not-for-profits would be reported as program expense.

> **OBSERVATION:** See how FIN-42 (Accounting for Transfers of Assets in Which a Not-for-Profit Organization Is Granted Variance Power) of FAS-116 changes this presentation for an organization acting as an agent or a pass-through entity.

Management and general costs   Management and general costs are those costs that cannot be identified as being related to a certain program or fund-raising activity. These costs support the operation of the organization's board activities, business management, bookkeeping, and/or other management functions. Management and general costs also include the cost of the organization's annual report or any other public dissemination of information about the organization's use of contributions received. Generally the salaries of the chief officers of the organization and their staff would be charged to management and general costs, unless it can be demonstrated that a portion of the time paid is devoted directly to supervising a program service or fund-raising function. In these cases, the not-for-profit organization may allocate salary costs among the various functions.

Fund-raising costs   Fund-raising costs are incurred to benefit the organization through contributions of money, time, or donated goods. These costs typically involve personnel, mailing and printing of solicitations, or fund-raising merchandise. The total of these costs

should be reported in the financial statements, and the major types
of fund-raising costs or fund-raising programs should be disclosed.

Fund-raising costs incurred in one year may have significant
benefits in succeeding years. Because it is difficult to determine
future benefits, accounting standards require these costs to be expensed as incurred. The exceptions to this standard are the following
instances:

- If a fund-raising expense is directly related to, and specifically
  identified with, contributions that are restricted for future periods, it may be appropriate to defer the expense of these costs
  where it is clear that the contributor's intention is that these
  costs be covered by the contribution.
- Costs incurred for materials or printing for a fund-raising campaign that has not begun in the reporting period.

Allocation of costs among various functions   Costs incurred by
the organization may apply to various functions of the organization.
For example, an employee may perform certain program functions
as well as certain management and general functions. In these instances it is appropriate to allocate these costs among those functions
that are benefited. SOP 78-10 did not prescribe a method to be used
to allocate these costs, but it did require appropriate disclosures on
the amounts allocated and the methods used.

SOP 98-2 provides guidance for allocation of *costs of joint activities*,
defined as:

> the costs of conducting joint activities that are not identifi-
> able with a particular component of the activity. For ex-
> ample, the cost of postage for a letter that includes both fund-
> raising and program components is a joint cost. Joint costs
> may include the costs of salaries, contract labor, consultants,
> professional fees, paper, printing, postage, event advertising,
> telephones, airtime, and facility rentals. [SOP 98-2, glossary]

For a more in-depth discussion of SOP 98-2, see below and Chapter 4, "Expenses."

Grants

FAS-116 (Accounting for Contributions Received and Contributions
Made) and the 1996 Audit Guide titled *Not-for-Profit Organizations*
provide significant discussion for accounting for grants. They should
be consulted to understand the appropriate accounting treatment
and disclosures.

Tax Allocations

SOP 78-10 recommended the use of deferred taxes to reflect the tax effects that the difference in the timing has on the reporting of financial statement report income and taxable income. These taxes may be excise taxes on investment income of foundations or income taxes on unrelated business income. The SOP did not require the use of a certain method for deferring taxes.

Supersessions

The AICPA Not-For-Profit Organizations Committee has issued an Audit and Accounting Guide titled *Not-for-Profit Organizations* that supersedes SOP 78-10 in its entirety. However, the guidance on certain transactions in SOP 78-10 that remains GAAP has been retained.

FASB STATEMENT NO. 116

FAS-116 (Accounting for Contributions Received and Contributions Made) was issued to set standards for the accounting of contributions received or made. Although primarily aimed at the not-for-profit community, it also applies to the contributions made by for-profit entities. FAS-116 also addresses donor-imposed restrictions on contributions and accounting for contributions of donated services and collections of artworks.

FAS-116 applies to contributions and promises to give. It does not apply to reciprocal transfers or exchange transactions, in which the donor or giver is provided goods or services in exchange for his or her contribution.

A *contribution* is a voluntary, unconditional, and nonreciprocal transfer of cash or assets to an organization. It also can take the form of a cancellation of a liability. Contributions have the following four characteristics:

1. They are unconditional.
2. They are nonreciprocal transfers (no goods or services are provided for contribution).
3. They are made voluntarily.
4. They include the transfer of assets to a new owner.

The following are *not* contributions, and FAS-116 does not apply to them:

- *Exchange transactions*—In an exchange transaction, each party gives and receives goods or services, transfers that, in effect, are purchases.

- *Agency transactions*—In an agency transaction, the receiving organization acts as an agent or trustee for the donor.

- *Tax exemptions*—Tax exemptions include tax abatements, tax incentives, and transfers from governmental units to business enterprises.

- *Conditional transfers*—Conditional transfers are transactions that may become contributions upon the occurrence of a future uncertain event.

Some contributions may be donor-restricted. Donor-restricted contributions are not dependent on the occurrence of a future event and therefore are not conditional. Rather, the donor has stipulated the purpose for which the contribution was made or the period of time over which the contribution must be used.

It is very important to identify transactions properly as contributions, exchanges, or other types of transactions. The timing of the recognition of income may be very different among these types of transactions. In an exchange transaction, revenue and expenses are matched. A misclassification of the nature of the transaction may not match the expenses to the related income. Amounts the organization receives as an agent are not revenues to the organization, and the expenditures are not expenses of the organization.

Some transactions may be part exchange and part contribution. A contribution is recognized to the extent that the value received exceeds the value given. If the value received by the resource provider is nominal compared to the amount transferred, a contribution and an expense would be recorded.

An organization must look carefully at its funding sources to determine if its support is an exchange, a contribution, or both. Funding may be supplied in the form of grants, awards, memberships, or sponsorships.

Funding Sources

Grants and awards   To classify a grant or award transaction properly, the organization must determine if the giver is getting something of value in exchange. Often, this is not an easy determination. If no value is received and the transaction meets the criteria for a contribution, then the standards established by FAS-116 would apply. To the extent that the grant is an exchange, revenue would be recognized when it is earned.

Example: ABC Research Center is given a grant to study the effects of a new chemical directly related to the donor's business. The research must be conducted as specified by the donor. The results of this research will be available only to the donor for one year after the research is completed. ABC may publish the results after that year.

This transaction is an exchange transaction. The donor specified how the research was to be performed. The public benefit was second to that of the donor. The donor is given a competitive edge with its one-year head start.

Example: XYZ Corporation gives a grant to the Y Museum. In return, XYZ is allowed the private use of the museum for its annual corporate party.

In this transaction, the portion of the grant that exceeds the value of the use of the premises is a contribution. The value of the use of the premises is an exchange.

Membership dues   Many organizations offer memberships and charge dues. To determine what portion of membership dues are contributions, the organization should consider the goods or services provided to the members. If the value of the benefits derived is less than the dues paid, then part of the dues may be contributions. Member benefits have value even if the members choose not to use them.

Example: A public television station has a membership drive during which donors who contribute $25 may receive a keyring and donors who contribute $100 may receive a tote bag. The value of these benefits is nominal compared to the contribution given. In this instance, the full amount given is recorded as a contribution and the expense of goods given is recorded as a fund-raising expense.

Example: Members of a not-for-profit theater company receive a monthly newsletter on current theater events and a subscription to one season of the company's productions. The value of the newsletter is $36 and the value of the one-season subscription is $400. Therefore, $436 of the one-year membership price is an exchange and the rest is a contribution.

Sponsorships   Individuals or enterprises may sponsor an event, newsletter, or program of a not-for-profit organization. Sponsors may or may not receive benefits from their donations, which therefore could be accounted for as contributions, exchanges, or part contribution and part exchange. Each transaction must be examined individually to determine what benefits, if any, are derived by the donor.

> **Example:** A medical not-for-profit organization publishes a monthly newsletter. A pharmaceutical company sponsors the June issue. The acknowledgment on the newsletter reads, "This issue has been made possible through an educational grant from ABC Pharmaceutical Company." No other rights, assets, or benefits are given to the donor.
> The acknowledgment of this sponsor is a nominal and incidental benefit, and the sponsor's donation is treated as a contribution.

> **Example:** Same facts as in the previous example, except that separate information about a new product of the pharmaceutical company and a trial sample are enclosed with the newsletter.
> In this example, the pharmaceutical company is receiving advertising and marketing benefits having more than nominal or incidental value. The fair market value of the advertising and marketing should be subtracted from the amount given by the sponsor to determine the amount that would be treated as a contribution.

> **Example:** XYZ Corporation sponsors a not-for-profit opera company's performance of *La Boheme*. XYZ gives the company $15,000 as sponsor of this event. XYZ receives 50 tickets to the performance. The opera normally charges $20 each for these seats. XYZ receives no other benefits.
> The value of the contribution is $14,000, and $1,000 (the value of the tickets) is treated as ticket or box office income.

Exchange transactions As shown in all of the above examples, not-for-profit organizations must examine each transaction to determine if it is a contribution or an exchange transaction. Some key elements that indicate that a donation is an exchange transaction are:

- Donor is receiving goods or services in return.
- Donor reserves the rights to copyrights, patents, or other intangible assets.
- Items being sponsored or funded by grants have direct value to donor and little or no value to the organization's program services or the general public.

- Items are made available to the public only after giver has an exclusive right for a period of time.
- Failure to perform or to deliver by a certain date results in a penalty.
- Giver prescribes the method rather than expresses the goals.

Once the organization determines the proper classification of the transaction, the proper accounting treatment can be applied.

Accounting for Contributions

Under FAS-116, contributions should be recognized as revenues or gains in the period in which they are received. They should be measured at their fair value. Contributions of cash, marketable securities, or notes generally are easy to value. Other types of contributions, however, may be difficult to value. In these cases, fair value may be determined by analyzing the prices at which similar items are sold in the normal course of business, not in a liquidation sale or forced sale. Fair value also may be determined by the present value of expected future cash flows.

Examples of determining values are as follows:

- *Buildings or real estate*—Value can be determined through appraisals by real estate brokers based on sales of similar real estate within the same geographic area.
- *Jewelry*—Value can be based on appraisals by jewelers based on similar gems and weight.
- *Contributed services*—Value can be determined using an hourly rate based on what the service provider would charge for the number of hours donated.
- *Contributed rent*—Value can be determined using square footage charges based on similar rental properties.

If a major uncertainty about the value of an item remains, an amount should not be recognized. Also, amounts should not be recognized for items that are saved for potential future use in scientific or educational research and that have no alternate value.

Accounting for Unconditional Promises to Give

An *unconditional promise to give*, also known as a *pledge*, is a contribution and is recorded as revenue at its fair value when received.

Short-term   If the promise is expected to be fulfilled within one year, the value of the items promised would be recorded at their net realizable value. Net realizable value may be determined on the basis of prior experiences.

> **Example:** C Organization usually collects 95% of the pledges made during its phone-a-thons. On December 1, 199X, it received $100,000 of pledges from its one-day phone-a-thon. Based on past experience, C Organization would recognize $95,000 as contribution revenue on December 1, 199X.
>
> After all collections are made, any shortfalls or surplus in actual collections should be recognized as an adjustment in contribution revenue. If the organization collects $96,000, an extra $1,000 of contribution revenue should be recorded.

Long-term Long-term unconditional promises to give are valued at the present value of estimated future cash flows. The accruals of interest on the discounted amount are accounted for as additional contributions.

> **Example:** On December 30, 19X1, Mr. Y unconditionally promises to give Not-for-Profit C five annual payments of $10,000 commencing on December 31, 19X1. The present value of this contribution at 10% (a risk-free rate of return appropriate for the expected term of the promise to give) is $41,377. The organization would make the following entries:
>
> On December 30, 19X1
>
> | | | |
> |---|---|---|
> | Contribution Receivable | 41,377 | |
> | Contribution Income | | 41,377 |
>
> To record contribution receivable and revenue.
>
> On December 31, 19X1
>
> | | | |
> |---|---|---|
> | Cash | 10,000 | |
> | Contribution Receivable | | 10,000 |
>
> To record the collection of the first annual payment.
>
> On December 31, 19X2
>
> | | | |
> |---|---|---|
> | Contribution Receivable | 3,286 | |
> | Contribution Income | | 3,286 |
>
> To record the interest accrual on discounted receivable as contribution revenue.
>
> | | | |
> |---|---|---|
> | Cash | 10,000 | |
> | Contribution Receivable | | 10,000 |
>
> To record the collection of the second annual payment.

On December 31, 19X3

Contribution Receivable	2,583	
Contribution Income		2,583

To record the interest accrual on discounted receivable as contribution revenue.

Cash	10,000	
Contribution Receivable		10,000

To record the collection of the third annual payment.

This would continue until the contribution had been received in full. A recap of the contribution revenues recorded will be:

Year 1	$41,377
Year 2	3,286
Year 3	2,583
Year 4	1,806
Year 5	948
	$50,000

The entire $50,000 will be recorded as contribution revenue when the promise is fulfilled.

OBSERVATION: FASB has issued an Exposure Draft, "Using Cash Flow Information and Present Value in Accounting Measurements," a proposed Statement of Financial Accounting Concepts that discusses these types of calculations.

Accounting for Donor-Imposed Restrictions

Not-for-profit organizations must classify contributions received as:

- Unrestricted
- Temporarily restricted
- Permanently restricted

These classifications are based on restrictions imposed by the donor, not on restrictions imposed by the organization's governing board or management.

Unrestricted   Unrestricted contributions are those contributions that are free of donor restrictions on their usage. Unrestricted contributions also can include contributions with restrictions that limit the usage of the contribution to an extent no more specific than the broad limits resulting from the nature of the not-for-profit organization's normal activities. Unrestricted revenues also include contributions that may be paid in future years, as long as the donor has not restricted their use.

> **Example:** Donor X contributes $10,000 to Organization Y, a not-for-profit medical education organization whose charter states that the organization will not conduct research. Donor X states this $10,000 may be used to further the education in the medical field but may not be used for research. This restriction is no more specific than the nature of the organization's operations, and the $10,000 does not need to be treated as a restricted contribution.

Restricted Contributions with donor-imposed restrictions are classified as either temporarily restricted or permanently restricted. *Temporarily restricted contributions* have donor-imposed restrictions that may be removed by (1) the passage of time or (2) an act of the organization. *Permanently restricted contributions* are those contributions with restrictions that can never be removed, such as an endowment fund. The restrictions can be from the donor's stipulation (e.g., a letter from the donor that the contribution can be used only to purchase new books for the library), or they may be implicit (e.g., amounts received in a capital improvements fund-raising drive may be used only for capital improvements). Donor-imposed restrictions that are fulfilled in the same period they are received may be recorded as unrestricted support provided that the organization discloses and consistently applies this accounting policy.

Contributions with donor-imposed restrictions are recorded as restricted revenues in the period in which they are received and increase temporarily or permanently restricted net assets.

Long-term promises to give generally are treated as restricted revenues unless the donor explicitly states that the contribution is intended for current usage.

An organization will recognize the expiration or removal of the restriction upon the passage of time or when the stipulated usage has been fulfilled. Upon the expiration, a reclassification is reported on the statement of activities. *Reclassifications* are items that simultaneously increase one net asset class and decrease another.

> **Example:** Donor X contributes $10,000 to Organization Y and stipulates that the money must be used to purchase new textbooks. This temporarily restricted contribution will be reclassified to unrestricted as soon as Organization Y acts to purchase the specified books.

> **Example:** Donor X contributes $100,000 to Organization Y
> and stipulates that the not-for-profit organization is to invest
> the money to provide a permanent source of income for schol-
> arships. The $100,000 contribution is permanently restricted.

Accounting for Conditional Promises to Give

A *conditional promise to give* is a transaction that depends on an
occurrence of a future and uncertain event. A conditional promise to
give is not recognized until the conditions are substantially met. At
this point the promise would become unconditional and the related
accounting rules would apply. A conditional promise would be
deemed as unconditional if chances of not meeting the conditions
are remote.

> **Example:** Often, organizations receive promises of matching
> gifts. These promises are conditional on the organization rais-
> ing a specified amount of money. If the organization is success-
> ful in raising the amount, the condition would be met and the
> conditional promise would become an unconditional promise.
> At that point, revenue and an asset would be recognized.

> **Example:** If an entity gives an organization an amount of
> money that will become a contribution if certain future condi-
> tions are met, the money should be accounted for as a refund-
> able advance until the conditions are met. The revenue would
> be recognized or refunded if the condition is not met.

Accounting for Donated Services

Donated services received by an organization should be recorded at
fair value if the services:

1. Create or enhance a nonfinancial asset (land, building, equipment, furniture, inventory), or
2. Require specialized skills that the provider possesses and that
   normally have to be purchased. These service providers can be
   lawyers, accountants, doctors, nurses, carpenters, architects,
   teachers, or other professionals.

Donated services not meeting either of these two criteria would
not be recognized.

The fair value of donated services can be estimated using hourly
rates, costs for similar projects, salary rates, etc.

Example: A CPA pays the bills and posts the cash receipts of a not-for-profit organization on a voluntary basis. The CPA's services do not require a specialized skill, so the donated service would not be recorded. However, if the CPA prepares a financial statement for the organization and prepares its related tax returns, the donated services require a specialized skill and would be recognized accordingly. The donated services can be measured using the billing rate the CPA charges his or her other clients.

Example: A contractor builds a theater for a community playhouse. The value of the donated materials and supplies is $50,000. Upon completion, the theater is appraised at $200,000. The playhouse would recognize a contribution of services in the amount of $150,000, as these services created a nonfinancial asset, required a specialized skill, and normally would have been purchased.

All organizations receiving donated services are required to include certain disclosures in their financial statements. Disclosures should include information about the program or activity benefited and the nature and extent of contributed services. The amount recognized in the reporting period also should be disclosed. These disclosures may be made for donated services that are not recognized, if practicable.

Accounting for Donated Collection Items

An organization is not required to recognize the value of contributions of works of art or historical treasures if it meets all of the following requirements:

1. The collection is held for public viewing, exhibition, education, or research instead of for investment or financial gain.

2. The collection is cared for, preserved, and protected by the organization.

3. The organization has a policy that requires the proceeds of sales of these items to be reinvested in other collections also available for public use. A policy that the sales proceeds would be used for the preservation and protection of other collections is not sufficient.

Donations of collections are required to be recognized as assets and revenues if all three of these requirements are not met.

When initially adopting this accounting principle, organizations are encouraged to capitalize the collections retroactively or prospectively. Organizations should not capitalize collections on a selective basis. If the organization begins on a prospective basis, the line item on the balance sheet may be titled "Collections Acquired from July 1, 1995," with the appropriate disclosure about this prospective method. Organizations retroactively capitalizing collections can value these items at the cost or market value at the time of acquisition, or at current cost or market value.

If an organization chooses not to recognize as revenue the donations of collections, it should disclose the accounting policy, the description of its collections, and their relative significance. Disclosures should be made for items that are destroyed, stolen, or lost.

Disclosures

Unconditional promises to give Organizations that have received unconditional promises to give need to disclose the amount of these promises that are receivable within one year, the amount receivable in one to five years, the amount receivable in more than five years, and the amount of the allowance for uncollectible contributions. A sample disclosure follows.

Contributions Receivable

As of December 31, 199X, the organization has unconditional contributions receivable as follows:

Due within 1 year	$ 10,000
Due within 1 to 5 years	40,000
Due after 5 years	30,000
	80,000
Present value discount	(17,500)
Allowance for uncollectible accounts	(1,000)
Contributions receivable	$ 61,500

Conditional promises to give Disclosure of conditional promises should include the total amount promised and a description of the condition. Grouping of similar type contributions is encouraged for each type of conditional gift. A sample disclosure follows.

As of December 31, 199X, the organization has been promised $200,000 from contributors. The organization will receive $100,000 upon raising $300,000 for the building of a new theater. The organization will receive $100,000 upon the establishment of a new acting school.

FASB STATEMENT NO. 117

Not-for-profit organizations traditionally have reported their external financial statements in various forms with differing contents. The reporting organizations generally looked to the AICPA Industry Guides for their reporting needs. However, the different Guides had their own prescribed formats and contents. In addition, they were not consistently followed by all like-kind organizations. This resulted in many inconsistencies in the presentation of financial statements. The external readers of these financial statements were left with the difficult challenge of comparing various organizations' results of operations and financial position.

In conjunction with FAS-116, FAS-117 (Financial Statements of Not-for-Profit Organizations) seeks to improve the comparability and usefulness of financial statements by resolving inconsistent accounting treatments and presentations. All financial statements of not-for-profit organizations should contain certain common information that presents the entity's financial position as a whole. Also, not-for-profit organizations should present similar transactions the same way.

According to FAS-117, not-for-profit organizations should present financial information and disclosures in a format similar to that used by for-profit entities. The financial statements under FAS-117 will provide external users with more consistent and relevant information and with a better tool for assessing the organization, how it conducts its programs and services, and its ability to continue its programs based on its financial resources. In addition, the new presentation will include information on the organization's liquidity, how the organization earned and expended its cash flows, how the organization obtained financial resources, how the organization repaid borrowings, and the future repayment terms that remain.

> **OBSERVATION:** FAS-117 allows flexibility in the financial statement formats to be used by not-for-profit organizations. Little documentation is currently available from which to derive accurate examples of all the possible formats. Accordingly, the original edition of **GAAP for Not-for-Profit Organizations** ad-

dressed the most common format. This and subsequent editions will present examples of new formats as they come into favor.

> **OBSERVATION:** Some examples of complete sets of financial statements prepared in accordance with FAS-117 are presented in Appendix A.

According to FAS-117, all not-for-profit organizations must present a complete set of financial statements that includes:

- Statement of financial position
- Statement of activities
- Statement of cash flows
- Accompanying notes to the financial statements

The financial statements should cover the entire not-for-profit organization and not piecemeal segments or funds. This presentation is especially true of colleges, universities, and museums. Under FAS-117, the focus of the financial statements is no longer on the components of individual funds, but on the not-for-profit organization as a whole. Fund accounting will continue to be allowed, but it will not be required. Financial statements that focus on the not-for-profit organization as a whole are more informative and useful for financial statement users.

> **OBSERVATION:** Not-for-profit organizations present information in the financial statements in fashions that are most easily understood by their finance committees and management. There continues to be significant diversity in practice.

Statement of Financial Position

The statement of financial position (or "balance sheet") presents the financial position of the organization at a moment in time, usually the end of the reporting period. It demonstrates the organization's financial resources and informs readers about the organization's ability to provide its program services or products. The statement of financial position also supplies information on an organization's liquidity, which helps financial statement users determine the organization's *financial flexibility*, defined by FASB as "the ability of an entity to take effective actions to alter amounts and the timing of cash flows so it can respond to unexpected needs and opportunities." The statement of financial position may show an entity's need for external financing.

The statement of financial position must report and focus on the organization as a whole and must show the organization's total assets, liabilities, and net assets. The statement of financial position must present the following six elements:

1. Total assets

2. Total liabilities

3. Unrestricted net assets

4. Temporarily restricted net assets

5. Permanently restricted net assets

6. Total net assets

ABC Organization
Statement of Financial Position
December 31, 199X

Total Assets	$ XX,XXX
Total Liabilities	$ XX,XXX
Net Assets:	
Unrestricted	XX,XXX
Temporarily Restricted	XX,XXX
Permanently Restricted	XX,XXX
Total Net Assets	XX,XXX
	$ XX,XXX

As seen in the illustration, the fund accounting model is no longer required and the format used is similar to the format used by business enterprises. However, organizations may still believe it is appropriate to present information in a columnar format. This format may be used, as long as the basic information is presented. Organizations wanting to show separate funds may report the basic information shown below.

ABC Organization
Statement of Financial Position
December 31, 199X

	Unrestricted	Temporarily Restricted	Permanently Restricted	Total
Total Assets	$ XX,XXX	$ XX,XXX	$ XX,XXX	$ XX,XXX
Total Liabilities	$ XX,XXX	$ XX,XXX	$ XX,XXX	$ XX,XXX
Net Assets:				
Unrestricted	XX,XXX			XX,XXX
Temporarily Restricted		XX,XXX		XX,XXX
Permanently Restricted			XX,XXX	XX,XXX
Total Net Assets	XX,XXX	XX,XXX	XX,XXX	XX,XXX
Total Liabilities and Net Assets	$ XX,XXX	$ XX,XXX	$ XX,XXX	$ XX,XXX

OBSERVATION: It is not necessary to come to subtotals for current assets and current liabilities (classified balance sheet) to be in conformity with generally accepted accounting principles for not-for-profit organizations.

OBSERVATION: Organizations may further disaggregate the separate classifications and present an operating fund and plant fund, for example, as separate components under the unrestricted class of net assets.

Classifications of assets and liabilities   The statement of financial position must present relevant information about the organization's:

- Liquidity
- Financial flexibility
- Interrelationships of assets and liabilities

Liquidity   Liquidity of an asset or liability is determined by its convertibility or nearness to cash. Assets and liabilities should be classified in order of liquidity. Grouping of assets and liabilities into similar or like-kind accounts is very useful in assessing liquidity. Organizations also should consider presenting classified balance sheets. ARB-43 (Restatement and Revision of Accounting Research Bulletins), Chapter 3A, provides guidance for classifying current assets and current liabilities. Liquidity of items also can be disclosed in footnote form.

Disclosures relating to when an organization will collect payments on a long-term grant or contribution are very useful to external readers. Similarly, if the not-for-profit organization has a long-term note payable that is to be paid out over a number of years, the organization should present the portion due every year in a manner similar to that used by for-profit entities. The not-for-profit organization should present a long-term debt maturity schedule and disclose encumbrances of assets.

Financial flexibility Financial flexibility is measured by the organization's ability to use its financial resources to meet program needs, pay maturing debt, or meet any unexpected cash requirements or opportunities. Disclosures regarding restrictions on the use of assets, compensating balances in cash accounts, and maturity of long-term assets or liabilities are useful for determining financial flexibility.

> **OBSERVATION:** At the time of this writing, FASB is studying various aspects of accounting for financial instruments, including measuring at fair value and the characteristics of a liability.

Interrelationships of assets and liabilities When grouping assets, the not-for-profit organization must consider donor-imposed restrictions. For example, cash received by an organization with donor-imposed restrictions to spend the money on new long-term research should *not* be included in regular operating cash.

Classification of net assets All balance sheets must include, on the face of the statement, the following three classes of net assets:

1. Unrestricted
2. Temporarily restricted
3. Permanently restricted

These classifications are based on donor-imposed restrictions. A restriction imposed by the governing board of the organization or by management does not affect the classification.

Unrestricted funds are those without any donor-imposed restrictions. Most organizations receive contributions that limit their usage. If the restriction is so broad that the organization can use the funds in its normal course of business without violating its bylaws, then the contribution may be classified as unrestricted funds. Organizations themselves may impose limitations on the use of contributions. These restrictions will not affect the classification, but they may be disclosed in the notes to the financial statements or presented on the face of the balance sheet.

Temporarily restricted net assets are those contributions with restrictions imposed by the donor. These restrictions may be removed by the:

- Passage of time
- Performance or act of the organization

If the donor specifies that a contribution must be used to support specified future periods, only the passage of time will remove the restriction. A purpose restriction is imposed on a contribution if the donor stipulates that it be used for a certain program, event, or particular use.

Net assets with permanent restrictions are those contributions that the donor stipulates must be used in perpetuity for a particular purpose. These are also known as *true endowment funds.* Examples of these follow:

- A member donates a sculpture with the provision that it may not be sold and that it must be preserved by the museum and must be displayed and open to the public.
- A university receives a donation that stipulates that the money must be invested to provide a permanent source of income for scholarships.

Information about the types of restrictions on assets and the amounts restricted is useful to external readers and is required by FAS-117. This information may be disclosed in notes or presented on the face of the statement.

Statement of Activities

The statement of activities is similar to the statement of support, revenue, and expenses and changes in fund balance described in the superseded AICPA Audit and Accounting Guides. The purpose of the statement of activities is to provide relevant information about:

- Transactions and other events and circumstances that change the amount and nature of net assets;
- The relationships of those transactions, and the relationships among other events and circumstances; and
- How the organization's resources are used to provide various programs or services.

A not-for-profit organization's statement of activities is similar to a for-profit enterprise's income statement and measures the performance of the organization during the reporting period. The statement of activities provides external users with a reporting period's performance and with information to further present expenditures for programs in relation to income and support.

Four required elements are presented in the statement of activities:

1. Change in total net assets or change in equity
2. Change in unrestricted net assets
3. Change in temporarily restricted net assets
4. Change in permanently restricted net assets

As with the statement of financial position, the statement of activities should focus on the entity as a whole. FASB was concerned with the titles of "Net Assets" and "Equity." Accordingly, in keeping with its views of reporting on the whole, the FASB did not want to emphasize funds and so avoided using the term "Fund Balance."

The following is an example of a statement of activities:

ABC Organization
Statement of Activities
Year Ended December 31, 199X

Changes in unrestricted net assets:		
Revenue, gains, and other support:		
Contributions	$	9,500
Service income		7,750
Interest income		630
Net unrealized and realized gain on investments		590
Other income		70
Net assets released from restrictions		6,100
Total unrestricted revenue, gains, and other support		24,640
Expenses:		
Program		5,980
Management and general		13,060
Fund-raising		1,690
Total expenses		20,730
Increase in unrestricted net assets		3,910
Changes in temporarily restricted net assets:		
Contributions		1,675
Interest income		795
Net assets released from restrictions		(6,100)
Increase in temporarily restricted net assets		6,370

Changes in permanently restricted net assets:

Contributions	1,985
Interest income	5,225
Net unrealized and realized gains on investments	770
Increase in permanently restricted net assets	7,980
Increase in net assets	18,260
Net assets, beginning of year	25,685
Net assets, end of year	$43,945

As illustrated in the example, contributions in each of the net asset classes increase the net asset balances. As mandated by FAS-116, contributions without donor-imposed restrictions would be included in unrestricted revenues. Revenue and expense items should be reported in homogenous groups. Likewise, contributions with donor-imposed restrictions should be included in their respective net asset classification based on the type of restriction. However, if donor-imposed restrictions are met within the same reporting period of the contribution, the contribution may, at the organization's option, be reported as unrestricted support. If used, this policy must be disclosed in the notes to the financial statements and consistently applied.

Revenues and support must be reported in gross amounts. The major categories of revenues should be presented (e.g., contribution, program service income, etc.). Investment income may be reported at net amounts, provided the amount of expenses is disclosed in the notes or on the face of the statement. Gains and losses on investments may be reported net of any increase or decrease in unrestricted net assets. However, if the donor has placed restrictions on the net gains, then the net gains would be classified as temporarily or permanently restricted based on the donor's wishes. The only other allowable netting is with peripheral or incidental transactions.

The reporting of expenses is extremely important to external users of financial statements because it provides information about the cost of services provided and how the organization used its support. Because of this importance, organizations need to report expenses by functional classification as a part of the statement of activities or in the notes to the financial statements. Expenses, always classified as decreases in unrestricted net assets, should be reported in major classes of program services and supporting activities such as management and general or fund-raising. The presentation of expenses in natural classifications, such as salaries, rent, depreciation, telephone, or consultants, is encouraged but not required, except for voluntary health and welfare organizations, which are required to present this information in a matrix format in a separate financial statement.

An example of this matrix is shown in Table 2-2.

Table 2-2: ABC Organization
Schedule of Expenses
Year Ended December 31, 199X

	Total	Education Program	Arts Program	Management and General	Fund Raising
Rent	$ 45,000	$ 11,000	$ 10,000	$ 19,000	$ 5,000
Salaries	17,257	7,253	6,119	2,885	1,000
Benefits	4,616	1,836	1,569	967	244
Professional	13,258	5,850	4,750	1,790	868
Printing	7,867	4,298	1,622	821	1,126
Insurance	6,300	2,700	2,400	1,000	200
Depreciation	5,200	2,200	2,100	750	150
Total	$ 99,498	$ 35,137	$ 28,560	$ 27,213	$ 8,588

Reclassifications   Reclassifications are items that increase one net asset class while simultaneously decreasing another class. An example would be the earlier illustration of the statement of activities. Included in changes in unrestricted net assets are net assets released from restrictions in the amount of $6,100. The $6,100 is also reported as a decrease in changes in temporarily restricted net assets. Reclassifications can be triggered by the passage of time that removes a donor restriction or by an act of the organization that removes a restriction. Reclassifications must be reported separately from revenues and expenses.

Special events   Not-for-profit organizations often hold special galas or events to raise funds. Generally, FAS-117 requires the reporting of revenues from these events in a gross amount. If the event is an ongoing or major activity, it should be reported by gross revenues and expenses. However, if the event is peripheral or incidental, the organization may report the net amounts (revenues – expenses). The frequency and significance of the event is a major factor in determining whether one is peripheral or incidental.

Example: A not-for-profit annual celebrity luncheon accounts for 40 percent of the not-for-profit organization's revenues. Reporting the net amount of this event would not be appropriate, because it is not incidental.

Statement of Cash Flows

The statement of cash flows provides information about the sources and uses of cash during the reporting period. The statement of cash flows is useful to external readers because it provides information about how:

- Cash was received by the organization to support its operations.
- Cash was expended to provide its programs.
- Changes in cash reconcile to the cash in net assets.

The statement provides relevant information that supports the statement of financial position in terms of the organization's liquidity, financial flexibility, ability to meet obligations, and need for external financing. The statement reports the sources and uses of cash from:

- Operating activities
- Investing activities
- Financing activities

FAS-117 amended FAS-95 (Statement of Cash Flows) to extend to not-for-profit organizations the same reporting requirements applicable to for-profit enterprises. FAS-117 added a few amendments for not-for-profit organizations, including:

- The receipt of investment income or contributions that are restricted by the donor to be used for long-term purposes, such as the purchase of equipment or to increase endowments, should be reported as cash flows from financing activities.
- Interest and dividends that are restricted by the donor for long-term purposes are not to be included in cash flows from operations.

The statement of cash flows reports the change in cash and cash equivalents during the reporting period. *Cash equivalents*, as defined in FAS-95, are short-term, highly liquid investments that are both:

- Readily convertible to known amounts of cash; and
- So near their maturity that they present insignificant risk of changes in value because of changes in interest rates.

As a general rule, investments purchased with an original maturity of three months or less are considered cash equivalents. Commercial paper, money markets, certificates of deposits, and Treasury bills all fall into this category. The notes to the organization's financial statements should disclose its policies regarding determination of cash equivalents. Any change in the organization's policy is a change in accounting principle and necessitates the restatement of prior year's financial statements that are presented.

FAS-95 requires the flows of cash amounts to be reported on a gross basis. This is more informative to external users than showing net amounts. Generally, netting of amounts is permitted if the reporting of gross amounts is not needed to understand the operating, investing, and financing activities. For example, if the organization is receiving or disbursing funds of a client, the reporting of net transactions would be acceptable.

Classifications of cash flows   Cash flows are to be reported as investing, financing, or operating activities. *Investing activities* are those transactions that relate to the acquisition or disposition of debt of other entities or equity instruments or land, plant, and equipment or other productive assets, or the making or collecting of loans. *Financing activities* are those transactions that relate to obtaining resources and providing a return or repayment thereof. *Operating activities* are all transactions that are not classified as investing or financing activities.

Inflows from Investing Activities

- Proceeds from the sales of stocks or bonds of other enterprises
- Proceeds from the sale of equipment or buildings
- Proceeds from insurance policies that cover damage or theft of property, plant, or equipment
- Collections of loans made by the organization
- Proceeds from the sale of works of art

Outflows from Investing Activities

- Purchases of stocks or bonds of other enterprises
- Purchases of property, plant, or equipment
- Loans made by the organization
- Purchases of works of art

Inflows from Financing Activities

- Receipts from the collection of contributions that have donor-imposed restrictions stating they must be used for long-term purposes
- Receipts of contributions that create permanently restricted or temporarily restricted annuity trusts or life income funds

- Proceeds from the issuance of notes, mortgages, bonds, or other borrowings
- Proceeds from the issuance of equity (in a consolidated financial statement where an organization has a for-profit subsidiary)
- Interest or dividend income that has a donor-imposed restriction on its usage to increase a permanent or temporary endowment

Outflows from Financing Activities

- Repayment of loans, mortgages, bonds, or other borrowings
- Refunds of contributions that were described in financing outflows
- Payments of dividends or repurchase of stock also known as treasury stock (in a consolidated financial statement where an organization has a for-profit subsidiary)

Inflows from Operating Activities

- Receipts from contributions or grants except those described in financing activities
- Receipts from program service income, sale of goods, or tuition
- Receipt of interest or dividends on investments or loans
- Settlement of lawsuits or proceeds from insurance claims other than those related to long-term assets

Outflows from Operating Activities

- Payment of salaries, vendors, and suppliers
- Payment of taxes or fees
- Payment of interest on loans or any borrowings
- Payment of grants or contributions

Format of the cash flows statement   The statement of cash flows must present the net cash provided or used in operating, investing, and financing activities and the change in cash and cash equivalents during the reporting period. When reporting cash flows from operating activities, the not-for-profit organization may use one of two methods: the direct method or the indirect method.

Not-for-profit organizations using the direct method, which is encouraged by FAS-95, report the major classes of gross cash receipts and disbursements. The following are reported separately:

- Cash received from program services or sales of goods
- Cash collected from contributions
- Interest and dividends received
- Other receipts from operating activities
- Cash paid to suppliers, to vendors, and for salaries
- Interest paid
- Income taxes paid
- Contributions or grants paid
- Payments of other operating activities

A separate reconciliation of change in net assets to cash flows from operating activities also must be provided. This reconciliation is similar to that used in the indirect method. A sample statement of cash flows for a not-for-profit organization using the direct method follows:

ABC Organization
Statement of Cash Flows (Direct Method)
Year Ended December 31, 199X

Cash Flows from Operating Activities:	
Cash received from contributions	$ 24,360
Cash received from performance fees	14,240
Cash paid to vendors, suppliers, and employees	(28,995)
Interest received	168
Interest paid	(1,690)
Income taxes paid	(498)
Grants paid	(4,280)
Net cash provided by operating activities	3,305
Cash Flows from Investing Activities:	
Purchase of fixed assets	(1,750)
Collection of note receivable	650
Proceeds from sale of investments	4,300
Purchase of investments	(12,500)
Net cash used in investing activities	(9,300)

Cash Flows from Financing Activities:

Proceeds of contributions restricted for building construction	10,000
Proceeds of long-term debt financing	7,500
Payments on long-term debt	(695)
Net cash provided by financing activities	16,805
Net increase in cash and cash equivalents	10,810
Cash and Cash Equivalents, beginning of year	65,211
Cash and Cash Equivalents, end of year	$ 76,021

Reconciliation of change in net assets to net cash provided by operating activities:

Change in net assets	$ 5,532
Adjustments to reconcile change in net assets to net cash provided by operating activities:	
Depreciation	665
Contributions restricted for building construction	(10,000)
Loss on sale of investments	130
Change in contributions receivable	3,890
Decrease in prepaid expenses	350
Increase in interest receivable	(715)
Decrease in security deposits	500
Increase in accounts payable	2,003
Increase in grants payable	950
Net cash provided by operating activities	$ 3,305

Not-for-profit organizations using the indirect method report the net cash flow information by reporting the reconciliation of the change in net assets to net cash provided by (or used in) operating activities. This method begins with the change in net assets. Major classes of reconciling items are then presented. These reconciling items remove (1) the effects of all deferrals of past cash receipts or payment (e.g., the net increase or decrease in a receivable or payable or the net increase or decrease in deferred income) or (2) the effects of all items whose cash effects are investing or financing cash flows (e.g., depreciation or amortization, or gains and losses on the sale of securities or long-term assets). A sample statement of cash flows for a not-for-profit organization using the indirect method follows:

ABC Organizations
Statement of Cash Flows (Indirect Method)
Year Ended December 31, 199X

Change in net assets	$ 5,532
Adjustments to reconcile change in net assets to net cash provided by operating activities:	
Depreciation	665
Loss on sale of investments	130
Contributions restricted for building construction	(10,000)
Change in contributions receivable	3,890
Decrease in prepaid expenses	350
Increase in interest receivable	(715)
Decrease in security deposits	500
Increase in accounts payable	2,003
Increase in grants payable	950
Net cash provided by operating activities	3,305
Cash Flows from Investing Activities:	
Purchase of fixed assets	(1,750)
Collection of note receivable	650
Proceeds from sale of investments	4,300
Purchase of investments	(12,500)
Net cash used in investing activities	(9,300)
Cash Flows from Financing Activities:	
Proceeds of contributions restricted for building construction	10,000
Proceeds of long-term debt financing	7,500
Payments on long-term debt	(695)
Net cash provided by financing activities	16,805
Net increase in cash and cash equivalents	10,810
Cash and Cash Equivalents, beginning of year	65,211
Cash and Cash Equivalents, end of year	$ 76,021

Supplemental Disclosures of Cash Flow Information:
Cash Paid During the Year for:
Interest $ 1,690

Noncash transactions   Information about investing or financing transactions that do not result in cash receipts or disbursements must be disclosed on the statement of cash flows. It may be disclosed in a narrative or schedule. Examples of noncash transactions are:

- Receipt of securities, works of art, or equipment as contributions
- Acquisition of an asset through a capital lease
- Refinancing of debt
- Contributed services that create or enhance a long-term asset or that require specialized skills
- Exchange of a noncash asset for another noncash asset

Foreign currency transactions   Organizations that have foreign currency transactions should report the foreign currency cash flows using exchange rates that were in effect at the time of the cash flow. A weighted-average exchange rate for the period may be used if it is substantially the same as the rate in effect at the time of the cash flow. The effect of the exchange rate on cash balances is a separate line item in reconciling the change in cash and cash equivalents.

FASB STATEMENT NO. 124

In November 1995, FASB issued FAS-124 (Accounting for Certain Investments Held by Not-for-Profit Organizations). This Statement is effective for fiscal years beginning after December 15, 1995.

FAS-124 affects investments in equity securities with readily determinable fair values and all investments in debt securities. It also establishes disclosure requirements for most investments held by not-for-profit organizations.

Guidance related to FAS-124 is contained in the AICPA Audit and Accounting Guide *Not-for-Profit Organizations,* issued June 1996.

FAS-124 does not provide new standards for investments in equity securities accounted for under the equity method or for investments in consolidated subsidiaries. FASB is considering these topics for all entities and, in October 1995, issued an Exposure Draft of a proposed Statement titled "Consolidated Financial Statements: Policies and Procedures). This Exposure Draft, which has not resulted in a Statement of Financial Accounting Standards, is discussed in Chapter 7, "Organizational Issues."

> **OBSERVATION**: FASB issued a revised Exposure Draft in February 1999.

Investments covered by FAS-124 should be measured at their fair value in the statement of financial position. Gains and losses on investments should be reported in the statement of activities as increases or decreases in unrestricted net assets, unless their use is temporarily or permanently restricted by explicit donor stipulation or by law.

According to FAS-116, donor stipulations, to the extent that they exist, determine the classifications of gains and losses from sales of restricted endowment funds. Securities held in perpetuity because of donor restrictions also may result in gains or losses increasing or decreasing permanently restricted net assets because of local law. However, in the absence of donor restrictions or local law that restricts the use of gains, such gains will follow the treatment of investment income. Accordingly, gains will increase unrestricted net assets when investment income is unrestricted or will increase temporarily restricted net assets when investment income is temporarily restricted by the donor.

FAS-124 notes that not-for-profit organizations are not bound to one method for reporting investment return. Nor are they bound to one method for reporting operations. In fact, FASB has increased the flexibility for reporting because there is no preferred method. Accordingly, organizations have great latitude in reporting the required information. In the explanatory material that accompanies FAS-124, FASB points out that the not-for-profit organization should present the required information in a manner that will prove to be meaningful to the financial statement users. Accordingly, the information may be presented based on factors such as:

- *The nature of the underlying transactions*—The organization may choose to classify realized amounts as operating activities and it may choose to report unrealized amounts as nonoperating activities.
- *Budgetary designations*—The organization could elect to classify amounts computed under a spending rate or total return policy as operating activities and it may choose to report the remainder of investment return as nonoperating activities.
- *Reporting requirements for categories of investments used in Statement 115*—Some organizations may opt to classify investment income, including realized gains and losses, unrealized gains and losses on trading securities, and other-than-temporary impairment losses on securities, as operating activities and classify the remainder of investment return as nonoperating activities.
- *Other characteristics*—Finally, a not-for-profit organization can present its investment activities in a manner that will provide relevant and understandable information for donors, creditors, and other users of financial statements

Disclosures

Not-for-profit organizations should disclose the following for each balance sheet:

- The carrying amount of investments by category (e.g., equity securities, U.S. Treasury securities, corporate debt securities, mortgage-backed securities, oil and gas properties, and real estate)
- Which basis is used to determine the reported value for investments that are neither equity securities with readily determinable fair values nor debt securities
- Which method(s) and significant assumptions were used by the organization in its process to estimate the fair values of investments other than financial instruments if reported at fair value
- The amount by which the fair value of the reported assets for all donor-restricted endowment funds is less than the level required by donor stipulations or law

Also, for each balance sheet, not-for-profit organizations should disclose the nature and carrying amount for each individual investment or group of investments that represents a significant concentration of market risk.

For each period for which a statement of activities is presented, an organization should disclose the following:

- The composition of investment return, including investment income, net realized gains or losses on investments reported at other than fair value, and net gains or losses on investments reported at fair value
- If investment return is separated into operating and nonoperating amounts, an analysis of investment return compared to amounts reported in the statement of activities and a description of the policy the organization used to determine the amount that is included in the measure of operations. When applicable, there should be disclosure of a change in that policy.

FAS-124 has the effect of changing the definition of *endowment fund* as contained in FAS-117. Instead of referring to *the principal of a permanent endowment* or *the principal of a term endowment*, FAS-124 refers to *the portion of a permanent endowment* or *the portion of term endowment* when describing how such portion must be maintained by the not-for-profit organization.

FASB STATEMENTS NO. 125 AND NO. 127

In June 1996, FASB issued FAS-125 (Accounting for Transfers and Servicing of Financial Assets and Extinguishments of Liabilities), in which the Board determined that accounting for financial assets should focus on control issues. A transfer of control (and accordingly, the recognition of a sale) occurs when **all** of the following conditions are met:

- The transferred assets are put beyond the reach of the transferring organization and its creditors
- The transferee organization has the right to pledge or exchange the transferred assets
- The transferor organization does not maintain effective control over the assets through an agreement that entitles or obligates the organization to repurchase or redeem the transferred assets

Beyond these control matters, FAS-125 added provisions relating to the derecognition of liabilities. In paragraph 16, FASB requires that a liability be derecognized if and only if either (a) the debtor pays the creditor and is relieved of its obligation for the liability or (b) the debtor is legally released from being the primary obligor under the liability either judicially or by the creditor. Therefore, a liability is not considered extinguished by an in-substance defeasance.

The Statement provides guidance for accounting for transactions in certain instances:

- Transfers of partial interests
- Servicing of financial assets
- Securities lending transactions
- Repurchase transactions
- Wash sales
- Loan syndications and participations
- Risk participations in banker's acceptances
- Factoring arrangements
- Transfers of receivables with recourse
- Extinguishments of liabilities

Then, in December 1996, FASB issued FAS-127 (Deferral of the Effective Date of FASB Statement No. 125), to defer the effective date of certain provisions of FAS-125, in response to concern about the ability of certain entities to comply with FAS-125 on a timely basis. FAS-127, which generally is effective for transfers and servicing of financial assets and extinguishments of liabilities occurring after December 31, 1996 (with earlier or retroactive application not permitted), caused a one-year deferral of certain sections of FAS-125— specifically, paragraph 15, relating to Secured Borrowings and Collateral, and paragraphs 9–12, as they relate to repurchase agreement, dollar-roll, securities lending, and similar transactions.

> **OBSERVATION:** FASB has issued two staff guides regarding the implementation of FAS-125 and continues to address additional questions.

FASB STATEMENT NO. 126

Also in December 1996, FASB issued FAS-126 (Exemption from Certain Required Disclosures about Financial Instruments for Certain Nonpublic Entities), to amend FAS-107 (Disclosures about Fair Values of Financial Instruments). An organization that FAS-126 makes exempt from the FAS-107 requirements to disclose fair values of financial instruments is one that meets **all** of the following:

- Is a *nonpublic entity*—one that is other than an organization whose debt or equity securities trade in a public market either on a stock exchange (domestic or foreign) or in the over-the-counter market, including one whose securities may be quoted only locally or regionally; an entity that files with a regulatory agency in connection with the possible sale of any class of debt or equity securities in a public market; or an entity that is controlled by an entity described above.

- Has total assets of less than $100,000,000 on the balance sheet date

- Has not held or issued any derivative financial instruments, other than loan commitments, during the reporting period

For comparative financial statements, if disclosures are not required in the current period, the disclosures for the earlier year(s) may be omitted. If disclosures are required for the current period, prior-year information need not be included if the disclosures were not required in the earlier period.

The Statement is effective for periods ending after December 15, 1996.

FASB STATEMENT NO. 129

Disclosure information about capital structure becomes effective for financial statements for periods ending after December 15, 1997. It applies to all entities that issued securities addressed within the statement. The FASB, in issuing Statement No. 129 (Disclosure of Information about Capital Structure), expanded the disclosure requirements about capital structure to all entities instead of just public companies as previously required. APB Opinion No. 15 excluded non-public companies from these disclosure requirements.

Securities are evidence of an entity's debt or ownership or a related right. The term includes an entity's options, warrants, debt, and stock.

An organization must disclose in its financial statements the rights and privileges of its outstanding securities—including, for debt securities, the sinking fund requirements.

FASB STATEMENTS NO. 128, NO. 130, AND NO. 131

FAS-128 (Earnings per Share), FAS-130 (Reporting of Comprehensive Income), and FAS-131 (Disclosures about Segments of an Enterprise and Related Information) do not apply to not-for-profit organizations and will not be discussed in this book.

FASB STATEMENT NO. 132

In February 1998, the FASB issued FAS-132 (Employers' Disclosures about Pensions and Other Post Retirement Benefits) as an amendment to FAS-87, -88, and -106. This Statement does not amend the accounting for these plans, but instead modifies the required disclosures of these plans. The FASB's intent for this new standard was to provide disclosures about the benefit plans that are concise, understandable, and uniform in application.

This Statement supersedes the disclosure requirements of FAS-87, -88, and -106. It also provides disclosure requirements for public companies and non-public companies. A non-public company can elect to provide a reduced disclosure about its benefit plans. The following discussion will address disclosures only for non-public companies. The required disclosures for not-for-profit organizations are:

1. The benefit obligation, fair value of plan assets, and funded status of the plan

2. Employer contributions, participant contributions, and benefits paid

3. The amounts recognized in the statement of financial position, including the net pension and other postretirement benefit prepaid assets or accrued liabilities and any intangible asset recognized pursuant to paragraph 37 of Statement 87, as amended

4. The amount of net periodic benefit cost recognized pursuant to paragraph 37 of Statement 87, as amended

5. On a weighted average basis, the following assumptions used in the accounting for the plans: assumed discount rate, rate of compensation increase (for pay-related plans), and expected long-term rate of return on plan assets

6. The assumed health care cost trend rate(s) for the next year used to measure the expected cost of benefits covered by the plan (gross eligible charges), and a general description of the direction and pattern of change in the assumed trend rates thereafter, together with the ultimate trend rate(s) and when the rate is expected to be achieved

7. If applicable, the amounts and types of securities of the employer and related parties included in plan assets, the approximate amount of future annual benefits of plan participants covered by insurance contracts issued by the employer or related parties, and any significant transactions between the employer or related parties and the plan during the period

8. The nature and effect of significant nonroutine events, such as amendments, combinations, divestitures, curtailments, and settlements

If the organization has two or more defined benefit plans or defined benefit postretirement plans, the disclosure information may be reported in the aggregate. If the disclosures are reported in the aggregate, then for all plans in which the benefit obligation exceeds the plan assets, the organization must disclose the aggregate benefit obligation and the aggregate fair value of plan assets for those plans. Prepaid benefit costs and accrued benefit obligations recognized on the statement of financial position must be reported separately.

Defined Contribution Plans

An organization must disclose the expense recognized from a defined contribution or postretirement plan separately from the amount expensed under a defined benefit plan. The organization needs to disclose the nature and effect of significant changes to the defined contribution plan, such as change in the contribution rate, termination, business combination, or eligibility.

Multiemployer Plans

An organization must disclose the amounts recognized from a contribution to a multiemployer plan. Disclosure must also include items that affect comparability, similar to those disclosures in a defined contribution plan.

Effective Date

This Statement became effective for fiscal years beginning after December 15, 1997. In comparative financial statements, restatement is not required unless the information is not readily available. In those instances, the information that is not available must be disclosed in the comparative financial statements.

FASB STATEMENT NO. 133

In June 1998 the FASB issued FAS-133 (Accounting for Derivative Instruments and Hedging Activities). This pronouncement:

- Defines *derivatives*
- Requires that all derivatives be carried at fair value, and
- Provides for hedge accounting when certain conditions are met.

Although the effective date for implementation of the new pronouncement is for all fiscal quarters of fiscal years beginning after June 15, 2000, the new standard does permit early adoption. At the time of this writing, FASB has delayed the implementation of the provisions of FAS-133 for one year. It is not anticipated that significant changes will be made, because a number of entities have adopted the Statement early. The effect, if any, on financial statements of not-for-profit entities is unknown. However, to the extent that such entities had investments in funds that use derivative instruments as part of their strategies, those investments may already be marked to market because of the provisions of FAS-124.

Application to Not-for-Profit Organizations

FASB addresses accounting by not-for-profit organizations in the Summary section of FAS-133. An organization that has invested in derivative instruments should recognize the change in the instruments' fair values as a change in net assets in the period in which the change occurs. If an instrument is a fair value hedge, the organization would recognize the change in the fair value attributable to the risk being hedged. Because of the format of the statement of activities, organizations may not use the special hedge accounting for derivatives. FAS-133 does not address the reporting of the change in fair value when the not-for-profit organization presents an operating measure in the statement of activities. Each organization that does present such an operating measure will need to decide how best to present this information.

Definitions

Derivative Instrument—a financial instrument or other contract that has all three of the following characteristics:

1. It has one or more of the following—specified interest rate, security price, commodity price, foreign exchange rate, index of prices or rates, or other variable (the *underlying*) **and** one or more *notional amounts* (a number of currency units, shares, bushels, pounds, or other units specified in the instrument) or payment provisions or both;

2. It has no required initial net investment, or the amount may be small; and

3. Its terms require or permit net settlement, it can readily be settled net by a means outside the contract, or it provides for delivery of an asset that puts the recipient in a position not substantially different from net settlement.

This last requirement relates to a contract that has settlement provisions in which:

- Neither party is required to deliver an asset that is associated with the underlying items identified in 1., above, or that has a value equal to the notional amount; or

- One of the parties **is required** to deliver such an asset, but there is a market opportunity that allows the recipient to receive the equivalent of a net settlement; or

- One of the parties **is required** to deliver such an asset, but that asset is readily convertible to cash or is itself a derivative instrument.

Financial Instrument—cash, evidence of ownership interest in an entity, or a contract that (a) imposes on one entity a contractual obligation to deliver cash or another financial instrument to a second entity or exchange other financial instruments on potentially unfavorable terms with the second entity; **and** (b) conveys to that second entity a contractual right to receive cash or another financial instrument from the first entity or to exchange other financial instruments on potentially favorable terms with the first entity.

Early Adoption May Be Desirable

Certain organizations may be able to take advantage of relaxed hedge accounting requirements—for certain foreign currency transactions, for example.

Fair Value

In the past, certain organizations were required to report, in the notes to the financial statements, the fair value of financial instruments. With the issuance of FAS-133, these derivative instruments will be valued and presented in the financial statements. This will result in greater scrutiny of these instruments by auditors, creditors, and other users of not-for-profit organizations' financial statements. Financial statement preparers may need to become more sophisticated in order to determine the appropriate assumptions and to make the computations required by FAS-133.

> **OBSERVATION:** Potential donors may review more closely the investment policies and investment results of organizations that make significant use of derivative instruments as part of their financial strategies.

Hedge Accounting

To qualify for hedge accounting, the derivative instrument must hedge an exposure to risk, but it is not required to reduce the risk, per se. Formal documentation is required at inception of the hedging relationship, and the entity's risk management objective and strategy for undertaking the hedge—including identification of the hedging instrument, the hedged item, the nature of the risk being hedged, and how the hedging instrument's effectiveness will be assessed.

> **OBSERVATION:** Currently, hedge accounting or settlement (accrual) accounting for derivatives is based primarily on designation and matching of the derivative with the hedged instrument. Organizations without formal risk management policies that encompass all of the FAS-133 requirements for hedge accounting need to become aware of the requirements and

prepare adequate documentation when they adopt this standard, so that they will qualify for hedge accounting.

STATEMENT ON AUDITING STANDARDS NO. 69

A typical opinion paragraph from an auditor's report is shown below.

In our opinion, the financial statements referred to above present fairly, in all material respects, the financial position of ABC, Inc., as of December 31, 199X, and the changes in its net assets and its cash flows for the year then ended, in conformity with generally accepted accounting principles.

SAS-69 (The Meaning of "Present Fairly in Conformity with Generally Accepted Accounting Principles" in the Independent Auditor's Report) was issued to explain the phrase "present fairly in conformity with generally accepted accounting principles" by introducing a hierarchy of applicable accounting principles. The auditor must use judgment when determining if the accounting principles used have general acceptance and are appropriate for the particular use. These principles should make the financial statements informative, concise, understandable, and not misleading.

As stated in SAS-69, *generally accepted accounting principles* (GAAP) is a term that encompasses the conventions, rules, and procedures necessary to define accepted accounting practice at a particular time. These conventions, rules, and procedures are the standard for measuring financial presentation. The auditor uses professional judgment in determining the financial presentation within these rules, guidelines, and standards. The auditor's opinion that the financial statements are fairly presented is based on the judgment that the accounting principles used (1) are generally accepted; (2) are appropriate for the circumstances; (3) make statements understandable, informative, and not misleading; (4) classify and summarize statements in a meaningful way; and (5) reflect the underlying transactions and events.

Exhibit 2-1 presents the GAAP hierarchy. The standard-setters referred to in the GAAP hierarchy are:

- Financial Accounting Standards Board
- Accounting Standards Executive Committee
- Emerging Issues Task Force
- Governmental Accounting Standards Board
- American Institute of Certified Public Accountants

Exhibit 2-1
GAAP and Governmental GAAP Hierarchies

	Nongovernmental Entities	*State and Local Governments*
Category A	FASB Statements and Interpretations, APB Opinions, and Accounting Research Bulletins	GASB Statements and Interpretations, AICPA and FASB pronouncements if made applicable to state and local governments by a GASB Statement or by the AICPA
Category B	FASB Technical Bulletins, AICPA Industry Audit and Accounting Guides, and AICPA Statements of Position	GASB Technical Bulletins, and the following pronouncements if specifically made applicable to state and local governments by the AICPA: AICPA Industry Audit and Accounting Guides and Statements of Position
Category C	Consensus positions of the FASB Emerging Issues Task Force and AICPA Practice Bulletins	Question-and-answer documents published by the GASB staff as well as industry practices widely recognized and prevalent
Category D	AICPA accounting interpretations, question-and-answer documents published by the FASB, industry practices widely recognized and prevalent	Consensus positions of the GASB Emerging Issues Task Force (if established) and AICPA Practice Bulletins if specifically made applicable
Other Accounting Literature	Other accounting literature, including FASB Concepts Statements; APB Statements; AICPA Issues Papers; International Accounting Standards Committee Statements; GASB Statements, Interpretations, and Technical Bulletins; pronouncements of other professional associations or regulatory agencies; AICPA Technical Practice Aids; and accounting textbooks, handbooks, and articles	Other accounting literature, including GASB Concepts Statements; pronouncements in Categories A through D of the hierarchy for governmental entities when not specifically made applicable to state and local governments; APB Statements; FASB Concepts Statements; AICPA Issues Papers; International Accounting Standards Committee Statements; pronouncements of other professional associations or regulatory agencies; AICPA Technical Practice Aids; and accounting textbooks, handbooks, and articles

Financial Accounting Standards Board

The Financial Accounting Standards Board (FASB) is composed of seven members appointed by the Financial Accounting Foundation (FAF). Members serve five-year terms, have diverse backgrounds, and are knowledgeable in the accounting, finance, and business arenas. In addition, FASB employs a staff of professionals. Its mission is to establish and improve standards for financial accounting and reporting.

FASB issues several types of pronouncements, which have varying degrees of authority within the GAAP hierarchy, but it is most known for its Statements of Financial Accounting Standards. These standards of financial reporting are recognized under Rule 203 of the AICPA Code of Professional Conduct and under the Securities and Exchange Commission (SEC) Accounting Series Release No. 150. Statements are issued after Exposure Drafts are circulated, public hearings are held, and written responses to Exposure Drafts are considered.

FASB also issues Interpretations, which have the same authority as Statements. Interpretations explain or clarify existing Statements. They are issued relatively infrequently and require less due process before issuance than do the Statements.

The FASB staff occasionally issues Technical Bulletins, which are not restricted to addressing existing standards. Technical Bulletins may give guidance that differs from standards in certain circumstances, but they cannot create new accounting practices or conflict with fundamental accounting practices. Technical Bulletins are usually presented in a question-and-answer format.

FASB also issues Statements of Financial Accounting Concepts, which do not establish new standards and are not intended to invoke the application of Rule 203 of the AICPA Code of Professional Conduct. In the GAAP hierarchy, Concepts Statements have the lowest level of authority and are simply an additional source of guidance in financial accounting and reporting problems.

Accounting Standards Executive Committee

The Accounting Standards Executive Committee (AcSEC) is the senior technical body of the AICPA. AcSEC is composed of 15 CPAs, who are members of the AICPA, and representatives from education and public and private accounting. AcSEC members usually serve three-year terms, monitoring the financial reporting standard-setting process and the activities of the AICPA accounting standards technical committees.

Statements of Position present guidance on financial reporting problems that can be followed until standards are set. Statements of Position clarify, update, and revise Audit and Accounting Guides.

Before they can be issued, Statements of Position must be agreed to by at least two-thirds of AcSEC.

Audit and Accounting Guides address the accounting and auditing of specialized industries or entities and are prepared by various committees of the AICPA. Sections of these Guides that deal with financial reporting must be approved by a majority of AcSEC.

AcSEC also issues Practice Bulletins, which give present AcSEC members' views on financial reporting issues not addressed by FASB or GASB. Practice Bulletins also require approval by two-thirds of AcSEC.

The AICPA Accounting Standards Division prepares Issue Papers to provide information on financial accounting and reporting issues it believes should be considered by FASB or GASB. Issue Papers present a neutral discussion of the issue in question by giving an overview of current practices, existing literature, recent developments in practice, and arguments on alternative solutions. They may include advisory conclusions or recommendations and require the approval of a majority of AcSEC for issuance.

Emerging Issues Task Force

The Emerging Issues Task Force (EITF) was established by the FASB in 1984 to give guidance on new and emerging issues affecting financial reporting. The EITF has 13 members who are senior technical partners of major national CPA firms and representatives of major associations of financial statement preparers. The Chief Accountant of the SEC and a member of AcSEC participate in the Task Force meetings as observers. The EITF Abstracts report the accounting issues discussed, the results of the discussion, and the consensus reached.

Governmental Accounting Standards Board

The Governmental Accounting Standards Board (GASB) was formed in 1984 as a FASB equivalent for governmental accounting. GASB issues Statements, Interpretations, Technical Bulletins, and Concepts Statements similar to those issued by the FASB. Governmental entities must comply with a public-sector hierarchy, which is different from the private-sector hierarchy presented in Exhibit 2-1. GASB pronouncements hold the same level of authority in the public-sector (or governmental GAAP) hierarchy as FASB pronouncements do in the private-sector (or GAAP) hierarchy.

American Institute of Certified Public Accountants

Committee on Accounting Procedures From 1939 to 1959, the AICPA Committee on Accounting Procedures issued 51 Accounting

Research Bulletins (ARBs). ARBs hold the same level of authority as FASB Statements in the GAAP hierarchy.

Accounting Principles Board   In 1959, the Accounting Principles Board (APB) continued the responsibilities of the Committee on Accounting Procedures. From 1962 to 1973, the APB issued 31 Opinions. These Opinions have the same level of authority as FASB Statements in the GAAP hierarchy.

STATEMENT ON AUDITING STANDARDS NO. 78

This Statement on Auditing Standards amends SAS-55 (Consideration of the Internal Control Structure in a Financial Statement Audit). The effect of this document is to redefine and change the description of *internal control* contained in SAS-55 to correspond to the definition and description contained in *Internal Control—Integrated Framework*, published by the Committee of Sponsoring Organizations of the Treadway Commission. The Auditing Standards Board (ASB) of the AICPA stated in SAS-78 that the COSO report, as it is known, has come to be viewed throughout the *economy* as an "accepted framework for sound internal control . . . and its acceptance will continue to grow." SAS-78 is important to all U.S. auditees, including not-for-profit organizations, because independent auditors may revise their financial statement audits; for recipients of federal financial assistance, the new OMB Circular A-133 *Compliance Supplement* incorporates SAS-78 for audits of financial statements for periods beginning on or after January 1, 1997.

The COSO report, SAS-78, and the *Compliance Supplement* identify "five interrelated components" of internal control consisting of the control environment (providing discipline and structure and acting as the basis for the other components); risk assessment (providing the basis for managing the risks identified and analyzed by the entity as being relevant to the achievement of the organization's objectives); control activities (actions and the policies and procedures taken by the organization to strengthen the likelihood that the directives of management are followed); information and communication (provided by the organization to its people to allow them to fulfill their responsibilities); and monitoring (the activities of the organization that permit the evaluation of the internal control related performance over time).

Organizations and auditors must keep in mind that internal control should provide reasonable assurance regarding the achievement of objectives related to (a) reliability of financial reporting, (b) effectiveness and efficiency of operations, and (c) compliance with applicable laws and regulations.

SAS-78 discusses the following topics:

- Application of the components to a financial statement audit
- Limitations of an entity's internal control
- Consideration of internal control in planning an audit, and
- Application to small and mid-sized entities.

In the latter section, the ASB notes that size does matter, meaning that smaller entities may use less formal means to ensure that internal control objectives are achieved. Active management involvement and the organization's culture may play an important role in achieving the internal control objectives and allowing the auditor to properly assess control risk.

STATEMENT ON AUDITING STANDARDS NO. 82

In SAS-82 (Consideration of Fraud in a Financial Statement Audit), the ASB provides guidance to auditors in fulfilling the "responsibility to plan and perform the audit to obtain reasonable assurance about whether the financial statements are free of material misstatement, whether caused by error or fraud." The Statement, which is effective for audits of financial statements for periods ending on or after December 15, 1997, "describes fraud and its characteristics, and requires the auditor to *specifically assess the risk of material misstatement due to fraud*" [emphasis added].

ASB identifies two types of misstatements that are relevant to the auditor:

1. Misstatements arising from fraudulent financial reporting
2. Misstatements arising from misappropriation of assets

Regarding the first type, the auditor should be concerned with "intentional misstatements or omissions of amounts or disclosures in the financial statements to deceive financial statement users."

For the second type, the auditor should be concerned with the potential for theft of assets through embezzlement, stealing, or payment for goods or services not received by the organization.

When fraud exists, often there are circumstances that cause the misstatement to occur:

- *Pressure or incentive to commit fraud*—pressure for management to achieve certain results; individuals living beyond their means
- *Perceived opportunity to do so*—the individual believes that he or she can circumvent internal control

SAS-82 discusses in depth such topics as:

1. Assessment of the risk of material misstatement due to fraud
2. The auditor's response to the results of the assessment, includ-
    ing specific responses to misstatements arising from fraudu-
    lent financial reporting and specific responses to misstatements
    arising from misappropriation of assets
3. Evaluation of audit test results
4. Documentation of the auditor's risk assessment and response
5. Communications about fraud to management, the audit com-
    mittee, and others

STATEMENT OF POSITION 87-2

> **OBSERVATION:** The AICPA has issued SOP 98-2 (Accounting
> for Costs of Activities of Not-for-Profit Organizations and State
> and Local Governmental Entities That Include Fund Raising).
> This Statement, which will be discussed in the following sec-
> tion, is effective for financial statements for years beginning on
> or after December 15, 1998.

Although SOP 87-2 was superseded by the AICPA Audit and Accounting Guide, *Not-for-Profit Organizations*, a discussion of the SOP's
provisions is useful, and has been incorporated into this Guide's
Chapter 13, "Expenses, Gains, and Losses."

Joint costs occur when an organization combines a fund-raising
appeal with a program or management and general function within
one activity. For example, an educational organization may publish
a quarterly newsletter that includes educational articles and articles
on industry developments and other program-related issues. In
addition, a page may be devoted to the organization's fund-raising
appeal, requesting contributions and providing a return envelope.
Should the costs to prepare and distribute the newsletter be attributed to program or to fund-raising, or should they be allocated to
both?

This issue was first addressed in 1964 in the Voluntary Health and
Welfare Industry Standards. Those standards proposed the *primary
purpose concept*, which noted that no allocation of joint costs would
be made because the main function of the activity would be charged.

Statement of Position 78-10 also addressed this issue and stated:

> If an organization combines the fund-raising function with a
> program function (for example, a piece of educational litera-
> ture with a request for funds), the costs should be allocated to
> the program and fund-raising categories on the basis of the
> use made of the literature, as determined from its content,
> the reasons for its distribution, and the audience to whom it
> is addressed.

Because of the nonuniform accounting treatment of these joint costs, AcSEC issued SOP 87-2 (Accounting for Joint Costs of Informational Materials and Activities of Not-for-Profit Organizations That Include a Fund-Raising Appeal) to set a standard for the accounting of joint costs that include a fund-raising appeal. SOP 87-2 gives guidance on when it is appropriate to allocate these joint costs, but does not address *how* to allocate these costs. SOP 87-2 applies only to those activities that include a fund-raising appeal; it does not apply to the allocation of costs between other multipurpose functions.

Under SOP 87-2, joint costs that include a fund-raising appeal should not be allocated, and should be reported solely as fund-raising expenses, if it cannot be shown that a program or management and general function has been involved. Conversely, if it can be shown that a bona fide program or management and general function has been performed, then the joints costs should be allocated between the program or management and general function and the fund-raising function.

Key elements in demonstrating that a bona fide program or management and general function has been performed include:

- *Content of the non–fund-raising portion of the activity*—How does the information provided further the organization's not-for-profit objectives? What is the extent of educational materials provided?
- *Audience targeted*—Is the audience selected because its members may have a need or an interest in the organization's services or is it selected because of its members' past giving or ability to support the organization?
- *Action requested of the recipients*—As stated in the SOP, "Unless an appeal is designed to motivate its audience to action other than providing financial support to the organization, all costs of the appeal should be charged to fund raising."
- *Other evidence of the reason for the activity*—Other evidence may include minutes of board of directors meetings or written instructions regarding the activity.

STATEMENT OF POSITION 98-2

(This SOP supersedes certain paragraphs of the AICPA Audit and Accounting Guide, *Not-for-Profit Organizations.*)

Since its issuance in 1987, SOP 87-2 has been criticized for many reasons. It is not specific enough; it lacks guidance on allocation of costs; and in general it lacks detailed applications for its usage. In addition, SOP 87-2 has been criticized for its excessive and unreasonable allocations, mainly by organizations whose program costs consist primarily of joint-cost allocations.

In September 1993, the Not-for-Profit Organizations Committee of the AICPA issued an Exposure Draft of a proposed SOP titled "Accounting for Costs of Materials and Activities of Not-for-Profit Organizations and State and Local Governmental Entities That Include a Fund-Raising Appeal." The new SOP supersedes the provisions of SOP 87-2 and attempts to provide better and more detailed guidance. A wide range of events, campaigns, and telethons would be considered joint activities if they include a fund-raising function and a program or management and general function. Under the new SOP, all costs associated with a fund-raising appeal would be reported as fund-raising expenses unless a bona fide program or management and general function has been conducted.

To demonstrate that a bona fide function exists, three criteria must be present:

1. Purpose
2. Audience
3. Content

Purpose   The SOP notes that:

> [t]he purpose criterion is met if the purpose of the joint activity includes accomplishing program or management and general functions.

Several factors may aid in the identification of the purpose of the activity. According to SOP 98-2, the activity being reviewed for allocation "should call for specific action by the audience" to help achieve the organization's mission. SOP 98-2 provides examples to help determine if, in fact, the activity is not solely fund-raising in nature. The SOP makes clear that "[a]sking the audience to make contributions is not a call for specific action . . . that will help accomplish" the organization's mission. The purpose test would be met if a program activity with a fund-raising appeal was also conducted using the same medium (i.e., direct mail) without an appeal. However, the non–fund-raising activity should be performed to the same extent as, or to a greater extent than, the activity with an appeal. Other indications that a bona fide purpose other than fund-raising exists include:

- Qualifications and duties of those who are performing the activities
- Likelihood that the activity would be conducted if it did not have the fund-raising appeal
- Measurement of the results or accomplishments of the program

If compensation or performance evaluation is solely or substantially based on the amounts raised, then all of the activity's costs would be charged to fund-raising expense.

Audience The audience addressed is critical in determining whether an allocation is appropriate. If the activities are aimed at a particular audience or if the audience is selected based on its likelihood to contribute, then the costs would be charged to fund-raising. To qualify for a cost allocation, the audience must be selected based on its program participation (i.e., "need to use . . . the specific action called for by the joint activity") or its ability to meet the organization's nonfinancial goals; or it must have reasonable potential for the use of the management and general components of the activity.

Content To support the assertion that a bona fide program or management and general function has been conducted, the content of the materials or activity must further the not-for-profit organization's mission or the "activity fulfills one or more" of the organization's management and general responsibilities. These activities or materials should motivate the audience to take action or participate in ways other than financial support. If the content solely describes the organization and its needs, and provides information on how funds are provided and used, then these expenses would be charged to fund-raising.

The SOP also addresses allocation methods, which would be based on the degree to which the activities were benefited by the costs incurred. It does not require or prescribe a specific method; however, it does provide certain examples of allocation methods.

Disclosures Disclosures that are required by the SOP include:

- The types of materials and activities involving joint costs
- That costs have been allocated and the methods used
- Total amounts allocated in the reporting period
- Amount allocated to each functional category

See Chapter 4, "Expenses," for more discussion of the issues surrounding joint costs.

STATEMENT OF POSITION 93-7

SOP 93-7 (Reporting on Advertising Costs) provides guidance on the advertising activities of all entities. The SOP notes that fund-raising for not-for-profit organizations is not advertising and, accordingly, is not within the scope of the SOP. However, certain disclosures are required and certain principles apply:

- Total advertising costs for a period must be disclosed.
- Advertising costs should be expensed as incurred or when the advertising first takes place, except for direct-response advertising, when it is expected to result in future benefits.

The Audit Guide notes that:

> Advertising by a not-for-profit organization . . . includes activities to create or stimulate a desire to use the organization's products or services that are provided without charge.

When the products or services are provided without charge, no future benefit to the organization should be expected and, accordingly, there is no basis for continued capitalization of the advertising costs after the first time the advertising takes place.

STATEMENT OF POSITION 94-2

Although SOP 94-2 was superseded by the AICPA Audit and Accounting Guide, *Not-for-Profit Organizations,* a discussion of its provisions is useful.

SOP 94-2 (The Application of the Requirements of Accounting Research Bulletins, Opinions of the Accounting Principles Board, and Statements and Interpretations of the Financial Accounting Standards Board to Not-for-Profit Organizations), also known as "the Applicability SOP," was issued by AcSEC in September 1994. Confusion exists because some people believe that not-for-profit organizations are exempt from all ARBs, APB Opinions, and FASB Statements unless the Bulletin, Opinion, or Statement specifically states that it applies to not-for-profits. Others believe that the ARBs, APB Opinions, and FASB Statements do apply to not-for-profit organizations.

Paragraph 7 of FAS-117 states that a set of financial statements includes information required by generally accepted accounting principles that do not specifically exempt not-for-profit organizations. In addition, FASB Interpretation No. 40 (Applicability of Generally Accepted Accounting Principles to Mutual Life Insurance and Other Enterprises) stresses that pronouncements apply to not-for-profit organizations unless the pronouncement specifically exempts them. In light of these two sources, AcSEC doubted the necessity of this SOP, but decided to issue it because it provides explicit guidance for not-for-profit organizations. The SOP concludes that not-for-profit organizations should implement the provisions of ARBs, APB Opinions, and FASB Statements and Interpretations unless the pronouncement specifically exempts not-for-profit organizations. FASB Statements issued after SOP 94-2 apply to all not-for-profits unless specifically exempted.

Certain pronouncements are industry-specific, such as FAS-50 (Financial Reporting in the Record and Music Industry). According to SOP 94-2, a not-for-profit that operates within an industry covered by an industry-specific pronouncement should follow the guidance of that industry-specific pronouncement concerning the recognition and measurement of the transaction, but should follow the display guidance of FAS-117 and the AICPA Audit and Accounting Guides, even if it conflicts with the industry-specific pronouncement.

The SOP expanded guidance on certain pronouncements where the application of their provisions were unclear. Expanded guidance is discussed in the following sections.

APB Opinion No. 16

Under APB Opinion No. 16 (Business Combinations), two methods of accounting for business combinations are allowable. The purchase method and the pooling-of-interests method are acceptable, but are not interchangeable. Business combinations must meet specific conditions to use the pooling-of-interests method. If all conditions are not met, then the combination would be treated as a purchase. The conditions for applying the pooling-of-interests method include the exchange of common stock of the combining companies. Because of this criterion, not-for-profits generally would not meet the conditions and would be precluded from using the pooling-of-interests method. However, AcSEC felt that, under certain circumstances, the pooling-of-interests method would be a better presentation than the purchase method. Therefore, SOP 94-2 allows not-for-profit organizations to use the pooling-of-interests method under certain circumstances, even if there is no exchange of stock.

> **OBSERVATION:** FASB is reviewing the accounting requirements contained in APB Opinion No. 16 for business combinations. FASB members are attempting to further limit the use of the pooling-of-interests method. Management and boards of not-for-profit entities should watch the progress of FASB in this area, as there may be changes to the rules regarding the use of pooling-of-interests method that will have an impact on how financial statements will look after a strategic alliance between organizations.

APB Opinion No. 21

As discussed in APB Opinion No. 21 (Interest on Receivables and Payables), business transactions often can involve the exchange of cash, property, goods, or services for a note or similar financial instrument. If the stated interest rate is below the prevailing market rates, the face amount of the note or instrument may be less than the value of the asset or service exchanged. Opinion No. 21 requires the note or instrument to be recorded at its present value to properly record the transaction and the interest income or expense in subsequent years.

Under FAS-116, the appropriate measure of the fair value of an unconditional promise to give is the present value of estimated future cash flows using a discount rate commensurate with the risks involved. When APB Opinion No. 21 was issued, the Board did not consider whether its provisions applied to these promises to give. SOP 94-2 requires that not-for-profit organizations apply APB Opinion No. 21 to these unconditional promises.

Other Pronouncements

SOP 94-2 acknowledges that certain pronouncements do not fit the fund reporting models in the Audit Guides or FAS-117. The SOP allows the preparers of the financial statements to exercise their judgment to determine the best financial statement presentation when these pronouncements apply. The pronouncements are:

- APB Opinion No. 9 (Reporting the Results of Operations)

- APB Opinion No. 26 (Early Extinguishment of Debt), as amended by:

  — APB Opinion No. 30 (Reporting the Results of Operations— Reporting the Effects of Disposal of a Segment of a Business, and Extraordinary, Unusual, and Infrequently Occurring Events and Transactions)

  — FAS-4 (Reporting Gains and Losses from Extinguishment of Debt)

  — FAS-76 (Extinguishment of Debt)

  — FAS-125 (Accounting for Transfers and Servicing of Financial Assets and Extinguishments of Liabilities)

- FAS-52 (Foreign Currency Translation)

- FAS-109 (Accounting for Income Taxes)

Effective Dates

The effective date for SOP 94-2 is for financial statements issued for fiscal periods beginning after December 15, 1994, except for those not-for-profit organizations with less than $5 million in total assets and $1 million in annual expenses. For those organizations, the effective date is for fiscal years beginning after December 31, 1995.

STATEMENT OF POSITION 94-3

The funding of not-for-profit organizations has become more difficult as governments decrease their support of not-for-profit organizations and as public support in general decreases. Not-for-profit organizations are beginning to look for additional funding methods, including interrelationships with for-profit entities and other not-for-profit organizations. Certain not-for-profit organizations have formed for-profit subsidiaries as additional funding sources.

The AICPA issued SOP 94-3 (Reporting of Related Entities by Not-for-Profit Organizations) to provide guidance on the reporting of related entities. It amends and makes uniform the guidance concerning reporting related entities in the following superseded AICPA publications:

- *Audits of Voluntary Health and Welfare Organizations*
- *Audits of Colleges and Universities*
- *Audits of Certain Nonprofit Organizations*
- SOP 78-10

SOP 94-3 does not apply to entities covered by the AICPA Audit Guide *Audits of Providers of Health Care Services*, and its guidance is aimed at investments in for-profit entities and financially interrelated not-for-profit entities.

> **OBSERVATION:** In February 1999, FASB issued an Exposure Draft (Consolidated Financial Statements: Purpose and Policy). The written comments and the due process hearings surrounding this Exposure Draft could result in a new set of accounting pronouncements relating to the consolidation of entities as the definitions of *control* are refined.

Investments in For-Profit Entities

If a not-for-profit organization has a controlling financial interest in a for-profit entity through the direct or indirect ownership of a majority voting interest, then the for-profit entity should be consolidated in the not-for-profit organization's financial statements. Not-for-profits should follow the guidance of ARB-51 (Consolidated Financial Statements), as amended by FAS-94 (Consolidation of All Majority-Owned Subsidiaries). Consolidation is required for all majority-controlled for-profit subsidiaries, even though the subsidiaries may have very dissimilar or diverse operations. FAS-94 eliminated the exception for nonhomogeneity as a basis for excluding majority-controlled subsidiaries.

If the not-for-profit organization has less than a 50 percent interest in the voting stock of a for-profit entity and can exercise significant control, then the organization should account for its investment using the equity method of accounting. The not-for-profit should follow the guidance in APB Opinion No. 18 (The Equity Method of Accounting for Investments in Common Stock). The related disclosures required by Opinion No. 18 also apply to not-for-profit organizations.

SOP 94-3 allows an exception to this rule. Although superseded, certain Audit Guides relating to some not-for-profit organizations allowed the organizations to report their investments at market value. SOP 94-3 allows these not-for-profit organizations to continue to account for their investments in this manner instead of using the equity method.

Financially Interrelated Not-for-Profit Organizations

The lack of ownership does not preclude the consolidation of two or more interrelated not-for-profit organizations. Organizations may be related to each other not only through ownership, but also through control and economic interest. *Control*, as defined in the SOP, is the direct or indirect ability to determine the direction of management and the policies through ownership, contract, or otherwise. *Economic interest*, as stated in the SOP, exists if (1) the other entity holds or uses significant resources that must be used for the unrestricted or restricted purposes of the reporting not-for-profit organization, either directly or indirectly by producing income or producing services, or (2) the reporting organization is responsible for the liabilities of the other organization.

For interrelated not-for-profits, the specific scenarios encountered will determine if the presentation of consolidated financial statements is required or allowed. Some examples follow.

> **Example:** If an organization has a controlling financial interest in another not-for-profit through the direct or indirect ownership of a majority voting interest, then the reporting organization should consolidate the other not-for-profit. If control is

likely to be temporary or the reporting organization does not control the other not-for-profit organization, then consolidation would be prohibited. Ownership is generally not associated with not-for-profits. However, certain membership organizations issue membership certificates or stock. Certain not-for-profit organizations also issue stock.

Example: If a reporting not-for-profit organization has both control of another not-for-profit organization, as evidenced by a majority ownership or a majority voting interest in the board of the other entity, and an economic interest in the other organization, then the organization would consolidate its financial statements. Consolidation would be prohibited if control was likely to be temporary or if the control was not with the majority ownership.

The following example demonstrates a majority voting interest in the board of another entity.

Example: XYZ Organization has a nine-member board. To approve board action a simple majority is required. The ABC Organization appointed five of its board members, officers, or employees to serve on the board of XYZ Organization. In this scenario, ABC has a majority voting interest in XYZ's board. Assume those same five board members, officers, and employees of the ABC Organization serve on XYZ's board, but ABC does not have the ability to appoint XYZ's board members. In this case, ABC does not have a majority voting interest in the XYZ board.

A not-for-profit organization with an economic interest in another not-for-profit may have control over the other entity through means other than by majority ownership or voting interest (e.g., through contract or affiliation agreement). Unless this control is likely to be temporary, consolidation would be permitted, but it is not required. If the reporting organization elects not to consolidate, then the following disclosures would be required:

- Identification of the other not-for-profit and the nature of its relationship with the reporting organization that results in control
- Summarized financial data of the other organization that includes information about:
  — Total assets, liabilities, net assets, revenues, and expenses

— Resources that are held for the benefit of the reporting organization or the resources under its control

— The disclosures required by FAS-57 (Related Party Disclosures)

An organization may have control over another organization but may lack an economic interest or vice versa. In these instances, consolidation is not permitted, and the disclosures required by FAS-57 should be made. Organizations that are currently presenting consolidated financial statements in conformity with SOP 78-10 may continue to do so, even if they lack control or economic interest.

Consolidated Disclosure Requirement

When presenting consolidated financial statements, the reporting organization must disclose any restrictions on the controlled organization imposed by entities outside of the reporting entity. It should also disclose any unavailable net assets of the controlled organization that are not for use of the reporting organization.

SOP 94-3 includes flowcharts to aid in its implementation. The flowcharts are reproduced in Figures 2-1 and 2-2.

SOP 94-3 became effective for financial statements of entities with fiscal years beginning after December 15, 1994. Organizations with less than $5 million in total assets and less than $1 million in annual expenses have an effective date for fiscal years beginning after December 15, 1995. The AcSEC encourages those organizations early adopting the provisions of FAS-117 to early adopt the provisions of this SOP as well.

STATEMENT OF POSITION 94-6

AcSEC issued SOP 94-6 (Disclosure of Certain Significant Risks and Uncertainties) in December 1994 to address issues related to the disclosure of certain significant risks and uncertainties. SOP 94-6 applies to those financial statements prepared in accordance with generally accepted accounting principles applicable to nongovernmental entities. The disclosures relate to those risks and uncertainties that may significantly affect items reported in the financial statements in the near term. Disclosures required by this SOP relate to the nature of the organization's operations, use of significant estimates, and the current vulnerability caused by certain categories of concentrations.

As stated above, SOP 94-6 applies to both for-profit and not-for-profit organizations. However, this chapter will address the SOP and its applications for the not-for-profit community.

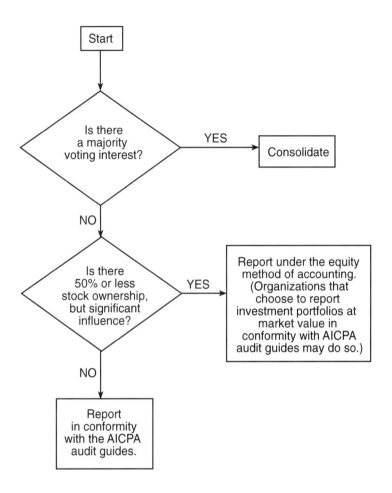

Figure 2-1: *Ownership of a For-Profit Entity*

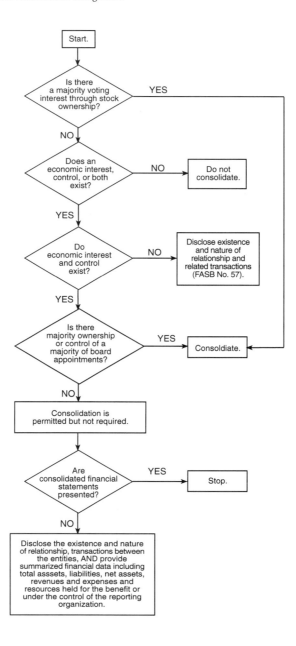

Figure 2-2: Relationship with Another Not-for-Profit Organization

Certain disclosures required by SOP 94-6 may have already been made in accordance with other FASB pronouncements. The disclosure requirements of SOP are not meant to change those requirements; they are meant to supplement those disclosures.

Disclosures required by the SOP include:

1. Nature of operations
2. Use of significant estimates in the preparation of the financial statements
3. Use of certain significant estimates
4. Current vulnerability caused by certain concentrations

These disclosure requirements are specifically *not* applicable to the following:

1. Those associated with management or key personnel
2. Proposed changes in government regulations
3. Proposed changes in accounting principles
4. Deficiencies in internal controls
5. Possible effects of God, war, or sudden catastrophes

Nature of Operations

Under SOP 94-6, the nature of the operations of the not-for-profit should be disclosed in the financial statements. The disclosure should include a description of its principal or major services or programs, as well as where these services are performed, and the major classes of funding or revenue sources. The major services, programs, and funding sources do not have to be quantified, but information should be provided about their relative importance. An illustrative disclosure follows.

The ABC Organization, located in New York City, is dedicated to the instruction and development of youth in the performing arts through educational workshops and classes. A major portion of its funding is from individual contributions and tuition received from its classes and workshops.

Use of Estimates and Certain Significant Estimates

To prepare financial statements in accordance with generally accepted accounting principles, not-for-profit organizations must use management's estimates. The financial statements need to disclose this fact, and SOP 94-6 provides the following sample disclosure:

The preparation of financial statements in accordance with generally accepted accounting principles requires management to make estimates and assumptions that affect the reported amounts of assets and liabilities and disclosure of contingent assets and liabilities at the date of the financial statements and the reported amounts of revenues and expenses during the reporting period. Actual results could differ from those estimates.

Management uses certain significant estimates in the preparation of its financial statements. These may include those estimates described in FAS-5 (Accounting for Contingencies) and FASB Interpretation No. 14 (Reasonable Estimation of the Amount of a Loss). The use of estimates should be disclosed when both of the following criteria are met:

1. There exists a reasonable possibility that, in the *near term*, the estimate of the effect on the financial statements of a condition, situation, or set of circumstances that existed at the date of the financial statements will change due to one or more future confirming events.[1]

2. The change would have a material effect on the financial statements.

If both conditions are met, then the required disclosure would include a description of the nature of the estimate and would indicate that "it is at least reasonably possible that a change in the estimate will occur in the near term."

Additional disclosures are required for loss contingencies, as described in FAS-5. FAS-5 requires an estimated loss from a loss contingency to be accrued by a charge to income or change in net assets, if both of the following conditions are met:

1. Information is available prior to the financial statement issuance that indicates it is probable an asset has been impaired, or a liability incurred, at the date of the financial statements.

2. The amount of the loss can be reasonably estimated.

The disclosure should include an estimate of the possible loss, the range of the loss, or a statement that an estimate cannot be made.

---

[1] SOP 94-6 defines *near term* as a period of time not to exceed one year from the date of the financial statements.

While not required, a description of the factors that may affect the estimates may be helpful to readers.

The terms *probable, reasonably possible,* and *remote* are used as follows:

> *Probable*—The future event or events are likely to occur.

> *Reasonably possible*—The chance of the future event or events occurring is more than remote but less than likely.

> *Remote*—The chance of the future event or events occurring is slight.

The disclosure requirements of SOP 94-6 are meant to supplement those of FAS-5. A major difference between SOP 94-6 and FAS-5 is that FAS-5 does not distinguish between long-term and near-term contingencies.

The amount of an estimate reported on a financial statement is *not* the determination of the materiality for a disclosure. The materiality, for disclosure purposes, is based on the effect that using a different estimate would have on the financial statements. SOP 94-6 may require a disclosure even if the estimate results in reporting no amount or an immaterial amount.

SOP 94-6 provides several examples of items that meet the requirements for disclosure based on estimates that are sensitive to change in the near term:

- Inventory and specialized equipment subject to technological obsolescence
- Capitalized motion picture film production costs or computer software costs
- Valuation allowances for loans
- Environmental remediation-related obligations
- Litigation-related obligations
- Contingent liabilities or guarantees of obligations of other entities
- Amounts reported as obligations for pensions and post-employment benefits

SOP 94-6 provides the following events or changes in circumstances that may demonstrate when estimates are sensitive to a change in the near term:

- Significant decrease in the market value of an asset
- Change in the manner or extent that an asset is used

- Adverse changes in legal factors or adverse changes within the business environment
- Assets with a history of losses and projected continued losses

Some sample disclosures follow.

Guarantee of Debt of Another Entity

A Organization is contingently liable under certain debt obligations of B Organization, an affiliate. At December 31, 19X1, the amount of those debt obligations is $1,000,000. B Organization is experiencing financial difficulties and may not be able to pay its annual debt obligation of $100,000 in 19X2. Although B Organization is developing new funding sources, it is reasonably possible that it may not be able to make all of its required payments on the loan. A Organization may be responsible for a portion of the debt payment due in 19X1 and in future years. No amount has been recorded in the organization's financial statements pending the outcome of the B Organization's fund-raising efforts.

Environmental Damage

The ABC Museum has recorded a provision for $500,000 for the estimated cost of an environmental cleanup on the property where the museum is located. The actual cost may vary and could possibly be up to $2,000,000 depending on the extent of environmental damage found. The cleanup is expected to be completed within the next two years.

Litigation

The ZZ Organization has tentatively agreed to settle a civil suit brought against it by the United States for environmental damages it caused in the construction of its new facilities in the amount of $200,000. The proposed settlement is subject to court approval. The court may double this assessment pending the outcome of certain environmental tests. It is expected that the results of these tests will not double the settlement, and the case is expected to be resolved with one year.

Current Vulnerability Caused by Certain Concentrations

Not-for-profit organizations generally have a specific purpose or a venue in which they operate. Because of their purposes, they may operate in the field of the sciences, art, education, or any other field. Because of limitations in a given industry or field, risk may be greater than the potential risk had there been greater diversification.

Several categories of concentrations exist, including the following:

- Concentrations in the volume of business transacted with a particular customer, supplier, lender, grantor, or contributor
- Concentrations in revenue from particular products, services, or fund-raising events
- Concentrations in the available sources of supply of materials, labor, or services, or of licenses or the rights used in the organization's operations
- Concentrations in the market or geographic area where the organization conducts its operations

Not-for-profit organizations would disclose these types of risks associated with the above concentrations if all of the following are met:

- The concentration exists at the date of the financial statements.
- The concentration makes the organization vulnerable to the risk of a near-term severe impact.
- It is at least reasonably possible that the events that could cause the severe impact will occur in the near term.

The disclosures should ensure that they inform the readers of the nature of the risk caused by the concentrations. Additionally, the following specific disclosures are required for two types of concentration risks:

1. If the organization has collective bargaining agreements, the financial statements must disclose the percentage of the labor force covered under the collective bargaining agreement and the percentage of the labor force covered by an agreement that expires within one year of the financial statements.
2. If an organization has offices or operations located outside of the organization's home country, it must disclose the carrying amount of the net assets and their geographic location.

An example follows.

Contributor Concentration

The City Theatre Company is a not-for-profit organization supported by individual contributions and performance fees. One major contributor provides 25 percent of the support of the Company.

Revenue Concentration

The City Theatre Company is a not-for-profit organization supported by individual contributions and performance fees. Twenty-five percent of its operating revenue is derived from its annual "theatre night" fund raiser.

Concentrations other than those discussed above may exist. For example, FAS-105 contains disclosure requirements for certain risks not addressed by SOP 94-6.

According to SOP 94-6, these disclosures are based on the facts and management's knowledge at the time of the issuance of the financial statements. A severe impact caused by a concentration that was not disclosed is not necessarily an error or noncompliance, if the appropriate judgment was used at the time of issuance. Conversely, disclosing a risk of concentration does not imply the occurrence or nonoccurrence of the event.

Effective Date

SOP 94-6 became effective for financial statements with fiscal years ending after December 15, 1995. For organizations issuing interim financial statements, SOP 94-6 became effective for interim statements subsequent to the year in which the SOP is first applied.

STATEMENT OF POSITION 98-1

In March 1998, the AICPA issued SOP 98-1 (Accounting for the Costs of Computer Software Developed or Obtained for Internal Use), which is applicable to all nongovernmental entities and effective for financial statements for fiscal years beginning after December 15, 1998.

Given the lack of authoritative guidance on accounting for costs of computer software developed or obtained for internal use, practice had become diverse, with some entities capitalizing certain costs and other entities expensing them. In December 1996, the AcSEC issued an Exposure Draft of a proposed SOP, which drew approximately 130 comment letters.

SOP 98-1 is intended to provide guidance on accounting for the costs of computer software developed or obtained for internal use and on determining whether computer software is for internal use. Costs of software developed or obtained can be classified into several different categories, including:

- Software to be sold, leased, or otherwise marketed as a separate product or as part of a product or process,
- Software to be used in research and development,
- Software to be developed for others under a contractual arrangement, or
- Software for internal use.

SOP 98-1 applies to costs that fall into the last category. Accounting for costs of reengineering activities, which are often associated with new or upgraded software applications, is not within the scope of SOP 98-1. These costs should be expensed as incurred, as set forth in the conclusions reached in EITF Issue No. 97-13, "Accounting for Costs Incurred in Connection with a Consulting Contract or an Internal Project That Combines Business Process Reengineering and Information Technology Transformation."

Definition

SOP 98-1 characterizes internal-use software as software acquired, internally developed, or modified solely to meet an entity's internal needs. During the software's development or modification, there should be no existing substantive plan and no plan in development to market the software externally. An appendix to SOP 98-1 provides examples of when computer software would or would not be considered internal use.

For example, for a not-for-profit organization to purchase or develop software to process its contributions receivable would be considered internal use. However, if the same organization develops the system for sale as well as for internal use, had a marketing plan before the project is complete, has a history of selling software that it also uses internally, and can reasonably be expected to implement the plan, then the software would be considered to be for other than internal use.

Stages of Computer Software Development and Effect on Related Accounting Treatment

SOP 98-1 illustrates the various stages and related process of computer software development, which include a preliminary project stage, an application development stage, and a post-implementation/operation stage.

Costs incurred during the *preliminary project stage* should be expensed as they are incurred. The activities giving rise to these costs might include:

- Making strategic decisions to allocate resources between different projects
- Determining performance requirements and system requirements
- Inviting vendors to perform demonstrations
- Exploring alternative means of achieving specified performance requirements
- Determining that technology needed to achieve performance requirements exists
- Selecting a vendor from which to obtain software
- Selecting a consultant to assist in the development or installation of the software.

Costs incurred during the *application development stage*—as well as costs to develop or obtain software that allows for access to or conversion of old data by new systems—should be capitalized. However, any training costs and data conversion costs that are incurred during this stage should be expensed as incurred.

Post-implementation/operation stage costs, which would include internal and external training and maintenance costs, should be expensed as incurred.

Internal costs incurred for maintenance should be expensed as incurred. Internal costs incurred for upgrades and enhancements, and external costs incurred for *specified* upgrades and enhancements, would be capitalized or expensed based on the guidance noted above regarding the different development stages. For any costs related to upgrades or enhancements to be capitalized, it must be probable that *additional* functionality will result for existing internal-use software. External costs related to maintenance, *unspecified* upgrades and enhancements, and costs under agreements combining the two generally should be recognized in expense over the contract period on a straight-line basis. If an entity cannot separate costs between maintenance and upgrades and enhancements on a reasonably cost-effective basis, then such costs should be expensed.

Capitalization of costs, as defined below, should begin (1) when the preliminary project stage is completed, (2) when management implicitly or explicitly authorizes and commits to funding a computer software project, and (3) when it is probable that the project will be completed and the software will be used to perform the intended function. When this last criterion no longer becomes probable, no further costs should be capitalized, and impairment should be addressed. Capitalization should cease no later than when the project is considered to be substantially complete and ready for its intended use—that is, when all substantial testing is completed.

When existing software is replaced, unamortized costs of the old software should be expensed when the new software is ready for its intended use.

Capitalizable Costs

Capitalizable costs include external direct costs of materials and services consumed in developing or obtaining the software, payroll and payroll-related costs for employees who are directly associated with and who devote time to the project, and interest costs incurred while the software is being developed. General and administrative and overhead costs should *not* be capitalized.

When an entity purchases software from a third party and the price includes multiple elements, the entity should allocate the cost among the individual elements based on objective evidence of fair value and not necessarily on the separate prices stated within the contract.

Impairment

Impairment should be recognized and measured in accordance with FAS-121 (Accounting for the Impairment of Long-Lived Assets and for Long-Lived Assets to Be Disposed Of). FAS-121 might be applicable when a significant change occurs in the extent or manner in which the software is used or expected to be used, when a significant change is made in the software program, or when the software is not expected to provide substantial service potential.

In addition, excessive costs of developing or modifying such software over original expectations might give rise to impairment considerations. For example, if a not-for-profit organization begins to develop internal-use software for use in a specific program and that software can be used for only that program, a discontinuation of the program would indicate that impairment should be reviewed in accordance with FAS-121.

When it is no longer probable that the software will be completed and placed in service, the organization should report the asset at the lower of the carrying amount or fair value, if any, less costs to sell. A rebuttable presumption exists that the fair value of such uncompleted software is zero. SOP 98-1 provides some examples of situations—including lack of budgeted expenditures for the project and significant cost overruns—that indicate when software may no longer be completed and placed in service.

Amortizing Capitalized Costs

Amortization of capitalized costs should take place on a straight-line basis, unless another systematic and rational basis is more representative of the software's use. Factors such as obsolescence, technology, and competition should be taken into account. Amortization should begin when the software is ready for its intended use, which would be after all substantial testing is completed.

Application

SOP 98-1 should be applied to internal-use software costs incurred in fiscal years beginning after December 15, 1998, including those in progress upon initial application. The initial application should take place as of the beginning of the first fiscal year. Earlier application is encouraged in fiscal years in which annual financial statements have not been issued. Any costs incurred before the application of the SOP, whether capitalized or not, should not be adjusted to the amounts that would have been capitalized if the SOP had been in effect when the costs were incurred. Amortization and impairment, as set forth in this SOP, should be applied to any unamortized costs that continue to be reported as assets after the effective date.

STATEMENT OF POSITION 98-3

In March 1998, the AICPA issued SOP 98-3 (Audits of States, Local Governments, and Not-for-Profit Organizations Receiving Federal Awards) to provide guidance regarding the performance of audits in accordance with the Single Audit Act Amendments of 1996 (the "Act") and Office of Management and Budget (OMB) Circular A-133 (the "Revised A-133"), titled *Audits of States, Local Governments, and Non-Profit Organizations* (June 1997 Revision). In addition to the Act and the Revised A-133, SOP 98-3 incorporates guidance from SAS-74 (Compliance Auditing Considerations in Audits of Governmental Entities and Recipients of Governmental Financial Assistance) and *Government Auditing Standards* (1994 Revision).

As explained more fully in this Guide in Part IV, Chapter 15, "Office of Management and Budget," the Act and the Revised A-133 resulted in certain changes to the standards by which audits of organizations receiving federal awards must be performed. These changes included the following:

- The threshold requiring an audit was changed from $25,000 of federal awards received to $300,000 of federal expenditures.
- Reports are now due within nine months following year-end, compared with thirteen months under the prior guidance.

- Major programs, which were previously determined based on dollars expended, are determined by the independent auditor under a risk-based approach.
- The number of reports required by the independent auditor was reduced significantly.
- Reportable findings and questioned costs, which in the past were basically *all* reported, are now determined based on certain criteria and thresholds.
- The auditee is now responsible for preparation and submission of the Schedule of Expenditures of Federal Awards, a report summarizing the status of the prior-year findings, and a corrective action plan.
- The auditor and the auditee must together prepare a data collection form, which summarizes the federal awards and audit results.

The applicability of the Act and the Revised A-133 is described in SOP 98-3, which supersedes the guidance in SOP 92-9 (Audits of Not-for-Profit Organizations Receiving Federal Awards) and Part II, "Audits of Federal Financial Assistance," of the AICPA Audit and Accounting Guide *Audits of State and Local Governmental Units.*

SOP 98-3 provides an overview of the auditor's responsibilities (1) in performing an audit of federal awards; (2) in testing and reporting on the Schedule of Expenditures of Federal Awards; (3) for reporting; (4) for considering internal control and performing tests of compliance with applicable laws, regulations, and program compliance requirements; and (5) for testing and reporting in a program-specific audit. Examples of the required reports under *Government Auditing Standards* and the Revised A-133 are also presented.

The Statement is intended merely to provide guidance and is not a complete manual of procedures; nor should it replace the auditor's judgment about the audit work. Given the complexity and variety of federal award programs and the additional audit requirements imposed by certain states, auditors must continue to use professional judgment to tailor the procedures to each particular engagement.

The effective dates of this guidance should be applied as provided for in the related literature (i.e., the Act and the Revised A-133, which are effective for audits of fiscal years beginning after June 30, 1996). The remaining provisions of SOP 98-3 are effective for fiscal years beginning after June 30, 1996, in which the related fieldwork commenced on or after March 1, 1998. Earlier application is encouraged.

STATEMENT OF POSITION 98-5

The AICPA's Accounting Standards Executive Committee (AcSEC) issued SOP 98-5 (Reporting on the Costs of Start-Up Activities) to provide guidance on the financial reporting of start-up costs. *Start-up costs* for development-stage and operating entities are defined as:

> those one-time activities related to opening a new facility, introducing a new product or service, conducting business in a new territory, conducting business with a new class of customer or beneficiary, initiating a new process in an existing facility, or commencing some new operation.

For not-for-profit organizations, these start-up activities could be represented by, for example, a new program or the opening of a new treatment or rehabilitation facility. In the Illustrations accompanying SOP 98-5, AcSEC includes a scenario in which an existing not-for-profit organization is opening its first shelter to house the homeless. An analysis of some of the related costs results in the following:

Start-up costs within the scope of the SOP	*Costs outside of the scope of the SOP*
Employee salary-related costs related to needs and feasibility studies	Costs of fund-raising
Staff recruiting and training	Costs of leasehold improvements and furniture (other than amortization and depreciation during the start-up period
Rent, security, insurance, and utilities during the start-up period	Government fees, registration fees, and inspection costs
Consultant fees for developing policies and procedures for operating the shelter	Architect fees for the addition
Amortization and depreciation, if any, of leasehold improvements and furniture during the start-up period	Advertising costs to publicize the shelter
Costs of the certified social workers until normal operating capacity is reached	

The activities contemplated by SOP 98-5 occur in the periods before an organization commences operations and after operations have begun, but before "normal productive capacity" is reached. AcSEC defines *normal productive capacity* as:

> the average level of operating activity that is sufficient to fill the demand for an entity's products or services over a period of time.

The SOP incorporates into the term *start-up activities* similar terms that have had wide use. These terms include *preoperating costs, preopening costs,* and *start-up costs*. AcSEC did not try to identify costs that should be included in the definition of *start-up activities,* because it believes that the organizations themselves are "best capable of identifying those costs." It does believe, however, that it can identify items that should be excluded from the definition of *start-up activities*. These would include:

- Costs of acquiring or developing tangible assets
- Costs of acquiring intangible assets from third parties
- Costs that are eligible to be capitalized as part of inventory, long-lived assets, or some other internally developed intangible assets
- Costs that relate to research and development costs and certain types of regulation
- Costs of fund-raising incurred by not-for-profit organizations
- Costs of raising capital
- Organization costs

Costs of long-lived assets or those capitalized as part of inventory are addressed in other authoritative literature.

SOP 98-5 amends several currently effective pronouncements:

- SOP 81-1 (Accounting for Performance of Construction-Type and Certain Production-Type Contracts)
- SOP 88-1 (Accounting for Developmental and Preoperating Costs, Purchases and Exchanges of Take-off and Landing Slots, and Airframe Modifications)
- Audit and Accounting Guide titled *Audits of Casinos*
- Audit and Accounting Guide titled *Construction Contractors*
- Audit and Accounting Guide titled *Audits of Federal Government Contractors*

The conclusion reached in SOP 98-5 is simply that **costs of start-up activities should be expensed as incurred**. AcSEC reached its conclusion using the underlying principle that "it is unnecessary to distinguish between the objectives for undertaking start-up activities." AcSEC believes that, in current practice, there is not a clear distinction between preopening/preoperating costs and start-up costs and the accounting treatment accorded to each.

While it considered that capitalization of the cost of start-up costs was a possibility, AcSEC concluded that "no evidence has been identified that demonstrates a causal relationship between start-up costs incurred and related future economic benefits; therefore, AcSEC reasons that those costs should be expensed as incurred."

AcSEC reached the conclusion that the value of disclosure of the cost of start-up activities for the period and the total of such costs expected to be incurred was outweighed by the costs of recordkeeping required to separately identify such costs. Accordingly, the SOP does not require organizations to make these disclosures.

SOP 98-5 was effective for financial statements of fiscal years beginning after December 15, 1997, with earlier application permitted. However, restatement of previously issued financial statements was not permitted. The initial application of this Statement will be at the beginning of the fiscal year in which it is adopted and will be reported as a cumulative effect of a change in accounting principle in accordance with Accounting Principles Board Opinion No. 20.

STATEMENTS ON AUDITING STANDARDS
NO. 59 AND NO. 64

Many not-for-profit organizations today are faced with soaring costs and fixed or declining funding resources. State and local governments are trimming their own budgets and may be spending less on public support of not-for-profit organizations. In addition, many private citizens are significantly reducing their contributions to not-for-profit organizations. In this environment of declining support, not-for-profit organizations may be forced to cease operations or continue operations only by using available resources. The auditor has the responsibility to determine if the entity has the ability to continue as a going concern for a reasonable amount of time, one year from the financial statement date. SAS-59 (The Auditor's Consideration of an Entity's Ability to Continue as a Going Concern) and SAS-64 (Omnibus Statement on Auditing Standards—1990) provide the auditor with guidance for auditing an organization for which factors exist that raise doubts about ongoing operations.

The auditor must evaluate conditions that existed or events that occurred before the completion of the fieldwork that may indicate substantial doubt about the ability of the organization to continue as a going concern. In the planning and design of the audit program, the auditor does not have to design specific tests and procedures to identify a going-concern issue, but should assess the results of all audit procedures performed and the results of the gathering of evidential matter. In the performance of the audit, the auditor should become aware of certain conditions or events that may indicate adverse conditions. The auditor should then expand the information-gathering process to determine if there is substantial doubt about the ability of the organization to continue as a going concern.

SAS-59 lists certain procedures that may identify conditions or events that indicate a going-concern problem:

- Analytic review procedures
- Review of subsequent events
- Review of compliance with the terms of loan agreements
- Reading of the minutes of board of directors meetings or other committee reports
- Inquiry of the organization's legal counsel about the existence of litigation, claims, or assessments
- Confirmation with related or third parties about the details regarding the arrangements to provide or maintain financial support

Conditions and events that can indicate going-concern issues include:

- *Negative trends*—Negative trends may be ongoing and continued losses, continued deficiencies in net asset categories, declining financial ratios, or adverse cash flows. They also can be loss of support of substantial contributors or cutbacks in government sponsorship or funding.
- *Other indications of possible financial difficulties*—Other indications of possible financial difficulties may be defaults on debt payments or covenants, denial of credit from suppliers, restructuring of debt, or the disposal of assets. Changes in demographic or social changes also can adversely affect not-for-profit organizations. The auditor should be alerted if the organization begins to use endowment funds to support its operations.
- *Internal matters*—Internal matters that may indicate going-concern issues are uneconomic long-term commitments, dependence on the success of a particular event or project, and the need to revise operations significantly or to seek new sources or methods for funding. Infighting among board members or management may indicate going-concern problems. The loss of the organization's tax status or activities that may endanger its tax status also are matters to be considered.
- *External matters*—External matters that may indicate going-concern issues are litigation against the organization, new laws

that adversely affect charitable giving, the loss of a major donor, or catastrophes. Adverse publicity regarding other not-for-profit organizations' spending or scandals also may negatively affect the operations of an organization in a similar field.

If, after conducting the procedures listed, the auditor believes substantial doubt exists about the organization's ability to continue as a going concern for a reasonable period of time, then the auditor has the responsibility to:

- Obtain information regarding how management plans to deal with the these adverse conditions and events.
- Determine if the plans can be effectively implemented.

Consideration of Management's Plans

When evaluating management's plans for dealing with declining circumstances, the auditor should consider the following:

Plans to Dispose of Assets
- The existence of restrictions on assets from donor-imposed or state and legal restrictions, or loan restrictions or encumbrances
- The marketability of the assets management plans to sell
- The possible direct or indirect effects of the disposition of the assets

Plans to Borrow Money or Restructure Debt
- The availability of debt financing, including the existing credit lines or committed credit arrangements or the availability of the sale-leaseback of assets
- Existing or anticipated restructuring of debt
- Whether current debt provisions allow additional financing and the availability of assets for collateral

Plans to Delay or Reduce Expenditures
- Apparent feasibility of plans to reduce program, management and general, or fund-raising expenses; postpone maintenance programs; or lease rather than purchase assets
- The possible direct or indirect effects of reduced or delayed expenditures

Plans to Increase Size of Ownership in Membership Organizations or to Obtain Additional Sources of Revenues

- Apparent feasibility of obtaining additional membership or additional supporters and contributors
- Apparent feasibility of new fund-raising campaigns

The auditor may need to obtain additional evidential matter or perform additional auditing procedures to evaluate management's plans. For example, the auditor may look at debt agreements to determine if the assets that management plans to sell are free of encumbrances.

As part of its plans, management may provide the auditor with projections of future operations or cash flows. The auditor needs to obtain information and evidence from management to support its claims and assumptions. Using his or her knowledge of the organization, the industry, and the organization's management, the auditor may become aware of factors or events that are not reported, or are improperly reported, in the prospective financials. In this case, the auditor should discuss these matters with management and may request a revision of the projections.

If, after evaluating management's plans, the auditor concludes that substantial doubt exists about the organization's ability to continue as a going concern, the auditor should:

- Disclose the organization's possible inability to continue as a going concern for a reasonable period of time, and
- Include in the auditor's report, an explanatory paragraph, following the opinion paragraph, reflecting the auditor's conclusion.

SAS-59 suggests that the following information be disclosed:

- Pertinent conditions and events giving rise to the assessment of the substantial doubt about the entity's ability to continue as a going concern for a reasonable period of time
- Possible effects of such conditions and events
- Management's evaluation of the significance of those conditions and events and any mitigating factors
- Possible discontinuance of operations
- Management's plans (including relevant prospective financial information)
- Information about the recoverability or classification of recorded asset amounts or the amounts or classification of liabilities

The explanatory paragraph in the auditor's report should read as follows:

The accompanying financial statements have been prepared assuming that the ABC Organization will continue as a going concern. As discussed in Note X to the financial statements, the Organization has suffered recurring losses from operations and has a deficiency in net assets that raises substantial doubt about its ability to continue as a going concern. Management's plans in regard to these matters are also described in Note X. The financial statements do not include any adjustments that might result from the outcome of this uncertainty.

A sample disclosure is presented below.

Note X. Going Concern

As shown in the financial statements, the organization has recurring losses from operations and has not been in compliance with certain financial covenants. These factors raise substantial doubt about its ability to continue as a going concern.

Management has begun a cost reduction program, which includes a reduction in salaries and fringe benefits. Additionally, the organization has scaled backed several of its service programs. Management is also continuing discussions with its bank to restructure its long-term debt, including extending the maturity date and making interest-only payments through the next fiscal year.

Management believes these factors will allow it to achieve greater cash flows from operations. The financial statements do not include any adjustments that might be necessary if the organization is unable to continue as a going concern.

If the auditor's consideration of management's plans has alleviated his or her substantial doubt about the organization's ability to continue as a going concern, the auditor should consider disclosing the following information:

- Principal conditions and events that initially caused the substantial doubt
- Possible effects of the conditions or events
- Any mitigating factors, including management's plans

FASB STATEMENT NO. 93

Background

Depreciation spreads the cost of an asset over its useful life of service and provides a matching of its usage to related income benefits. The method used to depreciate assets must be systematic and rational for a period equal to the property's estimated useful life. The cost basis used for depreciation is historical cost less any estimated salvage value. Depreciation is not intended to be a valuation but is intended to be an allocation of cost over a period of time.

Accounting for depreciation of long-lived assets is not a new concept to for-profit entities. However, some not-for-profit organizations, in particular colleges, universities, and religious organizations, were not required to record depreciation until recently. SOP 78-10 recommended depreciation accounting, but did not establish enforceable standards. FAS-32 (Specialized Accounting and Reporting Principles and Practices in AICPA Statements of Position and Guides on Accounting and Auditing Matters) organized the alternative accounting methods allowed under generally accepted accounting principles according to which methods were "preferable" to others. Depreciation accounting was described as preferable for not-for-profit organizations, but FAS-32 stopped short of requiring entities to change their specialized accounting and reporting methods.[2] SOP 74-8 (Financial Accounting and Reporting by Colleges and Universities) did not recommend its usage or nonusage. The AICPA Audit and Accounting Guides titled *Audits of Hospitals* and *Audits of Voluntary Health and Welfare Organizations* required depreciation accounting.

In August 1987, the FASB issued FAS-93 (Recognition of Depreciation by Not-For-Profit Organizations), which established standards that require all not-for-profit organizations to adopt depreciation accounting. The Statement required the disclosure requirements of APB Opinion No. 12 (Omnibus Opinion—1967), paragraph 5, which are as follows:

    a. Depreciation expense for the period,

    b. Balances of major classes of depreciable assets, by nature or function, at the balance-sheet date,

    c. Accumulated depreciation, either by major classes of depreciable assets or in total, at the balance-sheet date, and

    d. A general description of the method or methods used in computing depreciation with respect to major classes of depreciable assets.

---

[2] In November 1992, FAS-32 was superseded by FAS-111 (Rescission of FASB Statement No. 32 and Technical Corrections).

According to FAS-93, assets whose useful lives are extraordinarily long, such as land, works of art, or historical treasures, may not have to account for depreciation. To be excluded from the provisions of FAS-93, an asset must meet the following two conditions:

1. The asset individually must have cultural, aesthetic, or historical value that is worth preserving perpetually.

2. The holder of the asset must have the technological and financial ability to protect and preserve essentially undiminished the service potential of the asset and must be doing so.

An organization adopting the provisions of FAS-93 must apply the accounting change retroactively. The adjustments for this accounting change would be made to the beginning net assets balances of the earliest year presented in the financial statements or in the current year if a single-year presentation is used. In the year the Statement is adopted, the disclosures should include the nature of the restatement and the effect on net income for each of the periods presented.

Depreciation accounting relies on estimates for useful lives of assets. Estimates for salvage values and useful lives can change greatly from the time the asset is purchased to the time the organization adopts FAS-93. If the asset's useful life and salvage value is presently known but was not known at the time the asset was placed in service, the information known currently may be used when applying FAS-93.

Effective Date

When issued, FAS-93 was to become effective for financial statements with fiscal years beginning after May 15, 1988. However, FAS-99 (Deferral of the Effective Date of Recognition of Depreciation by Not-For-Profit Organizations) changed the effective date to financial statements issued for fiscal years beginning on or after January 1, 1990. This delay in effective date was in response to the January 1988 issuance of GASB Statement No. 8 (Applicability of FASB Statement No. 93, "Recognition of Depreciation by Not-for-Profit Organizations," to Certain State and Local Governmental Entities), which recommended that public colleges and universities *not* adopt the provisions of FAS-93. FASB reconsidered its position and decided to postpone the effective date of FAS-93, but not to rescind it. The Board also encouraged FAS-93's usage for those organizations permitted, but not required, to use it.

FASB STATEMENT NO. 105

FAS-105 (Disclosure of Information About Financial Instruments with Off-Balance Sheet Risk and Financial Instruments with Concentrations of Credit Risk) was the first phase of the FASB's project on disclosure policies regarding financial instruments. The FASB followed up on FAS-105 by issuing FAS-107, as discussed in the following section, which establishes additional disclosure policies designed to improve the financial statements.

In response to foreign exchange rate and interest rate volatility, tax law changes, and deregulation, many new innovative financial instruments are being created. FAS-105 was issued to provide disclosures for financial instruments that have off-balance-sheet risks and concentrations of credit risks.

FAS-105, as amended by FAS-107, defines a *financial instrument* as cash, evidence of an ownership interest in an entity, or a contract that both:

1. Imposes on one entity a contractual obligation (a) to deliver cash or another financial instrument to a second entity or (b) to exchange other financial instruments on potentially unfavorable terms with the second entity, and
2. Conveys to the second entity a contractual right (a) to receive cash or another financial instrument from the first entity or (b) to exchange other financial instruments on potentially favorable terms with the first entity.

Financial instruments have certain risks of accounting loss. According to FAS-105, "an accounting loss is the loss that may be recognized as a direct result of the rights and obligations of a financial instrument." These risks may be:

- *Credit risks*—The possibility of loss due to failure of another party to perform in accordance with contract terms
- *Market risks*—The possibility of loss due to future changes in market prices that affect the value of the financial instruments
- *Risk of theft or physical loss*

FAS-105 addresses only credit and market risks.

Generally, assets recorded on the balance sheet are subject to a loss that is limited to their recorded value. However, certain financial instruments may be subject to losses that exceed their recorded values. This may occur if these financial instruments have conditional rights or obligations that expose the organization to greater losses. This is known as off-balance-sheet risk. An example of this provided by FAS-105 is an interest-rate swap contract providing for a net settlement of cash receipts and payments that conveys a right to receive cash at current interest rates. The swap may impose an obligation to deliver cash if interest rates change in the future. Because this instrument may have a potential for losses that exceed the recorded value, it has an off-balance-sheet risk.

Off-balance-sheet risks do not apply exclusively to assets. They may apply to liabilities that have guarantees or obligations that may exceed the value recorded on the balance sheet. An organization also may have financial instruments not recorded on its statement of net assets that are subject to off-balance-sheet risks. These types of instruments may include forward interest rate agreements that, unless a loss is incurred, are not recognized until settlement.

Financial instruments with off-balance-sheet risk include standby and commercial letters of credit, loan commitments, financial guarantees, interest rate caps or floors, recourse obligations on receivables sold, repurchase agreements, futures contracts, and interest-rate or foreign currency swaps.

Disclosure of Extent, Nature, and Terms of Financial Instruments with Off-Balance-Sheet Risk

Organizations with financial instruments with off-balance-sheet risk of accounting loss must disclose the following by class of financial instrument:

- Face or contract amount. (A notional amount may be used if there is no face or contract amount.)
- The nature and terms of the financial instrument including a discussion of credit and market risk, cash requirements, and the related accounting policies used.

In its discussion of credit risk, the organization should disclose:

- The amount of accounting loss the entity would incur if any party to the financial instrument failed completely to perform according to the terms of the contract or if the collateral or other security, if any, for the amount due proved to be of no value to the entity
- The entity's policy of requiring collateral or other security to support financial instruments subject to credit risk, information about the entity's access to that collateral or other security, and the nature and a brief discussion of the collateral or other security supporting those financial instruments

FASB STATEMENT NO. 107

FAS-107 (Disclosures About Fair Value of Financial Instruments) sets standards for the disclosure of the fair value of financial instruments for all entities. FAS-107 was the result of the FASB's extensive financial instrument project, which also resulted in FAS-105. It requires all entities to disclose the fair value of most financial instruments, including the method or methods and significant assumptions used to determine the fair value. FAS-107 does not address or change any requirements for the recognition, measurement, or classification of financial instruments.

Certain organization have been exempted by FAS-125 (Exemption from Certain Required Disclosures about Financial Instruments for Certain Nonpublic Entities) from the FAS-107 requirements. These are entities with *all* of the following attributes:

- The entity is a nonpublic entity.
- The entity's total assets are less than $100 million on the date of the financial statements.
- The entity has not held or issued derivative financial instruments during the reporting period.

Financial Instruments

FAS-107 defines a *financial instrument* as cash, evidence of an ownership interest in an entity, or a contract that both:

1. Imposes on one entity a contractual obligation (a) to deliver cash or another financial instrument to a second entity or (b) to exchange other financial instruments on potentially unfavorable terms with the second entity, and

2. Conveys to the second entity a contractual right (a) to receive cash or another financial instrument from the first entity or (b) to exchange other financial instruments on potentially favorable terms with the first entity.

In simpler terms, the financial instruments are cash, an equity interest in an entity or contractual obligations that end with the delivery of cash, or an ownership interest in an entity. The FASB uses the term *financial instrument* within its definition since "any number of obligations to deliver financial instruments can be links in a chain that qualifies a particular contract as financial instruments."

Certain financial instruments are exempted from the requirements of FAS-107, including:

- Employers' and plans' obligations for pension benefits, post-retirement benefits, employee stock option plans, and other forms of deferred compensation arrangements

- Substantively extinguished debt covered by FAS-76

- Insurance contracts, other than financial guarantees and investment contracts

- Lease contracts

- Warranty obligations and rights

- Unconditional purchase obligations

- Investments accounted for under the equity method

- Minority interests and equity investments in consolidated subsidiaries

- Equity instruments issued by the reporting organization

Fair Value

A financial instrument's *fair value* is "the amount at which the instrument could be exchanged in a current transaction between willing parties, other than in a forced or liquidation sale." For certain financial instruments, fair value is readily available, such as the quoted market price if the instrument is publicly traded. Often, however, a quoted market price is not available. In these cases, an estimate of the fair value should be used.

Management can use various methods to arrive at a best estimate of fair value. The cost or carrying value of receivables or payables with a short maturity or a very short term generally will approximate the fair value. Similarly, loan instruments that reprice frequently, such as adjustable rate loans, and that do not have significant credit risks, generally would have a cost value that approximates its fair value.

For other financial instruments, management should look to the market value of similar types of instruments. For example, certain financial instruments may be "custom tailored" and may not have a quoted market rate. However, similar instruments without the custom tailoring may have quoted rates. Management may estimate a fair value based on those market rates adjusted for the custom tailoring. Similarly, for long-term loans, estimates of fair value may be based on the quoted market price of traded loans with similar rates, terms, and credit risks.

The fair value of a loan may be estimated using a discounted value of the future cash flows of the loan. The discount rate used should consider the prevailing interest rates for similar loans and the credit risks associated with the loans.

Disclosures

The FASB requires organizations to disclose the fair value of financial instruments, where it is practicable to estimate the value. The organizations also must disclose the method and significant assumptions used to value the financial instruments. When management deems it not practicable to estimate the fair value of financial instruments, the following information must be disclosed:

- Relevant information about the financial instrument, including, if applicable, the interest rate, carrying amount, and maturity
- Reasons it is not practicable to estimate the fair value

These disclosure requirements do not extend to regular trade payables or receivables.
A sample disclosure is shown below.

Note X. Fair Value of Financial Instruments

The estimated fair value of cash and cash equivalents and short-term debt approximates its carrying amount because of the short maturity of those instruments.

Long-term debt with a carrying value of $1,000,000 has a fair value of $1,050,000. The fair value of the long-term debt was estimated using a discounted cash flow analysis, based on the organization's current borrowing rates for similar types of borrowing arrangements.

Disclosure of Concentrations of Credit Risk of All Financial Instruments

According to FAS-107, an organization should disclose the following for all significant individual or concentrations of credit risks arising from financial instruments:

- Information about the (shared) activity, region, or economic characteristic that identifies the concentration
- The amount of accounting loss due to credit risk the entity would incur if parties to the financial instruments that make up the concentration failed completely to perform according to the terms of the contracts and the collateral or other security, if any, if the amount due proved to be of no value to the entity

- The entity's policy of requiring collateral or other security to support financial instruments subject to credit risk, information about the entity's access to that collateral or other security, and the nature and a brief discussion of the collateral or other security supporting those financial instruments

Group concentrations of credit risk are those that have two or more parties engaged in activities with activities and economic characteristics, which would be affected by changes in economic or other conditions. Financial instruments not covered by FAS-107 are:

- Insurance contracts, other than financial guarantees and investment contracts

- Unconditional purchase obligations that are guided by FAS-47 (Disclosure of Long-Term Obligations)

- Pensions, postretirement health and welfare benefits, stock options, and deferred compensation arrangements

- Pension plan's financial instruments

- Substantively extinguished debt

A sample disclosure follows.

Financial instruments that potentially subject the organization to concentrations of credit risk consist principally of cash equivalents and accounts receivable. The organization limits the amount of credit exposure to any one financial institution and invests cash in accounts with high credit quality. The organization's accounts receivable have a limited concentration of credit risk because of the dispersion of receivables from different industries and geographies.

Financial instruments that expose the organization to off-balance-sheet risk include lease guarantees where the organization is contingently liable as guarantor of certain leases assigned to third parties because of reorganizations and office closings. The minimum rental guarantees under these assigned leases are $200,000 for the years ended December 31, 19X1 and 19X2, and aggregate $500,000 for the remaining lease terms, which expire through 19X6. Management of the organization believes that the likelihood of a significant loss from these guarantees is remote because of a wide dispersion of third parties and legal recourse available to the organization should these parties fail to perform under the agreements.

The Y Organization uses interest-rate swaps to reduce its exposure to fluctuations in interest rates. At December 31, 19X1, the organization has outstanding interest-rate swap agreements, in the aggregate amount of $1,000,000, which fix the organization's interest rate on borrowings at 6%. Management considers the credit risk of these interest swaps to be minimal, as these contracts are with financial institutions with high credit ratings.

FASB STATEMENT NO. 63

As part of its establishment of reporting standards for specialized industries and practices, the FASB issued FAS-63 (Financial Reporting by Broadcasters) to target the broadcasting industry. FAS-63 sets standards for the recognition of rights acquired, or obligations incurred, under a license agreement and its related valuation, and for the recognition of advertising income. The FASB used SOP 75-5 (Accounting Practices in the Broadcasting Industry) as a framework for developing FAS-63.

As defined in FAS-63, a *broadcaster* is an entity or an affiliated group of entities that transmits radio or television program material. A broadcaster may be an independent station or may have a network affiliation. Broadcasters other than network-affiliated broadcasters generally acquire rights under a license agreement to broadcast several programs or a series of programs from producers or distributors. This right allows the broadcasters to air these programs over a period of time, known as the *license period*. The price for these rights is usually paid in installments over a period of time that is almost always less than the license period. Network-affiliated broadcasters do not incur a program cost for network programs. Instead, they receive compensation based on the advertising sold by the network.

As stated in FAS-63, the broadcaster reports the right acquired or the obligation incurred when *all* of the following conditions have been met:

- The cost of each program is known or reasonably determined.
- The program material has been accepted by the licensee in accordance with the conditions of the license agreement.
- The program is available for its first showing or telecast.

Except when a conflicting license prevents usage by the licensee, restrictions under the same license agreement or another license agreement with the same licenser on the timing of subsequent showings should not affect this availability condition.

The purchased rights should be classified as current or noncurrent based on the estimated timing of the airing. A liability should be classified based on the payment terms.

FAS-63 requires the asset or liability arising from the transaction to be reported at either of the following values:

- The present value of the liability, to be calculated in accordance with the standards promulgated by APB Opinion No. 21
- The gross amount of the liability

The purchased rights are to be amortized over a life based on the estimated number of times the program will be aired or the life of the agreement if the contract provides for unlimited broadcasts or the number of broadcasts cannot reasonably be estimated. Accelerated methods of amortization must be used when the first showing is more valuable then subsequent showings.

Purchased rights should be reported at the lower of unamortized costs or net realizable value on a program-by-program, series, or package basis, as appropriate for the circumstances. The writedown to net realizable value would be recorded as a charge to income and would establish a new cost basis.

A common industry practice includes the bartering of unsold advertising time for products or services. These transactions should be reported at the fair value of the assets or services received. For example, XYZ Broadcaster has unsold advertising time on an upcoming miniseries. If XYZ barters the advertising time to ABC Airline Company in return for airline travel, XYZ should record the transaction at the fair value of the airfare received. APB Opinion No. 29 (Accounting for Nonmonetary Transactions) provides guidance for these types of transactions. Because bartering arrangements generally do not occur simultaneously, the following would occur:

- If the commercial is aired, then a receivable should be recorded for the fair value of goods or services to be received.
- A liability should be recorded if the goods or services are received before the commercial is broadcast.

Network-affiliation agreements are intangible assets that should be reported on the balance sheet and amortized using the straight-line method over the life of the agreement or a period not to exceed 40 years. Upon termination of the agreement, the unamortized cost would be written off, unless the network affiliation is replaced or is under agreement to be replaced. The fair value of the new network affiliation is compared with the unamortized cost. If the unamortized cost exceeds the fair value of the replacement affiliation, a loss would be recorded for that amount. If the fair value of the replacement affiliation exceeds the unamortized cost, there would be no recognition of income.

FAS-63 also requires that disclosures be made for commitments for license agreements that have been executed but are not reported.

PART II
ACCOUNTING FOR NOT-FOR-PROFIT ORGANIZATIONS

CHAPTER 3
REVENUES

CONTENTS

CHAPTER 3
REVENUES

CROSS-REFERENCES

2000 MILLER NOT-FOR-PROFIT REPORTING: Chapter 2, "Overview of Current Pronouncements"

2000 MILLER GAAP GUIDE: Chapter 42, "Revenue Recognition"

2000 MILLER GAAP IMPLEMENTATION MANUAL: Chapter 36, "Revenue Recognition"

2000 MILLER GOVERNMENTAL GAAP GUIDE: Chapter 9, "Revenues"

Revenues of a not-for-profit organization are increases in its assets or settlement of its liabilities derived from the activities that constitute the organization's ongoing major or central operations. Accordingly, these revenues could result from contributions of cash, other assets, and services from other entities. Revenues also could arise from exchange transactions in which the organization provides "goods or services to members, clients, students, customers, and other beneficiaries for a fee." Revenues do not include increases in the entity's net assets that result from "peripheral or incidental transactions." The organization will need to consider its activities and determine which are its ongoing major or central operations. For similar types of transactions, one organization may report revenue and another a gain.

> **Example:** Sales of computer equipment by a college store should be reported as revenues if such sales are considered part of the college's ongoing major or central activities. Sales of old computer equipment used in a museum's administrative offices, however, would be reported as gains if such sales are peripheral and if the equipment was sold above book value [NPO, par. 12.03].

PLEDGES RECEIVABLE

FAS-116 (Accounting for Contributions Received and Contributions Made), which is effective for fiscal years beginning after December 15, 1994, applies to contributions of cash and other assets, including promises to give. It defines a *promise to give* as:

> A written or oral agreement to contribute cash or other assets to another entity.

Promises to give, also known as *pledges*, may be written or verbal. When the promise to give is not in writing, the organization should document internally the receipt of such promise if the transaction is to be recorded as an increase to net assets. This documentation could be in the form of a confirmation letter or an entry in a log.

A not-for-profit organization will recognize these promises to give in its financial statements when there is sufficient evidence in the form of verifiable documentation that a promise was made and received. Accounting for contributions depends on whether the donor has imposed conditions or restrictions, or both, on the contribution or pledge.

Conditional and Unconditional Promises

Conditional promise   A *donor-imposed condition* specifies a future and uncertain event the occurrence or failure of which gives the donor the right of return of the assets transferred or releases the promisor from the obligation to transfer the assets promised. The AICPA, in its Audit and Accounting Guide *Not-for-Profit Organizations*, cites the example of a matching fund as evidence of a conditional promise to give.

> **Example:** A foundation promises a not-for-profit organization matching funds, if the organization can raise $30,000. The not-for-profit organization must raise $30,000 to meet the condition before it is entitled to the matching funds.

> **Example:** A promise that stipulates that the donated assets will not be transferred unless the recipient organization establishes a new, specific program is another example of a conditional promise.

A not-for-profit organization receiving a conditional promise to give will *not* record the receipt of a contribution. The contribution will not be recorded until the conditions have been substantially met. However, if the possibility that the condition will not be met is *remote* (the chance of the future event or events not occurring is slight), the donee organization may record the receipt of a contribution.

> **OBSERVATION:** The donor's requirement that an annual report be sent to the donor or any other administrative condition may be evidence that the condition will not be met is remote.

Unconditional promise   Unconditional promises to give are also known as pledges. They are recorded as contributions when received. Unconditional promises to give may be donor-restricted as to what the contribution can be used for or when the contribution can be used.

Determining the nature of a promise   FAS-116 recognizes that the determination of whether a promise is conditional or unconditional can be difficult, especially if the promise contains donor stipulations that do not clearly state whether the right to receive payment or delivery of the promised assets depends on meeting those stipulations. The FASB notes:

> A promise containing stipulations that are not clearly unconditional shall be presumed to be a conditional promise.

Assets that have been received but are subject to return if conditions are not met should be reported as refundable advances until the conditions have been substantially met. A condition imposed by the donor could relate to a program for which the organization must incur costs before the donor will recognize the contribution. For example, if a day-care organization receives a sum of money to be used for providing meals to home-bound clients, revenue would not be recognized until costs are incurred to fulfill that new program. The AICPA Guide titled *Not-for-Profit Organizations* notes:

> When the likelihood of the conditions not being met is remote and the contribution is recognized, a contingent liability should also be disclosed describing the nature of the transaction and the obligation that would result in the event that the conditions are not met in the future.

Not-for-Profit Organizations also notes that some conditions may be met in stages rather than because of a single event. It states that a "portion of those contributions should be recognized as revenue as each of those stages is met." For example, if the $30,000 matching fund covers a period of time and is not an "all or nothing" contribution, as contributions are received toward that total from other donors, the conditions would be met and the promise to give would become unconditional. As amounts are received, a portion of the original conditional promise would be recognized as contribution revenue.

Restrictions

A *donor-imposed restriction* limits the use of contributed assets; it specifies a use that is more specific than broad limits resulting from the nature of the organization, the environment in which it operates, and the purposes specified in its articles of incorporation or bylaws, or comparable documents for an unincorporated association.

Some restrictions imposed by donors may permanently limit the use of the assets received. Others may stipulate that the assets may be used in a particular period (time restriction), for a particular purpose (e.g., to construct a laboratory for research), or for a particular program (e.g., to feed homeless people in a shelter).

The restrictions could be explicitly expressed in the documentation that the donee uses to transfer the asset, or they could be implicit in the circumstances surrounding the receipt of the contributed assets. For example, if the solicitation material that resulted in a donation of assets indicates that the money was being sought for a particular purpose, there would be evidence of the donor's intent to restrict the contribution to that purpose.

Contributions received with donor-imposed restrictions are recorded as permanently restricted or temporarily restricted net assets in the year of receipt. They are measured at their fair values.

When the donor-imposed temporary restriction has been satisfied, the net assets released from restriction are transferred to the unrestricted net asset classification.

GRANTS AND CONTRACTS RECEIVABLE

Explanatory material in FAS-116 notes that three transaction characteristics identify contributions. These are:

- Nonreciprocal transfers
- Transfers to or from entities other than owners
- Transfers made or received voluntarily

Exchange transactions are reciprocal transfers in which each party receives and gives up equal value. Some exchange transactions appear to be contributions, but a careful assessment of the transaction characteristics will allow the organization to determine whether the recipient of a transfer of assets has given up an asset or incurred a liability of equal value.

According to the AICPA Audit and Accounting Guide titled *Not-for-Profit Organizations*, exchange transactions for not-for-profit organizations are "reciprocal transfers in which each party receives and sacrifices something of approximately equal value" (par. 5.10).

Recognizing Receivables

Revenues from exchange transactions are recognized, measured by the increase of related assets, in accordance with the accrual basis of accounting—in a manner similar to that used by for-profit entities.

Valuation Allowances

In accordance with the accrual basis of accounting, receivables are reported net of an allowance for uncollectible amounts. The allowance, which will be disclosed on the face of the balance sheet or in the notes to the financial statements, will be based on management's experience with collecting receivables, aging of the receivables, and subjective matters (e.g., results of collection efforts and history with a particular customer/grantor or class of customers/grantors).

Revenue Recognition

Revenue is recorded in the statement of activities as increases in unrestricted net assets. Revenue is generally reported gross, but it is permissible to list the related expenses together with the revenue and the net subtotaled.

THIRD-PARTY REIMBURSEMENTS

Health care organizations and other not-for-profit organizations that provide services for a fee (e.g., child welfare organizations, United Cerebral Palsy organizations, or day-care centers) often receive funding from parties other than the recipient of the service. The funding is based on contracts between the service provider and the funding source (third-party payer).

> **Example:** A State Education Department reimburses a day-care center a per diem sum of money for each child attending.

When these arrangements are in place, the not-for-profit organization reports gross revenue on the accrual basis at its established rates for services provided. Often, the organization does not expect to collect the published rate because of the contracts with the third-party payer. When the latter situation occurs, the not-for-profit organization will accrue an amount that will reduce reported gross revenues to the expected net service revenue. This net service revenue is reported in the statement of operations of the service provider.

Many third-party payers will not determine the ultimate revenue to be paid to service providers until after an analysis is performed—retrospectively. The third-party payers will review cost reports submitted by the service providers to determine the appropriateness of the establish rate. Provisional rates are determined in advance of the audits of the cost reports, and the third-party payers will make periodic interim payments to the service providers based on the provisional rates.

Clearly, then, one of the most significant issues facing preparers, auditors, and users of not-for-profit organizations whose funding is heavily dependent on third-party payers is the accuracy of the estimates of the amounts ultimately to be received for the services and reported as revenues and accounts receivable in the year that the service is provided.

In some instances the rates to be paid to the service provider are set in advance—prospectively. Although the intent of the prospective rate is to determine the amounts that the service provider will be paid during the contract period, these, too, may be subject to retrospective adjustment. Accordingly, the financial statement preparer and auditor must be aware of the rate-setting environment in which the service provider operates and the various contracts entered into by the service provider.

The AICPA Audit and Accounting Guide *Health Care Organizations* notes:

> Under a retrospective system, an entity may be entitled to receive additional payments or may be required to refund amounts received in excess of amounts earned under the system. Although final settlements are not made until a subsequent period, they usually are subject to reasonable estimations and are reported in the financial statements in the period in which services are rendered. Differences between original estimates and subsequent revisions are included in the statement of operations in the period in which the revisions are made and disclosed, if material (par. 5.07).

The foregoing accounting is based on the premise that the estimates are based on facts and circumstances available to the organization at the time of recording the contractual allowances. Revisions that are subsequently made because of errors in the use of the facts available as of the original balance sheet date will be reported as prior-period adjustments in the year the errors are discovered.

SPLIT-INTEREST GIFTS

Split-interest gifts arise when donors enter into arrangements that benefit a not-for-profit organization and others. Three of the more common split-interest arrangements are charitable gift annuities, trusts held by third parties, and charitable remainder trusts.

> **Example:** In a charitable gift annuity, the donor contributes assets to the organization in exchange for the organization's promise to pay a fixed amount for a specified period of time to the donor or to payees designated by the donor. For example, if NPO Not-for-Profit Organization and Donor D enter into an agreement under which assets are transferred from D to NPO, NPO may agree to pay a stated dollar amount annually to D's spouse until the spouse dies.

> **Example:** In some circumstances, a donor may establish a trust that is administered by a party other than the not-for-profit organization. The terms of the trust held by a third party may provide for the organization to receive income earned on the trust assets in perpetuity.

> **Example:** In a charitable remainder trust, a donor establishes and funds a trust with specified distributions to be made to a designated beneficiary over the trust's term. Upon termination of the trust's term, the organization will receive any assets remaining in the trust and, depending on the donor's wishes, may have unrestricted or restricted use of them. For example, Donor D establishes a trust with NPO as trustee. D's spouse is to receive an annual distribution equal to a specified percentage of the fair market value of the trust's assets for life. Income on the assets remain in the trust until the spouse dies, at which time the remaining assets are distributed to NPO for use as a permanent endowment.

Split-interest gifts take several forms and, depending on the form used, will involve different concerns for the organization. Some arrangements may require the organization to comply with state insurance regulations; some may result in losses for the organization; all involve significant recordkeeping and the potentially sophisticated use of assumptions relating to interest/discount rates and market trends for investment vehicles. The not-for-profit organization also may incur fees for attorneys and other professionals in making certain that the organization fulfills all of the obligations associated with these arrangements.

Recognition and Measurement Principles

Organizations named in split-interest agreements should account for these agreements as part contribution, part exchange transaction. The assets received are recorded at their fair value. Liabilities incurred, such as an agreement to pay an annuity to the donor, also should be recognized.

The part of the agreement that represents the unconditional transfer of assets in a voluntary nonreciprocal transaction should be recognized at fair value in the statement of activities as revenue if the transaction is part of the organization's major activities. If the transaction is peripheral or incidental, it should be recognized as gain. As with other gifts, the contribution revenue should not be recognized until the benefits to be received become unconditional.

As with all transactions involving promises to give, circumstances will dictate whether the agreement should be considered conditional. For example, if an unrelated third party (e.g., a bank or trust company, a foundation, or a private individual) has substantive discretion over when or to whom benefits of an agreement are distributed, the agreement should be considered conditional.

Revocable split-interest agreements are conditional promises to give, and accordingly, the assets received should be accounted for as refundable advances.

Initial recognition   When contribution revenue is recognized in the organization's financial statements, it should be measured at fair value.

In a lead interest trust—under which the organization receives the distributions during the agreement's term—the fair value can be estimated directly based on the present value of the estimated future distributions the organization expects to receive. In a remainder interest agreement—under which the organization receives assets at the end of the agreement's term—the fair value may be estimated based on the fair value of the assets contributed by the donor minus the present value of the expected payments to be made to other beneficiaries. Factors to be considered include the estimated return on the invested assets during the expected term of the agreement, the contractual payment obligations under the agreement, and an appropriate discount rate. Contributions received generally will be recorded as increases in temporarily restricted net assets, unless the donor has permanently restricted the organization's use of future distributions of assets or unless the organization has the immediate right to use the assets it receives without restrictions. For example, under many charitable gift annuity agreements, the assets received from the donor are held by the organization as part of its general assets and are available for its unrestricted use.

When the organization is the trustee or has control over the assets, cash and other assets should be recognized at fair value at the date of the initial recognition. If the assets, or a portion of the assets, are being held for the benefit of others, a liability equal to the present value of the expected future payments to be made to the other beneficiaries also should be recognized at the date of the initial recognition.

During the agreement's term During the agreement's term, the not-for-profit organization may gain new information regarding the assumptions used at the time of the initial recognition of the agreement in the organization's records. For example, the donor's life expectancy may change. When such changes arise, the not-for-profit organization should add a caption to its statement of activities titled "Changes in the Value of Split-Interest Agreements."

The changes will be classified as temporarily restricted, permanently restricted, or unrestricted net assets, depending on the original classification used when the contribution initially was recognized. Similarly, when the organization is the trustee for the agreement, income earned on the controlled assets, gains, and losses, and distributions made to the other beneficiaries under the agreements, should be reflected in the organization's accounts.

Termination of the agreement Upon termination of the split-interest agreement, related asset and liability accounts should be closed. Remaining asset and liability amounts should be recognized as changes in the value of split-interest agreements and classified as changes in the appropriate net asset classification.

Financial Statement Presentation

Assets and liabilities recognized under split-interest agreements should be disclosed as separate line items in the balance sheet or in the notes to the financial statements. Contribution revenue and changes in the value of recognized split-interest agreements should be disclosed as separate line items in the statement of activities or in the notes to the financial statements.

Disclosures

Generally accepted accounting principles mandate the following disclosures relating to the split-interest agreements:

- Description of the general terms of the existing split-interest agreements
- Basis used for valuing recognized assets
- Discount rates and actuarial assumptions used to calculate present values

- For split-interest agreements that give rise to unconditional promises to give, the amounts of promises expected to be collected in less than one year, in one to five years, and in more than five years
- For conditional promises to give, the total amounts promised and a description and the amount of each group of agreements having similar characteristics

Charitable Gift Annuity

In a charitable gift annuity, the donor contributes assets to the organization in exchange for the organization's promise to pay a fixed amount for a specified period of time to the donor or to payees designated by the donor. The not-for-profit organization holds the assets received as general assets, and the annuity liability is a general obligation of the organization.

> **Example:** ABC Not-for-Profit Organization and Donor D enter into an agreement under which assets are transferred from D to ABC. ABC agrees to pay a stated dollar amount annually to D's spouse until the spouse dies. ABC recognizes the agreement in the period in which the contract is executed. The assets received are recorded at fair value, and an annuity payment liability is recognized at the present value of the expected future cash flows to be paid to D's spouse. Contribution revenue will be recognized as the difference between these two amounts. In subsequent periods, payments to the spouse will reduce the liability, and accretion of the initial discount, and changes in the investment return and life expectancy of D's spouse will be recognized as changes in the value of split-interest agreements in the statement of activities. Upon the death of D's spouse, the annuity liability is closed and a change in the value of split-interest agreements should be recognized.

Journal entries   The AICPA Audit and Accounting Guide titled *Not-for-Profit Organizations* lists the following journal entries to be recorded in relation to charitable gift annuities:

Creation of the annuity:

Assets (dr)	XXXX	
Annuity Payment Liability (cr)		XXXX
Contribution Revenue—Unrestricted (cr)		XXXX

Note: Assets are measured at fair value, liabilities at the present value of expected future cash flows to be paid to the annuity beneficiary.

Over the term of the annuity:

Annuity Payment Liability (dr)	XXXX	
Cash (cr)		XXXX

Note: Payment is to annuity beneficiary.

Change In Value Of Split-Interest		
Agreements—Unrestricted (dr)	XXXX	
Annuity Payment Liability (cr)		XXXX

Note: Accretion of discount on liability and recording of any change in the life expectancy of the beneficiary—debit and credit could be reversed.

Termination of the annuity:

Annuity Payment Liability (dr)	XXXX	
Change In Value Of Split-Interest		
Agreements—Unrestricted (cr)		XXXX

Note: To close the annuity payment liability.

Trust Funds

In some circumstances, a donor may establish a trust that is administered by a party other than the not-for-profit organization. The terms of the trust may provide for the organization to receive income earned on the trust assets in perpetuity. The trust's grantor (donor) will establish what restrictions, if any, apply to the use of the income. Accordingly, the income will be considered increases in the net asset classification that matches the donor stipulations. In this circumstance, the organization has received an unconditional promise to give that should be recognized as a contribution and as an asset when the organization is made aware of the existence of the trust. As with any long-term receivable, the fair value of the asset is the present value of the estimated future cash flows from the trust.

Although the income from the trust may be classified as unrestricted or restricted, depending on the stipulation of the donor, the present value of the trust's assets will be recognized as a permanently restricted net asset. The recorded value will change each year as annual evaluations of the assets are performed. Changes arising from these annual evaluations will be recognized in the statement of activities as permanently restricted gains or losses.

Journal entries The AICPA Audit and Accounting Guide titled *Not-for-Profit Organizations* lists the following journal entries to be recorded in relation to perpetual trust funds:

Creation of the trust:

Beneficial Interest In Perpetual Trust (dr)   XXXX
     Contribution Revenue—Permanently
        Restricted (cr)   XXXX

Note: Assets and revenue are measured at present value based on the expected future cash flows to the organization (generally measured by the fair value of the assets contributed to the trust).

Each year:

Cash (dr)   XXXX
     Contributions Revenue (Unrestricted Or
        Temporarily Restricted) (cr)   XXXX

Note: Income is received from trust (net asset class based on stipulations of the trust instrument or organizational policy).

Beneficial Interest In Perpetual Trust (dr)   XXXX
     Gain Or Loss—Permanently Restricted (cr)   XXXX

Note: To adjust asset for changes in present value of expected cash flows—debit and credit could be reversed.

Charitable Remainder Trust

In a charitable remainder trust, a donor establishes and funds a trust with specified distributions to be made to a designated beneficiary over the trust's term. Upon termination of the trust's term, the organization will receive any assets remaining in the trust and, depending on the donor's wishes, will have unrestricted or restricted use of them.

> **Example:** Donor D establishes a trust with ABC Not-for-Profit Organization as trustee. D's spouse is to receive an annual distribution equal to a specified percentage of the fair market value of the trust's assets for life. Income on the assets remain in the trust until the spouse dies, at which time the remaining assets are distributed to ABC for use as a permanent endowment.
>
> - ABC recognizes the contribution in the period in which the trust is established.
> - The liability to D's spouse is recorded at the present value of the estimated future cash flows to be distributed over the spouse's expected life.
> - The contribution, classified as permanently restricted, is the difference between the fair value of the assets and the liability recorded by ABC.

In subsequent periods:

- Income earned on the assets and related gains and losses and distributions paid to D's spouse are reflected in the trust's assets and liability accounts.

- Accretion of discount, revaluations of present values, and changes in actuarial assumptions are recognized in the statement of activities as a change in the value of split-interest agreements in the permanently restricted net asset classification.

When D's spouse dies:

- The liability account is closed, and any balance is recognized as a change in the value of split-interest agreements in the permanently restricted net asset class.

Example: If ABC is not the trustee and does not exercise control over the assets contributed to the trust, ABC should record the agreement as an unconditional promise to give, at the present value of the estimated future benefits to be received when the trust assets are distributed.

Adjustments to the receivable to reflect the accretion of the discount, revaluation of the present value of the estimated future payments to D's spouse, and changes in actuarial assumptions during the term of the trust are recognized as changes in the value of split-interest trust agreements.

Upon the death of D's spouse:

- The receivable is closed.

- The assets received are recognized at fair value.

- Any difference is reported as a change in the value of split-interest agreements in permanently restricted net assets.

Journal entries The AICPA Audit and Accounting Guide titled *Not-for-Profit Organizations* lists the following journal entries to be recorded in relation to charitable remainder trusts:

Creation of the trust:

Assets Held In Charitable Remainder Trust (dr)	XXXX	
Liability Under Trust Agreement (cr)		XXXX
Contribution Revenue—Permanently Restricted (cr)		XXXX

Note: Assets are measured at fair value; liability is measured at the present value of expected future payments to be made to the beneficiary.

Over the term of the trust:

Assets Held In Charitable Remainder Trust (dr)	XXXX	
Liability Under Trust Agreement (cr)		XXXX

Note: Trust income and change in fair value of assets held in trust, to the extent recognized.

Liability Under Trust Agreement (dr)	XXXX	
Assets Held In Charitable Remainder Trust (cr)		XXXX

Note: Payment to beneficiary.

Liability Under Trust Agreement (dr)	XXXX	
Change In Value If Split-Interest		
Agreements—Permanently Restricted (cr)		XXXX

Note: Accretion of discount and adjustment of liability to reflect change in actuarial assumptions—debit and credit could be reversed.

Termination of the trust:

Liability Under Trust Agreement (dr)	XXXX	
Change In Value Of Split-Interest		
Agreements—Permanently Restricted (cr)		XXXX

Note: To close liability.

Endowment Assets (dr)	XXXX	
Assets Held In Charitable Remainder Trust (cr)		XXXX

Note: To close trust and recognize assets available for use.

ENDOWMENT GIFTS

Definition

FAS-117 (Financial Statements of Not-for-Profit Organizations) defines *endowment fund* as "an established fund of cash, securities, or other assets to provide income for the maintenance of a not-for-profit organization" (FAS-117, par. 168).

The AICPA Audit and Accounting Guide titled *Not-for-Profit Organizations* defines *endowment fund* as:

> An established fund of cash, securities, or other assets to provide income for the maintenance of a not-for-profit organization . . . Endowment funds generally are established by donor-restricted gifts and bequests to provide a permanent endowment, which is to provide a permanent source of in-

come, or a term endowment, which is to provide income for a specified period. . . . A board-designated endowment, which results from an internal designation, is not donor-restricted and is classified as unrestricted net assets. [glossary]

Generically, the term *endowment fund* often is used to include the "true endowments" defined above and also (1) term endowment funds and (2) quasi-endowment funds. Term endowment funds and quasi-endowment funds relate to:

- Funds whose principal may be expended after a stated period of time, or after the occurrence of a particular event.
- Funds that the governing board of the organization has decided should be set aside for investment. The board could set these funds aside for purposes similar to those of true endowments or term endowments.

Endowments are set aside for the production of income for current and future needs of the organization. Whereas the principal of "true endowments" is nearly inviolate (with few exceptions) and whereas term endowment funds do not become available to the organization until the time restriction or purpose restriction has been met, quasi-endowment funds may be redesignated by the organization's governing board and returned to general use.

Accounting for Endowments

As prescribed by FAS-116, not-for-profit organizations must distinguish between contributions received with donor-imposed restrictions and contributions received without restrictions. The donor may place permanent or temporary restrictions on the use of the assets contributed.

True endowments fall under the classification of permanently restricted net assets, while term endowments generally are reported as temporarily restricted net assets. Quasi-endowment funds are created by the organization's governing body and are appropriations of unrestricted net assets. These funds should be identified as unrestricted net assets and should be included under that caption on the balance sheet. However, the financial statements of the organization may identify such funds as "quasi-endowment." In these cases, the purpose for which the fund was established should be explained in the notes to the financial statements.

A not-for-profit organization's accounting system generally maintains separate records for each fund, each with its own cash and investments, unless the organization maintains pooled investment funds that include the investments of more than one fund.

The organization's management must be cognizant of provisions that affect the type of investments permitted by the donor (e.g., the funds should not be pooled with funds of other donors, or the income may be used only for a particular purpose).

Accounting for endowment funds requires the not-for-profit organization to evaluate the sources of net assets that arise from the funds. Interest and dividends, and gains and losses, may have different accounting treatments depending on the donor's stipulations. FAS-117 notes, "Income from donor-restricted permanent or term endowments may be donor-restricted and increase either temporarily restricted net assets or permanently restricted net assets."

Gains and losses should be reported as changes in permanently restricted net assets if donor stipulations or law prohibits expenditure. If there are no donor restrictions on gains, they should be reported as increases in unrestricted net assets if the income is reported as unrestricted. If income is restricted, the gains should be reported as increases in temporarily restricted net assets.

Some organizations use the "total return concept" to manage endowment fund investments. The AICPA Industry Audit and Accounting Guide titled *Not-for-Profit Organizations* defines *total return* as:

> A measure of investment performance that focuses on the overall return on investments, including interest and dividend income as well as realized and unrealized gains and losses on investments. Frequently used in connection with a spending-rate formula to determine how much of that return will be used for fiscal needs of the current period. [glossary]

Use of this approach will result in the organization recognizing as income for unrestricted purposes some portion of the gains that otherwise would be considered additions to the restricted net assets classification. This approach should be followed only after consultation with legal counsel regarding the nature of the instruments that establish the endowment. The superseded AICPA Industry Audit Guide *Audits of Colleges and Universities* notes:

> Practically all total return approaches emphasize the use of "prudence" and a "rational and systematic formula" in determining the portion of gains which may be appropriated for expenditures and call for the protection of endowment principal from the loss of purchasing power (inflation) as a primary consideration before appropriating gains.

SOP 78-10 (Accounting Principles and Reporting Practices for Certain Nonprofit Organizations), superseded when the AICPA Audit and Accounting Guide titled *Not-for-Profit Organizations* became final, further emphasizes the subjectivity of the total return concept:

> While all of the total return approaches emphasize the use of prudence and a rational and systematic formula, those matters are subjective and not susceptible to measurement.

When Endowment Gifts Can Be Used

The Uniform Management of Institutional Funds Act (UMIFA) attempts to provide guidance to organizations and their advisers about the ability of an organization to use the endowment funds and increases associated with gains. As mentioned in Chapter 5, "Assets," UMIFA provides a standard for the use of gains associated with invested endowment funds.

Notwithstanding the accounting for endowment funds, a not-for-profit organization should not use its funds until it has considered state and local laws, has studied the instrument establishing the endowment, and has consulted with legal counsel familiar with the requirements of the state.

RESTRICTED GIFTS

FAS-116 requires not-for-profit organizations to distinguish among those contributions received that increase permanently restricted net assets, those that increase temporarily restricted net assets, and those that increase unrestricted net assets. It also requires recognition of the expiration of donor-imposed restrictions in the period in which the restrictions expire.

Distinguishing restrictions from conditions provides a challenge to the not-for-profit organization. The organization must determine if the donor-imposed condition on the transfer of assets or a promise to give specifies an uncertain, future event whose occurrence or failure to occur gives the donor a right of return of the assets or releases the donor from the obligation to transfer assets promised.

A donor-imposed restriction, according to FAS-116, limits the use of assets contributed to the organization. The restriction limits the use of the assets to one that is more specific than broad limits resulting from the nature of the organization, the environment in which it operates, and the purposes specified in its corporate documents.

Revenue Recognition

Donor-imposed conditions cause a not-for-profit organization to delay recognition of contribution revenue until the organization substantially meets the donor's conditions. Restrictions imposed by the donor do not delay revenue recognition.

Contributions whose uses are restricted by the donor are reported as increases of temporarily or permanently restricted net assets in the period they are received. Temporary restrictions may include limiting an asset's use to a specific purpose or to a later time period or until a specific date.

FAS-116 discusses reporting of restricted contributions by not-for-profit organizations. The restriction may be explicit or may be ascertained from the circumstances surrounding the gift. Donor-restricted net assets are reported as such in the statement of activities, except that contributions with restrictions that are met in the same period in which the contribution is received may be reported as unrestricted if the organization is consistent in this practice from period to period and discloses this policy in the notes to its financial statements (FAS-116, pars. 14–16).

Determining Restrictions

The AICPA Audit and Accounting Guide *Not-for-Profit Organizations* notes that restrictions may result implicitly from the circumstances surrounding receipt of a contributed asset. For example, a promise to give, with the stipulation that if the organization runs a specific program this year the donor will contribute $1,000 each year for the next three years, should be included in unrestricted net assets, but an unconditional promise to give with payments due in future periods may be included in temporarily restricted net assets, because the implicit intention is to support the activities of future periods.

Careful consideration of the terms of the promise to give will determine if the donor intended to place a condition or a restriction on the use of the assets. If there is only a remote possibility that the conditional purpose of the donation will not be met, the organization may recognize receipt of a contribution. The revenue recognized will increase temporarily restricted net assets, unless the organization has adopted the policy for donor-restricted contributions whose restrictions are met in the current period, under which the revenues are reported as unrestricted.

Recognizing Reclassifications

The expiration of donor-imposed restrictions on contributions should be reported in the period or periods in which (1) a donor-stipulated time period has elapsed or (2) the not-for-profit organization has fulfilled a donor-stipulated purpose for which the contribution was restricted. If the contributor stipulates two or more donor-imposed restrictions, the expiration of the restriction should be reported in the period in which the last remaining restriction is satisfied.

In certain circumstances, costs may be incurred for purposes for which both unrestricted and temporarily restricted net assets are available. For example, the cost of supplies, which otherwise might be reported as a decrease in unrestricted net assets, may meet donor-imposed restrictions on net assets to support the specific program for which the supplies were purchased. The restriction on the contribution will be met to the extent of the expense incurred unless the purpose of the expense is directly attributable to another specific external source, such as a conditional promise to give or to a cost-reimbursement contract.

CONDITIONAL GIFTS AND GRANTS

A *conditional promise to give* is a promise to give that depends on the occurrence of a specified future and uncertain event to bind the promisor.

The AICPA Audit and Accounting Guide titled *Not-for-Profit Organizations* notes:

> Because of the uncertainty about whether they will be met, conditions imposed by resource providers may cast doubt on whether the resource provider's intent was to make a contribution, to make a conditional contribution, or to make no contribution. As a result of this uncertainty, donor-imposed conditions should be substantially met by the organization before the receipt of assets (including contributions receivable) is recognized as a contribution.

Ascertaining the difference between a restriction and a condition is difficult at times. The organization must determine if the donor's intent is to limit the use of donated assets, or if the donor has created a barrier to be overcome before the assets transferred or promised become contributions.

A condition creates a situation that will lead to a return of cash or other assets transferred if the uncertain future event does not occur. Because conditions can vary significantly, the likelihood of meeting the condition ranges from "probable" to "remote." If a reasonable possibility exists that the condition will not occur, and thus the transferred assets will not be retained by the organization, the assets will be accounted for as a refundable advance (FAS-116, par. 60).

Examples of Implementing Rules

When a conditional gift is received, the organization will not recognize the contribution revenue until the donor-imposed conditions have been substantially met. If Donor A provides funding for an outreach program, the revenue will not be recognized until the program has begun. Donor B may provide a matching fund that will permit the organization to retain a portion of the grant as certain levels of donations from others are reached. In that situation, the organization will recognize revenue when the preset level of matching is attained. In some instances, the organization must spend money before the conditions are considered fulfilled. The revenue from these conditional grants may be recognized when the qualifying costs are incurred.

DEFERRED REVENUE/REFUNDABLE ADVANCES

Under SOP 78-10, *deferred revenue and support* was defined as (SOP 78-10, App. A):

> Revenue or support received or recorded before it is earned, that is, before the conditions are met, in whole or in part, for which the revenue or support is received or is to be received.

The AICPA Audit and Accounting Guide titled *Not-for-Profit Organizations* notes that "a transfer of assets with a conditional promise to contribute them should be accounted for as a refundable advance until the conditions have been substantially met or the conditions have been explicitly waived by the donor." However, certain donor-imposed conditions are such that the likelihood of not meeting the conditions is remote (e.g., filing Form 990). In those circumstances, the organization need not consider the requirement to be a condition that would delay recording the receipt of contribution revenue.

Measurement

Revenue is measured at the fair value of the asset received. Accordingly, quoted market prices, estimates based on quoted market prices of similar assets, independent appraisals, or the present value of estimated future cash flows may be used to determine the amount of the contribution to be recognized in the organization's financial statements.

Revenue Recognition

As noted in the previous section titled "Conditional Gifts and Grants," revenue should be recognized as revenue when the conditions upon which the gift or grant depends are substantially met. Some examples of how to ascertain whether the conditions have been met and whether the donor stipulations are restrictions or conditions are discussed in paragraphs 57–68 of FAS-116 and paragraphs 5.23–5.34 of *Not-for-Profit Organizations*.

The organization also must determine if the conditions are being substantially met in stages. It may be appropriate to recognize revenue as stages are met. *Not-for-Profit Organizations* furnishes the example of a matching grant under which the donor will match contributions received up to $100,000 over a six-month period. As contributions are received from others, the conditions would be met and the promise to give would become unconditional for the portion received.

Another example involves an organization that must incur certain costs to earn the contribution. As those costs are recognized by the organization, the conditions would be satisfied and the revenue recognized.

MEMBERSHIP DUES

Revenue Recognition

Appendix C of SOP 78-10 contains examples of sample financial statements for the various types of organizations that fall under its requirements. Exhibit 3D contains sample notes to the financial statements of a country club. In this section, SOP 78-10 includes the following note.

Membership Dues and Initiation Fees

Membership dues are recognized as revenue in the applicable membership period. Initiation fees are recorded as revenue in the period in which the fees are due.

The AICPA Audit and Accounting Guide *Not-for-Profit Organizations* notes that an organization that receives dues from its members should determine which portion is a contribution and which portion may be considered an exchange transaction (because the organization's members receive tangible or intangible benefits as a result of membership). Benefits received in an exchange transaction could include a newsletter, a professional journal, or the use of facilities such as a gym.

Not-for-Profit Organizations includes a list of indicators that may help an organization determine the amount that is recognized as contribution and the amount that is recognized as an exchange transaction. This list includes the following indicators:

Expressed Intent Concerning Purpose of Dues Payment

- If the request for membership dues describes the dues as being used to provide benefits to the general public or to the organization's service beneficiaries, those dues are considered a contribution.
- If the request for membership dues describes the dues as providing economic benefits to members or to other organizations or individuals designated by or related to the members, those dues are considered an exchange transaction.

Extent of Benefits

- If the benefits to members are negligible, the dues are considered a contribution.
- If the substantive benefits to members may be available to nonmembers for a fee, the dues are considered an exchange transaction.

Not-for-Profit Organization's Service Efforts

- If the organization provides service for members and nonmembers, the dues are considered a contribution.
- If the organization benefits are provided only to members, the dues are considered an exchange transaction.

Duration of Benefits

- If the duration of benefits is not specified, the dues are considered a contribution.
- If the benefits are provided for a defined period and an additional payment of dues is required to extend benefits, the dues are considered an exchange transaction.

Qualifications for Membership

- If membership is available to the general public, the dues are considered a contribution.
- If membership is available only to individuals who meet certain criteria, the dues are considered an exchange transaction.

Methods for Determining Deferrals

If an exchange transaction has occurred, the revenue associated with membership dues should be recognized over the period to which the dues relate. When the organization expects to receive fees in the future to cover services to members in future periods, nonrefundable initiation and life membership fees should be recognized in the financial statements of the period in which the fees become receivable. If the organization expects that these future services will not be covered by additional fees to be received, the nonrefundable amounts received "should be recognized as revenue over the average duration of membership, the life expectancy of members, or other appropriate time period" (NPO, par. 5.16).

FEES FOR SERVICES

Revenue Recognition

Not-for-profit organizations may enter into transactions that will give rise to revenues because the organization is providing goods or services for a fee. The transactions may be with members, clients, students, customers, and others. These "exchange transactions" and the accounting therefor should be guided by "the relationship of the transaction to the organization's activities" (NPO, par. 12.03). Examples of exchange transactions are payments for tuition, low-cost day care, nursing services, or research.

Revenue arising from an exchange transaction that is part of the ongoing purpose of the not-for-profit organization is accounted for in a manner similar to the methods that for-profit entities use for reporting revenue. The revenue would be determined using accrual accounting principles. The amount recognized would be measured by the increase in assets or the decrease in liabilities resulting from the transaction. *Not-for-Profit Organizations*, for example, notes that interest on loans made to students and to other individuals or organizations should be recognized as revenue when earned (NPO, par. 12.04, footnote 2).

Restricted versus Unrestricted Determination

The revenue recognized in exchange transactions is reported gross unless it is reduced by regularly provided discounts such as reduced rates or free services. In these situations, revenue should be reported net of the discounts. Expenses that are directly related to these revenues may be reported in the statement of activities sequentially with the revenues.

If exchange transactions arise in the normal course of the organization's operations, and if no donor restrictions are placed on the assets received, the resulting revenues are reported as increases in unrestricted net assets in the organization's statement of activities. The organization is permitted, because of the flexibility provided by FAS-117, to classify the revenues using operating and nonoperating categories, or other useful breakdowns, in the statement of activities.

Presentation of Fees from Related Entities

In September 1994, the AICPA issued SOP 94-3 (Reporting of Related Entities by Not-for-Profit Organizations), which, at that time, amended the AICPA Industry Audit Guides *Audits of Voluntary Health and Welfare Organizations* and *Audits of Colleges and Universities,* the AICPA Audit and Accounting Guide *Audits of Certain Nonprofit Organizations,* and SOP 78-10. SOP 94-3 provides guidance primarily on the following:

1. Reporting investments in for-profit majority-owned subsidiaries

2. Reporting investments in common stock of for-profit entities that are not subsidiaries

3. Reporting financially interrelated not-for-profit organizations

Financially interrelated not-for-profit organizations may be related through ownership, control, and economic interest.

The financial reporting and disclosures required for related entities vary, depending on which of the three situations apply, as discussed in Chapter 2, "Overview of Current Pronouncements." When consolidation is the mode of reporting, fees from related entities are eliminated as part of the interorganization entry. If consolidated financial statements are not presented, the notes to the financial statements of the reporting not-for-profit organization should contain the following:

- Identification of the other organization and the nature of its relationship with the reporting organization that results in control

- Summarized financial data of the other organization, including:

  — Total assets, liabilities, net assets, revenue, and expenses

  — Resources that are held for the benefit of the reporting organization or that are under its control

- A description of the transactions for each of the periods for which statements of activities are presented, and other information deemed necessary to an understanding of the effects of the transactions on the financial statements

- The dollar amounts of transactions for each of the periods for which statements of activities are presented, and the effects of any change in the method of establishing the terms from that used in the preceding period

- Amounts due from or to related parties as of the date of each balance sheet presented and, if not otherwise apparent, the terms and manner of settlement

CHAPTER 4
EXPENSES

CONTENTS

CHAPTER 4
EXPENSES

Expenses of a not-for-profit organization are decreases in its assets or incurrences of liabilities for the purpose of carrying out the activities that constitute the organization's ongoing major or central operations. Losses are distinguished from expenses in that they are decreases in net assets as a result of peripheral or incidental transactions. The costs of providing care to patients in a hospital are clearly expenses; however, the costs associated with operating the hospital's gift shop are probably peripheral and would not be included in the measurement of results of operations in the statement of activities.

GROSS VERSUS NET PRESENTATIONS

A not-for-profit organization should report both revenues and expenses on a gross basis to help explain the relationships of its ongoing major or central operations and activities (FAS-117, par. 24). Exceptions apply for investment income, which can be reported net of related expenses. Even in this situation, the amount of investment-related expenses for custodial fees and investment advisory fees should be reported either on the face of the financial statements or in the notes to the financial statements.

FASB recognizes that some activities and transactions peripheral or incidental to the organization's purpose will result in gains and losses. These activities may be reported net (FAS-117, par. 25). For example, a college bookstore may sell computers as part of its ongoing activities, transactions that are reported gross in the statement of activities. However, if that same bookstore were to sell the computers that it used for its own internal purposes, the transactions would be recognized net of related costs of disposal.

Many organizations consider special events to be peripheral to their activities. However, FASB notes that special events are often ongoing and major activities for not-for-profit organizations. The organization must determine the significance of the special events to its activities and report the revenues and expenses on a gross basis if deemed to provide useful information about the organization's resources. For more information on special events, see Chapter 2, "Overview of Current Pronouncements."

ALLOWABLE AS CHARGES TO TEMPORARILY AND PERMANENTLY RESTRICTED NET ASSETS

In the due process activities it undertook before issuing FAS-117 (Financial Statements of Not-for-Profit Organizations), the FASB asked commentators whether all expenses should be classified as decreases in unrestricted net assets or whether those expenses financed by restricted resources should be reported as decreases in their respective net asset classifications. Although most respondents did not agree, FASB concluded that "not-for-profit organizations should report expenses as decreases in unrestricted net assets" (FAS-117, pars. 133 and 135).

OPERATING VERSUS NONOPERATING CONCEPTS

When considering the presentation of the statement of activities, the FASB determined that not-for-profit organizations should have latitude in presenting information that is similar to that given to for-profit organizations. As part of its activities before the issuance of FAS-117, the FASB decided that a not-for-profit organization may, if it wishes, determine how to classify its revenues, expenses, gains, and losses—either as operating or nonoperating—in its statement of activities (FAS-117, par. 67).

If an intermediate measure of operations is reported, the FASB requires that it be included in the financial statement that, at a minimum, reports the change in unrestricted net assets for the period (FAS-117, par. 68). FASB also requires that the organization's financial statements describe the nature of the reported operations. SOP 94-6 (Disclosure of Certain Significant Risks and Uncertainties) requires all organizations that present financial statements in accordance with generally accepted accounting principles to do the following (SOP 94-6, par. 10):

> Include a description of the major products or services the reporting entity sells or provides and its principal markets, including the locations of those markets. . . . Not-for-profit organizations' disclosures should briefly describe the principal services performed by the entity and the revenue sources for the entity's services. Disclosures about the nature of operations need not be quantified; relative importance could be conveyed by use of terms such as *predominately, about equally,* or *major and other.*

An organization might present such information about a measure of operations in the financial statements in the following manner:

Operating revenues and support:

    Fees for services

    Operating support

    Net assets released from restrictions

        Total operating revenues and support

Operating expenses:

    Programs

    Management and general

    Fund raising

        Total operating expenses

            Change in unrestricted net assets from operations

Other changes:

    (Increases and decreases in items considered to be nonoperating)

        Change in unrestricted net assets before effects of discontinued operations, extraordinary items, and changes in accounting principles

Discontinued operations

Extraordinary items

Changes in accounting principles

Change in unrestricted net assets

Unrestricted net assets at beginning of year

Unrestricted net assets at end of year

FUNCTIONAL ALLOCATION OF EXPENSES

Not-for-profit organizations incur costs to operate their businesses—programs designed to carry out the organizations' purposes, manage their finances, raise funds, and inform donors and others who provide resources about the programs. To provide information about costs to users of financial statements, organizations classify expenses as relating to program services, fund-raising, or management and general. These classifications should be clearly identified in the statement of activities, as mandated by FAS-117, and should be presented as decreases in unrestricted net assets.

Allocations of Costs—Methods and Principles

Many organizations will be unable to separately identify an element of expense as program services or supporting services (fund-raising or management and general). Accordingly, the costs that cannot be separately identified must be allocated among the various classifications. The AICPA Audit and Accounting Guide *Not-for-Profit Organizations* identifies examples of expenses that may require allocation among the various classifications of costs to be disclosed in the statement of activities:

- Salaries and fringe benefits of individuals performing more than one function
- Rent and other occupancy costs
- Depreciation
- Professional fees

Voluntary health and welfare organizations must report expenses by "natural classification" (e.g., salaries, rent, interest, depreciation). In addition to requiring voluntary health and welfare organizations to report expenses in this way, FAS-117 *encourages* other not-for-profit organizations to do the same.

There is no one correct way to perform the allocation; it could be performed using several bases. The following is taken from the superseded AICPA Industry Audit Guide *Audits of Voluntary Health and Welfare Organizations* (AVHWO, par. 6.16):

1. A study of the organization's activities may be made at the start of each fiscal year to determine the best practicable allocation methods. This study should include an evaluation of the preceding year's time records or activity reports of key personnel, the use of space, the consumption of supplies and postage, etc. The results of this study should be reviewed periodically and revised where necessary to reflect significant changes in the nature or level of the organization's current activities.

2. Daily time and expense records may be kept by all employees who spend time on more than one function and may be used as a basis for allocating salaries and related costs. These records should indicate the nature of the activities in which the employee is involved.

3. Automobile and travel costs may be allocated on the basis of the expense or time reports of the employees involved.

4. Telephone expense may be allocated on the basis of use of the extensions, generally following the charge for the salary of the employee using the telephone, after mak-

ing direct charges for toll calls or other service attributable to specific functions.

5. Stationery, supplies, and postage costs may be allocated based on a study of their use.

6. Occupancy costs may be allocated on the basis of a factor determined from a study of the function of the personnel using the space involved.

7. The depreciation and rental of equipment may be allocated based on asset usage.

Office of Management and Budget (OMB) Circular A-122 (Cost Principles of Nonprofit Organizations) notes in Attachment A that:

> In general, any cost element or cost-related factor associated with the organization's work is potentially adaptable for use as an allocation base provided (i) it can readily be expressed in terms of dollars or other quantitative measures (total direct costs, direct salaries and wages, staff hours applied, square feet used, hours of usage, number of documents processed, population served, and the like) and (ii) it is common to the benefiting functions during the base period.

Thus, the not-for-profit organization should evaluate its programs and operations to determine the allocation base that is most reasonable in the circumstances.

Distinguishing Between Program and Supporting Activities

Program services are an organization's activities that fulfill its purposes or mission. These activities may take the form of goods and services being distributed to beneficiaries, customers, or members. These are the purpose for which the organization exists, and they often relate to several major programs.

Supporting services are those costs that are not program-related and that include management and general expenses and fund-raising costs. Management and general expenses include general recordkeeping, financing, and all other activities that are not directly program- or fund-raising-related.

Fund-raising activities include those activities that involve solicitation of contributions from donors. The nature of costs varies and may include maintaining donor mailing lists and fund-raising campaign costs (including the salaries of personnel connected with the campaign). These costs, along with those related to program services, will be reported as decreases in unrestricted net assets, in accordance with FAS-117.

Accounting for Costs of Activities That Include Fund-Raising

As discussed in Chapter 2, "Overview of Current Pronouncements," the subject of joint costs of mailings was addressed by the AICPA Accounting Standards Executive Committee (AcSEC). AcSEC has issued Statement of Position 98-2 (Accounting for Costs of Activities of Not-for-Profit Organizations and State and Local Governmental Entities That Include Fund Raising). Until the issuance of the new AICPA Audit Guide, SOP 87-2 (Accounting for Joint Costs of Informational Materials and Activities of Not-for-Profit Organizations That Include a Fund-Raising Appeal) was the effective pronouncement guiding the accounting for these transactions. The new SOP amends the Audit Guide. SOP 98-2 is effective for financial statements for years beginning on or after December 15, 1998, but the AICPA encouraged earlier application in fiscal years for which financial statements have not been issued. Also, retroactive application is permitted but not required if comparative financial statements are presented.

Organizations will use communications that contain a request for funds for a variety of other reasons:

- To describe the organization's purpose
- To educate and motivate the public
- To inform prospective donors why funds are needed

The conclusions in SOP 98-2 (par. 7) include the following:

> If any of the criteria [purpose, audience, and content] are not met, all of costs of the joint activity should be reported as fund-raising costs, including costs that otherwise might be considered program or management and general costs if they had been incurred in a different activity. . . . Costs of goods or services provided in exchange transactions that are part of joint activities, such as direct donor benefits of a special event (for example, a meal), should be not be reported as fund-raising.

Joint activities   Joint activities are activities that are part of the fund-raising function and have elements of a program, management and general, or membership development function. SOP 98-2 provides "illustrations of applying the criteria . . . to determine whether a program or management and general activity has been conducted." These illustrations are in-depth analyses to ascertain whether an activity has purpose, audience, and content. Among the illustrations are the following:

An entity with a mission to prevent drug abuse publishes an annual report stating that one of its objectives is to assist parents in preventing their children from abusing drugs. The audience to which informational material about the dangers of drug abuse is mailed includes the parents of all junior high school students. The mailing encourages parents to speak to their children about the dangers of drug abuse. It includes a request for contributions. The SOP concludes that all three criteria have been met because of the following:

- *Purpose*—The informational material calls for specific action by the recipient, to help accomplish the entity's mission: to counsel children about the dangers of drug abuse.
- *Audience*—The audience has been selected based on the perceived potential for use of the action called for by the informational material.
- *Content*—This criterion has been met because of the material's call for specific action by the recipient that will help the entity accomplish its mission.

It is expected that not all situations will be as straightforward as the foregoing. Careful analysis will be needed to meet the rules that permit allocation of joint costs, rather than having them classified all as fund-raising.

For example, an entity's mailings to a roster of recent prior donors for renewal also includes "messages about the effects and early warning signs of [a] disease and specific action that should be taken to prevent it." The entity notes that there is no correlation between the recent contributions and participation in the program. AcSEC concluded that the purpose and content criteria were met, but not the audience criterion because there is a "rebuttable presumption that the audience is not met because the audience includes prior donors." In this instance, the audience's need to use the information in the program component "was an insignificant factor in its selection."

Space does not permit the description of the many illustrations included in the SOP.

Appendix F of SOP 98-2 describes some joint activities cost allocation methods, and potential drawbacks, including:

- The "physical units" method, which allocates the costs based on the units of output—e.g., lines, square inches—attributed to each of the materials and activities;
- The "relative direct cost" method, which allocates the costs based on the respective direct costs of the components; and
- The "stand-alone joint-cost-allocation" method, which allocates the costs to each component "based on a ratio that uses estimates of costs of items included in joint costs that would have been incurred had the components been conducted independently."

Appendix G of SOP 98-2 provides alternative (narrative and tabular) illustrations of disclosures required by the SOP:

- The types of activities for which joint costs have been incurred;
- A statement that such costs have been allocated; and
- The total amount allocated during the period and the portion allocated to each functional expense category.

The SOP also *encourages* the disclosure of the amount of joint costs for each kind of joint activity, if practical.

The narrative example follows:

Note X. Allocation of Joint Costs

In 19XX, the organization conducted activities that included requests for contributions, as well as program and management and general components. Those activities included direct mail campaigns, special events, and a telethon. The costs of conducting those activities included a total of $310,000 of joint costs, which are not specifically attributable to particular components of the activities (joint costs). [*Note to reader: The following sentence is encouraged but not required.*] Joint costs for each kind of activity were $50,000, $150,000, and $110,000, respectively. These joint costs were allocated as follows:

Fund-raising	$180,000
Program A	80,000
Program B	40,000
Management and general	10,000
Total	$310,000

Joint costs   These are the costs of conducting joint activities that are not identifiable with a particular component of the activity. Examples of joint costs include salaries, facilities rental, contract labor, consultants, paper, and training. They may also include postage, telephones, airtime, and facility rentals.

Bona fide program or management and general function   SOP 98-2 notes that the "purpose criterion is met if the purpose of the joint activity includes accomplishing program or management and general functions." For a bona fide program or management and general function to exist, the following elements must be present:

- *Purpose*—For an activity to have a purpose other than fund-raising, it must not result in compensation or fees for performing the activity that are based on the amounts raised. If performance is evaluated substantially on the activity's effectiveness in raising funds, all costs of the activity should be charged to fund-raising. The following are situations indicating that the purpose of the activity is not only for fund-raising purposes:

— A similar program or management and general component is conducted without the fund-raising appeal using the same medium, and on a scale that is similar to or greater than the scale on which it is conducted with the appeal.

— Evaluation of the results of the activity is based on a process that identifies program results and program goals, but not on its effectiveness in raising funds.

— The qualifications and duties of the personnel carrying out the activity are indicative of an individual who is performing other than fund-raising activities (e.g., not members of the fund-raising department).

— Tangible evidence of the activity exists that supports the existence of a bona fide program or management and general component of the activity.

• *Audience*—The population is selected principally on the basis of its need for the program or because it can assist the entity in meeting its program goals other than by financial support provided to the entity. Examples of the latter would be the appeal going to a broad segment of the population and a broad population segment that would benefit from the appeal, or if the appeal went to the population that would benefit most from the program. An audience selected on the basis of its ability to give—for example, prior donors—indicates a fund-raising activity.

• *Content*—To indicate that a bona fide program activity exists, the materials or activity should indicate what action the recipient should perform to further the organization's mission; it should not be related to financial support. The activity should benefit the recipient of the appeal or should benefit society. To indicate that the activity is for management and general purpose, the materials and activities should inform the audience about the organization's stewardship or how it is carrying out its program(s).

ACCOUNTING FOR
GRANT AND CONTRACT EXPENSES

A not-for-profit organization will incur expenditures for a variety of purposes, and depending on their nature, those expenditures will be classified as assets, reductions of liabilities, program costs, management and general costs, or fund-raising costs. Expenditures are also classified and reported in a variety of ways for different purposes (e.g., general-purpose financial statements, reporting in accordance with requirements under terms of federal awards, for reimbursement purposes). How the expenditures are reported does *not* depend on the source of the cash used (e.g., restricted donations).

The AICPA Audit and Accounting Guide *Not-for-Profit Organizations* cites paragraph 80 of FASB Concepts Statement No. 6 (Elements of Financial Statements), as a source for the definition of *expenses*. The Concepts Statement's definition is as follows:

> Expenses are outflows or other using up of assets or incurrences of liabilities (or a combination of both) from delivering or producing goods, rendering services, or carrying out other activities that constitute the entity's ongoing major or central operations.

Direct versus Indirect Costs

OMB Circular A-122 provides definitions of *direct* and *indirect costs*, as follows:

> Direct costs are those that can be identified specifically with a particular final cost objective: i.e., a particular award, project, service, or other direct activity of an organization.
>
> Indirect costs are those that have been incurred for common or joint objectives and cannot be readily identified with a particular final cost objective. . . . After direct costs have been determined and assigned directly to awards or other work as appropriate, indirect costs are those remaining to be allocated to benefiting cost objectives.

According to OMB Circular A-122, costs of "activities performed primarily as a service to members, clients, or the general public" are treated as direct costs and are allocated an equitable share of indirect costs. Examples are as follows:

- Maintaining membership rolls, subscriptions, publications, and related functions

- Providing services and information to members, legislative or administrative bodies, or the public

- Conducting promotions, lobbying, and performing other types of public relations

- Attending and planning meetings and conferences, except those held to conduct the general administration of the organization.

Circular A-122 notes that expenditures may not be charged to an award as a direct cost if any other cost incurred for the same purpose, in like circumstances, was allocated to an award as an indirect cost. Also, if an expenditure has been allocated to an award as a direct cost, a cost incurred for the same purpose in similar circumstances may not be allocated as an indirect cost.

Circular A-122 notes that "because of the diverse characteristics and accounting practices of nonprofit organizations, it is not possible to specify the types of costs which may be classified as indirect costs in all situations." The following typical indirect costs are listed (A-122, par. C.2):

- Depreciation or use allowances on buildings and equipment
- Cost of operating and maintaining facilities
- Salaries and expenses of executive officers, personnel administration, and accounting

Certain activities, such as fund-raising, may not be charged to federal awards. Accordingly, a not-for-profit organization charging costs to awards or against contracts must understand the nature of what may be allowable. For more information on allowable costs, see Chapter 15, "Office of Management and Budget."

OMB Circular A-122 notes that an indirect cost rate may be computed in a simplified manner if the organization has only one major function, or if all of its major functions benefit from its indirect costs to approximately the same degree. When the organization has several major functions and they do not all benefit from its indirect costs to approximately the same degree, the indirect costs should be allocated to the functions by means of a "base which best measures the relative degree of benefit" (A-122, par. D.1.b).

Simplified allocation method   An organization using the simplified allocation method will identify and separate total costs into direct or indirect pools and remove unallowable costs from the pools. The allowable indirect costs will be divided by an equitable distribution base to determine the indirect cost rate that will be used to distribute indirect costs to individual awards. Circular A-122 notes that the distribution base may be total direct costs (excluding capital expenditures) or direct salaries and wages.

Multiple allocation base method   A multiple allocation base method will be used when the organization's indirect costs do not uniformly benefit its major functions. Indirect costs will be accumulated into separate groupings to be allocated to the functions benefited by means of a base "which best measures the relative benefits." The organization will develop an indirect cost rate for each separate indirect cost pool identified (A-122, par. D.3.a).

Direct allocation method The direct allocation method will be used by organizations that treat all except general administration and general expenses as direct costs. Organizations will be required to identify joint costs and allocate them to the different activities with which the benefits of the joint costs are associated.

Program versus Management and General Costs

Program and management and general costs are discussed in some detail in the previous section on the functional allocation of expenses. Costs of program services, including grants to other entities, are reported separately from management and general costs and fund-raising costs on the organization's statement of activities.

Classifications of program services for voluntary health and welfare organizations might include research, public health education, professional education and training, and community services. Colleges' or universities' program services may include some or all of the following: instruction, research, public service, academic support, student services, institutional support, operation and maintenance of plant, and scholarships and fellowships. For other not-for-profit organizations, the list of program activities will depend on the organization and its purpose.

Costs of management and general activities "are those that are not identifiable with a single program, fund-raising activity, or membership-development activity but that are indispensable to the conduct of those activities and to an organization's existence. They include oversight, business management, general recordkeeping, budgeting, financing, soliciting revenue from exchange transactions, such as federal contracts and related administrative activities, and all management and administration except for direct conduct of program services or fund-raising activities" (NPO, par. 13.29).

Restricted versus Unrestricted Expenses

A not-for-profit organization reports expenses in its statement of activities. FAS-117 directs that expenses of the organization be reported as decreases in unrestricted net assets. The absence or presence of restrictions on the use of an organization's resources depends on the source of the funds.

In paragraphs 133–137, FAS-117 concludes that all expenses should be classified as decreases in unrestricted net assets. FASB's conclusion was based on the contention that the source of the funds to carry out an activity does not make the expenditure donor-restricted. Managment makes decisions about activities and when to use particular resources for the activities. To provide funding for these expenses, the FASB permits not-for-profit organizations to reclassify resources from temporarily restricted net assets to unrestricted net assets when managment determines that restricted resources are available for the particular activity.

FASB permits netting of revenues and expenses in only a few limited circumstances. These instances include investment revenues (net of custodial fees and investment advisory fees) and amounts resulting from peripheral or incidental transactions or from other events and circumstances that may be a result of conditions not in the control of the organization and its management. In FAS-117, paragraph 25, the FASB uses an example of an entity that sells land and buildings no longer needed for its ongoing activities to indicate a type of transaction that is reported net in the statement of activities. The revenue from the sale is reported less the cost of the asset sold and the costs of making the sale (e.g., fees and permits).

Chapter 5
ASSETS

CONTENTS

Chapter 5
ASSETS

This chapter covers some of the asset classifications that are peculiar to the not-for-profit community (e.g., promises to give or pledges, collections, and pooled investments). Other assets such as cash, receivables arising from the ongoing and central activities of an entity, and prepaid expenses are treated the same in the books and financial statements of not-for-profit and for-profit entities. Detailed information about the recording of these assets can be found in the *Miller GAAP Guide*.

CROSS-REFERENCES

2000 MILLER NOT-FOR-PROFIT REPORTING: Chapter 2, "Overview of Current Pronouncements"; Chapter 6, "Liabilities"; Chapter 9, "Note Disclosures"; Chapter 16, "Cost Accounting Standards"

2000 MILLER GAAP GUIDE: Chapter 12, "Depreciable Assets and Depreciation"; Chapter 28, "Investments in Debt and Equity Securities"

2000 MILLER GAAP IMPLEMENTATION MANUAL: Chapter 25, "Investments in Debt and Equity Securities"

2000 MILLER GOVERNMENTAL GAAP GUIDE: Chapter 14, "Assets"; Chapter 31, "General Fixed Assets Account Group"

2000 MILLER GAAS GUIDE: Section 336

INVESTMENTS AND INVESTMENT EARNINGS

Not-for-profit organizations carry investments for varying reasons. Generally, they have investment portfolios for unrestricted funds to earn additional income until such time as the funds are to be used for program or other purposes. They also have portfolios of restricted funds and endowment funds. These investment portfolios frequently are invested in pools of various funds, the income from which should be allocated equitably among the participating funds.

Investments may have been purchased by or donated to the not-for-profit organization. As required by FAS-116 (Accounting for Contributions Received and Contributions Made), the organization should include investments received from donors in classifications of net assets guided by the donors' intentions. Some investments received or purchased with donated funds may be prohibited from being included in investment pools because of the donors' expressed intent for the use of the contribution.

The publication of FAS-124 (Accounting for Certain Investments Held by Not-for-Profit Organizations) eliminated the alternative valuation methods that previously had been available to not-for-profit organizations. Investments in equity securities with readily determinable fair values and all investments in debt securities should be reported at fair value in the statement of financial position.

The requirements of FAS-124 are covered beginning on page 161, below.

Under the fair market value method, the unrealized appreciation or depreciation should be identified separately and included in the appropriate section of the statement of activities, as required by FAS-117 (Financial Statements of Not-for-Profit Organizations). Organizations that continue to use fund accounting in the general ledger and other books of account should record the unrealized appreciation or depreciation in the activities of the appropriate fund.

Accounting for Income, Gains, and Losses

Investment income and realized gains and losses on investments of unrestricted funds should be reported as unrestricted revenue. Unrealized gains and losses related to such funds also are reported in unrestricted revenue.

For investments of donor-restricted funds, other than endowment funds, income and gains should be included in the revenue of the restricted funds unless legally available for unrestricted purposes. Losses, both realized and unrealized, should be reported as a loss of the restricted fund, unless legal restrictions require otherwise.

For investments of endowment funds, investment income is available for unrestricted purposes and should be included in the revenue of the unrestricted fund unless the donor has restricted the use of the income, in which case the income should be included in the revenue of the appropriate restricted fund. Traditionally, realized gains and losses on investments of endowment funds have been considered as principal transactions. Accordingly, the restrictions placed on the original principal of the endowment have been applied to the net realized gains.

With the issuance of FAS-116, accounting for endowment income and gains or losses changed significantly for many organizations that previously included all assets, including cumulative interest earnings, and gains or losses in the endowment fund.

FAS-116 recognizes three types of net assets related to endowments: (1) the original principal, (2) income consisting of interest and dividends, and (3) gains or losses due to appreciation or depreciation (realized and unrealized) of investments. Each of these sources of net assets must be considered separately under FAS-116. Treatment of income on the endowment is often specifically stipulated in the endowment instrument, while the treatment of gains or losses often is not addressed. If the endowment instrument is silent on both income and gains or losses, then local law must be observed. Unless specific donor stipulations or local laws restrict the endowment's income and gains or losses in some way, these items are considered *unrestricted*.

Income and net appreciation from endowments may be subject to temporary restrictions related to time or purpose. For example, a time restriction may require that interest income from an endowment be spent during or after a specific period. A purpose restriction, such as a requirement that endowment interest be used to fund scholarships for students who have demonstrated financial need, may focus on a specific objective. In this case, the endowment-related asset is temporarily restricted until it is given to a student as a scholarship. At that point, the funds have been expended for their specified purpose and the asset is no longer restricted. FAS-117 provides guidelines for reporting such transfers between unrestricted and restricted net assets.

Certain states permit not-for-profit organizations in certain circumstances to consider net realized gains on investments of endowment funds to be available for unrestricted use. When this approach is permitted by a state, the designated amount of appreciation transferred to unrestricted funds should be reflected in the financial statements as a transfer of fund balance.

Most states have adopted the Uniform Management of Institutional Funds Act (UMIFA). Under UMIFA, in the absence of any donor restrictions, an endowment fund's net appreciation is to be used for the purposes for which the endowment was established, subject to a standard of business care and prudence. Net appreciation is the excess of the fair value of the assets of an endowment fund over the historic dollar values of the fund. Historic dollar, which equals the value of the original gift or gifts that established the endowment fund value, may not be impaired. Historic dollar value does not change unless new gifts are added to the fund or unless the donor requires that some or all of the gains be added to the fund. If the fair value of the assets is less than the historic dollar value, no amount of net appreciation is available for expenditure.

Not-for-profit organizations commonly have endowments that are more than 100 years old. In these circumstances, the original endowment instrument may no longer be available, if it ever existed in written form. The amount of effort to be spent in establishing each individual endowment's restriction should be based on a cost–benefit analysis. The most important factor in such an analysis is the amount of the individual endowment in question relative to the organization's total endowment fund. If no written guidance exists or can be reasonably found with respect to an individual endowment's historic value or donor stipulations, local law should be followed. In those states that have adopted it, UMIFA provides that the "determination of historic dollar value made in good faith by the institution is conclusive."

Total Return Concept

Some organizations, with the advice of their legal counsel, have adopted a "total return" approach to their management of endowment fund investments. According to the total return concept, (1) gains are not the same as principal and accordingly may be spent and (2) total investment return should include yield plus or minus gains and losses. Organizations using this concept account for the portion of gain used for general operating purposes as revenue rather than as a transfer to the operating funds. Under the total return approach, organizations use prudence and a formula based on historic returns on investments to determine the portion of the gains used for operating expenditures. The AICPA Audit and Accounting Guide, *Audits of Colleges and Universities,* superseded by the new Audit Guide *Not-for-Profit Organizations,* describes several methods for computing the "total return" and emphasizes "the protection of endowment principal from the loss of purchasing power (inflation) as a primary consideration before appropriating gains."

Investment Pools

Not-for-profit organizations frequently pool investments of various funds (e.g., operating, restricted, and endowment). The realized and unrealized gains and losses and income must be allocated equitably among the sources of the investments in the pool. Accordingly, investment pools should be operated on the market value method. Each operating, restricted, and endowment fund is assigned a number of units based on the relationship of the market value of all investments at the time they are pooled.

Investment pool income should be allocated to participating funds based on the number of units held by each fund. When the use of income has been restricted by the donor (e.g., in an endowment fund), it may be necessary to segregate gains and losses from income because the gains and losses may revert to the separate funds differently than the income.

FASB Statement No. 124

In November 1995, FASB issued FAS-124 (Accounting for Certain Investments Held by Not-for-Profit Organizations). FAS-124 affects investments in equity securities with readily determinable fair values and all investments in debt securities. It also establishes disclosure requirements for most investments held by not-for-profit organizations.

FAS-124 supersedes the guidance contained in the following AICPA Audit and Accounting Guides:

- *Audits of Colleges and Universities*
- *Audits of Voluntary Health and Welfare Organizations*
- *Audits of Providers of Health Care Services*
- *Audits of Certain Nonprofit Organizations*

The provisions of FAS-124 have been incorporated into the final language of the following new Guides issued by the AICPA:

- *Not-for-Profit Organizations*
- *Health Care Organizations*

As part of its deliberations regarding this topic, FASB considered amending FAS-115 (Accounting for Certain Investments in Debt and Equity Securities) to extend its coverage to not-for-profit organizations, as FAS-115 and FAS-124 apply to the same classes of investments. FASB decided that it must first resolve the issues of accounting for contributions and financial statement display before applying the requirements of FAS-115 to not-for-profit organizations. FAS-115 specifically excluded not-for-profits.

FAS-124 does not provide new standards for investments in equity securities accounted for under the equity method or for investments in consolidated subsidiaries. FASB is considering these topics for all entities and, in October 1995, issued an Exposure Draft of a proposed Statement titled "Consolidated Financial Statements: Policies and Procedures." This Exposure Draft is discussed in Chapter 7, "Organizational Issues."

Investments covered by FAS-124 should be measured at their fair value in the statement of financial position. Gains and losses on investments should be reported in the statement of activities as increases or decreases in unrestricted net assets, unless their use is temporarily or permanently restricted by explicit donor stipulation or by law.

According to FAS-116, donor stipulations, to the extent that they exist, determine the classifications of gains and losses from sales of restricted endowment funds. Securities held in perpetuity because of donor restrictions also may result in gains or losses increasing or decreasing permanently restricted net assets because of local law. However, in the absence of donor restrictions or local law that restricts the use of gains, such gains will follow the treatment of investment income. Accordingly, gains are "unrestricted if the investment income is unrestricted or are temporarily restricted if the investment income is temporarily restricted by the donor" (FAS-124, par. 11).

One area of confusion that existed in earlier guidance related to losses on investments of a donor-restricted endowment fund. Preparers of financial statements were trying to understand in which class of net asset the losses should be reported. FAS-124 clarifies the accounting.

The organization must first look to donor stipulations and local law governing endowments. In the event that there are no such stipulations or law, losses on the investments of a donor-restricted endowment fund must first reduce temporarily restricted net assets. This reduction will be to the extent that donor-imposed temporary restrictions on the net appreciation of the fund have not been met before the loss occurs. Unrestricted net assets are reduced for any loss remaining.

FAS-124 notes that when losses reduce a donor-restricted endowment fund below the level required by the donor or by law, gains that restore the fair value of the fund's assets to the required level are classified as increases in unrestricted net assets in the statement of activities.

Accordingly, gains on endowment funds that are in a deficit position relative to the historic value, and for which the donor or local law has not stipulated restrictions, first will be classified as increases in unrestricted net assets up to the level required to remove the deficiency. Further gains will increase temporarily restricted net assets, if the donor has stipulated a use for the income. If no use for the income has been stipulated by the donor, further gains will increase unrestricted net assets.

FAS-124 notes that not-for-profit organizations are not bound to one method for reporting investment return. Nor are they bound to one method for reporting operations. In fact, FASB notes that there is no preferred method for reporting. Accordingly, organizations have great latitude in reporting the required information. In the explanatory material that accompanies FAS-124, FASB points out that the not-for-profit organization should present the required information in a manner that will prove to be meaningful to the financial statement users. Accordingly, the information may be presented based on (FAS-124, par. 102):

- The nature of the underlying transactions, such as classifying realized amounts as operating activities and unrealized amounts as nonoperating activities

- Budgetary designations, such as classifying amounts computed under a spending rate or total return policy as operating activities and the remainder of investment return as nonoperating activities

- The reporting requirements for categories of investments used in Statement 115, such as classifying investment income, realized gains and losses, unrealized gains and losses on trading securities, and other-than-temporary impairment losses on securities (that is, all items included in net income of a business enterprise) as operating activities and classifying the remainder of investment return as nonoperating activities

- Other characteristics that provide information that is relevant and understandable to donors, creditors, and other users of financial statements

Disclosures According to FAS-124, not-for-profit organizations should disclose the following for each balance sheet (FAS-124, pars. 14–16):

- The aggregate carrying amount of investments by major types (e.g., equity securities, U.S. Treasury securities, corporate debt securities, mortgage-backed securities, oil and gas properties, and real estate)

- The basis for determining the carrying amount for investments other than equity securities with readily determinable fair values and all debt securities

- The method(s) and significant assumptions used to estimate the fair values of investments other than financial instruments if those other investments are reported at fair value

- The aggregate amount of the deficiencies for all donor-restricted endowment funds for which the fair value of the assets at the reporting date is less than the level required by donor stipulations or law

Also, for each balance sheet, not-for-profit organizations should disclose the nature and carrying amount for each individual investment or group of investments that represents a significant concentration of market risk.

For each period for which a statement of activities is presented, not-for-profit organizations should disclose the following:

- The composition of investment return including, at a minimum, investment income, net realized gains or losses on investments reported at other than fair value, and net gains or losses on investments reported at fair value
- A reconciliation of investment return to amounts reported in the statement of activities if investment return is separated into operating and nonoperating amounts, together with a description of the policy used to determine the amount that is included in the measure of operations and a discussion leading to a change, if any, in that policy

FAS-124 has the effect of changing the definition of *endowment fund* as contained in FAS-117. Instead of referring to *the principal of a permanent endowment* or *the principal of a term endowment*, FAS-124 refers to *the portion of a permanent endowment* or *the portion of a term endowment* when describing how such portion must be maintained by the not-for-profit organization.

Definitions Not-for-profit organizations should consider the following:

> *Debt security*—In addition to creditor relationships with another enterprise, debt securities are also (a) redeemable preferred stock and (b) a collateralized mortgage obligation (CMO) (or other instrument) that is issued in equity form but is required to be accounted for as a nonequity instrument regardless of how that instrument is classified (that is, whether equity or debt) in the issuer's statement of financial position. The term *debt security* excludes option contracts, financial futures contracts, lease contracts, and swap contracts.

> *Equity security*—An instrument representing an ownership interest in another enterprise (e.g., common, preferred, or other capital stock) or the right to acquire (e.g., warrants, rights, and call options) or dispose of (e.g., put options) an ownership interest in an enterprise at fixed or determinable prices. The term *equity security* does not include convertible debt or redeemable preferred stock.

FIXED ASSETS

Depreciable Assets

Depreciable assets of not-for-profit organizations include those assets that are used to provide goods and services to beneficiaries, customers, and members. This classification of assets does not include collection items. For more information about items in a collection and how they are recorded in the accounts of a not-for-profit organization, see the next section, titled "Works of Art and Historical Treasures." The fixed assets classification is not intended to include long-lived tangible assets that are held for investment purposes.

Items that should be considered among the fixed asset accounts and that are depreciated over their expected economic useful life include the following:

- Land improvements, buildings and building improvements, equipment, furniture and office equipment, library books, and motor vehicles
- Capital leased property and equipment
- Leasehold improvements
- Contributed use of facilities and equipment that were capitalized in accordance with FAS-116

SOP 78-10 (Accounting Principles and Reporting Practices for Certain Nonprofit Organizations), now superseded by the new Audit Guide, required not-for-profit organizations to capitalize fixed assets, and "organizations that have not previously capitalized their fixed assets should do so retroactively." Purchased fixed assets are recorded at cost. Those fixed assets that have been donated to the organization should be recorded at their fair value at the date of the gift and should be classified as permanently restricted, temporarily restricted, or unrestricted net assets depending on donor restrictions and the organization's accounting policy. When organizations record fixed assets for the first time and the assets' historical costs or fair market values on the date of donation are not available, another reasonable basis should be used to record the assets in the books of account.

Nondepreciable Assets

Certain long-lived tangible assets held by a not-for-profit organization are not depreciated. These include:

- Land used as a building site
- Construction in progress

When considering prior practices relating to accounting for the costs of fixed assets of not-for-profit organizations, the FASB rejected the notion that certain assets, such as landmarks, monuments, cathedrals, and historical treasures, should not be depreciated. In FAS-93 (Recognition of Depreciation by Not-for-Profit Organizations), the

FASB notes that the term *collections* should apply to a group of assets that is not inexhaustible. Accordingly, FAS-93 concluded that assets such as landmarks and monuments should be depreciated unless the individual works of art or historical treasures have economic benefit or service potential that is used up so slowly that their estimated useful lives are extraordinarily long. That characteristic exists if there is verifiable evidence to demonstrate (a) that the asset has cultural, aesthetic, or historical value worth preserving perpetually and (b) that the holder has both the technological and the financial ability to protect and preserve the service potential of the asset and in fact is doing that.

Verifiable evidence includes documentation from individuals who possess the skills needed to evaluate items in a collection, such as art historians and archeologists. Auditors who rely on these individuals to support a client's assertion that certain items should not be depreciated should follow the AICPA guidance for determining the experts' qualifications. In accordance with SAS-73 (Using the Work of a Specialist), auditors should review the experts' accomplishments, memberships, and standing in the profession before relying on opinions and documentation provided.

Funding Depreciation or Depreciation Reserve

In certain circumstances, organizations provide resources for renewal and replacement of physical plant. These resources will be provided as a result of board action or agreement with outside agencies to maintain these funds. The outside agencies (e.g., HUD or other source providing mortgage financing) will reach agreement with the organization regarding the amounts to be provided each year and how the funds should be segregated in the organization's accounts. The funding of replacement reserves is based on decisions made by the organization's management. Accordingly, replacement reserves are not the basis used for determining depreciation.

Accounting for Replacement Reserves

As a rule, replacement fund assets are divided between board-designated (unrestricted) funds and funds that are restricted by donors or by agreements with the agencies providing the funding for the fixed assets (e.g., by bond indenture). According to the superseded Guide, *Audits of Colleges and Universities* (ACU, par. 9.14):

> Funds for renewals and replacements arise from mandatory and voluntary transfers from current funds and income and gains on investments of these funds. In some cases governmental appropriations and other gifts and grants are made

specifically for these purposes and recorded as direct additions to the restricted portion of the fund balance.

Deductions from the fund balance consist primarily of expenditures for renewals and replacements of plant, some of which may be considered as additions to plant assets in the investment-in-plant subgroup, and some may be renewals and replacements of a type not ordinarily capitalized. Other deductions might include losses on investments of these funds and transfers of funds back to unrestricted current assets.

WORKS OF ART AND HISTORICAL TREASURES

FAS-116 defines *collections*. These are assets that are works of art or treasures held by the organization for public exhibition, education, or research in furtherance of public service rather than financial gain. These assets must be protected, kept unencumbered, cared for, and preserved. To be considered a collection, the assets should be subject to an organizational policy that requires the proceeds of items that are sold to be used to acquire other items for collections. Examples include paintings held by a museum and original musical scores held by a library.

Capitalization Policies

Under the terms of prior guidance available to not-for-profit organizations, in SOP 78-10, "it is often impracticable to determine a value for such collections and accordingly… they need not be capitalized." SOP 78-10 pointed out that collections often are very valuable to organizations, constituting "the largest assets" owned. The SOP encouraged organizations to capitalize collections if records and values do exist. As will be seen, FAS-116 continues this guidance.

Management Practices

Organizations should catalog and control the collections, because they represent, in many cases, the most significant assets owned by museums, art galleries, botanical gardens, libraries, etc.

Accounting for Collections

The accounting for collections depends on the policies adopted by the not-for-profit organization. FAS-116 does not require that organizations capitalize assets included in collections. When initially adopting the provisions of FAS-116, not-for-profit organizations will be able to choose one of the following three options:

1. Capitalizing their collections, including all items acquired in prior periods that have not been capitalized previously and all items acquired in future periods
2. Capitalizing only those items acquired after initial adoption of FAS-116
3. Not capitalizing any items

The accounting for collections depends on which option is elected. If the organization elects to capitalize acquisitions in the collection, those items in the collection that were acquired in exchange transactions would be recognized as assets and as contributions in the appropriate net asset class at fair value.

If the organization does not elect to capitalize collections, no assets are recognized from the acquisition of collection items. Cash flows associated with these collections (e.g., sales, insurance recoveries, and purchases) are reported in the financial statements as investing activities. In addition, an organization that follows the policies described in (2) and (3), above, will make the following disclosures in the notes to the financial statements:

- Description of the collections
- Relative significance of the collections
- Organization's accounting and stewardship policies
- Description of collection items given away, damaged, destroyed, lost, or otherwise deaccessed during the period (or disclose their fair value)

When contributions for collections include items that have significant uncertainties about their future service potential or economic benefit, the organization should not recognize any value in the financial statements.

Amortization and Depreciation Policies

The AICPA Audit Guide provides examples of financial statement disclosures relating to collections. Paragraph 7.14 illustrations relate to (1) organizations that capitalized collections before the issuance of FAS-116; (2) organizations that capitalize collections retroactively upon initial adoption of FAS-116; (3) organizations that capitalize their collections prospectively upon initial adoption of FAS-116; and (4) organizations that do not capitalize collections. These examples follow.

(1) Note X: Summary of Significant Accounting Policies

The organization has capitalized its collections since its inception. If purchased, items accessioned into the collection are capitalized at cost, and if donated, they are capitalized at their appraised or fair value on the accession date (the date on which the item is accepted by the Acquisitions Committee of the Board of Trustees). Gains or losses on the deaccession of collection items are classified on the statement of activities as unrestricted or temporarily restricted support depending on donor restrictions, if any, placed on the item at the time of accession.

(2) Note X: Summary of Significant Accounting Policies

In 19X1, the organization capitalized its collections retroactively in conformity with FASB Statement No. 116. To the extent that reliable records were available, the organization capitalized collection items acquired prior to 19X1 at their cost at the date of purchase or, if the items were contributed, at their fair or appraised value at the accession date (the date on which the item was accepted by the Acquisitions Committee of the Board of Trustees). Other collection items, particularly those acquired prior to 19X1 when detailed curatorial records began to be maintained, have been capitalized at their appraised or estimated current market value. In some cases, collection items held solely for their potential educational value or historical significance were determined to have no alternative use and were not assigned values for the purpose of capitalization. The collections capitalized retroactively were determined to a total value of $11,138,100. This amount is reflected as a change in accounting principle on the statement of activities.

(3) Note X: Summary of Significant Accounting Policies

Collection items acquired on or after July 1, 19X0: Accessions of these collection items are capitalized at cost, if the items were purchased, or at their appraised or fair value on the accession date (the date on which the item is accepted by the Acquisitions Committee of the Board of Trustees), if the items were contributed. Gains or losses from deaccessions of these items are reflected on the statement of activities as changes in the appropriate net asset classes, depending on the existence and type of donor-imposed restrictions.

Collection items acquired prior to July 1, 19X0: Collection items accessioned prior to July 1, 19X0, were recorded as decreases in unrestricted net assets, if the items were purchased. No financial statement recognition was made for contributed collection items. Proceeds from insurance recoveries or deaccessions of these items are reflected on the statements of activities as changes in the appropriate net asset classes, depending on the existence and type of donor-imposed restrictions.

Note Y: Accounting Change

In 19X1, the organization adopted FASB Statement No. 116. The organization has determined that the cost to capitalize its collections retroactively would be excessive because records of the cost of purchased items and of the fair value at the date of contribution of donated items are unreliable or do not exist. However, such information is available for current-year acquisitions and will be maintained on an ongoing basis. Therefore, the organization has elected to capitalize prospectively all collection items acquired after July 1, 19X0, the date of initial adoption of FASB Statement No. 116.

Note Z: Collections

The organization's collections are made up of artifacts of historical significance, scientific specimens, and art objects. Each of the items is cataloged for educational, research, scientific, and curatorial purposes, and activities verifying their existence and assessing their condition are performed continuously.

During 19X1, a significant number of American pioneer artifacts from the 1800s were destroyed while in transit to an exhibition in which they were to be displayed. Because these items were purchased prior to July 1, 19X0, the insurance proceeds of $22,000, which reimbursed the organization in full for the artifacts' fair value, are reflected as an increase in unrestricted net assets on the statement of activities. No other collection items were deaccessioned in 19X1 or 19X0.

(4) Note X: Summary of Significant Accounting Policies

The collections, which were acquired through purchases and contributions since the organization's inception, are not recognized as assets on the statement of financial position. Purchases of collection items are recorded as decreases in unrestricted net assets in the year in which the items are acquired, or as temporarily or permanently restricted net assets if the assets used to purchase the items are restricted by donors. Contributed collection items are not reflected on the financial statements. Proceeds from deaccessions or insurance recoveries are reflected as increases in the appropriate net asset classes.

Note Z: Collections

The organization's collections are made up of artifacts of historical significance, scientific specimens, and art objects that are held for educational, research, scientific, and curatorial purposes. Each of the items is cataloged, preserved, and cared for, and activities verifying their existence and assessing their condition are performed continuously. The collections are subject to a policy that requires proceeds from their sales to be used to acquire other items for collections.

During 19X1, a significant number of American pioneer artifacts from the 1800s were destroyed while in transit to an exhibition in which they were to be displayed. These artifacts were contributed in 19XX, with a restriction that limited any future proceeds from deaccessions to acquisitions of artifacts from a similar period. As a result, the insurance proceeds of $22,000, which reimbursed the organization in full for the artifacts' fair value, are reflected as an increase in temporarily restricted net assets on the statement of activities. No other collection items were deaccessioned in 19X1 or 19X0.

CHAPTER 6
LIABILITIES

CONTENTS

Chapter 6
LIABILITIES

CROSS-REFERENCES

2000 MILLER NOT-FOR-PROFIT REPORTING: Chapter 2, "Overview of Current Pronouncements"; Chapter 5, "Assets"; Chapter 11, "Display of Certain GAAP Transactions"; Chapter 16, "Cost Accounting Standards"

2000 MILLER GAAP GUIDE: Chapter 16, "Extinguishment of Debt"; Chapter 24, "Interest Costs Capitalized"; Chapter 31, "Long-Term Obligations"; Chapter 47, "Troubled Debt Restructuring"

2000 MILLER GAAP IMPLEMENTATION MANUAL: Chapter 7, "Capitalization and Expense Recognition Concepts"; Chapter 16, "Extinguishment of Debt"; Chapter 41, "Troubled Debt Restructuring"

2000 MILLER GOVERNMENTAL GAAP GUIDE: Chapter 17, "Liabilities"; Chapter 30, "General Long-Term Debt Account Group"

Liabilities of not-for-profit organizations are similar to those of for-profit entities. FAS-116 (Accounting for Contributions Received and Contributions Made) provides guidance on liabilities relating to promises to give. That guidance is discussed in this chapter. Not-for-profit organizations often incur debt for construction of facilities under tax-exempt financing arrangements, or they may incur liabilities through the promotion of split-interest agreements, discussed at length in Chapter 3, "Revenues." Liabilities also may be incurred for unrelated business income tax, for excise tax on investment earnings of certain foundations, and for holding assets to be given to other organizations under agency arrangements. Agency transactions have come under media scrutiny because of litigation in several jurisdictions. FASB continues to look at these transactions with the intent of publishing clarifying guidance as Interpretations of FAS-116; as a result, FASB Interpretation (FIN) No. 42 (Accounting for Transfers of Assets in Which a Not-for-Profit Organization Is Granted Variance

Power) has been published. An Exposure Draft of a proposed new Statement addressing these issues was issued in 1998. A final Statement, FAS-136 (Transfers of Assets to a Not-for-Profit Organization or Charitable Trust That Raises or Holds Contributions for Others), was issued just before this book went to press. Liabilities for payroll, payroll taxes, and those related to the normal operating expenses of entities are covered in pronouncements that apply to for-profit organizations. These are discussed in the 2000 *Miller GAAP Guide*.

AGENCY TRANSACTIONS

FAS-136 (Transfer of Assets to a Not-for-Profit Organization or Charitable Trust That Raises or Holds Contributions for Others) is effective for financial statements for periods beginning after December 15, 1999. The organization may apply it by restating the financial statements of all years presented, or by recognizing the cumulative effect of the change in accounting in the year of change.

This Statement requires a "recipient organization" that accepts assets from a resource provider, the "donor," on behalf of another entity, the "beneficiary," to transfer the assets received to the beneficiary or to use the assets on behalf of the donor-specified beneficiary. When the intermediary entity receives the assets, it should recognize a liability to the specified beneficiary.

The recipient organization should recognize a contribution, however, if the donor grants variance power to the recipient organization. A contribution also will be recognized if the recipient organization and the beneficiary are financially interrelated organizations. Organizations are financially interrelated when one organization has the ability to influence the operating and financial decisions of the other and one organization has an ongoing economic interest in the net assets of the other.

A beneficiary of rights to assets in a charitable trust must recognize such rights unless the donor has explicitly granted variance power to the recipient organization. The beneficial interest, recognized as a receivable, is measured at fair value and remeasured at each subsequent balance sheet date.

The Statement describes four situations in which the transfer of assets must be accounted for as a liability by the recipient organization and as an asset by the resource provider. In each situation, the transfer is revocable or reciprocal:

1. The resource provider may retain the ability to redirect the use of the assets to another beneficiary.

2. The resource provider attaches a condition to the transfer, or the transfer is revocable or repayable.

3. The recipient organization is controlled by the resource provider, and the beneficiary is unaffiliated.

4. The resource provider specifies itself as the beneficiary, and the transfer is not an equity transaction. In this situation, the resource provider records an interest in the net assets of the recipient organization.

If the resource provider is a not-for-profit organization and names itself or an affiliate as the beneficiary, the following disclosures must be made:

- The identity of the recipient organization;

- Whether variance power was granted to the recipient, and a description of the terms of the variance power;

- The terms under which there will be distributions to the resource provider or its affiliate; and

- The aggregate amount recognized in the balance sheet for the related transfers, and whether it will be recorded as an interest in the net assets of the recipient organization or as another asset.

LIABILITIES FOR PLEDGES TO GIVE OR GRANT COMMITMENTS

Some not-for-profit organizations pledge money to other organizations. For example, private foundations often make contributions to other not-for-profit organizations in the form of pledges to support research or other programs.

FAS-116 establishes accounting standards for organizations that make contributions. Generally, these contributions, which include unconditional promises to give, should be recognized as expenses of the organization in the period made.

Contributions are unconditional transfers of assets in a voluntary, nonreciprocal transfer. The term *assets* includes cash or other assets including securities, land, buildings, use of property, materials and supplies, services, and unconditional promises to give in the future. FAS-116 notes that for a promise to give to be recognized in the financial statements, there must be verifiable evidence that a promise was made to and received by a not-for-profit organization.

Unconditional promises to give are recognized in the financial statements of the organization in the period in which made. Conditional promises to give are recognized in the period in which the conditions on which they depend are substantially met. FAS-116 also notes that a conditional promise to give is considered unconditional if the possibility that the condition will not be met is remote.

As with organizations that record contributions received, the determination of whether a promise to give is conditional or merely restricted (and therefore unconditional) will depend on the stipulations contained in the promise to give. When the donor stipulations are ambiguous, the promise to give will be deemed to be conditional. Accordingly, evidence of donor intentions should be in the form of written or verifiable oral communications—written agreements, pledge cards, oral communications documented by tape recording, written contemporaneous registers, written confirmations, etc.

Paragraph 61 of FAS-116 states that the imposition of a condition allows the transferor of assets to retain a right of return of transferred assets. The FASB concludes "that if a transferor imposes a condition, a reasonable possibility exists that the condition will not occur."

Foundations responding to the Exposure Draft for FAS-116 were concerned that the final Statement should make clear whether administrative requirements should be considered a condition for the purposes of recognizing a multiyear grant. The FASB noted that the foundations were concerned that "trivial" conditions may allow an organization to avoid recognition of promises to give. Accordingly, if the possibility that the condition will not be met is remote (the chance of the future event or events not occurring is slight), the donor organization may record the conditional promise to give as a contribution made.

The AICPA Guide notes that "[u]nconditional promises to give should be recognized at the time the donor has an obligation to transfer the promised assets in the future, which generally occurs when the donor approves a specific grant or when the recipient is notified."

Disclosure Requirements

Paragraph 10.08 of SOP 78-10 notes that organizations that make grants to others should disclose, in the notes to the financial statements, commitments for unpaid grants that have not been recorded as liabilities for promises to give, in accordance with FAS-5 and FAS-47. The disclosures should list, for the total amount of the recorded liability for unconditional promises to give, the following amounts: those due in less than one year, in one to five years, and in more than five years. For those amounts payable in more than one year, the unamortized discount should also be disclosed.

LONG-TERM DEBT

Generally, liabilities of not-for-profit organizations are similar to those of business entities. Accounting for long-term debt, however, is generally different because of the type of accounting used. Fund accounting, most often used by not-for-profit organizations, segregates assets, liabilities, and fund balances into self-balancing account groupings that observe the limitations and restrictions placed on the resources available to the organization. Resources are classified according to their nature and purposes.

Debt Reserve Funds

Many not-for-profit organizations that have significant plant and equipment (e.g., hospitals, colleges, and universities) maintain plant funds in their books of accounts. Included among these funds are the liabilities for mortgages or bonds payable and asset accounts related to the amounts deposited with trustees under the terms of the indenture.

The deposits with trustees could be on account for renewal and replacement of plant, or they could be used for the retirement of indebtedness and payment of interest on the debt. The funds will increase when transfers are made from unrestricted funds for payment of interest and principal. Other sources of additions to the funds include income earned and gains on sales of investments held in the funds, and donor-designated gifts, grants, and governmental appropriations for debt retirement.

The debt reserve funds will be reduced by payments of principal and interest, trustee fees and expenses, and losses on investments of the funds.

Capitalizing Interest on Tax-Exempt Financing

Generally accepted accounting principles (FAS-34 [Capitalization of Interest Cost], amended by FAS-62 [Capitalization of Interest Cost in Situations Involving Certain Tax-Exempt Borrowings and Certain Gifts and Grants]) note that interest should be capitalized as part of the cost of certain assets. To qualify, assets must require a period of time for an organization to get them ready for their intended use. Examples are assets that an organization constructs for its own use (such as facilities).

When funds are available from gifts or grants received by the organization for the restricted purpose of acquiring assets that would ordinarily qualify for interest capitalization, FAS-62 notes that interest should not be capitalized.

The cost that is permitted to be capitalized consists of interest costs of assets financed with tax-exempt borrowing reduced by any interest earned on the temporary investment of the proceeds from the debt. The period covered is from the date of the borrowing until the date that the qualifying assets are ready for their intended use.

In these circumstances, interest cost and interest earned on borrowings not intended to be used for the acquisition of these qualified assets should not be capitalized. The interest cost on these borrowings may be capitalized on other qualifying assets.

Consider the following:

---

a. The organization will construct a clinic at a cost of $10 million, to be financed from three sources:
   (1) $4 million foundation grant restricted to use for the specified project, payable $1 million per year
   (2) $4 million tax-exempt borrowing at an interest rate of 5 percent ($200,000 per year)
   (3) $2 million from operations
b. The entity has $10 million in other borrowings that are outstanding throughout the construction of the clinic. The interest rate on those borrowings is 6 percent. Other qualifying assets of the organization never exceed $5 million during the construction period.
c. The proceeds from the borrowing and the initial phase of the grant are received 1 year in advance of starting construction on the clinic and are temporarily invested in interest-bearing investments yielding 7 percent. Interest income earned from temporary investments is not reinvested.
d. Construction of the clinic will take 4 years after start of construction to complete.
e. The [following table] sets forth the amount of interest to be capitalized as part of the entity's investment in the clinic.
f. Over the course of construction the net cost of financing is $487,000, the sum of the interest capitalized for the 5 years. Accordingly, the entity's total net investment in the clinic will be $10,487,000.

	Year				
	19X1	19X2	19X3	19X4	19X5
	(amounts in thousands)				
(1) Assumed average qualifying assets	$ 0	$ 2,000	$ 5,000	$ 8,000	$ 9,000
(2) Average funding received					
borrowing	4,000	4,000	4,000	4,000	4,000
grant	1,000	2,000	3,000	4,000	4,000
(3) Average temporary investments ((2) – (1), not less than zero)[1]					
borrowing	4,000	3,000	1,000	0	0
grant	1,000	1,000	1,000	0	0

	Year				
	19X1	*19X2*	*19X3*	*19X4*	*19X5*
	(amounts in thousands)				
(4) Interest earned ((3) x 7 percent)					
borrowing	280	210	70	0	0
grant	70	70	70	0	0
(5) Average qualifying assets in excess of borrowing, grant, and interest earned on grant[2]	0	0	0	0	790
(6) Interest cost capitalized—other borrowings ((5) x 6 percent)	0	0	0	0	47
(7) Interest cost—tax-exempt borrowings	200	200	200	200	200
(8) Interest capitalized ((6) + (7) − (4)(a)[3]	(80)	(10)	130	200	247

[1] Balances of unexpended borrowings and unexpended grants can vary depending on the source from which the entity elects to disburse funds.

[2] That is, (1) average qualifying assets minus the sum of (2) (average funding received plus (4)(b) cumulative interest earned on grant), not less than zero.

[3] Note that amounts in parentheses are reductions in the cost of the asset.

Arbitrage Considerations

Organizations that issue tax-exempt bonds are required to file certain information returns for Internal Revenue Service (IRS) purposes.

Generally, interest income earned on an arbitrage bond is not exempt from tax unless the bond issuer rebates to the United States the arbitrage profits that are earned from investing the bond proceeds in higher-yielding investments. Proceeds that are to be used to finance construction expenditures are excepted from the filing requirements if the issuer elects to pay a penalty equal to 1½ percent of the difference between the unexpended proceeds and the required expenditure amount. This election must be made before the bonds are issued.

The exception applies when bond issuers anticipate completing construction within two years, and intend either to spend or to designate a specific portion of the proceeds for that purpose. Issuers must also spend 10 percent of an issue within six months of issuance, 45 percent by the end of the first year, 75 percent within 18 months, 95 percent within two years, and 100 percent within three years. An additional penalty of 3 percent must be paid to terminate the election.

Bond/Debt Financing Costs

APB Opinion No. 21 (Interest on Receivables and Payables), paragraph 16, notes that the costs related to the issuance of debt should be reported in the balance sheet as deferred charges. Discounts or premiums resulting from the issuance of debt are not assets or liabilities that are separable from the underlying instruments, but rather result "from the determination of present value." Accordingly, the amounts of these discounts or premiums are reported in the balance sheet as a deduction from or an addition to the face amount.

Defeasance

In certain circumstances, an organization will extinguish debt before its due date. Any organization may refinance debt or pay it off early to reduce interest costs. Prior to June 1996, FAS-76 (Extinguishment of Debt) governed the accounting for extinguishment of debt. For extinguishments of debt occurring after December 31, 1996, FAS-125 (Accounting for Transfers and Servicing of Financial Assets and Extinguishments of Liabilities) provides new guidance. FAS-76 notes that the debt can be removed from the balance sheet in the following instances:

- The debtor pays the creditor and is relieved of all its related obligations, including the debtor's reacquisition of its outstanding debt securities, regardless of whether the securities are canceled or held as so-called treasury bonds.
- The debtor is legally released from being the primary obligor under the debt—judicially or by the creditor—and it is probable that the debtor will not be required to make future payments with respect to that debt under any guarantees.
- The debtor places cash or other assets in an irrevocable trust to be used only for the satisfaction of scheduled payments of both interest and principal of a specific obligation, and the possibility that the debtor will be required to make future payments with respect to that debt is remote. In this situation, called in-substance defeasance, debt is extinguished without the debtor being legally released from being the primary obligor under the debt obligation.

The FASB established high standards for qualifying for in-substance defeasances of debt. For example, if the assets to be deposited into the irrevocable trust are not cash, they must bear certain characteristics. Also, the debt to be extinguished must be of a certain type. The assets in the trust must be monetary assets that are "essentially risk-free as to the amount, timing, and collection of interest and principal." Essentially risk-free monetary assets are limited to direct obligations of the U.S. government.

Direct obligations of the U.S. government are securities that are backed by U.S. government obligations as collateral under an arrangement by which the interest and principal payments on the collateral generally flow immediately through to the holder of the security.

The debt to be considered extinguished by an in-substance defeasance must be debt with fixed maturities and fixed payment schedules. The debt may not have variable terms that do not permit advance determination of debt service requirements (e.g., debt with a floating interest rate).

The difference between the amount paid for extinguishing the debt, including cash and the present value of securities used for the acquisition, and the net carrying amount of the debt should be recognized in the statement of activities of the period of extinguishment and should not be amortized to future periods. The net carrying amount of the debt consists of the amount due at maturity, adjusted for unamortized premium, discount, and cost of issuance.

FAS-125 is more succinct. The liability may be removed from the debtor's accounts "if and only if it has been extinguished." There are two circumstances in which a liability has been extinguished:

- The debtor pays the creditor and is relieved of its obligation for the liability.
- The debtor is legally released from being the primary obligor under the liability, either judicially or by the creditor.

Fund Accounting Considerations Modified to Reflect Net Asset Classifications

When reporting the funds segregated for plant renewal or replacement, or for debt servicing—interest and mortgage amortization payments—the not-for-profit organization is required to divide fund balances into appropriate net asset classifications. Accordingly, those funds designated by the organization's governing board will be classified as unrestricted. Resources segregated by agreement with the funders or trustees under terms of indentures also will be classified as part of unrestricted net assets, but the assets will be listed separately from other cash and investments, as well as funds that have been restricted by contributors, will be classified as temporarily or permanently restricted.

INTERFUND TRANSFERS/BORROWINGS

Many not-for-profit organizations use fund accounting for internal record keeping purposes. This method of accounting segregates assets, liabilities, and fund balances into separate self-balancing groups to record transactions related to specific activities, programs, donor restrictions, etc. Before the issuance of FAS-117, organizations that maintained their records using fund accounting generally issued financial statements that presented the self-balancing funds or groupings of funds with similar purposes.

Often these separate funds will reflect *interfund balances*, which can arise from transfers for operating purposes or to cover temporary shortfalls in assets held for a specific purpose (e.g., resulting from management's decision not to liquidate investments until maturity). Because the separate funds, or groups of funds, are self-balancing, equal amounts of assets and liabilities will be reflected and, accordingly, total net assets will not be increased or decreased as a result of these transactions.

Legal Requirements

In some situations, the not-for-profit organization may be required to maintain reserve funds for renewals, replacements, or debt service. Also, donors may establish endowments that have permanent or temporary restrictions on the use of principal. If these balances must be maintained, the not-for-profit organization may have to use other funds to provide resources for temporary use (e.g., payment of custodian or trustee fees). In these cases, an interfund transaction will be recorded.

Financial Presentation

Before the issuance of FAS-117, organizations that presented financial statements using fund accounting displayed the interfund balances within the separate fund or fund group balance sheets. With the adoption of FAS-117, not-for-profit organizations must change the presentation. According to FAS-117, receivables and payables between fund groups are not assets or liabilities of the organization. Accordingly, the balance sheet should not contain these classifications when displaying total assets or liabilities.

Financial statement preparers are not precluded from displaying interfund items in the balance sheet.

CHAPTER 7
ORGANIZATIONAL ISSUES

CONTENTS

CHAPTER 7
ORGANIZATIONAL ISSUES

CROSS-REFERENCES

2000 MILLER NOT-FOR-PROFIT REPORTING: Chapter 2, "Overview of Current Pronouncements"; Chapter 11, "Display of Certain GAAP Transactions"

2000 MILLER GAAP GUIDE: Chapter 4, "Business Combinations"; Chapter 8, "Consolidated Financial Statements"; Chapter 15, "Equity Method"; Chapter 43, "Segment Reporting"

2000 MILLER GAAP IMPLEMENTATION MANUAL: Chapter 6, "Business Combinations"; Chapter 11, "Consolidated Financial Statements"; Chapter 15, "Equity Method"; Chapter 37, "Segment Reporting"

2000 MILLER GOVERNMENTAL GAAP GUIDE: Chapter 14, "Assets"; Chapter 17, "Liabilities"; Chapter 27, "Proprietary Funds"

2000 MILLER GAAS GUIDE: Section 411

BUSINESS SEGMENTS
AND DISCONTINUED OPERATIONS

For financial statements of public business enterprises for periods beginning after December 15, 1997, the Financial Accounting Standards Board has issued FAS-131 (Disclosures about Segments of an Enterprise and Related Information). This Statement has the effect of superseding FAS-114 (Financial Reporting for Segments of a Business Enterprise). FAS-131 does not apply to nonpublic business enterprises or to not-for-profit organizations. Accordingly, it is not discussed in this volume.

Requirements for reporting segment information in accordance with generally accepted accounting principles prior to that date are presented in FAS-14 (Financial Reporting for Segments of a Business

Enterprise), as affected by several subsequent pronouncements, including, but not limited to, FAS-18 (Financial Reporting for Segments of a Business Enterprise—Interim Financial Statements), FAS-30 (Disclosure of Information About Major Customers), FAS-95 (Statement of Cash Flows), FAS-131 (Disclosure About Segments of an Enterprise and Related Information), and FASB Technical Bulletin No. 79-5 (Meaning of the Term "Customer" as It Applies to Health Care Facilities under FASB Statement No. 14).

The principles relating to accounting for and reporting discontinued operations are included in APB Opinion No. 30 (Reporting the Results of Operations—Reporting the Effects of Disposal of a Segment of a Business, and Extraordinary, Unusual, and Infrequently Occurring Events and Transactions), as amended by FAS-4 (Reporting Gains and Losses from Extinguishment of Debt) and FAS-109 (Accounting for Income Taxes).

Discontinued Operations

Generally accepted accounting principles for accounting and reporting of discontinued operations are summarized below:

> The results of discontinued operations and the gain or loss on disposal shall be reported in the income statement separately from continuing operations but not as an extraordinary item. If a loss is expected from the discontinuance of a business segment, the estimated loss shall be provided for as of the measurement date. If a gain is expected, it shall be recognized when realized.

Relation to Program Classifications

Segments of a not-for-profit organization are those services or programs that constitute the major purpose for the organization's existence. These services equate to the organization's major programs. Footnote 6 to FAS-117 (Financial Statements of Not-for-Profit Organizations) points out that readers of a not-for-profit organization's financial statements would benefit from having information about both program revenues and program expenses.

To provide information about service efforts, and to help users of financial statements understand and assess the results of a not-for-profit organization's efforts, FAS-117 requires a not-for-profit organization's statement of activities or notes to the financial statements (FAS-117, par. 26) to report expenses by their functional classification, i.e., major classes of program services and supporting activities. Continuing an earlier requirement, voluntary health and welfare organizations also must report information about expenses by their natural classification, e.g., salaries, rent, electricity, interest expense, depreciation, awards and grants to others, and professional fees, in a matrix format in a separate financial statement.

A not-for-profit organization may choose to discontinue one of its major classes of programs. This occurrence would be accounted for in a fashion similar to the practices for-profit entities use to account for a discontinued business segment. A not-for-profit organization will recognize a loss when previously recognized assets are expected to provide reduced or no future benefits. Not-for-profit organizations should consider using FAS-121 (Accounting for the Impairment of Long-Lived Assets and for Long-Lived Assets to Be Disposed Of) to determine the appropriateness of valuation when "events or changes in circumstances indicate that the carrying amount of the assets may not be recoverable" (NPO, par. 9.09). Formats A, B, and C of FAS-117, Appendix C, illustrate possible displays of losses in a statement of activities. Losses are included as decreases in unrestricted net assets when the related asset was classified as unrestricted. Losses on restricted net assets (e.g., an actuarial loss on annuity obligations) are reflected as decreases in the appropriate classification (e.g., temporarily restricted net assets).

Relation to Multi-Entity Not-for-Profit

In certain circumstances, not-for-profit organizations may control, directly or indirectly, the activities or finances of another entity. The accounting in these circumstances is guided by SOP 94-3 (Reporting of Related Entities by Not-for-Profit Organizations). The disclosures required by the SOP include information about the separate organizations in consolidated or combined financial statements, or financial information about related entities included on the equity basis—for-profit investees that are less than 50-percent–owned by the reporting organization, or have other significant relationships with the reporting organization. The disclosures required by SOP 94-3 are:

- Identification of the other not-for-profit organization and the nature of its relationship with the reporting organization that results in control
- Summarized financial data of the other organization that includes information about:
  - Total assets, liabilities, net assets, revenues, and expenses
  - Resources that are held for the benefit of the reporting organization or the resources under its control
  - The disclosures required by FAS-57 (Related Party Disclosures)

A more detailed explanation of SOP 94-3 is included in Chapter 2, "Overview of Current Pronouncements."

CONSOLIDATIONS AND COMBINATIONS

In consolidated financial statements, related organizations are presented as a single entity. Consolidation often occurs because the reporting entity, or parent, owns more than 50 percent of the other entities. Combined financial statements present a group of entities in a single set of financial statements because there is an overriding economic interest in the combined assets, liabilities, and results of operations of the group. This could occur when one individual owns all of the businesses and uses the entities as security for a loan. It would not be considered a consolidation because there is no "parent" in the group.

FASB is currently studying the "reporting entity" and what accounting is appropriate for reporting entities. To date, generally accepted accounting principles for entities other than not-for-profit organizations are substantially contained in FAS-94 (Consolidation of All Majority-Owned Subsidiaries) and ARB-51 (Consolidated Financial Statements). Principles of accounting for investments in related entities of not-for-profit organizations are contained in SOP 94-3.

The AICPA will reconsider its conclusions regarding reporting investments in related entities when FASB completes its project.

FASB Statement No. 94

Consolidated financial statements present results of operations and the financial position of a parent company and its subsidiaries as if they were a single entity. As noted in ARB-51, "There is a presumption that consolidated financial statements are more meaningful than separate statements and that they are usually necessary for a fair presentation when one of the companies in the group directly or indirectly has a controlling financial interest in the other companies."

Normally, ownership of a majority voting interest is evidence of a controlling financial interest. Exceptions to this general rule follow:

- Control is likely to be temporary.
- Control does not rest with the majority owner.

According to FAS-94, other majority-owned subsidiaries should be consolidated with the majority owner's financial statements.

There may be circumstances in which the parent–subsidiary relationship does not exist, but a set of combined financial statements of commonly controlled entities would be more meaningful than separate statements of the components of the controlled group. ARB-51 cites the example of an individual owning a controlling interest in several entities that are related in their operations. Another example of a situation in which to provide combined financial statements as the most meaningful presentation may be entities under common management.

Statement of Position No. 94-3

SOP 94-3 is discussed in detail in Chapter 2, "Overview of Current Pronouncements." However, one situation included in SOP 94-3 is especially applicable to consolidations/combinations. This situation is analyzed below.

Investments in common stock of for-profit entities wherein the not-for-profit organization has a 50 percent or less voting interest   Investments in common stock of for-profit entities wherein the not-for-profit organization has a 50 percent or less voting interest should be reported in accordance with the principles contained in APB Opinion No. 18 (The Equity Method of Accounting for Investments in Common Stock). SOP 94-3 notes that "organizations that choose to report investment portfolios at market value in conformity with the AICPA Audit Guides (which permit an electing organization to report investment portfolios at market) may do so instead of applying the equity method to investments covered." Furthermore, APB Opinion No. 18 states:

> Investors shall account for investments in common stock of corporate joint ventures by the equity method.

> The equity method of accounting for an investment in common stock should also be followed by an investor whose investment in voting stock gives it the ability to exercise significant influence over operating and financial policies of an investee even though the investor holds 50 percent or less of the voting stock.

APB Opinion No. 18 notes that the ability to exercise significant influence may be indicated in several ways:

> Determining the ability of an investor to exercise such influence is not always clear and applying judgment is necessary to assess the status of each investment. In order to achieve a reasonable degree of uniformity in application, an investment (direct or indirect) of 20 percent or more of the voting stock of an investee should lead to a presumption that in the

absence of evidence to the contrary an investor has the ability to exercise significant influence over an investee. Conversely, an investment of less than 20 percent of the voting stock of an investee should lead to a presumption that an investor does not have the ability to exercise significant influence unless such ability can be demonstrated.

Use of the equity method of accounting by a reporting organization requires the following disclosures:

- The name of each investee and percentage of ownership of common stock

- The accounting policies of the investor with respect to investments in common stock

- The difference, if any, between the amount at which an investment is carried and the amount of the underlying equity in net assets and the accounting treatment of the difference

- The aggregate value of the identified investment based on the quoted market price, if available

- Summarized information on assets, liabilities, and results of operations of the investees, if the investments are, in the aggregate, material in relation to the financial position or results of operations of the reporting organization

- Material effects of possible conversions of convertible securities, exercises of outstanding options or warrants, or contingent issuances of an investee

Disclosures The disclosures required by FAS-57 (Related Party Disclosures) that relate to these organizations are:

- The nature of the relationship involved

- For each of the periods for which statements of activities are presented, a description of the transactions, including those for which there are no amounts involved, and such other information necessary for a user to understand the effects of the transactions on the financial statements

- For each of the periods for which statements of activities are presented, the dollar amounts of transactions and the effects of any change in the method of establishing the terms among the related parties from that used previously

- As of the date of each balance sheet presented, amounts due from or to related parties and, if not otherwise apparent, the terms and manner of settlement

The existence of control or an economic interest, but not both, will preclude consolidation. In these circumstances, the disclosures required by FAS-57 should be made in the notes to the financial statements. There is an exception to this rule—not-for-profit organizations that historically have presented consolidated financial statements in accordance with the terms of SOP 78-10 (Accounting Principles and Reporting Practices for Certain Nonprofit Organizations) may continue to do so.

Finally, consolidated financial statements should disclose any restrictions made by entities other than the reporting organization on distributions from the other not-for-profit organization to the reporting organization, and any resulting unavailability of the net assets of the other organization for use by the reporting not-for-profit.

Proposed Statement

> **OBSERVATION:** FASB continues to review the issues surrounding consolidations and control. In February 1999 FASB issued an Exposure Draft of a Statement of Financial Accounting Standards titled "Consolidated Financial Statements: Purpose and Policy." If adopted as drafted, this Statement would require a parent to consolidate all subsidiaries (entities that the parent controls) unless, as stated in FAS-94, control is temporary at the time that the entity becomes a subsidiary. The Exposure Draft includes a definition of *control.* Control in this situation is the ability of one entity to direct the policies and management over the activities of another entity. This ability increases the benefits and limits the losses to the parent from the subsidiary's activities. FASB refers to this as "nonshared decision-making ability." FASB expects to issue a final Statement relating to this matter in the fourth quarter of 1999.

Late in 1995, the FASB issued an Exposure Draft of a proposed Statement titled "Consolidated Financial Statements: Policy and Procedures." The proposed Statement, which will apply to not-for-profit organizations, establishes "when entities should be consolidated and how financial statements should be prepared."

In the Exposure Draft, FASB notes that it is especially interested in comments relating to the proposed definition of *control* and whether it is "operational." Accordingly, we may see changes before the final Statement is issued. The Exposure Draft defines *control* as the power of one organization to use or direct the use of the assets of another entity. This can be achieved through control of the other entity's policies and budgets. The controlling organization would be able to control financing activities, investing activities, and operations of the other entity. The controlling organization may be able to make decisions affecting personnel and compensation. FASB notes that control is exclusionary: If one organization controls another, no other entity is able to exercise that control.

Although it includes illustrations of the application of the proposed Statement, FASB further asked respondents to the Exposure Draft for suggestions that would improve guidance about control relationships.

A parent entity would consolidate all entities that it controls. The controlled entities, subsidiaries, would be included in the consolidated financial statements unless control is temporary at the time the entity becomes a subsidiary. The Exposure Draft includes descriptions of circumstances indicating temporary control, which is discussed in the later section titled "Temporary Control." The entity will continue to be included in the consolidated financial statements of its parent until the parent's control ceases to exist.

Consolidated financial statements are designed to report, for the benefit of shareholders, creditors, and other resource providers, the financial position, results of operations, and cash flows of the reporting entity. The reporting entity includes the parent and its subsidiaries, and the result of the process provides information as if "all of the resources of the affiliates were held and all their activities were conducted by a single entity."

The Exposure Draft incorporates certain long-standing presumptions:

- Consolidated financial statements are more meaningful than the separate financial statements of affiliated entities.
- Consolidated financial statements are usually necessary for a fair presentation if one of the entities controls the resources and activities of the others.
- Omission of information about an entity's assets, liabilities, revenues, expenses, gains, and losses impairs the relevance of the financial statements.
- The notes to the financial statements should contain certain disaggregated information for a full understanding of the transactions and amounts reported in the consolidated financial statements.

The Exposure Draft recognizes that power to control need not be unrestricted. Laws, regulations, and contractual agreements impose limits on the controlling entity's use of the assets of a subsidiary. For not-for-profit organizations, the Exposure Draft recognizes that donor restrictions can, to an extent, control the not-for-profit organization's decision-making powers. However, a controlling organization should be able to remove restrictions and direct the use of the individual assets of a controlled entity by using the assets to further the controlling entity's mission.

Legal versus effective control   Paragraph 13 of the Exposure Draft differentiates between *legal control* of an entity and *effective control*. *Legal control* is attained by holding sufficient rights to unconditionally elect or appoint a majority of an entity's governing board; by provisions of a partnership agreement; or by other contractual arrangement. Legal control is exemplified by a majority ownership of shares in a corporation that issues only a single class of stock.

Effective control is attained by other than unconditional legal control, e.g., owning a large minority voting interest coupled with other favorable circumstances.

When legal control does not exist, the existence of effective control must be assessed from relevant facts and circumstances. The Exposure Draft notes that effective control is presumed to exist if (1) there is no evidence to the contrary and (2) an organization has one or more of the following:

a. Ownership of a large minority voting interest without another party or organized group of parties having a significant interest.

b. The ability to control the process of nominating candidates for another entity's governing board and to cast a majority of the votes cast in an election of board members.

c. The unilateral ability to obtain a majority voting interest through ownership of securities or other rights that may be converted into a majority voting interest at the option of the holder without assuming risks in excess of the expected benefits from the conversion.

d. A relationship with another entity established by the organization that has no voting stock or member voting rights and whose charter, bylaws, or trust instrument (1) cannot be changed by entities other than its creator (sponsor) and (2) that limits the second entity, including the powers of its board, to activities that the creating organization can schedule (or can initiate) to provide substantially all future net cash inflows or other future economic benefits to the creating organization.

e. The unilateral ability to dissolve the other entity and assume control of its assets, subject to claims against those assets, without assuming economic costs in excess of the expected benefits from that dissolution.

f. A sole general partnership interest in a limited partnership.

Temporary control   FAS-94, which currently applies to consolidations, discusses the concept of *temporary control*. If adopted, the new Statement will supersede FAS-94, so the descriptions of circumstances that would indicate temporary control of an entity may become determining factors in the future. Both FAS-94 and the Exposure Draft would preclude inclusion of an entity in consolidated financial statements if control is temporary.

Paragraph 16 of the Exposure Draft notes that "a subsidiary shall not be consolidated if control is temporary at the date it becomes a subsidiary." Indications of temporary control include:

- An obligation of the parent to relinquish control within one year of the date of acquisition.

- A management decision, as of the date of acquisition, to dispose of the newly acquired subsidiary. A plan for such action exists, and the expectation of disposition within one year is reasonable.

- Circumstances existing at the date of acquisition, outside the control of management, that make it likely that more time will be required to complete the ultimate disposition. To illustrate this point, the Exposure Draft uses the example of a proposed sale of a newly acquired subsidiary that is subject to regulatory approval.

Basic consolidation procedures Not-for-profit organizations rarely prepare consolidated financial statements. If the existing Exposure Draft is adopted as a final Statement, guidance on the consolidation procedure will be established for not-for-profit organizations, and some of the basic tenets of preparing consolidated financial statements will apply:

Intercompany Transactions and Balances

- All intercompany transactions and balances and profits or losses on transactions between affiliates included in the consolidated group shall be eliminated.

- When a noncontrolling interest exists, the effects on equity of eliminating intercompany profits and losses that remain within the consolidated group will be "allocated between the controlling interest and the noncontrolling interest on the basis of their proportionate interests in the selling affiliate."

- Intercompany investments in equity securities of affiliates will be eliminated.

- Shares of the parent organization held by a subsidiary will not be reported as outstanding stock in the consolidated financial statements.

- Intercompany investments in debt securities originally issued to third parties will be reported, at the end of the reporting period, as constructively retired.

- Related gains or losses will be attributed to the issuing affiliate and allocated between the controlling and noncontrolling (if any) interests based on their proportionate interest in the issuing affiliate.

Reporting Noncontrolling Interest in Subsidiaries

- The aggregate amount of the noncontrolling interest in subsidiaries will be reported in consolidated financial statements as a separate component of equity.

  > **Note:** The prevailing current practice in the United States is to report the noncontrolling interest in a subsidiary (minority interest) in a caption between liabilities and equity and, accordingly, the Exposure Draft's requirement represents a significant departure.

- Footnote 5 of the Exposure Draft instructs that not-for-profit organizations are controlled, normally, by entities with 100 percent interest. If a noncontrolling interest does exist, the underlying amounts related to each of the individual components of that entity's unrestricted net assets, temporarily restricted net assets, and permanently restricted net assets should not be separately reported on the face of a consolidated statement of financial position.

- The net income or loss of a subsidiary will be allocated to the noncontrolling interest proportionately with the noncontrolling interest in the subsidiary's net income or loss.

- Losses in excess of the noncontrolling interest's basis should be allocated to the controlling interest.

- Profits occurring after the incurrence of excess losses will first be allocated to the controlling interest to the extent of such excess losses in the preceding bulleted item.

- Net income allocated to the noncontrolling interest will be deducted from consolidated net income to compute the controlling interest's share.

- The consolidated statement of activities of a not-for-profit organization will, on its face, report net income allocable to both the controlling and noncontrolling interests.

Acquisition of a subsidiary　In the Exposure Draft, FASB proposes a fundamental change in the manner of reporting the assets and liabilities of a subsidiary acquired in a business combination accounted for as a purchase under APB Opinion No. 16 (Business Combinations).

Current Practice	Exposure Draft
Only the portion of the assets and liabilities acquired that is attributable to the parent is revalued.	All of the assets and liabilities of the acquired subsidiary are revalued.
The portion attributable to the noncontrolling interest is reported at historic value.	The portion attributable to the noncontrolling interest is reported at fair value.

Although more than half of the respondents to a Discussion Memorandum that preceded the Exposure Draft believed that current practice should be retained, FASB concluded that the purchase price of the transaction should be assigned to each of the identifiable assets acquired and liabilities assumed in relation to the full amount of their fair values at the date the parent–subsidiary relationship is established. Goodwill is the excess of the cost of the acquisition over the parent's share of the net amount assigned to those identifiable assets and liabilities.

This "economic unit" approach was supported by one-third of the respondents to the Discussion Memorandum. FASB believes that consolidated financial statements should "report on an entity that includes a parent and its subsidiaries," thereby rejecting the parent company view of consolidated statements that is the current practice. It explains in paragraph 115 of the Exposure Draft:

> Consolidated financial statements should include the identifiable assets and liabilities that a parent controls and for which it is accountable and those assets and liabilities should be measured by an attribute that possesses an appropriate balance of relevance and reliability.

This result is achieved by issuing financial statements that include the cost of an acquired subsidiary with identifiable assets and liabilities reported at fair value on the date of acquisition and the parent's share of goodwill purchased on the same date.

Changes in a parent's ownership interest in a subsidiary   A parent company may change its interest in a subsidiary. The resulting accounting changes are discussed in the following three paragraphs.

No loss of control   Changes in a parent's proportionate interest in a subsidiary that do not result in a loss of control are accounted for as equity transactions of the consolidated entity and will not result in gain or loss recognition. The amount of change in proportionate interest will be reported as an increase or decrease in additional paid-in capital and a corresponding change in the noncontrolling interest.

Disposition of entire interest   If a parent disposes of its entire interest in a subsidiary, gain or loss will be recognized in the change in net assets of a not-for-profit organization. The amount to be recognized will be the difference between the proceeds of sale (or fair value of contribution) and the carrying value of the subsidiary's assets in the consolidated financial statements, less its liabilities and noncontrolling equity, if any. Remaining goodwill associated with the subsidiary will be included in the subsidiary's assets.

Loss of control   If a parent disposes of a portion of its interest in a subsidiary and, thereby, no longer maintains control, gain or loss is recognized in the change in net assets of a not-for-profit organization. The amount to be recognized will be the difference between the proceeds of sale (or fair value of contribution) and the carrying value of the subsidiary's assets in the consolidated financial statements, less its liabilities and noncontrolling equity, if any, and less the remaining carrying value of the subsidiary's net assets. The remaining equity ownership is measured initially at the proportionate part of the interest in the carrying amount of the net assets of the subsidiary.

Accounting policies   The Exposure Draft mandates that parents and subsidiaries generally have the same accounting policies for similar transactions or events and the same fiscal periods, for purposes of preparing consolidated financial statements. Conformity is not required in certain circumstances. Generally accepted accounting principles, for example, permit a single entity to value some inventories using the first-in, first-out method and other inventories using the last-in, first-out method. If the parent and subsidiary have different inventories, they will be permitted to use different valuation methods.

When a change must be made in a subsidiary's accounting methods for the purpose of inclusion in consolidated financial statements, the effect of the change is allocated proportionately between the controlling and noncontrolling interests.

Accounting periods   The subsidiary's financial information should be for the same period as the parent's fiscal year. If it is not practicable to prepare consolidated financial statements using a single fiscal period, the notes to the financial statements should disclose that fact, why conformity is not practicable, and the period covered by the subsidiary's financial statements.

Combined financial statements   The Exposure Draft does not change the guidance in ARB-51, as it relates to combined financial statements. It acknowledges that such combined financial statements are useful in some circumstances (e.g., where one individual owns a controlling interest in several corporations that are related in their operations).

Disaggregated information about formerly unconsolidated major-ity-owned subsidiaries   The Exposure Draft does not change the guidance in FAS-94 to disclose certain information—summarized in-formation about the assets, liabilities, and results of operations—about unconsolidated majority-owned subsidiaries that were accounted for under APB Opinion No. 18 before the adoption of FAS-94.

BUSINESS COMBINATIONS

> **OBSERVATION:** FASB is currently examining the topic of busi-ness combinations and may determine that there is no need to have two methods—both the purchase accounting method and the pooling of interests method.

The accounting for a transaction in which "a corporation and one or more incorporated or unincorporated businesses are brought to-gether into one accounting entity" is governed by APB Opinion No. 16. At the conclusion of the transaction, the single entity carries on the activities of the previously separate, independent entities. These transactions are known as business combinations.

Two recognized methods are used to record business combina-tions: the *pooling-of-interests method* and the *purchase method*. As a result of the issuance of APB Opinion No. 16 in 1970, accountants recognize that a business combination can be treated under only one of the methods and that the methods are not interchangeable. Before the issuance of the Opinion, business combinations were recorded as "pooling," "purchase," or "part-pooling, part-purchase," depending on the needs of the parties and not necessarily based on the structure of the transaction itself.

Many FASB Statements have amended the original guidance of APB Opinion No. 16, and many AICPA and FASB Interpretations and a FASB Technical Bulletin have been issued to help accountants and others who deal with structuring business combinations under-stand the requirements of the Opinion. As new types of business combinations are structured by investment bankers and others, and as new transactions introduce nuances into the area of business combinations, the FASB Emerging Issues Task Force (EITF) will issue additional guidance.

The EITF, formed in 1984, is composed of members from public accounting and industry, FASB's director of research and technical activities, and observers from the SEC and the Accounting Stan-dards Executive Committee (AcSEC). SAS-69 (The Meaning of "Present Fairly in Conformity with Generally Accepted Accounting Principles" in the Independent Auditor's Report) places consensus positions of the EITF in the third-highest rank in the hierarchy of generally accepted accounting principles. (See the *2000 Miller Imple-mentation Manual* for comprehensive EITF coverage.)

Current authoritative accounting literature for not-for-profit organizations does not address business combinations in great detail. These transactions were not discussed in SOP 78-10, *Audits of Certain Nonprofit Organizations, Audits of Voluntary Health and Welfare Organizations,* or *Audits of Colleges and Universities.* The new AICPA Guides *Not-for-Profit Organizations* and *Health Care Organizations* include information about these transactions. Business combination transactions are covered by APB Opinion No. 16. Thus, not-for-profit organizations should follow the same principles for accounting for business combinations as for-profit entities.

Both of the new Guides discuss the pooling of interests method of accounting for a business combination. These transactions generally include an exchange of common stock of the combining organizations. Not-for-profit organizations generally do not issue common stock and, accordingly, would not meet the strict criteria imposed by APB-16 for this accounting treatment. The AICPA Accounting Standards Executive Committee (AcSEC) has determined that:

> circumstances exist under which reporting on the combination of two or more not-for-profit organizations (or that of a not-for-profit organization with a formerly for-profit entity) by the pooling of interests method better reflects the substance of the transaction than reporting by the purchase method. Therefore, not-for-profit organizations are, under certain circumstances, permitted to report by the pooling of interests method, even though they generally do not issue common stock. Such circumstances include the combination of two or more entities to form a new entity without the exchange of compensation.

Why should not-for-profit organizations be concerned with business combinations? Historically, few not-for-profit activities would result in such a transaction. However, as funding sources contract, and as government begins to review the efficiency and overhead of organizations with which it does business, more combinations of organizations will arise. The new guide *Health Care Organizations* notes (par. 11.02):

> Networks among health care organizations, both vertical and horizontal, are being formed continually and new organizational structures are being developed. The dynamics of change… and their impact on evolving organizational structures must be considered in defining the reporting entity.

Pooling of Interests Method

The pooling of interests method of accounting for business combinations is intended to present as a single interest two or more common stockholder interests that were previously independent, and the combined rights and risks represented by those interests. Certain conditions must be met for a business combination to be recognized as a pooling of interests transaction. Failure to meet these conditions results in the transaction being recognized in accordance with the purchase method. Two of the conditions refer to the essential attributes of the combining companies (APB-16, par. 45):

1. Each of the combining companies is autonomous and has not been a subsidiary or division of another corporation within two years before the plan of combination is initiated.

2. Each of the combining companies is independent of the other combining companies. In this situation, at the date of initiation of the plan of combination and consummation, the combining companies hold as intercorporate investments no more than 10 percent of the outstanding voting common stock of any combining company.

Seven of the conditions relate to the exchange of stock to effect the combination. Separate stockholder interests lose their identities and all share mutually in the combined risks and rights of the combined organization:

1. The combination is effected in a single transaction or is completed in accordance with a specific plan within one year after the plan is initiated. If litigation or action of a governmental authority causes a delay beyond one year, this condition is still met.

2. A corporation offers and issues only common stock with rights identical to those of the majority of its outstanding voting common stock in exchange for substantially all of the voting common stock interest of another company at the date the plan of combination is consummated. Cash may be offered for fractional shares or for shares held by dissenting shareholders, but to meet the "substantially all" condition, 90 percent or more of the stock must be included in the exchange.

3. None of the combining companies changes the equity interest of the voting common stock in contemplation of effecting the combination either within two years before the plan of combination is initiated or between the date the combination is initiated and the date it is consummated.

4. Each of the combining companies reacquires shares of voting common stock only for purposes other than business combinations, and no company reacquires more than a normal number of shares between the date the plan of combination is initiated and the date it is consummated. These other purposes could

include acquiring shares for reissuance as part of a stock option or compensation plan or other recurring distributions.

5. The ratio of the interest of an individual common stockholder to those of other common stockholders in a combining company remains the same as a result of the exchange of stock to effect the combination.

6. The voting rights to which the common stock ownership interests in the resulting combined corporation are entitled are exercisable by the stockholders.

7. The combination is resolved at the date the plan is consummated, and no provisions of the plan relating to the issue of securities or other consideration are pending. Accordingly, the combined entity does not agree to contingent issuance of additional shares or other consideration at a later date to the former stockholders of a combining corporation.

Three of the conditions relate to activities after a combination is consummated:

1. The combined corporation does not agree to retire or reacquire all or part of the common stock issued in the transaction.

2. There are no transactions or arrangements for the benefit of former stockholders of a combining company (e.g., loan guarantee secured by stock issued in the combination).

3. There is no plan by the combined corporation to dispose of a significant part of the assets of the combining companies within two years after the combination—other than those in the ordinary course of business and to eliminate excess capacity or duplicate facilities.

Purchase Method

Business combinations accounted for by the purchase method use the following basic principles:

1. Assets acquired by exchanging cash or other assets is recorded at cost—the amount of cash disbursed or fair value of the other assets.

2. Assets acquired by incurring liabilities is recorded at cost—the present value of the amounts to be paid in the future.

3. Assets acquired by issuing shares of stock are recorded at the fair value of the assets, measured either by the fair value of the

consideration given or by the fair value of the property acquired, whichever is the more clearly evident.

Differences between the costs assigned to the assets acquired, both tangible and identifiable intangible, less liabilities assumed, are accounted for as an intangible asset.

Alternative Presentations: Transfer of Assets or Gift

How the business combination transaction is structured will determine the accounting. Often, however, not-for-profit transactions don't include an exchange of stock or other consideration because there are no stockholders to receive the consideration.

The AICPA recognized that there often will be combinations of entities under common control. Interpretation No. 27 of APB Opinion No. 16 describes different situations that would be identified as entities under common control. There may be a single "owner" or a "sole-member" that has controlling interest in one or more other entities and there may be some outside interests as well.

Considerable judgment usually will be required to determine the substance of a combination involving one (or more) of several companies under common control. For example, it may be necessary to look beyond the form of the legal organizations to determine substance when an unincorporated business or a closely held corporation, owned by one or a few individuals who also control other entities, is involved since the dividing lines may not be as sharp as they would be in publicly held corporations with wide ownership interests.

In Interpretation No. 39 of APB Opinion No. 16, the AICPA notes that transfers and exchanges that do not involve outsiders are excluded from the considerations of the Opinion. It clarifies, however, that assets and liabilities transferred among organizations that are under common control (e.g., a parent and subsidiary) "would be accounted for at historical cost in a manner similar to that in pooling-of-interests accounting."

When consideration is given in the combination (e.g., liabilities assumed or monetary consideration paid), the transaction bears a resemblance to a purchase transaction and would be accounted for accordingly. The acquiring entity will have a basis in the acquired assets that will likely be different than that recorded by the combining organization.

PART III
EXTERNAL FINANCIAL REPORTING

CHAPTER 8
OVERVIEW OF
EXTERNAL FINANCIAL REPORTING

CONTENTS

CHAPTER 8
OVERVIEW OF
EXTERNAL FINANCIAL REPORTING

CROSS-REFERENCES

2000 MILLER NOT-FOR-PROFIT REPORTING: Chapter 8, "Overview of External Financial Reporting"

2000 MILLER GAAP GUIDE: Chapter 52, "Not-for-Profit Organizations"

2000 MILLER GOVERNMENTAL GAAP GUIDE: Chapter 34, "Certain Nonprofit Organizations"

NET ASSET CLASS MODEL

Before the issuance of FAS-117, most not-for-profit organizations presented their financial statements according to the fund accounting model. For accounting purposes, entities using fund accounting classify their resources into funds for specific activities or objectives. This accounting method allows not-for-profit organizations to observe limitations on resources used for particular purposes.

When preparing their financial statements, not-for-profit organizations using the fund accounting model would sort their many funds (e.g., a college would use funds related to fixed assets, loan funds, debt, funds restricted by the board of trustees, operating funds, and endowment funds, etc.) into groups having similar characteristics. This presentation provided a high level of detail about the fund groupings, but it resulted in significant differences between for-profit and not-for-profit financial statements. In fact, the financial statements for one type of not-for-profit organization were often completely different than the financial statements for a second type of not-for-profit organization.

FAS-117 was issued in 1993 in an effort to make not-for-profit financial statements reflect the activities, financial position, and cash flows as a whole, resulting in a financial presentation that more closely resembles the financial statements of for-profit entities. To do this, FAS-117 establishes the net asset class accounting model, in which revenues serve to increase unrestricted net assets, temporarily restricted net assets, or permanently restricted net assets, regardless of what specific activities or objectives the resources would benefit.

FAS-117 is effective for financial statements issued for fiscal years beginning after December 15, 1994. For organizations with less than $5 million in total assets and less than $1 million in annual expenses, FAS-117 is effective for fiscal years beginning after December 15, 1995. Therefore, most not-for-profit organizations should now be using the net asset model to prepare their financial statements, with one exception. Not-for-profit organizations associated with governmental entities and that fall under GASB pronouncements are prohibited from implementing FAS-117. Government not-for-profit organizations will continue to use the fund accounting model.

> **OBSERVATION:** A sample set of financial statements in accordance with FAS-117 is presented in Appendix A. The sample uses a basic net asset approach.

> **OBSERVATION:** A sample set of financial statements in accordance with the fund accounting model is presented in Appendix B.

According to FAS-117, not-for-profit organizations should present financial information and disclosures in a format similar to that used by for-profit entities. The financial statements under FAS-117 will provide external users with more consistent and relevant information and with a better tool for assessing the organization, how it conducts its programs and services, and its ability to continue its programs based on its financial resources. In addition, the new presentation will include information on the organization's liquidity, how the organization earned and expended its cash flows, how the organization obtained financial resources, how the organization repaid borrowings, and the future repayment terms that remain.

> **OBSERVATION:** FAS-117 allows flexibility in the financial statement formats to be used by not-for-profit organizations. Because this Statement is just now being implemented, however, little documentation is currently available from which to derive accurate examples of all the possible formats. Accordingly, this edition of **Miller Not-for-Profit Reporting** will ad-

dress some common formats; see Appendix C. Subsequent editions will present additional examples of new formats as they are developed by the various industry groups. An AICPA Task Force currently is working on this project.

According to FAS-117, all not-for-profit organizations must present a complete set of financial statements, which includes:

- Statement of financial position
- Statement of activities
- Statement of cash flows
- Accompanying notes to the financial statements

The financial statements should cover the entire not-for-profit organization and not piecemeal segments or funds. This presentation is especially true of colleges, universities, and museums. Under FAS-117, the focus of the financial statements is no longer on the components of individual funds, but on the not-for-profit organization as a whole. Most organizations continue to use fund accounting for their internal accounting purposes. Financial statements that focus on the not-for-profit organization as a whole are believed to be more informative and useful for financial statement users.

STATEMENT OF FINANCIAL POSITION

The statement of financial position (or "balance sheet") presents the financial position of the organization at a moment in time, usually the end of the reporting period. It demonstrates the organization's financial resources and informs readers about the organization's ability to provide its program services or products. The statement of financial position also supplies information on an organization's liquidity, which helps financial statement users determine the organization's *financial flexibility*, defined by FASB as "the ability of an entity to take effective actions to alter amounts and the timing of cash flows so it can respond to unexpected needs and opportunities." The statement of financial position may show an entity's need for external financing.

The statement of financial position must report and focus on the organization as a whole and must show the organization's total assets, liabilities, and net assets. The statement of financial position must present the following six elements:

1. Total assets
2. Total liabilities

3. Unrestricted net assets
4. Temporarily restricted net assets
5. Permanently restricted net assets
6. Total net assets

Classification of Net Assets

All balance sheets must include, on the face of the statement, the following three classes of net assets:

1. Unrestricted
2. Temporarily restricted
3. Permanently restricted

These classifications are based on donor-imposed restrictions. A restriction imposed by the governing board of the organization or by management does not affect the classification.

Information about the types of restrictions on assets and the amounts restricted is useful to external readers and is required by FAS-117. This information may be disclosed in notes or presented on the face of the statement.

STATEMENT OF ACTIVITIES

The statement of activities is similar to the statement of support, revenue, and expenses and changes in fund balance described in the superseded AICPA Audit Guides. As stated in FAS-117, the purpose of the statement of activities is to provide relevant information about:

- The effects of transactions and other events and circumstances that change the amount and nature of net assets
- The relationships of those transactions, and the relationships among other events and circumstances
- How the organization's resources are used to provide various programs or services

A not-for-profit organization's statement of activities is similar to a for-profit enterprise's income statement and measures the performance of the organization during the reporting period. The statement of activities provides external users with a reporting period's performance and with information to further present expenditures for programs in relation to income and support.

Four required elements are presented on the statement of activities:

1. Change in net assets
2. Change in unrestricted net assets
3. Change in temporarily restricted net assets
4. Change in permanently restricted net assets

As with the statement of financial position, the statement of activities should focus on the entity as a whole.

Revenues and Support

Revenues and support must be reported in gross amounts. The major categories of revenues should be presented (e.g., contribution, program service income, etc.). Investment revenues may be reported at net amounts, provided the amount of expenses is disclosed in the notes or on the face of the statement. If the donor has placed restrictions on the net gains, then the net gains would be classified as temporarily or permanently restricted based on the donor's wishes. The only other allowable netting is with peripheral or incidental transactions.

Expenses

The reporting of expenses is extremely important to external users of financial statements because it provides information about the cost of services provided and how the organization used its support. Because of this importance, organizations should report expenses by functional classification as a part of the statement of activities or in the notes to the financial statements. Expenses, always classified as decreases in unrestricted net assets, should be reported in major classes of program services and supporting activities such as management and general or fund-raising. The presentation of expenses in natural classifications, such as salaries, rent, depreciation, telephone, or consultants, is encouraged but not required, except for voluntary health and welfare organizations, which are required to present this information in a matrix format in a separate financial statement.

STATEMENT OF CASH FLOWS

The statement of cash flows provides information about the sources and uses of cash during the reporting period. The statement of cash flows is useful to external readers because it provides information about how:

- Cash was received by the organization to support its operations.
- Cash was expended to provide its programs.
- Changes in cash reconcile to the cash in net assets.

The statement provides relevant information that supports the statement of financial position in terms of the organization's liquidity, financial flexibility, ability to meet obligations, and need for external financing. The statement reports the sources and uses of cash from:

- Operating activities
- Investing activities
- Financing activities

> **OBSERVATION:** For more information on the Statement of Cash Flows, please refer to Chapter 10, "Cash Flows."

The statement of cash flows must present the net cash provided or used in operating, investing, and financing activities and the change in cash and cash equivalents during the reporting period.

CHAPTER 9
NOTE DISCLOSURES

CONTENTS

CHAPTER 9
NOTE DISCLOSURES

Overview

FAS-116 (Accounting for Contributions Received and Contributions Made), FAS-117 (Financial Statements of Not-for-Profit Organizations), and FAS-124 (Accounting for Certain Investments Held by Not-for-Profit Organizations) set forth disclosures that should be included in a not-for-profit organization's complete set of general purpose financial statements. These disclosures are in addition to the requirements established elsewhere in generally accepted accounting principles and include the following:

- Revenue recognition
- Restricted net assets
- Service efforts
- Investments
- Functional expenses

SOP 98-2 (Accounting for Costs of Activities of Not-for-Profit Organizations and State and Local Governmental Entities That Include Fund-Raising) has added other items to be disclosed by not-for-profit organizations, including, for joint costs:

- Types of materials and activities involving joint costs
- Allocation methods
- Amounts allocated

Common disclosures required by generally accepted accounting principles, but not covered in this publication, include:

- Significant accounting policies
- Components of pension and other postretirement and postemployment benefits costs and the funded status of plans covered by FAS-87 (Employers' Accounting for Pensions), FAS-

106 (Employers' Accounting for Postretirement Benefits Other Than Pensions), FAS-112 (Employers' Accounting for Post-employment Benefits), and FAS-132 (Employers' Disclosures about Pensions and Other Postretirement Benefits)

- Lease disclosures required by FAS-13 (Accounting for Leases)

- Disclosure of certain financial instruments required by FAS-105 (Disclosure of Information About Financial Instruments with Off-Balance-Sheet Risk and Financial Instruments with Concentrations of Credit Risk) and FAS-107 (Disclosures About Fair Value of Financial Instruments), as amended

CROSS-REFERENCES

2000 MILLER GAAP FOR NOT-FOR-PROFIT ORGANIZATIONS: Chapter 2, "Overview of Current Pronouncements"; Chapter 3, "Revenues"; Chapter 5, "Assets"

2000 MILLER GAAP GUIDE: Chapter 28, "Investments in Debt and Equity Securities"; Chapter 42, "Revenue Recognition"

2000 MILLER GAAP IMPLEMENTATION MANUAL: Chapter 25, "Investments in Debt and Equity Securities"; Chapter 36, "Revenue Recognition"

2000 MILLER GOVERNMENTAL GAAP GUIDE: Chapter 9, "Revenues"; Chapter 14, "Assets"

2000 MILLER GAAS GUIDE: Section 431

REVENUE RECOGNITION

Contributions

Paragraph 14 of FAS-116 requires an organization to "distinguish between contributions received with permanent restrictions, those received with temporary restrictions, and those received without donor-imposed restrictions." Note 2f of the sample financial statements in Appendix A discloses the organization's accounting policies for receipts of contributions.

FAS-116 notes that "donor-restricted contributions whose restrictions are met in the same reporting period may be reported as unrestricted support provided that an organization reports consistently from period to period and discloses its accounting policy."

Long-Lived Assets

FAS-116 also states that an organization should disclose its accounting policy for gifts of long-lived assets received without donor restrictions on how long the donated asset must be used. The gift should be reported as restricted support if it is the organization's policy to imply a time restriction over the useful life of the donated assets. If the organization adopts such an accounting policy, it also must imply a time restriction on long-lived assets acquired with gifts of cash or other assets restricted for that purpose. If no policy is adopted and no donor restriction exists, gifts of long-lived assets should be reported as unrestricted support. In any case, FAS-116 states that the "organization shall disclose its accounting policy."

Donated Services

Not-for-profit organizations are often recipients of donated services; FAS-116 and the new Guide *Not-for-Profit Organizations* provide the basis for the required disclosures. The disclosures regarding donated services should include (NPO Guide, par. 5.63):

- The nature and extent of contributed services received by the organization
- A description of the programs or activities for which the services were used
- The amount of contributed services recognized during the period

Also, organizations are encouraged to report the fair value of contributed services received but not recognized in the financial statements.

Contributions Receivable

FAS-116 and the new Guide also provide information about disclosures that are required for the related receivables. The required disclosures allow the users of the statements to understand the liquidity of the contributions receivable. These disclosures include (NPO Guide, par. 5.63):

- Information about contributions pledged as collateral or otherwise limited as to use
- Information about the age of the unconditional promises to give, separating the total into amounts receivable in less than one year, amounts receivable in one to five years, and amounts receivable in more than five years
- Information about the related allowance for uncollectible promises receivable
- The amount of the unamortized discount related to promises to give that are expected to be collected over a period longer than one year
- The total amount of conditional promises to give and descriptions and amounts of each group of similar promises

RESTRICTED NET ASSETS

FAS-117 requires not-for-profit organizations to report information "about the nature and amounts of different types of permanent restrictions or temporary restrictions." The disclosures may be in the form of separate line items on the face of the balance sheet or in the notes to the financial statements. Notes 6 and 7 of the sample financial statements provided in Appendix A include the relevant information for temporarily restricted net assets and permanently restricted net assets (FAS-117, par. 14).

Organizations also disclose information about net assets released from restrictions either through the incurrence of expenses satisfying the restricted purpose or through the occurrence of events specified by donors. Note 8 to the sample financial statements in Appendix A provides an example of such disclosures.

SERVICE EFFORTS

The superseded AICPA Audit Guide titled *Audits of Voluntary Health and Welfare Organizations* required voluntary health and welfare organizations to report, in a separate financial statement, information about expenses by their functional classification—program services, management and general, and fund-raising—as well as by their natural classification—salaries, rent, interest, depreciation, etc. FAS-117 also contains this requirement and notes that the information should be in a matrix format.

For other organizations covered by FAS-117, FASB required financial statements to include information about service efforts, costs of services, and use of resources. The information may be on the face of a statement of activities or notes to financial statements. The information about expenses should be reported by their functional classification such as major classes of program services and supporting activities.

Not-for-profit organizations that are not voluntary health and welfare organizations are encouraged to provide information about expenses by their natural classification. Note 9 to the sample financial statements in Appendix A provides this information.

INVESTMENTS

FASB Statement No. 124

In December 1995, the FASB released FAS-124 (Accounting for Certain Investments Held by Not-for-Profit Organizations). FAS-124 affects the way in which not-for-profit organizations record their investments in equity securities with readily determinable fair values and investments in debt securities. The Statement was effective for annual financial statements issued for fiscal years beginning after December 15, 1995. Accordingly, many not-for-profit organizations implemented the provisions of FAS-124 in their fiscal years beginning July 1, 1996.

Investments not covered by FAS-124 are discussed in the new AICPA Guide.

Investments not covered by FAS-124 may generally be accounted for as follows:

Investment Type	Colleges and Universities	Voluntary Health and Welfare Organizations	Other Not-for-Profit Organizations
Purchased	Cost	Cost	Fair value or lower of cost or fair value
Contributed	Fair market or appraised value on date of gift	Fair market value at the date of gift	Fair value or lower of cost or fair value

Further guidance in the new AICPA Guide indicates that for:

- *Colleges and universities*—Other investments may also be reported at current market value or fair value, provided that the same attribute is used for all other investments.
- *Voluntary health and welfare organizations*—Other investments may be reported at market value, provided that the same attribute is used for all other investments and is disclosed.
- *Other not-for-profit organizations*—The same measurement attribute is to be used for all other investments.

The new Guide notes that the financial statements or the notes thereto should disclose the total return and the spending rate used for the current year's activities (NPO Guide, pars. 8.19–8.20).

FASB Statement No. 119

FAS-119 (Disclosure About Derivative Financial Instruments and Fair Value of Financial Instruments) requires certain disclosures about classes of investments in which not-for-profit organizations may place funds. Although guidance for preparing the related disclosures is covered elsewhere in the accounting literature (see, for example, the *Miller GAAP Guide*), the growing importance of these investments to organizations, and the relative newness of the accounting and disclosure requirements, makes this a useful topic for discussion.

FAS-119 requires organizations to disclose the amounts, nature, and terms of derivative financial instruments that are not subject to FAS-105, because they do not result in off-balance-sheet risk of accounting loss (NPO, par. 8.22).

In addition, FAS-119 requires the organization to distinguish between financial instruments held or issued for trading purposes and those held or issued for purposes other than trading. Also required are additional disclosures about those derivative instruments held for purposes other than trading and those accounted for as hedges of anticipated transactions.

FUNCTIONAL EXPENSES

The reporting of expenses is extremely important to external users of financial statements because it provides information about the cost of services provided and how the organization used its support. Because of this importance, organizations need to report expenses by functional classification as a part of the statement of activities or in the notes to the financial statements. Expenses, always classified as decreases in unrestricted net assets, should be reported in major classes of program services and supporting activities such as management and general or fund-raising. The presentation of expenses in natural classifications, such as salaries, rent, depreciation, telephone, or consultants, is encouraged but not required, except for voluntary health and welfare organizations, which are required to present this information in a matrix format in a separate financial statement.

An example of this matrix is shown in Table 9-1.

Table 9-1: ABC Organization Schedule of Expenses
Year Ended December 31, 199X

	Total	Education Program	Arts Program	Management and General	Fund Raising
Rent	$ 45,000	$ 11,000	$ 10,000	$ 19,000	$ 5,000
Salaries	17,257	7,253	6,119	2,885	1,000
Benefits	4,616	1,836	1,569	967	244
Professional	13,258	5,850	4,750	1,790	868
Printing	7,867	4,298	1,622	821	1,126
Insurance	6,300	2,700	2,400	1,000	200
Depreciation	5,200	2,200	2,100	750	150
Total	$ 99,498	$ 35,137	$ 28,560	$ 27,213	$ 8,588

The Guide *Not-for-Profit Organizations* notes that for all organizations (NPO, par. 13.27):

> If the components of total program expenses are not evident from the details provided on the face of the statement of activities . . . the notes to the financial statements should provide information about why total program expenses disclosed in the notes does not articulate with the statement of activities. The financial statements should also provide a description of the nature of the organization's activities, including a description of each of its major classes of programs, either on the statement of activities . . . or in the notes to the financial statements.

The following example was taken from the Guide.

Assume that a one-program organization has the following revenues and expenses:

Revenues:

Contributions	$ 8,460
Bookstore sales	2,150
Investment revenue	1,110
	$11,720

Expenses:

Salaries	$ 6,000
Merchandise cost of sales	1,450
Investment fees	60
Various other expenses	4,000
	$11,510

A statement of activities might report that information follows:

Changes in unrestricted net assets:

Contribution revenue		$ 8,460
Bookstore sales	$ 2,150	
Less: cost of sales	1,450	
gross profit on sales		700
Investment revenue (net of expenses of $60)		1,050
		10,210
Expenses:		
Program A	$ 7,120	
Management and general	2,100	
Fund raising	780	
		10,000
Increases in unrestricted net assets		$ 210

A note to the financial statements might appear as follows:

Expenses were incurred for the following:

	Total	Program A	Management and General	Fund Raising
Salaries	$ 6,000	$ 5,000	$ 400	$ 600
Cost of sales	1,450	1,450		
Investment fees	60		60	
Various other expenses	4,000	2,120	1,700	180
Total expenses	11,510	8,570	2,160	780
Less:				
Expenses deducted directly from revenues on the statement of activities:				
Cost of sales	(1,450)	(1,450)		
Investment fees	(60)	—	(60)	—

Total expenses reported by function on the statement of activities	$10,000	$ 7,120	$ 2,100	$ 780

The not-for profit organization also should disclose the amount of income taxes charged to expense and the nature of the activities that gave rise to the taxes.

CHAPTER 10
CASH FLOWS

CONTENTS

CHAPTER 10
CASH FLOWS

CROSS-REFERENCES

2000 MILLER NOT-FOR-PROFIT REPORTING: Chapter 2, "Overview of Current Pronouncements"; Chapter 14, "Payroll and Miscellaneous Requirements"

2000 MILLER GAAP GUIDE: Chapter 5, "Cash Flow Statement"; Chapter 32, "Nonmonetary Transactions"

2000 MILLER GAAP IMPLEMENTATION MANUAL: Chapter 8, "Cash Flow Statement"; Chapter 28, "Nonmonetary Transactions"

2000 MILLER GOVERNMENTAL GAAP GUIDE: Chapter 5, "Governmental Financial Reporting"

The statement of cash flows provides information about the sources and uses of cash during the reporting period. The statement of cash flows is useful to external readers because it provides information about how:

- Cash was received by the organization to support its operations.
- Cash was expended to provide its programs.
- Changes in cash reconcile to the cash in net assets.

The statement provides relevant information that supports the statement of financial position in terms of the organization's liquidity, financial flexibility, ability to meet obligations, and need for external financing. The statement reports the sources and uses of cash from:

- Operating activities
- Investing activities
- Financing activities

CHANGES TO FASB STATEMENT NO. 95

FAS-117 (Financial Statements of Not-for-Profit Organizations) states that, to be complete, a not-for-profit organization's financial statements must include a statement of cash flows for the reporting period. Also, the "primary purpose of a statement of cash flows is to provide relevant information about the cash receipts and cash payments of an organization during a period." The FASB amended FAS-95 (Statement of Cash Flows) to extend its provisions to not-for-profit-organizations and to amend certain paragraphs relating to cash flows from financing activities, as follows (FAS-117, pars. 6 and 29):

- Receiving restricted resources that the donor restricts for long-term purposes is financing activities.
- Receipts from contributions and investment income that the donor restricted for the purposes of acquiring, constructing, or improving property, plant, equipment, or other long-lived assets or establishing or increasing a permanent endowment or term endowment are financing activities.
- Operating cash flows should be reported by major class of gross receipts. For example, interest and dividends received are a major class. Interest and dividends that are for long-term purposes as restricted by donor are not part of operating cash receipts.
- Information about all non-cash investing and financing activities of an organization during a period that affect recognized assets or liabilities should be reported in related disclosures, e.g., obtaining a building or investment asset by receiving a gift.

CASH EQUIVALENTS

The statement of cash flows reports the change in cash and cash equivalents during the reporting period. *Cash equivalents*, as defined in FAS-95, are short-term, highly liquid investments that are both:

- Readily convertible to known amounts of cash; and

- So near their maturity that they present insignificant risk of changes in value because of changes in interest rates.

As a general rule, investments purchased with an original maturity of three months or less are considered cash equivalents. Commercial paper, money markets, certificates of deposits, and Treasury bills all fall into this category. The notes to the organization's financial statements should disclose its policies regarding determination of cash equivalents. Any change in the organization's policy is a change in accounting principle and necessitates the restatement of any prior year's financial statements that are presented.

NETTING

FAS-95 requires the flows of cash amounts to be reported on a gross basis. This is more informative to external users than showing net amounts. Generally, netting of amounts is permitted if the reporting of gross amounts is not needed to understand the operating, investing, and financing activities. For example, if the organization is receiving or disbursing funds of a client, the reporting of net transactions would be acceptable.

CLASSIFICATIONS OF CASH FLOWS

Cash flows are to be reported as investing, financing, or operating activities. *Investing activities* are those transactions that relate to the acquisition or disposition of debt or equity instruments or land, plant, and equipment or other productive assets, or the making or collecting of loans. *Financing activities* are those transactions that relate to obtaining resources and providing a return or repayment thereof. *Operating activities* are all transactions that are not classified as investing or financing activities.

Inflows from Investing Activities

- Proceeds from the sales of stocks or bonds of other enterprises
- Proceeds from the sale of equipment or buildings
- Proceeds from insurance policies that cover damage or theft of property, plant, or equipment
- Collections of loans made by the organization
- Proceeds from the sale of works of art

Outflows from Investing Activities

- Investment made of stocks, bonds, or other enterprises
- Purchases of property, plant, or equipment

- Loans made by the organization
- Purchases of works of art

Inflows from Financing Activities

- Receipts from the collection of contributions that have donor-imposed restrictions stating they must be used for long-term purposes
- Receipts of contributions that create permanently restricted or temporarily restricted annuity trusts or life income funds
- Proceeds from the issuance of notes, mortgages, bonds, or other borrowings
- Proceeds from the issuance of equity (on a consolidated financial statement where an organization has a for-profit subsidiary)
- Interest or dividend income that has a donor-imposed restriction on its usage to increase a permanent or temporary endowment

Outflows from Financing Activities

- Repayment of loans, mortgages, bonds, or other borrowings
- Refunds of contributions that were described in financing outflows
- Payments of dividends or repurchase of stock also known as treasury stock (on a consolidated financial statement where an organization has a for-profit subsidiary)

Inflows from Operating Activities

- Receipts from contributions or grants except those described in financing activities
- Receipts from program service income, sale of goods, or tuition
- Receipt of interest or dividends on investments or loans
- Settlement of lawsuits or proceeds from insurance claims other than those related to long-term assets

Outflows from Operating Activities

- Payment of salaries, vendors, and suppliers
- Payment of taxes or fees
- Payment of interest on loans or any borrowings
- Payment of grants or contributions

INDIRECT AND DIRECT METHODS

The statement of cash flows must present the net cash provided or used in operating, investing, and financing activities and the change in cash and cash equivalents during the reporting period. When reporting cash flows from operating activities, the not-for-profit organization may use one of two methods: the direct method or the indirect method.

FAS-95 encourages organizations to report cash flows from operating activities by major class of gross cash receipts, gross cash payments, and the net cash flow—the direct method. The following are reported separately:

- Cash received from program services or sales of goods

- Cash collected from contributions

- Interest and dividends received

- Other receipts from operating activities

- Cash paid to suppliers, to vendors, and for salaries

- Interest paid

- Income taxes paid

- Contributions or grants paid

- Payments of other operating activities

A separate reconciliation of change in net assets to cash flows from operating activities also must be provided. This reconciliation is similar to that used in the indirect method.

An organization that expects to report cash flows from operating activities first should review its internal reporting system to ascertain that the information is readily available. If it is not readily available, the organization may be required to make changes to its reporting system or create a secondary recordkeeping system to accumulate the gross data needed for the direct method of reporting.

Not-for-profit organizations using the indirect method report the net cash flow information by reporting the reconciliation of the change in net assets to net cash provided by (or used in) operating activities. This method begins with the change in net assets. Major classes of reconciling items are then presented. These reconciling items remove (1) the effects of all deferrals of past cash receipts or payment (e.g., the net increase or decrease in a receivable or payable or the net increase or decrease in deferred income) or (2) the effects of all items whose cash effects are investing or financing cash flows (e.g., depreciation or amortization, or gains and losses on the sale of securities or long-term assets).

The comprehensive sample financial statements shown in FAS-95 include a statement of cash flows prepared using the indirect method for reporting cash flows from operations. The cash flows from operations determined by the indirect method—adjusting the change in net assets to reconcile it to net cash flow from operating activities—should report the same amount for net cash flow from operations as the direct method.

Change in net assets is adjusted to remove the effects of all deferrals of past operating cash receipts and payments and all accruals of expected future operating cash receipts and payments, such as changes in receivables and payables, and the effects of all items whose cash effects are investing or financing cash flows (e.g., depreciation, amortization of goodwill, and gains and losses on sales of property, or gains and losses on extinguishment of debt).

> **OBSERVATION:** Sample statements of cash flows using both the direct and indirect methods are presented in Chapter 2, "Overview of Current Pronouncements."

TRANSACTIONS REPORTED IN THE STATEMENT OF CASH FLOWS

The AICPA Guide *Not-for-Profit Organizations* gives examples of the types of transactions that may be reported by not-for-profit organizations in a statement of cash flows:

- *Receipt of a cash contribution restricted for the acquisition of equipment*—Report as a financing cash inflow and an outflow from investing activities.

- *Receipt of a contributed asset not classified as cash or cash equivalent*—Adjust "Change in Net Assets" if the indirect method is used to determine cash flow from operating activities.

- *Equipment is purchased in period subsequent to that in which the restricted asset was received*—Report, in cash flows from investing activities, the proceeds of sale of the restricted asset (if not cash) and the cash used to acquire the equipment.

- *Cash equivalents not reported as such in the statement of cash flows*—Contributed assets with donor restrictions may be used to purchase securities that would ordinarily meet the definition of "cash equivalents" in FAS-95. These securities would be excluded from the "Cash and Cash Equivalents" caption. The donor restrictions involved could relate to endowment funds or to stipulations about the type of investments that can be purchased.

Noncash Transactions

Information about investing or financing transactions that do not result in cash receipts or disbursements must be disclosed on the statement of cash flows. It may be disclosed in a narrative or schedule. Examples of noncash transactions are:

- Receipt of securities, works of art, or equipment as a contribution
- Acquisition of an asset through a capital lease
- Refinancing of debt
- Contributed services that create or enhance a long-term asset or that require specialized skills
- Exchange of a noncash asset for another noncash asset

Foreign Currency Transactions

Organizations that have foreign currency transactions should report the foreign currency cash flows using exchange rates that were in effect at the time of the cash flow. A weighted-average exchange rate for the period may be used if it is substantially the same as the rate in effect at the time of the cash flow. The effect of the exchange rate on cash balances is a separate line item in reconciling the change in cash and cash equivalents.

CHAPTER 11
DISPLAY OF CERTAIN GAAP
TRANSACTIONS

CONTENTS

CHAPTER 11
DISPLAY OF CERTAIN GAAP TRANSACTIONS

CROSS-REFERENCES

2000 MILLER NOT-FOR-PROFIT REPORTING: Chapter 2, "Overview of Current Pronouncements"; Chapter 6, "Liabilities"; Chapter 7, "Organizational Issues"

2000 MILLER GAAP GUIDE: Chapter 16, "Extinguishment of Debt"; Chapter 18, "Foreign Operations and Exchange"; Chapter 31, "Long-Term Obligations"; Chapter 41, "Results of Operations"; Chapter 43, "Segment Reporting"

2000 MILLER GAAP IMPLEMENTATION MANUAL: Chapter 16, "Extinguishment of Debt"; Chapter 18, "Foreign Operations and Exchange"; Chapter 35, "Results of Operations"; Chapter 37, "Segment Reporting"

2000 MILLER GOVERNMENTAL GAAP GUIDE: Chapter 5, "Governmental Financial Reporting"; Chapter 14, "Assets"; Chapter 17, "Liabilities"; Chapter 27, "Proprietary Funds"; Chapter 30, "General Long-Term Debt Account Group"

2000 MILLER GAAS GUIDE: Section 411

SAS-69 (The Meaning of "Present Fairly in Conformity with Generally Accepted Accounting Principles" in the Independent Auditor's Report) establishes the rules that govern the hierarchy of generally accepted accounting principles for all entity types. For recording and reporting transactions of not-for-profit organizations, accountants are advised to follow FASB standards for all organizations unless there is accepted guidance specifically for the transaction type. The following transactions are not included in pronouncements that provide specific guidance for not-for-profit organizations, but are considered in FASB Statements or other pronouncements recognized as generally accepted accounting principles by the AICPA in SAS-69.

> **OBSERVATION:** The general guidance relating to these transaction types is discussed in more detail in the **Miller GAAP Guide**; however, they are presented here from a not-for-profit organization's viewpoint.

EXTRAORDINARY ITEMS

FAS-117 (Financial Statements of Not-for-Profit Organizations) does not change the reporting or definition of extraordinary items. APB Opinion No. 30 (Reporting the Results of Operations—Reporting the Effects of Disposal of a Segment of a Business, and Extraordinary, Unusual, and Infrequently Occurring Events and Transactions) reserves the "Extraordinary Items" caption for "the effects of events and transactions, other than the disposal of a segment of a business, that meet the criteria for classification as extraordinary."

Extraordinary items are events and transactions that are distinguished by their unusual nature *and* by the infrequency of their occurrence. Thus, *both* of the following criteria should be met to classify an event or transaction as an extraordinary item:

1. *Unusual nature*—The underlying event or transaction possesses a high degree of abnormality and is of a type clearly unrelated to, or only incidentally related to, the ordinary and typical activities of the enterprise, taking into account the environment in which the enterprise operates.

2. *Infrequency of occurrence*—The underlying event or transaction is of a type that would not reasonably be expected to recur in the foreseeable future, taking into account the environment in which the enterprise operates.

For not-for-profit organizations, reporting extraordinary items requires:

- Segregation on the face of the statement of activities and the use of the caption "Extraordinary Items";
- Disclosure of amounts for individual events or transactions that are deemed to be extraordinary; and
- Description of extraordinary events or transactions that are deemed to be extraordinary.

As with all entities, management of not-for-profit organizations will be required to exercise a great deal of judgment in the determination of transactions or events that will lead to the use of the "Extraordinary Items" caption. Events such as a loss of a major funding source should not be considered extraordinary, but gains or losses on the extinguishment of debt should.

FOREIGN TRANSLATION ADJUSTMENT ACCOUNTS

FASB addresses foreign currency translation in FAS-52 (Foreign Currency Translation). The purpose of the Statement is to:

- Provide information that is generally compatible with the expected economic effects of a rate change on an enterprise's cash flows and equity, and
- Reflect in consolidated statements the financial results and relationships as measured in the primary currency in which each entity conducts its business (referred to as its functional currency).

Many not-for-profit organizations conduct programs outside of the United States. For purposes of FAS-52, an entity can be a subsidiary, division, branch, or joint venture. Using the guidelines set forth in FAS-52, an organization must:

- Identify the functional currency of the entity's economic environment.
- Measure all elements of the entity's financial statements in the functional currency.
- Determine the appropriate exchange rate for translation from the functional currency to the reporting currency, if different.
- Determine the impact of changes in exchange rates on individual assets and liabilities that are receivable or payable in currencies other than the functional currency.

Translation adjustments result from the process of translating a foreign operation's financial statements from the functional currency into U.S. dollars. FAS-52 requires that translation adjustments be recorded and accumulated separately from net income until the foreign operation is disposed of or liquidated. However, not-for-profit organizations must show translation adjustments within the statement of activities as one of the components of changes in net assets. To avoid wide fluctuations in operating results resulting from translation adjustments, not-for-profit organizations may choose to record such adjustments within the statement of activities but after arriving at an operating measure such as Results of Operations. If this policy is followed, the translation adjustments should be disclosed on the statement of activities and the accumulated adjust-ments should be disclosed as a separate component of net assets (usually unrestricted). When the foreign operation is disposed of in whole or in part, or when liquidation of the investment in the foreign operation is substantially complete, the accumulated translation ad-justments should be written off as part of the gain or loss on disposal.

Not-for-profit organizations also should report *transaction gains and losses* as a result of transactions that are denominated in curren-cies other than the functional currency. Unless the transaction in which these currencies come into account is a hedge of a foreign currency commitment or a net investment in a foreign entity, the gains and losses arising from the transactions will be reported on the statement of activities as a component of operating activities.

GAIN OR LOSS ON EXTINGUISHMENT OF DEBT

FAS-125 (Accounting for Transfers and Servicing of Financial Assets and Extinguishments of Liabilities) has superseded FAS-76 (Extin-guishment of Debt) and FTB 84-4 (In-Substance Defeasance of Debt). It amends APB Opinion No. 26 (Early Extinguishment of Debt) to incorporate the authority of FAS-125 to define "transactions that the debtor shall recognize as an extinguishment of a liability."

APB Opinion No. 26 (Early Extinguishment of Debt) notes in paragraph 19 that "all extinguishments of debt are fundamentally alike." Accordingly, it concludes that the accounting for all extin-guishments should be the same regardless of how the transaction is accomplished.

FAS-4 (Reporting Gains and Losses from Extinguishment of Debt) notes in paragraph 8 that "gains and losses from extinguishment of debt that are included in the determination of net income shall be aggregated and, if material, classified as an extraordinary item."

FAS-76 permitted debtors to treat a liability as extinguished if they completed an "in-substance defeasance." The debtor would transfer risk-free assets to an irrevocable trust set up for the purpose of generating cash flows. This would approximate the scheduled interest and principal payments of the debt that was to be removed from the debtor's financial statements. FAS-125 notes that transfer-ring assets to the defeasance trust after interest rates have risen results in an economic loss to shareholders. These transactions do not meet either of the criteria for determining that a debt has been extinguished; that is:

- That the debtor pays the creditor and is relieved of its obliga-tion for the liability; or

- That the debtor is legally released from being the primary obligor, either judicially or by the creditor.

In all circumstances of debt extinguishment, the difference between the *reacquisition price* and the net carrying amount of the debt is recognized currently in the change in net assets of the period of extinguishment and is reported separately in the statement of activities.

> **OBSERVATION:** Defeasance is covered in more detail in Chapter 6, "Liabilities."

DISCONTINUED OPERATIONS

Discontinued operations are defined in APB Opinion No. 30 as the operations of a segment of a business that have been sold, abandoned, spun off, or otherwise disposed of or, although still operating, is the subject of a formal plan for disposal. The Opinion concludes:

> The results of continuing operations should be reported separately from discontinued operations and any gain or loss from disposal of a segment of a business . . . should be reported in conjunction with the related results of discontinued operations and not as an extraordinary item. Accordingly, operations of a segment that has been or will be discontinued should be reported separately as a component of income before extraordinary items and the cumulative effect of accounting changes (if applicable).

The gain or loss from the disposal of the segment should be disclosed on the face of the income statement or in related notes.

The *Not-for-Profit Organizations* Guide refers financial statement preparers to FAS-14 (Financial Reporting for Segments of a Business Enterprise) for guidance on the determination of major classes of programs and supporting activities (activities that may be considered segments). In footnote 7 to paragraph 13.26 of the Guide, the AICPA states:

> Applying paragraph 11 of FASB Statement No. 14 to not-for-profit organizations, the major classes of program services and supporting activities should be determined by (a) identifying the major programs and activities that an organization undertakes, (b) grouping those programs and activities by function, and (c) selecting those functions that are significant with respect to the organization as a whole.

> **OBSERVATION:** FAS-131 (Disclosures about Segments of an Enterprise and Related Information) has superseded FAS-14 for financial statements for periods beginning after December 15, 1997.

FUTURE CHANGES

As organizations continue to implement FAS-116 (Accounting for Contributions Received and Contributions Made), other transactions or events occurring in the life cycle of not-for-profit organizations may require interpretation of the existing literature for business entities.

CHAPTER 12
SERVICE EFFORTS
AND ACCOMPLISHMENTS

CONTENTS

Chapter 12
SERVICE EFFORTS
AND ACCOMPLISHMENTS

FASB CONCEPTS STATEMENT NO. 4

FASB Concepts Statement No. 4 (Objectives of Financial Reporting by Nonbusiness Organizations) discusses service efforts and accomplishments of not-for-profit organizations.

The Statement concludes that resource providers and others will find disclosure of information about an organization's service efforts and accomplishments useful in assessing the performance of an organization and in making contribution decisions, because:

- The accomplishments of not-for-profit organizations are not susceptible to measurement in terms of sales, profit, or return on investment, and

- The resource providers often do not have direct knowledge of the not-for-profit organization's programs, because they may not be users or beneficiaries of such programs.

Concepts Statement No. 4 notes that disclosures about programs should focus on how the organization's resources are used in providing different programs or services.

Finally, Concepts Statement No. 4 notes:

> Ideally, financial reporting also should provide information about the service accomplishments of a nonbusiness organization.

This information, in terms of goods or services produced and of program results "may enhance significantly the value of information provided about service efforts."

FASB STATEMENT NO. 117

FAS-117 (Financial Statements of Not-for-Profit Organizations) discusses the need for not-for-profit organizations to provide information about service efforts. The purpose of these disclosures is to "help donors, creditors, and others" assess the organization's cost of services and how it uses its resources.

Currently, voluntary health and welfare organizations report information about expenses in a matrix format in a separate financial statement. The matrix includes expenses by their functional nature (e.g., major classes of program services and supporting activities) on one axis and expenses by their natural classification (e.g., salaries, rent, interest) along the other axis. FAS-117 encourages but does not require other not-for-profit organizations to provide similar information about the *natural classification* of expenses in the financial statements or the notes thereto.

In footnote 6 of FAS-117, FASB notes that information about an organization's programs can be enhanced in several ways. An organization may present information in a manner that provides a measure of operations (e.g., reporting revenues together with related expenses). A hospital, for example, may present net patient service revenue with the costs of providing care, arriving at a subcaption that indicates the excess of revenues over expenses. Nonoperating activities (e.g., investment income and contributions affecting unrestricted net assets) would be reported separately.

FASB Special Report

A FASB Special Report, *Results of the Field Test of the Proposed Standards for Financial Statements of Not-for-Profit Organizations and Accounting for Contributions*, presents several possibilities for the presentation of operating results based on the Exposure Draft that led to FAS-117. The organizations that participated in the field test include a hospital, a university, an orchestral association, and a health care entity. The narrative that accompanies each of the statements of activities presented critiques the statement and notes the degree of flexibility employed by the organization and departures from the requirements of the Exposure Draft.

FAS-117 concluded that discussing disclosures about program inputs, outputs, and results in nonmonetary terms helps the users of the financial statements. The Statement cited information about applications, acceptances, admissions, enrollment and occupancy rates, and degrees granted as being helpful. Reporting that kind of information is possible, usually, in supplementary information or management explanations, or by other methods of financial reporting.

Because past pronouncements lacked an emphasis on measuring service accomplishments, the ability to do so "is generally undeveloped" (FASB:CON-4, par. 53). In the past, FASB has encouraged research to determine if such information can be reliably developed. FASB concluded, therefore, that FAS-117 precludes including information about service accomplishments in the financial statements, because such information is not measurable in "units of money" (FAS-117, par 54).

AICPA AUDIT AND ACCOUNTING GUIDE

In response to these limitations, the AICPA Guide *Not-for-Profit Organizations* states:

> The financial statements should provide information about program expenses. If the components of total program expenses are not evident from the details provided on the face of the statement of activities . . . , the notes to the financial statements should disclose total program expenses and should provide information about why total program expenses disclosed in the notes does not articulate with the statement of activities. The financial statements should also provide a description of the nature of the organization's activities, including a description of each of its major classes of programs, either on the statement of activities . . . or in the notes to the financial statements. [par. 13.27]

This guidance is in line with Concepts Statement No. 4 and recognizes that financial statements may not include information that is not reliably measured.

SAMPLE NARRATIVE DESCRIPTION

The FASB Special Report provides an example of a narrative description about the functions used in reporting expenses of an organization that participated in the field test:

The organization carries out its ministries through the following programs:

Broadcasting—Produces and transmits Christian programs in various languages to countries around the world. Broadcasting is done from its radio stations in Ecuador and affiliated broadcasting in Panama and South Texas. This area is carried out by the broadcasting and technical services divisions.

Hospital and medical service—Operates hospitals in Ohio and the jungle village of Shell in Ecuador. Community development assists rural areas in obtaining clean water, improved sanitation, better crops, etc. Mobile medical facilities provide medical and dental treatment to those in outlying areas. This area is carried out by the health care division.

Evangelism and Christian growth—Provides evangelism ministries, including counseling, film distribution, training seminars, and the production of Christian literature, records, cassettes, and Bible correspondence courses. This area is carried out by the Spanish ministries division. Spanish television programs are produced to be broadcast on local stations.

Home countries—Carries out ministries in the home countries of the missionaries. These activities include furlough and other ministries that promote missionary vision or spiritual growth within the local church or community, and the involvement of interested individuals in the work of missions throughout the world.

Management will have significant flexibility while providing this information in the financial statements, notes to the financial statements, and other locations in an organization's annual report. The users of financial statements will need to read the information critically because the information regarding service efforts and performance is not readily measurable. Auditors will need to satisfy themselves that the narrative information provided by management is consistent with information learned during the course of the audit.

Part IV
Regulatory Financial Reporting

CHAPTER 13
TAX REPORTING REQUIREMENTS

CONTENTS

CHAPTER 13
TAX REPORTING REQUIREMENTS

CROSS-REFERENCES

2000 MILLER NOT-FOR-PROFIT REPORTING: Chapter 2, "Overview of Current Pronouncements"

2000 MILLER GAAP GUIDE: Chapter 21, "Income Taxes"

2000 MILLER GAAP IMPLEMENTATION MANUAL: Chapter 20, "Income Taxes"

2000 MILLER GAAS GUIDE: Section 711

FEDERAL OVERVIEW

For federal purposes, all organizations exempt from tax under Internal Revenue Code (IRC) Section 501(a), including foreign organizations, are generally required to file certain returns. IRC Section 501(a) exempts from tax those organizations "described in subsection (c)" unless denied under IRC Section 502 or 503. These Sections refer to certain special-purpose organizations and to those "engaged in prohibited transactions." Exceptions to the filing requirements apply for certain smaller organizations with annual gross receipts that normally do not exceed $25,000, religious organizations and certain affiliates, and certain federally chartered organizations.

When filing returns when an application for exemption is pending, the not-for-profit organization should file as if its exemption has been recognized. The words "Application Pending" should appear at the top of the first page of the return, and a copy of the first page of the exemption application should be attached.

Background

The Internal Revenue Code provides the not-for-profit organization with an exemption from income taxes. IRC Section 501(c) lists those classes of organizations that are exempt, and that Section includes not only charitable organizations, but also certain employee benefit plans, state and local governments, labor unions, museums, cemeteries, credit unions, social clubs, trade associations, and many others.

The government recognizes, however, that some of the activities of these exempt organizations are carried out in direct competition with for-profit businesses that have owners who expect a return for their investment of time and money in the operations of the business. To prevent exempt organizations from competing unfairly, the expectation of excess income for distribution is nonexistent, and the federal government will impose an income tax on the portion of the exempt organization's revenues that are not related to its tax-exempt purposes. Not-for-profit organizations must guard against losing their tax-exempt status through careful monitoring of activities that might be deemed by the Internal Revenue Service to be unrelated business activity resulting in unrelated business income (UBI), which is discussed later in this chapter (section titled "Unrelated Business Income Tax").

In 1997, Congress passed the Taxpayer Relief Act of 1997. Following is a brief outline of key provisions that affect not-for-profit organizations.

TAXPAYER RELIEF ACT OF 1997

The Taxpayer Relief Act of 1997, signed into law on August 5, 1997, contains several provisions that affect not-for-profit organizations.

Estimated Tax Payment for a Private Foundation

The new law has extended the due date of the first-quarter estimate by one month. Effective for tax years beginning after August 5, 1997, the due date of a private foundation's first-quarter estimate is the fifteenth day of the fifth month of the tax year. For calendar-year organizations, the due date is May 15. This change was made to correspond with the filing due date of the previous year's Form 990. Congress felt that private foundations would be able to make more accurate estimated tax payments if they had additional time.

Intermediate Sanctions

Intermediate sanctions, as previously discussed, have been amended under the Taxpayer Relief Act. The IRS was given the authority to abate first-tier taxes on excess benefit transactions. The organization must demonstrate that the taxable event was due to reasonable cause rather than willful neglect and that the event was corrected within the correction period. This provision becomes effective, generally, for all excess benefit transactions occurring after September 14, 1997. During 1999, the IRS issued final Regulations related to intermediate sanctions.

Form 990 Reporting of Penalties

The Taxpayer Relief Act has added a provision, in a not-for-profit annual filing, for reporting the amount of taxes imposed on the organization or any organization manager during the taxable year. The following taxes incurred must be disclosed:

- Section 4911—Tax on excess expenditures to influence legislation
- Section 4912—Tax on disqualifying lobbying expenditures of certain organizations
- Section 4955—Taxes on political expenditures of Section 501(c)(3) organizations
- Any excise taxes on excess benefit transactions paid by the organization, organization manager, or disqualified person. Reimbursements that an organization pays to an organization manager with respect to these taxes must also be disclosed.

If the IRS has abated the first-tier penalty, then there is no reporting requirement.

The reporting requirements were effective with filings of returns for tax years beginning after July 30, 1996.

Unrelated Trade or Business

The Taxpayer Relief Act of 1997 added Code Section 513(i), "Treatment of Certain Sponsorship Payments," which provides that an unrelated trade or business does not include income from qualified sponsorships received by an organization. A person or company (the payor) may make a qualified sponsorship payment to an organization if there is no expectation or arrangement that the payor will receive any substantial return benefit. An acknowledgment of the payor's name, logo, or product line is not considered a substantial benefit. However, advertising carries a message to buy the payor's product, service, etc. If the payor receives a benefit through advertising products or services, then those qualified sponsorship payments would be considered unrelated business income.

Example: A medical not-for-profit organization publishes a monthly newsletter. The ABC Pharmaceutical Co. sponsors the December issue. The acknowledgment reads, "This issue has been made possible through an educational grant from ABC Pharmaceutical Co." No other rights or benefits pass to ABC Pharmaceutical Co. This sponsorship would not be subject to the unrelated business tax.

Example: Same facts as previous example, except that separate information about a new product of the pharmaceutical company and a trial sample are enclosed. This sponsorship would be subject to the unrelated business tax, because this would be considered advertising.

If a single payment is made to a not-for-profit organization, an allocation of a qualified sponsorship payment may be made. The fair market value of the benefit provided by the not-for-profit organization would be subject to the unrelated business tax.

The law provides that a "qualified sponsorship payment does not include any payment if the amount of such payment is contingent upon the level of attendance at one or more events, broadcast ratings, or other factors indicating the degree of public exposure to one or more events."

Income from Controlled Entities

Code Section 512(b)(13) was amended to expand the criteria for a controlled entity. Control of a corporation means ownership of more than 50% of the stock of the company. In a partnership, control means ownership of 50% or more of the profits or capital accounts. In any other entity, control means more than a 50% beneficial interest. Under the old laws, control was established at an level of 80% or higher. Aggregation rules for constructive ownership under Section 318 apply.

The effect of this change will be that more income received by not-for-profit organizations will be subject to the unrelated business tax. Interest, rent, royalty, and annuity payments that reduce the net income of a controlled for-profit organization and that reduce the entity's tax liability will be considered unrelated business income.

FILINGS REQUIRED

A not-for-profit organization, before it can claim exempt status, must apply for that status. Exempt status will be recognized in advance of operations if proposed operations can be described in sufficient detail to permit a conclusion that the organization will clearly meet the particular requirements of the IRC Section under which exemption is claimed. The organization must fully describe the activities in which it expects to engage, including the standards, criteria, procedures, or other means adopted or planned for carrying out the activities, the anticipated sources of receipts, and the nature of contemplated expenditures. Two IRS forms may be used for that purpose:

- **Form 1023 [Application for Recognition of Exemption under Section 501(c)(3)]**   Form 1023 must be filed within 15 months after the end of the month in which the organization was created. It is used by organizations applying for a ruling or determination on their tax-exempt status under IRC Sections 501(c)(3), 501(f), and 501(k). If the form is not filed within 15 months after the end of the month in which the organization was created, the organization will not qualify for exempt status during the period before the date of its application. However, notice is not required to be given to the IRS within 15 months if the organization (1) is a church, interchurch organization, or the like; (2) is not a private foundation and normally has gross receipts of not more than $5,000 in each tax year; or (3) is a subordinate organization covered by a group exemption letter, but only if the parent or supervisory organization submits a notice covering the subordinates in a timely manner.

- **Form 1024 [Application for Recognition of Exemption under Section 501(a), or for Determination under Section 120]**   Form 1024 must be filed as soon as the material and supporting documents needed to file a complete application can be obtained. A ruling or determination letter recognizing an exemption is usually effective as of the date of formation of an organization if its purposes and activities during the period prior to the date of the ruling or determination letter were consistent with the requirements for exemption.

Other forms also may be required from an organization requesting tax-exempt status:

- **Form 8718 [User Fee for Exempt Organization Determination Letter Request]**   Form 8718 is submitted with Form 1023 or Form 1024 to request a determination letter.

- **Form 872-C [Consent Fixing Period of Limitation Upon Assessment of Tax under Section 4940 of the Internal Revenue Code]**   Form 872-C must be filed by the same date as Form 1023 and should be filed in response to box (h), (i), or (j) of Part III, question 9, of Form 1023.

The tax returns for tax-exempt organizations are numerous. Filing requirements vary depending on the nature of the organization, its purpose, and its activities. The most basic and common tax return is **Form 990** [Return of Organization Exempt from Income Tax]. Due on or before the 15th day of the fifth month after the end of the annual accounting period, this return is filed by:

- Organizations exempt from tax under IRC Section 501(a) (excluding a church, religious activity, state institution, organization organized by an act of Congress, private foundation, etc.) and

- Nonexempt charitable trusts not treated as private foundations whose normal annual receipts are at least $25,000.

Gross receipts are $25,000 or less if the organization is:

- Up to a year old and has received, or donors have pledged, $37,500 or less during the first tax year;

- Between one and three years old and averaged $30,000 or less in gross receipts for the first two years; or

- Three or more years old and averaged $25,000 or less in gross receipts.

Accompanying Form 990 is **Schedule A** [Organization under 501(c)(3)—Supplementary Information]. As indicated by its title, this Schedule is filed by organizations described under IRC Section 501(c)(3), except private foundations that file Form 990-PF.

Form 990-PF [Return of Private Foundation] is due at the same time as Form 990, and is filed by organizations classified as private foundations under IRC Section 509(a) and nonexempt charitable trusts that are treated as private foundations under IRC Section 4947(a)(1).

Black Lung Benefit Trusts classified as exempt organizations under IRC Section 501(c)(2) and trustees or disqualified persons liable for tax under IRC Section 4951 or 4952, file **Form 990-BL** [Information and Initial Excise Tax Return for Black Lung Benefit Trusts and Certain Related Persons]. The due date for this form is the same as for Form 990. Any entity that has incurred taxes under IRC Section 4951 or 4952 will file Form 990-BL and **Schedule A (Form 990-BL)** [Computation of Initial Excise Taxes on Black Lung Benefit Trusts and Certain Related Persons]. Any person who has incurred liability for the excise tax on excess contributions under IRC Section 4953 will file **Form 6069** [Return of Excise Tax on Excess Contributions to Black Lung Benefit Trust under Section 4953 and Computation of Section 192 Deduction].

Generally, when organizations exempt from tax under IRC Section 501(a) have *gross* income from an unrelated trade or business of

$1,000 or more, they should file **Form 990-T** [Exempt Organization Business Income Tax Return] by the Form 990 due date.

Organizations that must file Form 990 and that have (1) gross receipts during the year that were less than $100,000 and (2) total assets at the end of the year that were less than $250,000 may file **Form 990EZ** [Short Form Return of Organization Exempt from Income Tax]. This return is due at the same time Form 990 is due (i.e., the 15th day of the fifth month following the close of the annual accounting period).

IRC Section 4947(a) indicates that a charitable trust should be treated as an organization described in IRC Section 501(c)(3) and a split-interest trust should be treated as a private foundation. **Form 1041** [U.S. Fiduciary Income Tax Return], and **Schedules A, B, D, G, J,** and **K-1**, are to be filed by a decedent's estate, by trusts, and by bankruptcy estates by the 15th day of the fourth month following the close of the annual accounting period. **Form 1041-A** [Trust Accumulation of Charitable Amounts] is filed by trusts that claim a charitable or other deduction under IRC Section 642(c) or split-interest trusts described in IRC Section 4947(a)(2) including charitable remainder trusts and pooled-income funds. Form 1041-A is due by the 15th day of the fourth month following the close of the annual accounting period.

Form 1041-ES [Estimated Income Tax for Fiduciaries] is filed on the 15th day of the fourth, sixth, and ninth months of the accounting year and the first month of the following accounting year when a fiduciary of an estate or trust must pay estimated tax (i.e., the estate or trust is expected to owe, after subtracting its withholding and credits, at least $500 in tax for the year).

Organizations described under IRC Section 501(d), religious and apostolic organizations, must file **Form 1065** [U.S. Partnership Return of Income] on or before the 15th day of the fourth month after the end of the annual accounting period.

Other organizations may be required to file returns on or before the 15th day of the third month after the end of the tax year. These include IRC Section 528 associations, homeowners, that would file **Form 1120-H** [U.S. Income Tax Return for Homeowners Association]. **Form 1120-POL** [Income Tax Return for Certain Political Organizations] should be filed by a political organization that is organized and operated primarily for the purpose of accepting contributions or making expenditures to influence the selection, nomination, election, or appointment of persons to public office, if such organization has any taxable income; or an IRC Section 501(c) organization that expends any amount for the purpose of influencing the selection, nomination, election, or appointment of any individual to public office.

All charitable reminder trusts described in IRC Section 664, pooled-income funds described in IRC Section 642(c)(5), and charitable lead trusts are required to file **Form 5227** [Split-Interest Trust Information

Return]. This return is due on April 15th. Generally, split-interest trusts created before May 27, 1969, are not required to file Form 5227. However, if any amounts were transferred to the trust after May 26, 1969, for which a deduction was allowed under any of the IRC Sections listed under IRC Section 4947(a)(2), Form 5227 must be filed for the year of the transfer and all subsequent years regardless of whether additional transfers are made. Charitable lead trusts and charitable remainder trusts whose charitable interests involve only war veterans' posts or cemeteries, described in IRC Sections 170(c)(3) and 170(c)(5), respectively, are not required to complete Parts VI and VII of Form 5227.

A charitable remainder annuity trust or unitrust is exempt from federal income tax for any tax year if it (1) was created after July 31, 1969, and (2) has no taxable unrelated business income for the tax year. Even though exempt from federal income tax, such a trust must file Form 5227 for the calendar year.

Private foundations that have engaged in certain transactions (e.g., self-dealing, failure to distribute income) and IRC Section 501(c)(3) organizations that are liable for the tax on excess lobbying expenditures as computed in Part VI of Schedule A, Form 990, or such IRC Section 501(c)(3) organizations that participate or intervene in any political campaign on behalf of or in opposition to any candidate for public office, must file **Form 4720** [Return of Certain Excise Taxes on Charities and Other Persons under Chapters 41 and 42 of the Internal Revenue Code]. This return is due:

- For private foundations, on or before the due date of Form 990-PF

- For 501(c)(3) organizations, on or before the unextended due date of Form 990 and Schedule A of Form 990 or by the due date for filing Form 990-PF or Form 5227

For affiliated group returns that have different tax years, the return will be due as prescribed in regulations.

When the annual information returns cannot be filed on a timely basis, the IRS allows organizations to file **Form 2758** [Application for Extension of Time to File; Certain Excise, Income, Information and Other Returns]. This form must be filed in duplicate before the due date of the return for which an extension is requested. This Form is filed by organizations filing Form 990, Form 990-BL, Form 990-PF, Form 4720, Form 990-T (Trust), and Form 6069. A corporate exempt organization filing Form 990-T or Form 1120-POL must file **Form 7004** for an automatic extension of time to file.

Certain organizations exempt under IRC Section 501(c)(3) may elect, or revoke a prior election, to come under the provisions of IRC Section 501(h) in making limited expenditures to influence legislation by filing **Form 5768** [Election/Revocation of Election by an

Eligible Sec. 501(c)(3) Organization to Make Expenditures to Influence Legislation]. The election must be signed and postmarked within the first taxable year to which it applies. The revocation must be signed and postmarked before the first day of the taxable year to which it applies.

When an exempt organization must pay taxes, the IRS provides forms for this purpose. **Form 990-W** [Estimated Tax on Unrelated Business Taxable Income or Tax-Exempt Organizations] is used by tax-exempt trusts or tax-exempt corporations that expect to owe tax of $500 or more. The payments are due April 15, June 15, September 15, and December 15 for organizations with calendar year ends, and the 15th day of the fourth, sixth, ninth, and twelfth months of the tax year for organizations with fiscal year ends. The estimated tax payments are filed with **Form 8109** [Federal Tax Deposit Coupon] and are deposited with the Federal Reserve Bank or a qualified depository for federal taxes.

Other federal tax forms that exempt organizations will use in certain circumstances are as follows:

- **Form 637 [Application for Registration (for Certain Excise Tax Transactions)]** Form 637 is used by entities that buy taxable articles tax-free or tax-reduced, sell taxable articles tax-free, or incur liability for gasoline, diesel fuel, or aviation fuel tax. There is no specific due date for this form.

- **Form 2670 [Credit or Refund—Exemption Certificate for Use by a Nonprofit Educational Organization]** Form 2670 is completed by a not-for-profit educational organization then given to a seller so the seller can claim a credit or refund of the manufacturer's excise tax or an exemption from the special fuels excise tax. There is no specific due date for this form.

- **Form 5578 [Annual Certification of Racial Nondiscrimination for a Private School Exempt from Federal Income Tax]** Form 5578 is used by any organization that claims exemption under IRC Section 501(c)(3) that operates, supervises, or controls a private school or schools and does not file Form 990 or Form 990EZ. This form is due by the 15th day of the fifth month following the end of the annual accounting period.

- **Form 8274 [Certification by Churches and Qualified Church-Controlled Organizations Electing Exemption from Employer Social Security Taxes]** Form 8274 is used by churches and qualified church-controlled organizations that are opposed for religious reasons to the payment of Social Security taxes. The organization files this form with the IRS after employees are hired but prior to the first date on which a quarterly employment tax return would otherwise be due from the electing organization.

- **Form 8282 [Donee Information Return]**   Form 8282 is used by original and successor donee organizations who sell, exchange, consume, or otherwise dispose of charitable property within two years after the date the original donee received the property. The form is filed with the IRS within 125 days after date of disposition.

- **Form 8300 [Report of Cash Payments Over $10,000 Received in a Trade or Business]**   Form 8300 is used by each person, including organizations exempt from tax, engaged in a trade or business who, in the course of such trade or business, receives more than $10,000 in cash in one transaction or two or more related transactions. The form is filed with the IRS by the 15th day after the date of the transaction. In addition to filing the form, the filer must provide a written statement to each person named in the Form 8300 on or before January 31 of the year following the calendar year in which this report is made.

Public Inspection of Tax Forms

The tax forms of exempt organizations are public documents. Anyone may inspect or request a copy of these tax forms at an IRS office by completing and submitting **Form 4506-A** [Request for Public Inspection or Copy of Exempt Organization Tax Form].

As a result of the Taxpayer Bill of Rights II, organizations must provide copies of their last three years' Form 990 as well as their exemption application immediately to anyone requesting copies at the organization's office and within 30 days to anyone requesting copies in writing. Penalties for noncompliance will be stiff—$5,000 for each request with which an organization fails to comply. The requirement applies to annual information returns of exempt organizations other than private foundations. Form 990-T, *Exempt Organization Business Income Tax Return*, is not subject to public inspection.

> **OBSERVATION:** The rule for immediate production of a copy of the forms does not apply if the request poses an unreasonable burden on the organization. An organization may be exempt from processing requests if it has made the documents widely available, such as by posting them on the organization's Web page. The organization may charge a reasonable fee for the copies, not in excess of $1.00 for the first page and $.15 for each subsequent page, plus actual postage costs.
>
> If an organization believes it is receiving a number of requests as part of a harassment campaign, it may not be required to comply with the requests.

Another Consideration for Federal Filers

An organization otherwise exempt from filing Form 990 because its normal gross receipts do not at least equal the prescribed minimum should nonetheless file a Form 990, by completing the heading, indicating that receipts were below the requisite minimum, signing the return, and sending it to the appropriate IRS Center. This will keep IRS records up to date and eliminate the need for the IRS to contact the organization at a later date to ask why no return was filed.

UNRELATED BUSINESS INCOME TAX

Organizations exempt from income taxes under Section 501(a) of the IRC can still incur an income tax. This results from the imposition of a tax on unrelated business income.

Unrelated business income is defined under IRC Sections 512 and 513 as gross income derived from a trade or business that is regularly carried on and that is not substantially related (other than to use the proceeds for charitable purposes) to the exempt purpose or function of the organization, less deductions directly related to carrying on this activity.

A trade or business is determined to be regularly carried on if there is a continual or frequent conduct of the activities.

> **Example:** Not-for-Profit Theatrical Company, in connection with its 25th anniversary, sells a silver commemorative coin at its season finale. This activity would not be considered regularly carried on and thus would be exempt from the unrelated business income tax.

> **Example:** Not-for-Profit Theatrical Company includes advertising in its programs at all of its productions. This activity would be considered regularly carried on and would be subject to the tax on unrelated business income.

A trade or business activity would be considered substantially related to the performance by the organization of its exempt purpose or function if the activity contributes importantly to the accomplishment of the exempt purposes.

> **Example:** In the above example of the Not-for-Profit Theatrical Company, the sale of advertising in its show programs does not contribute importantly to the exempt purpose of the theater company.

Example: An exempt zoo operates, on its grounds, a cafeteria that is open to its employees and to the public visiting the zoo. The cafeteria allows the viewing public as well as the zoo staff to remain at the zoo longer and not be forced to leave the grounds to eat elsewhere during mealtimes. This business would be considered to contribute importantly to the exempt purposes of the zoo.

Example: ABC University sponsors a touring exhibit of the works of a famous artist. It sells tickets for admittance to a viewing of the work to its students, its faculty, and the general public. This activity would be considered to have contributed importantly to the educational and cultural functions of the not-for-profit university.

Under Sections 512 and 513 of the IRC, an unrelated trade or business does *not* include the following:

- Any trade or business in which substantially all the work done to conduct the activity is performed for the organization without compensation
- For IRC Section 501(c)(3) organizations or colleges or universities defined in Section 511(a)(2)(B), activities carried on mainly for the convenience of the organization's members, students, employees, officers, or patients, or the sale of work-related clothes or equipment or vending machine items to 501(c)(4) organization's employees for their convenience at the place of business
- Sale of merchandise that was substantially received as contributions
- Qualified public entertainment activities that are regularly carried on by 501(c)(3), (4), or (5) organizations as one of their main exempt purposes
- Qualified convention and trade show activities regularly conducted to display industry products or to educate and promote industry products related to the exempt activity of the organization
- Certain hospital services where these services are performed at a facility not helping more than 100 people, and where the activities perform the exempt purposes and the fee charged does not exceed the cost incurred by the organization
- Bingo games not conducted on a commercial basis and not in violation of state law
- Qualified pole rentals by mutual or cooperative telephone or electric companies
- Sale of low-cost articles

> **OBSERVATION: Low-cost** means a cost less than $5 (which has been indexed for cost of living). The 1999 low-cost ceiling was $7.20, as adjusted for COLA.

- Interest, dividends, royalties, and annuities (except amounts received from controlled entities)
- Gains and losses from sales of securities or real property
- Rental income except for rental income from a controlled entity or from debt-financed property

Debt-Financed Property

Taxable unrelated business income under Section 513 also includes certain income from debt-financed property. IRC Section 514(b) defines *debt-financed property* as any property held to produce income with respect to which there is an acquisition indebtedness. This does not include real or personal property used substantially in the exempt function of the organization.

> **Example:** MLT Theater Company, an exempt organization, acquires a building and finances the purchase through a mortgage. MLT uses this property for its theatrical presentations and office. Although the property is debt-financed, it is **not** subject to unrelated business income tax.

> **Example:** LTT Not-for-Profit Organization rents an empty building to an unrelated corporation. This building was not subject to a mortgage during the year. The rental income would **not** be deemed unrelated business income, under the rental exception. If the building was subject to a mortgage, the rental income would be treated as unrelated business income subject to the tax because the property is debt-financed. The rental income would be subject to the unrelated business income tax even if the income is used for an exempt purpose.

Expense Deductions

Unrelated business income may be reduced by directly connected expenses to arrive at a taxable income. Deductions may be limited. For example, allowable deductions for meals and entertainment generally are limited to 50 percent of the amount paid. Organizations also are allowed a deduction for net operating losses, charitable contributions, and a $1,000 specific deduction.

Tax Rates

As provided for in IRC Sections 11 and 11(e), the following tax rate schedules should be applied to the taxable unrelated business income.

Tax Rate Schedule for Corporations

Unrelated business taxable income:

Over:	But not over:		Tax is:	Of the amount over:
$ 0	$ 50,000		15%	$ 0
50,000	75,000	$ 7,500	+25%	50,000
75,000	100,000	13,750	+34%	75,000
100,000	335,000	22,250	+39%	100,000
335,000	10,000,000	113,900	+34%	335,000
10,000,000	15,000,000	3,400,000	+35%	10,000,000
15,000,000	18,333,333	5,150,000	+38%	15,000,000
18,333,333	—		35%	0

Tax Rate Schedule for Trusts

Unrelated business taxable income:

Over:	But not over:		Tax is:	Of the amount over:
$ 0	$ 1,500		15%	$ 0
1,500	3,600	$ 225	+28%	1,500
3,600	5,500	813	+31%	3,600
5,500	7,500	1,402	+36%	5,500
7,500	—	2,122	+39.6%	7,500

Federal Filings

Organizations having gross income of $10,000 or more from an unrelated trade or business must file a **Form 990-T** [Exempt Organization Business Income Tax Return]. This return is due by the 15th day of the fifth month after the end of the tax year.

STATE OVERVIEW

Alabama

Alabama requires tax-exempt organizations with unrelated business income to file Form 20C. All tax-exempt organizations must file a copy of federal Form 990 or Form 990-T (for those organizations with gross unrelated business revenue of $1,000 or more).

Alaska

Alaska requires organizations that solicit contributions in the state to file an Annual Charities Registration Statement with the Department of Law. Form 08-196 (Nonprofit Biennial Report) is required from all not-for-profit organizations conducting business in the state, and Form 04-611 (Corporate Annual Return) is required for exempt organizations with unrelated business income. A copy of federal Form 990, 990-T, 990-PF, or 1120-POL should be attached to the Annual Return.

Arizona

All entities incorporated in Arizona must file Form INC0046. Most organizations with gross income of more than $25,000 must file Form 99. Also, tax-exempt organizations with unrelated business income must file Form 99T.

Arkansas

Arkansas requires all organizations soliciting contributions of more than $1,000 to file federal Form 990 and UBT Form 1100 CT.

California

California requires various filings. All exempt organizations must file Form 199 (Exempt Organization Annual Information Statement or Return). Exempt organizations with unrelated business income of $1,000 or more must file Form 109 (Exempt Organization Business Income Tax Return). Every corporation, association, or trustee holding assets for the public (except religious, educational, or charitable organizations, etc.) must file Form CT-2 (Periodic Report to the Attorney General of California) if gross assets or revenues exceed $25,000. Trusts must file Forms 541A and 541B.

Colorado

Colorado requires all exempt organizations to file Form CR-1 (Corporate Report). Tax-exempt organizations with unrelated business income must file Form 112.

Connecticut

Connecticut requires a one-time registration on Form CPC-63 of all organizations directly or indirectly soliciting funds from persons in the state. Form CPC-54 (Exempt Status Verification) is required from all charitable organizations that have neither solicited nor received contributions in excess of $25,000, that solicit or receive their contributions from not more than 10 persons, or that solicit contributions using unpaid officers or fund-raisers. Not-for-profit organizations also must file an annual report, Form CPC-60 (may be federal Form 990). This report must be audited by an independent CPA if gross revenues less government grants exceed $100,000.

Delaware

Delaware has no specific filing requirements for not-for-profit organizations.

District of Columbia

The District of Columbia requires the filing of Form 990 (copy of the DC Annual Report) by exempt organizations that filed federal Form 990. Exempt organizations that filed federal Form 990-T must file Form 990-T (federal form and copy of DC-20 Corporation Franchise Tax Return). All registered organizations except those having proceeds of less than $1,500 and using only volunteers for soliciting must file Form 990-PF, a copy of federal Form 990-PF, and Form BRA27 (two-year report for non-profit foreign and domestic corporations).

Florida

Florida requires that before beginning any solicitations, charitable organizations file a copy of the IRS Determination Letter with F-1120 for the first year they qualify as an exempt organization or the first year they are subject to the Florida income tax Code. All exempt organizations with unrelated business income must file Form 1120

(Florida Corporate and Emergency Excise Tax Return). Exempt organizations with proceeds of $10,000 or more must file federal Forms 990, 990-T, and 990-PF. If proceeds are less than $100,00, an independent CPA must issue a review report; an audit is required for annual reports of organizations with contributions of $100,000 or more. Form DR-5 (Application for Certification of Exemption) is required for exempt organizations that qualify for exemption from sales tax.

Georgia

Georgia requires the filing of Form 600T by all exempt organizations, which are required to file a Form 990-T with the federal government and have unrelated business income derived from Georgia sources. To apply for tax-exempt status, an organization must file Form 3605. Form C-100 (Annual Report) must be audited by a CPA if the organization has proceeds greater than $50,000. Also, the organization will have to file copies of federal Forms 99, 990-PF, and 990-T, if applicable.

Hawaii

Hawaii requires that exempt organizations having Hawaii unrelated business income of more than $1,000 file Form N-70NP (Exempt Organization Business Tax Return) along with a copy of federal Form 990-T. All organizations must file a domestic or foreign not-for-profit annual report.

Idaho

Idaho requires exempt organizations with unrelated business income to file Form 41 (Idaho Corporate Income Tax Return).

Illinois

Illinois requires exempt organizations with unrelated business income to file Form ILL-990T (Exempt Organization Income and Replacement Tax Return). All exempt organizations must file Form AG990-IL (Charitable Organization Supplement). This form must be accompanied by Form NP-102.10 (Articles of Incorporation), by federal Form 990, and by an independent CPA audit report if revenues exceed $150,000 or if the organization used a paid professional fundraiser that raised contributions in excess of $25,000.

Indiana

Not-for-profit organizations desiring to do business in Indiana must file Form IT-35A (Application to File as a Not-for-Profit Organization). In addition, all organizations must file Form 2423 (Annual Report of Non-profit Organization). All not-for-profit organizations must file Form IT-35AR (Return of a Not-for-Profit Organization Exempt from Indiana Gross Income Tax). Indiana requires exempt organizations with unrelated business income to file Form IT-20NP (Not-for-Profit Organization Return) together with federal Forms 990-T and 990.

Iowa

Not-for-profit organizations desiring to do business in Iowa must file Form IA 42-044 (Application to File for Exempt Status). Iowa requires exempt organizations with unrelated business income to file Form IA 1120 (Iowa Corporate Income Tax Return). All private foundations must file federal Form 990-PF along with Form IA 42-044.

Kansas

While not requiring any forms, Kansas requires exempt organizations doing business in the state to file an annual report and a Registration Statement for Charitable Organizations for Solicitations of Contributions. If proceeds exceed $100,000, an audit conducted by an independent CPA must be submitted along with a copy of federal Form 990.

Kentucky

Kentucky requires all not-for-profit organizations to file an annual report, but no form is required.

Louisiana

Louisiana requires all organizations desiring tax-exempt status to file the IRS Determination Letter for Initial Qualification for Tax-Exempt Status.

Maine

A charitable organization intending to conduct charitable fund-raising in Maine must register with the Department of Professional and Financial Regulation. Maine requires exempt organizations with unrelated business income to file Form 1120-ME (Corporate Income Tax Return) along with a copy of the organization's federal return. An annual report is required for exempt organizations doing business in the state, and if contributions exceed $30,000, an audit conducted by an independent CPA is required.

Maryland

Maryland requires exempt organizations with unrelated business income to file Form 500 (Corporate Income Tax Return). All tax-exempt organizations that have more than $25,000 in solicitations or that hire professional solicitors must register with the state. The applicable copies of federal Forms 990, 990-T, and 990-PF must be filed, or a Form COF-85 may be filed. If contributions exceed $100,000 and are below $200,000, a financial review conducted by an independent CPA is required. If contributions exceed $200,000, an audit performed by an independent CPA is required. An exempt organization may register with Maryland with Form COR-92 (Registration Statement for Charitable Organizations).

Massachusetts

Massachusetts requires all exempt organizations to file an annual report. Also, Form PC is required for all public charities other than religious organizations, and if contributions exceed $100,000, an audit conducted by an independent CPA is required. Form 3M (Income Tax Return for Clubs and Other Organizations Not Engaged in Business for Profit) is required to be filed only when the exempt organization has taxable dividends, interest, capital gains, or other miscellaneous taxable income.

Michigan

An exempt organization should file an Initial Charitable Trust/Solicitation Questionnaire to determine if registration or a license is required. Michigan requires exempt organizations with unrelated business income in excess of $40,000 to file Form C-8000 (Single Business Tax Annual Return-Corporations). All exempt organizations must file an annual report on Form CT-15. If contributions exceed $50,000, an audit conducted by an independent CPA is required.

Minnesota

Minnesota requires exempt organizations to file a charitable organization annual report. However, if total contributions are less than $25,000 and no professional fund-raiser is employed, the organization may file a notice of exemption. When contributions exceed $350,000, an audit conducted by an independent CPA is required. All organizations that solicit funds or hire professional fund-raisers must register with the state's Attorney General. Also, all private foundations must file Form 990-PF and all exempt organizations with $25,000 or more of proceeds must file Form 990.

Mississippi

Mississippi requires organizations desiring exempt status to file a copy of the IRS Determination Letter. Organizations with $25,000 or more of proceeds will file Form 990 (Return of Exempt Organizations). When contributions exceed $100,000, audited financial statements must also be submitted. In addition, an organization that has had a change in the character of its operation must file affidavits to that effect.

Missouri

Missouri has two forms that must be filed: (1) Form 1-A (Initial Registration Statement—Charitable Organization) for organizations that will solicit funds or employ professional fund-raisers and (2) Form 2-A (Annual Report) for all exempt organizations with more than $10,000 in proceeds.

Montana

Montana requires organizations that are exempt under federal law but not under Montana law and organizations with unrelated business income to file Form CLT-4 (Corporate License Tax Return). Exempt organizations with unrelated business income should file a copy of federal Form 990-T.

Nebraska

Nebraska requires exempt organizations that filed a federal Form 990-T to file Form 1120N (Corporate Income Tax Return). Exempt organizations soliciting contributions from the public should file federal Form 990.

Nevada

Nevada requires all exempt organizations soliciting public support to file federal Form 990 and to file an annual list of officers, directors, and agents of the not-for-profit organization.

New Hampshire

Except for churches, all exempt organizations must register with the state's Attorney General using Form NHCT-1 (Application for Registration). New Hampshire requires those organizations that file with the IRS to file Form NHCT-2 (Annual Report of Charitable Organizations) or, if an organization is filing federal Form 990, to simply sign Form NHCT-2 and submit it along with Form 990.

New Jersey

Every charitable organization that intends to solicit contributions from persons in New Jersey (except educational organizations; fraternal organizations; veterans' organizations; volunteer fire, ambulance, or rescue squads; and organizations formed to solicit on behalf of a specific individual) should file Form CRI-100 (Charitable Registration and Investigation). Organizations that receive less than $25,000 in contributions and do not use professional fund-raisers may file Form CRI-200 (short form registration) and may continue to annually renew this form as long as these requirements are met. An annual renewal Form CRI-300 R is required for those organizations not eligible to file the short form. Organizations receiving contributions over $100,000 must attach an audited financial statement.

New Mexico

A not-for-profit organization must file a Non-Profit First Report and must file an annual Non-Profit Corporate Report thereafter. Exempt organizations soliciting public support must file with the state's

Attorney General Charitable Organization Registry. New Mexico requires exempt organizations with unrelated business income to file Form CIT-1 (Corporate Income and Franchise Tax Return).

New York

New York requires all charitable organizations—except religious organizations, libraries, volunteer fire and ambulance squads, and veterans' organizations—that solicit or intend to solicit contributions in excess of $25,000 annually, or that pay for fund-raising, to file Form 410 (Registration Statement—Charitable Organizations). A registered charitable organization that receives total annual support of $25,000 or more or that made payments for fund-raising must file Form 497 (Annual Financial Report—Charitable Organizations). For organizations that do not reach the threshold, pages 1 and 2 of Form 497 are required. If amounts of contributions received are more than $25,000 and total revenue is less than $75,000, the organization must file a copy of federal Form 990 and attachments, with Form 497 attached as a cover sheet. If amounts of contributions received are more than $25,000 and total revenue is more than $75,000 but less than $150,000, Forms 990 and 497 must be accompanied by an independent accountant's review report. When the organization receives more than $25,000 in contributions and total revenue is in excess of $150,000, the forms should be accompanied by an independent auditor's opinion.

Form CT-13 (Unrelated Business Income Tax Report) is required for every organization and trust that is described in IRC Sections 511(a)(2) and (b)(2) and that is carrying on an unrelated trade or business. Form CT-247 (Application for Exemption from Corporate Franchise Taxes by a Not-for-Profit Organization) may be filed by organizations desiring exemption from New York State Franchise Tax. A number of conditions will permit the filing of this application for exemption:

- The entity must be organized and operated as other than for-profit.
- The entity must not have issued any stock.
- The entity must be exempt under IRC Section 501(a).
- No part of the entity's net earnings may inure to the benefit of any officer, director, or member.

In addition, any trustee holding and administering any property for charitable purposes must file NYCF-1 (Registration Form). Trustees not required to file annually and having gross receipts of $10,000 or less, and organizations with assets of less than $25,000, should file

Form NYCF-2A (Annual Report of Charitable Organization). Any private foundation, exempt organization, trustee, or executor must file Form NYCF-3 (Securities Schedule) if the property held is composed wholly or partly of securities. Form NYCF-4 (Tax Exempt Organizations) is used by trustees of any *inter vivos* or testamentary trust or by the executors of such trusts or estates.

North Carolina

North Carolina requires exempt organizations to file an initial application for licensing organizations to solicit charitable contributions. Thereafter, the organization must file Form DFS-6014 (Renewal Application to Licensing Organization to Solicit Charitable Contributions) along with Form DFS-6055 (Financial Summary). Exempt organizations subject to tax on unrelated business income must file Form CD-405 (North Carolina Corporate Franchise and Income Tax Return). An affidavit of Tax-Exempt Organization, accompanied by an independent CPA's report when gross receipts are $350,000 or more, is required for exempt organizations soliciting public support.

North Dakota

North Dakota requires Form 40 (North Dakota Corporation Income Tax Return) for exempt organizations with unrelated business income. Form 99 (North Dakota Information from Organization Exempt from Income Tax) is filed by all exempt organizations. An annual report is required from exempt organizations soliciting support.

Ohio

Every organization that solicits contributions in Ohio must file a Charitable Organization Registration Statement and Form CFR-1 (Charitable Trust Registration Form). Those exempt organizations with gross receipts of more than $5,000 or gross assets of more than $15,000 must file an annual financial report in the form of federal Form 990 or a certified copy of the financial statements.

Oklahoma

Oklahoma requires exempt organizations with unrelated business income to file Form 512-E (Return of Organization Exempt from

Income Tax). Exempt organizations soliciting public support must file an annual report.

Oregon

Oregon requires all charitable organizations holding assets in Oregon to file Form CT-12, Part I (Annual Report for Charitable Organizations) along with federal Form 990. In addition, all charitable organizations except religious, educational, cemetery, and child-care corporations are required to file Parts II and III (Annual Report—Charitable Organizations Report on Solicitation of Funds).

Pennsylvania

Pennsylvania requires all organizations that solicit funds to file Form BCO-10 (Registration Statement). For organizations with gross receipts of less than $25,000, including an audit, review, or compilation report is optional. The financial statements of organizations with gross receipts between $25,000 and $100,000 must be reviewed by an independent CPA. The financial statements of organizations with gross receipts of $100,000 or more must be audited by an independent CPA. Exempt organizations that file federal Form 990-PF are required to file that form with the Pennsylvania Department of Revenue.

Rhode Island

Rhode Island requires all exempt organizations to register with the state's Division of Tax. No form is required for this registration. Form N-13 (Annual Registration Required by the Organization) should be filed by all not-for-profit organizations, and if proceeds exceed $100,000, an audit is required. In addition, all charitable organizations that solicit funds should file Form 115-1-77 (Return of Organizations Exempt from Income Tax) and Form 115-2-78 (Application for Exempt from Registration Requirements of Charitable Organizations).

South Carolina

South Carolina requires all charitable organizations to register annually with the state's Division of Public Charities. No form is specified. All exempt organizations (except religious corporations; insurance, fraternal, beneficial, or mutual protection corporations; volunteer fire and rescue squads; certain cooperatives; building and loan associations or credit unions doing mutual business; and certain foreign corporations unless they have unrelated business income) should file Form SC990 (Return of Organizations Exempt from Income Tax).

South Dakota

South Dakota requires all domestic corporations authorized to do any business in the state to file an annual report with the Secretary of State. There is no specified form for this filing.

Tennessee

Tennessee requires exempt organizations that file federal Form 990-PF to file a copy as a Private Foundation Return with the state's Attorney General. In addition, organizations soliciting public support are required to file a Tax-Exempt Organizations Report with the state's Attorney General and submit a copy of federal Form 990. An audit by a CPA is required if proceeds are greater than $250,000.

Texas

In Texas, exempt organizations are required to furnish the state's Franchise Tax Board with a copy of the IRS Determination Letter.

Utah

Utah requires exempt organizations to file an affidavit with the Tax Commissioner showing the nature and purpose of the organization. Exempt organizations with unrelated business income should file Form TC-20 (Utah Corporate Tax Return).

Vermont

Vermont requires organizations desiring exempt status to file a copy of the IRS Determination Letter with the Vermont Department of Taxes. Not-for-profit organizations must file a biennial report with the Secretary of State Corporations Division.

Virginia

Virginia requires exempt organizations with unrelated business income to file Form 500 (Corporate Income Tax Return). In addition, exempt organizations soliciting public support should file federal Form 990 with the state's Office of Consumer Affairs.

Washington

Washington requires exempt organizations that solicit funds to file Form CHO-1 (Application to Register as a Charitable Organization), unless the solicitation is for political or religious purposes or is conducted entirely by volunteers and raises less than $5,000 of gross revenue.

West Virginia

West Virginia requires exempt organizations with unrelated business income that is subject to federal tax to file Form CNT-112 (Corporate Net Income Tax Return). In addition, all exempt organizations must file an annual Charitable Registration Statement. If contributions exceed $50,000, an audit by a CPA is required. All exempt organizations must file federal Form 990, and exempt organizations that file federal Schedule A to Form 990 must also file that schedule with West Virginia's Secretary of State.

Wisconsin

Wisconsin requires every organization that receives charitable contributions of more than $5,000 and employs no paid fund-raiser to file Form 308 (Charitable Organization Annual Report). When proceeds exceed $50,000, an audit by an independent CPA is required. Exempt organizations that have gross income of $1,000 or more from an unrelated trade or business and that file federal Form 990-T must file Form 4-T (Exempt Organization Business Franchise or Income Tax Return). In addition, all corporations registered with Wisconsin's Secretary of State must file Form 17 (Annual Report).

Wyoming

Wyoming requires all exempt organizations to file an annual report with the state's Secretary of State.

CHAPTER 14
PAYROLL AND
MISCELLANEOUS REQUIREMENTS

CONTENTS

Chapter 14
PAYROLL AND
MISCELLANEOUS REQUIREMENTS

Overview

Exempt organizations often find that the filing of government forms related to the employment of personnel and the withholding of taxes is an onerous burden. Specific reports and forms must be timely filed with the appropriate governmental federal and state agencies. Some of the forms are solely informational; others require the payment of taxes upon filing. In addition to federal requirements, state and local requirements apply. Penalties may be associated with noncompliance with filing due dates, and pervasive noncompliance could result in *criminal* penalties being assessed against the management of the entity.

> **OBSERVATION**: Payroll and miscellaneous requirements change often. This chapter represents the federal requirements in place at the time of publication. State and local requirements may apply to not-for-profit organizations and should be considered as well. Not-for-profit organizations should consult with their tax and other advisers to keep abreast of the most recent changes.

CROSS-REFERENCES

2000 MILLER NOT-FOR-PROFIT REPORTING: Chapter 2, "Overview of Current Pronouncements"; Chapter 10, "Cash Flows"

2000 MILLER GAAP GUIDE: Chapter 32, "Nonmonetary Transactions"

2000 MILLER GAAP IMPLEMENTATION MANUAL: Chapter 28, "Nonmonetary Transactions"

2000 MILLER GAAS GUIDE: Section 711

BACKGROUND

Federal Employer Identification Number

Exempt organizations must obtain an Employer Identification Number (EIN) if one of the following criteria is met:

- Wages are paid to one or more employees.

- Returns, statements, or other documents require use of an EIN.

- Withholding is required on income, other than wages, paid to nonresidents including individuals, corporations, and partnerships.

Each corporation in an affiliated group must file a separate application, but if several trades or businesses are operated by a single entity, only one EIN is required. The EIN can be obtained by writing or calling the Internal Revenue Service (IRS).

To request an EIN in writing, the employer should file **Form SS-4** [Application for Employer Identification Number] four to five weeks before the EIN is needed. To request an EIN by phone, the employer should call the Tele-TIN number assigned to its jurisdiction.

Employment Eligibility Verification

With certain exceptions, an employer must complete **Form I-9** [Employment Eligibility Verification] for any person who is hired to perform labor or services in return for wages or other remuneration. Exceptions are permitted for:

- Persons hired before November 7, 1966, who are continuing in their employment and have a reasonable expectation of employment at all times;

- Persons employed for casual domestic work in a private home on a sporadic, irregular, or intermittent basis who are paid less than $1,000 per calendar year;

- Persons who are independent contractors; and

- Persons who provide labor who are employed by a contractor providing contract services (e.g., employee leasing).

Form I-9 must be completed every time an employee is hired. The Form must be retained by the employer for three years after the date the employee begins work or one year after the employee's termination, whichever is longer. It need not be filed with any agency, but must be available for inspection by the Immigration and Naturalization Service and other U.S. agencies concerned with employment issues.

Employee's Federal Withholding Allowance

Each new employee must provide his or her employer with **Form W-4** [Employee's Federal Withholding Allowance Certificate] for the correct determination of federal withholding taxes. A withholding certificate remains in effect until the employer receives a new one except when exempt status is claimed by the employee. In this situation, a new certificate must be received by the employer by February 15 of each year an exemption from withholding is claimed by the employee. If the employee does not file a new certificate, the employer must deem the employee to be single with zero withholding allowances for the current year. A withholding certificate that replaces an existing one should result in the withholding tax being adjusted beginning no later than the start of the first payroll period ending on or after the 30th day from the date the new certificate was received.

Form W-4 is to be sent to the IRS for those employees employed at the end of the quarter who either:

- Claim more than 10 withholding allowances, or

- Claim complete exemption from withholding and whose wages normally exceed $200 per week.

The Certificates, and copies of written statements from employees to support the claims made on the certificates, should be sent with the employer's **Form 941** for the quarter. No other certificates are required to be filed unless requested in writing by the IRS.

Employer Tax Deposit Requirements

An employer's liability for taxes occurs when wages are paid, not when the payroll period ends. The frequency of tax deposits is determined by the amount of taxes owed. The deposits are made with preprinted forms provided by the IRS. The following summarizes the deposit rules for Social Security and federal withholding taxes:

Accumulated Liability	Frequency of Payment	Deposit Due Date
Less than $500 per quarter	None	No deposit is required. The withholdings may be paid with the tax return for the quarter.
Less than $50,000 in the four quarters of the lookback period	Monthly	Deposits must be made within 15 days after the end of the month.
More than $50,000 in the four quarters of the lookback period	Semiweekly	Deposits must be made on Wednesday and/or Friday, depending on which day of the week the not-for-profit organization makes payments. If the payment date is Wednesday through Friday, the deposit is due the following Wednesday; if the payment date is Saturday through Tuesday, the deposit is due the following Friday.
More than $100,000 on any day during the deposit period	Daily	Deposit is due on the next banking day after any day in which a liability is incurred.

Lookback period   The *lookback period* consists of four quarters beginning July 1 of the second preceding year and ending June 30 of the prior year. This period is applicable even if the entity did not report any taxes for any of the quarters. New employers' taxes for the lookback period are considered to be zero.

Backup withholding   An employer cannot combine backup withholding with other taxes on Form 941. Employers must treat backup withholding as a separate tax and deposit it separately following the same rules required for Social Security and federal withholding taxes. Form 941 no longer includes nonpayroll items. These are included on **Form 945** to be filed annually. Form 945 is used to deposit backup withholding and withholding from pensions, annuities, and gambling winnings.

Federal Tax Deposit Coupon

The IRS will send the taxpayer a deposit coupon booklet five to six weeks after an EIN has been requested and received by the organization. These preprinted coupons (Form 8109) should be used to make payments of employment taxes. If the organization has not yet received its initial supply of preprinted coupons, Form 8109-B may be used. The IRS has developed a tracking system that permits it to issue new coupon books to the employer automatically.

Separate coupons should be used for payroll taxes and nonpayroll taxes. The deposit coupons and a single payment, made payable to the depository, for all of the taxes to be deposited should be mailed or delivered to a financial institution that is qualified as a depository for federal taxes or to the Federal Reserve Bank (FRB) serving the applicable geographic area. Payments may be made in several different forms. Employers should check with their depositories or the applicable FRB branch to determine the form(s) they will accept. If the organization has not yet received an EIN, deposits must be made with the IRS Center rather than with a depository bank or FRB.

The IRS determines the timeliness of the deposits made by the date they are received by an authorized depository or FRB. Except for deposits of $20,000 or more for those taxpayers who are required to deposit taxes more than once a month, the IRS will consider a deposit timely if the organization can demonstrate that the deposit was mailed in the United States by the second day before the due date. When the due date falls on a Saturday, Sunday, or legal holiday, the next regular workday may be used for depositing taxes.

The organization/employer must maintain documentation of the payment because the IRS or the depository will not return a copy of the deposit coupon. This documentation becomes important when penalties for failure to deposit taxes when due are asserted against the organization. The penalty ranges from two percent to 15 percent depending on the lateness of the payment.

EMPLOYER TAX RETURN OBLIGATIONS—FEDERAL

Monthly Returns

Form 941-M [Employer's Monthly Federal Tax Return] Form 941-M is required from employers upon written notification from the IRS District Director. These forms generally are required from employers who have not complied with the requirements for filing returns or the payment/deposit of taxes reported on quarterly returns. Amounts reported on the twelve monthly reports for the year must agree with **Form W-3**, which reports the total of all W-2 Forms issued by the employer and filed with Social Security Administration.

Due dates   Form 941-M is due by the 15th day of the month following the reporting period.

Penalties   The penalty for failure to file the form when due is five percent of the unpaid tax for each month or part of a month that the form is late, up to a maximum of 25 percent of the unpaid tax.

Penalties also may be imposed for failure to file a complete and correct form when due. These penalties are denominated in dollar amounts rather than as a percentage of the unpaid tax:

- Fifteen dollars for each information form if the correct information is filed within 30 days after the due date, with a maximum penalty of $75,000 per year
- Thirty dollars for each information form if the correct information is filed more than 30 days after the due date but by August 1, with a maximum penalty of $150,000 per year
- Fifty dollars for each information form that is not filed at all or is not filed correctly by August 1, with a maximum penalty of $250,000 per year

Penalties also may be imposed for intentional disregard of the filing requirements ($100 minimum penalty and no maximum penalty for each information return) or for not paying tax when due ($\frac{1}{2}$ of 1 percent of the unpaid tax, for each month or part of a month the tax is unpaid, up to a maximum of 25 percent).

Quarterly Returns

Form 941 [Employer's Quarterly Federal Tax Return]   Form 941 is required from employers who withhold income tax, Social Security taxes, or both, except for:

- Seasonal employers for quarters when they regularly have no tax liability because they paid no wages
- Employers in certain jurisdictions
- Agricultural employers reporting Social Security and withheld income tax
- Employers who file Form 941-M monthly

Amounts reported on the four quarterly reports for the year must agree with Form W-3, the sum of all the employer's Forms W-2, which is filed with the Social Security Administration.

Due dates   A return is due for the first quarter in which income tax or Social Security taxes are required to be withheld. They are due regularly after that, as follows:

Quarter	Ending	Due Date
January–March	March 31	April 30
April–June	June 30	July 31
July–September	September 30	October 31
October–December	December 31	January 31

The IRS permits a 10-day grace period beyond these dates if all quarterly taxes have been deposited when due.

Organizations that have a tax liability for payroll items of $100,000 or more on any day, or are required to file on a semiweekly basis, must file **Schedule B** [Employer's Record of Federal Tax Liability] along with Form 941 and deposit the withheld taxes by the next banking day.

> **Note:** When a business reorganization or termination occurs, both the former employer and the new employer are required to file a return in the quarter in which the change occurs. Each organization reports only the wages applicable to the period for which it was the employer.

Penalties   A penalty may be imposed for failure to file the form when due. The penalty is five percent of the unpaid tax for each month or part of a month that the form is late, up to a maximum of 25 percent of the unpaid tax. There also are penalties for failure to file a complete and correct form when due. These penalties are denominated in dollar amounts rather than as a percentage of the unpaid tax:

- Fifteen dollars for each information form if the correct information is filed within 30 days after the due date, with a maximum penalty of $75,000 per year

- Thirty dollars for each information form if the correct information is filed more than 30 days after the due date but by August 1, with a maximum penalty of $150,000 per year

- Fifty dollars for each information form that is not filed at all or is not filed correctly by August 1, with a maximum penalty of $250,000 per year

Penalties also may be imposed for intentional disregard of the filing requirements ($100 minimum penalty and no maximum penalty for each information return) or for not paying tax when due (½ of 1 percent of the unpaid tax, for each month or part of a month the tax is unpaid, up to a maximum of 25 percent).

Annual Returns

Federal backup withholding   Backup withholding is required of organizations that pay reportable interest, dividends, or make miscellaneous payments if:

- The payee does not furnish the organization with a taxpayer identification number; or
- The organization is informed by the IRS or a broker that the taxpayer identification number is incorrect.

Organizations that are withholding agents file **Form 945** [Annual Return of Withheld Federal Income Tax] annually to report their backup withholding liability as well as taxes withheld from pensions, annuities, and certain gambling winnings. **Form 945-A** [Annual Record of Federal Tax Liability] should be attached to the Form 945 if the withholding agent is a semiweekly depositor or has accumulated a $100,000 withholding tax liability on any one day. However, the tax withheld should be deposited throughout the year following the same rules used for depositing Social Security and federal income taxes withheld.

Due dates   The due date for Form 945 is January 31; however, if all taxes have been paid on time, there is a 10-day grace period for filing the return.

Penalties   The penalty for failure to file the form when due is five percent of the unpaid tax for each month or part of a month that the form is late, up to a maximum of 25 percent of the unpaid tax. There also are penalties for failure to file a complete and correct form when due. These penalties are denominated in dollar amounts rather than as a percentage of the unpaid tax:

- Fifteen dollars for each information form if the correct information is filed within 30 days after the due date, with a maximum penalty of $75,000 per year
- Thirty dollars for each information form if the correct information is filed more than 30 days after the due date but by August 1, with a maximum penalty of $150,000 per year

- Fifty dollars for each information form that is not filed at all or is not filed correctly by August 1, with a maximum penalty of $250,000 per year

Penalties also may be imposed for intentional disregard of the filing requirements ($100 minimum penalty and no maximum penalty for each information return) or for not paying tax when due ($\frac{1}{2}$ of one percent of the unpaid tax, for each month or part of a month the tax is unpaid, up to a maximum of 25 percent).

Federal unemployment tax return   Organizations are required to file **Form 940** [Employer's Annual Federal Unemployment Tax Return] if they either pay wages of $1,500 or more in any calendar quarter or had one or more employees for some part of a day in any 20 different weeks and the employer is other than a household or agricultural employer during the current and prior years. However, tax-exempt organizations described specifically in IRC Section 501(c)(3) are not required to file.

Household employers are required to file if cash wages of $1,000 or more are paid in any calendar quarter in the current or prior years for household work in a private, local college club, or a chapter of a college fraternity or sorority.

Federal unemployment tax (FUTA) is a rate applied to the first wages paid during the calendar year to each employee. For 1995, for example, the base wages and rate were $7,000 and 6.2 percent, respectively. The organization is allowed a partial credit against the tax based on its state unemployment insurance liability.

Employers who timely pay all unemployment contributions to only one state and do not pay taxable FUTA wages that are exempt from state unemployment may qualify to file a simplified version of the FUTA return, **Form 940-EZ.**

When the organization's contributions to a certified state unemployment fund are paid by the due date of the federal return, a credit may be taken against the FUTA liability. Payments to the state unemployment fund do not qualify for the credit it they have been deducted or are deductible from employees' pay. In 1995, the credit could not exceed 5.4 percent of taxable wages.

Tax deposit requirements   The tax deposit requirements related to FUTA are as follows:

Accumulated Liability	Frequency of Payment	Deposit Due Date
Less than $50	Annual	Mail with Form 940 by January 31 of the following year.
$50 or more	Quarterly	End of the following month after each quarter.

If the amount due at the end of each quarter is less than $100, no deposit is required. The amount due should then be recomputed at the end of each succeeding quarter to determine if the cumulative liability is greater than $100. If it exceeds $100, a deposit must be made.

Due dates   The due date for Form 940 is January 31; however, if all taxes have been paid on time, there is a 10-day grace period for filing the return.

Penalties   The penalty for failure to file the form when due is five percent of the unpaid tax for each month or part of a month that the form is late, up to a maximum of 25 percent of the unpaid tax. There also are penalties for failure to file a complete and correct form when due. These penalties are denominated in dollar amounts rather than as a percentage of the unpaid tax:

- Fifteen dollars for each information form if the correct information is filed within 30 days after the due date, with a maximum penalty of $75,000 per year
- Thirty dollars for each information form if the correct information is filed more than 30 days after the due date but by August 1, with a maximum penalty of $150,000 per year
- Fifty dollars for each information form that is not filed at all or is not filed correctly by August 1, with a maximum penalty of $250,000 per year

Penalties also may be imposed for intentional disregard of the filing requirements ($100 minimum penalty and no maximum penalty for each information return) or for not paying tax when due ($\frac{1}{2}$ of 1 percent of the unpaid tax, for each month or part of a month the tax is unpaid, up to a maximum of 25 percent).

Supporting statement to correct information   Form 941c [Supporting Statement to Correct Information] is used to adjust income and Social Security tax information reported on any of the aforementioned forms (except Form 940). The correction form should be attached to the return for which an adjustment is being claimed, and corrections for more than one period may be made on a single statement. However, if different types of tax returns are being corrected, a separate statement should be filed for each type. Similarly, a separate return should be filed if reporting of both wages and tips is being corrected.

Form W-2c [Statement of Corrected Income and Tax Amounts] should be filed when corrections are made to the Social Security tax.

To request a refund of an overpayment, other than employee withholdings, the organization should file **Form 843** [Claim for

Refund and Request for Abatement]. This form also may be used to request an abatement of an overassessment of employee taxes, interest, and/or penalties.

Annual wage and tax statement   Form W-2 [Annual Wage and Tax Statement], which should be received by employees for a calendar year by January 31 of the following year, is used by organizations to report a variety of information including:

- All wages
- Tips
- Other compensation
- Federal and Social Security tax withheld
- Social Security wages
- Deferred compensation
- Advanced earned income credits

Other compensation, including certain taxable fringe benefits, can be included in gross income but is not subject to withholding tax. The following are examples of taxable fringe benefits:

- Employer-provided educational assistance in excess of a certain amount ($5,250 in 1994) is included in employee's income, unless the purpose is to maintain or improve skills required in the employee's current position.
- Employer-provided parking and commutation cost in excess of monthly floors (e.g., $155 and $60 for 1994, respectively) is includible.
- Amounts of scholarships or grants are generally not taxable income to an employee who is a candidate for a degree. However, if the individual is not a candidate for a degree, up to $300 per month, for up to 36 months, can be excluded from taxable income (these figures are subject to change). Amounts received by an individual for teaching, research, or other services required as a condition for receiving the scholarship or fellowship are not excludable.
- Employer-provided automobiles used strictly for the organization, or if personal use is de minimis, are not taxable income for the employee. The value of any significant personal use will be added to the employee's income.
- Parsonage allowance, the rental allowance paid or the rental value of a home provided to members of the clergy, is excludable from taxable income and need not be reported on a W-2. However, no exclusion will be allowed for allowances paid to a

member of the clergy who performs services for an employer that is not a religious organization.

- A statement of benefits should be given to each recipient of supplemental unemployment compensation benefits or third-party sick pay.

Due dates   Copy A of each Form W-2 is due at the Social Security Administration by the last day of February of the following year. These copies and copies of **Form 1099-R** [Distributions from Pensions, Annuities, Retirement or Profit-Sharing Plans, IRAs, Insurance Contracts, etc.] are filed by the end of February with the summary transmittal **Form W-3** [Transmittal of Wage and Tax Statement]. Extensions of time to file this form may be requested from the IRS on **Form 8809**. The amounts reported on the quarterly returns for payroll taxes withheld must agree with the transmittal. If an organization has 250 or more forms, then the information must be filed on magnetic media.

Penalties   The penalty for each failure to furnish a payee statement by the required date is $50, up to a maximum of $100,000 per calendar year. If the organization intentionally disregards the return filing, providing of payee statements, and correct information reporting requirements, a penalty of at least $100 per document may be imposed. In addition, there may be penalties for failure to file an information return or for filing with incorrect information:

- Fifteen dollars for each information form if the correct information is filed within 30 days after the due date, with a maximum penalty of $75,000 per year
- Thirty dollars for each information form if the correct information is filed more than 30 days after the due date but by August 1, with a maximum penalty of $150,000 per year
- Fifty dollars for each information form that is not filed at all or is not filed correctly by August 1, with a maximum penalty of $250,000 per year

Corrections   When Forms W-2 require correction, the organization files **Form W-2c** [Statement of Corrected Information and Tax Amounts], along with **Form W-3c** [Transmittal of Corrected Income and Tax Statement], with the Social Security Administration office where the original returns were sent.

Annual summary and transmittal of information returns   The IRS expects organizations to report certain payments on **Forms 1098, 1099, 5498**, and **W-2G**. For each type of form filed with the IRS, the organization should use **Form 1096** [Annual Summary and Transmittal of U.S. Information Returns].

Due dates Except for the transmittal accompanying Forms 5498, Form 1096 must be filed by February 28 of the following year. The Form 5498 transmittal is due May 31 of the following year.

Penalties Penalties are associated with each of the forms applicable to Form 1096.

Withholding certificate for pension and annuities Recipients of payments from annuity, pension, and certain other deferred compensation plans are required to file **Form W-4P** [Withholding Certificate for Pension or Annuity Payments] with the payers to inform them whether to withhold income tax and in what amount. The amount to be withheld will depend on whether the payment is periodic or nonperiodic.

A *periodic payment* is one that is included in income for tax purposes and is paid in installments at regular intervals over a period of more than one full year. Unless the recipient files Form W-4P, tax must be withheld on periodic payments as if the recipient were claiming three withholding allowances.

A taxable lump-sum distribution from a qualified pension or annuity plan is termed an "eligible rollover distribution." From such distributions, tax will be withheld at a flat rate of 20 percent unless the entire distribution is paid to an eligible retirement plan. The recipient cannot claim an exemption from the 20 percent withholding, unless the distribution is directly rolled over to an eligible plan or the distribution check is made out directly to an eligible plan.

The recipient should prepare and file Form W-4P with the payer as soon as possible. The payer, in turn, sends copies of the Form W-4P to the IRS.

Organizations that pay pension, annuity, or retirement amounts during the year must complete an annual statement, **Form 1099-R** [Distributions from Pensions, Annuities, Retirement or Profit-Sharing Plans, IRAs, Insurance Contracts, etc.]. Distributions from nonqualified plans are reported on Form W-2.

The payer must obtain from the recipient the correct taxpayer identification number and the payee's **Form W-9** to identify the appropriate amount of withholding. If Form W-9 is not returned to the organization within 60 days after the payer has provided the form to the recipient, the payments will be subject to backup withholding at a flat rate of 31 percent.

Due dates Generally, the organization should provide recipients of payments with Form 1099-R by January 31 of the following year, although the recipient may be furnished with the form any time after the final payment is made. Copy A of each Form 1099-R should be received by the IRS by February 28 of the following year accompanied by the transmittal Form 1096.

Penalties   For each form not issued when required, the IRS extracts a penalty of $25, with a maximum penalty of $15,000 per calendar year. For each IRA information report not issued when required, the penalty is $50. When the organization intentionally disregards the requirement for return filing, providing payee statements, and correct information reporting, the penalty could be at least $100 per document.

Prizes, awards, or other gambling winnings   Organizations that sponsor events that provide prizes to recipients (e.g., bingo, keno, raffles, sweepstakes, and drawings) are required to report winnings in certain circumstances. The threshold is $600 or more for lotteries, raffles, sweepstakes, and drawings; $1,200 for bingo; and $1,500 for keno. Winnings from horse racing, dog racing, or jai alai must be reported if the amount won is $1,200 or more and is at least 300 times the amount wagered.

The sponsor organization is required to withhold 28 percent of all winnings from any wagering transactions exceeding $5,000 (less the amount of the wager), if the amount of the proceeds is at least 300 times the amount of the wager. There is no withholding requirement for winnings from bingo, keno, or slot machines, or if no payment was required to enter a raffle or game of chance.

Noncash prizes are reported at their fair market value. The withholding requirements could be satisfied by the winner providing the organization with a check in the amount of the required withholding, or the organization must pay the withholding amount and gross-up the amount reported to reflect the payment of income taxes on the winner's behalf.

The reporting is done on **Form W-2G** [Certain Gambling Winnings]. The recipient signs this form to certify that no other person is entitled to any part of the winnings. The form also is used to furnish the payer the recipient's name, address, and tax identification number.

Form 5754 [Statement by Person(s) Receiving Gambling Winnings] is provided to the payer by the person to whom the winnings are paid when the individual receives the money for someone else, or as a member of group of winners on the same ticket. The form, signed by the person receiving the winnings only if tax is withheld, indicates the name, address, and taxpayer identification number of all other winners to whom the winnings are taxable.

Due dates   Form W2-G should be filed with Form 1096 by February 28 of the following year and provided to the recipient by January 31 of the following year. Form 5754 is not sent to the IRS.

Penalties   A $50 penalty per failure may be imposed on the payer for failure to furnish a correct statement by the required date or failure to sign the return or claim. A $50 penalty may be imposed on the payee for failure to furnish identification numbers. The maximum penalty is $100,000 per calendar year.

In addition, there may be penalties for failure to file correct information returns:

- Fifteen dollars for each information form if the correct information is filed within 30 days after the due date, with a maximum penalty of $75,000 per year
- Thirty dollars for each information form if the correct information is filed more than 30 days after the due date but by August 1, with a maximum penalty of $150,000 per year
- Fifty dollars for each information form that is not filed at all or is not filed correctly by August 1, with a maximum penalty of $250,000 per year

Recipients of miscellaneous income   Form **1099-MISC** [Statement for Recipients of Miscellaneous Income] must be completed for every person to whom the following types of payments are made:

- At least $600 in fees, commissions, prizes, and awards for services rendered, or other forms of compensation for services rendered for a trade or business by an individual who is not an employee
- Deferred compensation payments to former employees made in years subsequent to employment
- At least $10 in gross royalties payments before reduction for severance and other taxes that may have been withheld and paid
- At least $600 in wages or other compensation paid to an estate or beneficiary of a deceased
- Directors' fees in the year paid even though they may be subject to self-employment Social Security tax in the prior year because they were earned in that prior year
- At least $600 in payments, in the course of trade or business, to each provider of medical or health care services, including payments made by medical and health care insurers under health, accident, and sickness insurance programs
- Payments for which federal income tax is withheld under the backup withholding rules regardless of the amount of the payment
- At least $600 in prizes and awards that are not for services rendered
- At least $600 in rents paid to a reportable person

Reimbursement of expenses to an independent contractor must be included as reportable payments on Form 1099-MISC if the independent contractor is not required to make an accounting to the service recipient. If there is a proper accounting for the expenses, the reimbursement is not reported and is not taken into account in determining the $600 threshold.

As with other payments, the payer must obtain a proper taxpayer identification number or the payment will be subject to backup withholding at a flat rate of 31 percent.

Due dates   Form 1099-MISC should be filed with transmittal Form 1096 by February 28 of the following year. The form should be sent to the recipient by January 31 of the following year. A 30-day extension of time to file may be requested by use of Form 8809.

Penalties   A $50 penalty per failure may be imposed on the payer for failure to furnish a correct statement by the required date or failure to sign the return or claim. A $50 penalty may be imposed on the payee for failure to furnish identification numbers. The maximum penalty is $100,000 per calendar year.

In addition, penalties for failure to file correct information returns may be imposed, as follows:

- Fifteen dollars for each information form if the correct information is filed within 30 days after the due date, with a maximum penalty of $75,000 per year

- Thirty dollars for each information form if the correct information is filed more than 30 days after the due date but by August 1, with a maximum penalty of $150,000 per year

- Fifty dollars for each information form that is not filed at all or is not filed correctly by August 1, with a maximum penalty of $250,000 per year

Foreign person's income subject to withholding   Certain types of nonbusiness income paid to nonresident aliens, foreign partnerships, and foreign corporations are subject to a withholding tax at the flat rate of 30 percent. This rate may be reduced if a treaty is applicable. Generally, the following fixed or determinable periodic income is subject to the withholding tax:

- Interest

- Dividends

- Rents

- Royalties

- Salaries

- Wages

- Premiums

- Annuities

- Other gains

- Profits

- Income unless specifically exempt

To claim a treaty exemption, **Form 1001** [Ownership, Exemption, or Reduced Rate Certificate] must be filed with the withholding agent. The withholding agent is the payer. The payer may be an individual, trust, estate, partnership, corporation, government agency, association, or tax-exempt foundation.

The payers of U.S.-source income are required to withhold and deduct tax from such income at the rate in effect when payment is made and to report the amount withheld on **Form 1042S** [Foreign Person's U.S.-Source Income Subject to Withholding].

Withholding is *not* required for the following types of income:

- Income effectively connected with a U.S. trade or business other than compensation received for personal services, if the recipient has filed the annual **Form 4224** [Exemption from Withholding of Tax on Income Effectively Connected with the Conduct of a Trade or Business in the United States]

- Portfolio interest as defined

- Interest on bank deposits

- Income of foreign governments

The transmittal form for Copy A of Form 1042S is **Form 1042** [Annual Withholding Tax Return for U.S.-Source Income of Foreign Persons], which must be filed by every U.S. withholding agent who receives, controls, has custody of, disposes of, or pays a fixed or determinable annual or periodic income.

Due dates The due date for filing this form is no later than March 15 of the following year. An extension of time to file may be requested on **Form 2758** [Application for Extension of Time to File Certain Excise, Income, Information, and Other Returns].

Tax deposit coupons The withholding agent must deposit the tax withheld with an authorized financial institution or FRB using a federal tax deposit coupon (Form 8109). The requirements are:

Accumulated Liability	Frequency of Payment	Due Date
Less than $200	Annually	Pay with Form 1042 or deposit withholding by March 15 of the following year.
More than $200 but less than $2,000	Monthly	Deposit the taxes by the 15th day of the following month.
More than $2,000	Quarter –Monthly	Deposit the taxes within three banking days after the quarter-monthly period. A quarter-monthly period ends on the 7th, 15th, 22nd, and last day of the month.

Penalties   A penalty may be imposed for failure to furnish a Form 1042S to the payee by the required date. The penalty is equal to $50 per failure, with a maximum penalty of $100,000 per calendar year. Penalties may be imposed for failure to file a correct and complete Form 1042S, as follows:

- Fifteen dollars for each information form if the correct information is filed within 30 days after the due date, with a maximum penalty of $75,000 per year

- Thirty dollars for each information form if the correct information is filed more than 30 days after the due date but by August 1, with a maximum penalty of $150,000 per year

- Fifty dollars for each information form that is not filed at all or is not filed correctly by August 1, with a maximum penalty of $250,000 per year

Finally, the penalty for not filing Form 1042 when due, including extensions, is usually five percent of the unpaid tax for each month or part of a month the return is late, up to a maximum of 25 percent of the unpaid tax. The penalty for failure to deposit tax when due is usually ½ of 1 percent of the unpaid tax, for each month or part of a month the tax is unpaid, up to a maximum of 25 percent of the unpaid tax.

Exclusion of wages for services outside the United States   **Form 673** [Statement for Claiming Benefits Provided by Section 911 of the

Internal Revenue Code], completed and furnished by a U.S. citizen or resident, permits employers to exclude from withholding all or part of the wages paid for services performed outside the country. The election applies to the taxable year for which it was made, and to all subsequent years, until revoked by the taxpayer.

MISCELLANEOUS FILINGS

Quid Pro Quo Contributions

Charitable organizations are subject to a penalty if they fail to inform donors that quid pro quo contributions in excess of $75 are deductible only to the extent that the contributions exceed the value of goods or services provided by the organization. Solicitations or receipts issued by the organization must contain a written statement that:

- Informs the donor that the tax deductible amount of the contribution is limited to the excess of the amount contributed by the donor over the value of the goods or services provided by the organization, and

- Provides the donor with a good-faith estimate of the value of the goods or services furnished to the donor by the organization.

If the cost of the benefits provided to the donor is nominal, the statements in the solicitation are not required. Examples of proper language follow.

Special Events
Tickets are $100 per person. Forty dollars is the estimated value of the event. Sixty dollars of each ticket is tax deductible as a charitable contribution.

Auctions (Receipts Issued to Winning Bidders)
The estimated fair market value of this item is the price you paid for it. Therefore, none of your payment is tax deductible as a charitable contribution.

Admissions (When No Payment Is Required, but a Donation Is Suggested)

While there is no charge for admission, we request each visitor to make a tax deductible contribution of $ [X].

Raffle Tickets

Under federal law, the cost of this ticket is not tax deductible as a charitable contribution.

Memberships

Individual $75. Includes free admission, two invitations to the Spring Party, and a subscription to our magazine. Estimated value: $35.

Supporter $200. Includes free admission for two, four invitations to the Spring Party, a subscription to our magazine, and the Spring Catalog. Estimated value: $90.

Memberships are tax deductible as a charitable contribution to the extent your payment exceeds the estimated value.

Other Benefits (When the Aggregate Value of All Benefits Provided Is the Lesser of Two Percent of the Contribution Amount or $75 [for 1995], or Only Token Items Bearing an Organization's Name or Logo Costing Less Than $7.20 [for 1999] Are Provided)

Under IRS guidelines, the estimated value of [mention benefits received] is insubstantial; therefore, the full amount of your contribution is tax deductible.

Other Benefits (When More than Token Benefits Are Provided)

The estimated value of [mention benefits] is $10. Your contribution in excess of $10 is tax deductible as a charitable contribution.

Penalties   Penalties of $10 per contribution, $5,000 per particular fund-raising event or mailing, will be imposed on charities that fail to make the required disclosure, unless due to reasonable cause.

Substantiation Requirements for Gifts

Beginning in 1994, the IRS requires donors wishing to claim charitable tax deductions for contributions of $250 or more to obtain written substantiation from the donee organization prior to the due date of the donor's return. For this purpose, the written substantiation must acknowledge:

- The amount of cash contributed or a description of the property contributed;

- Whether the charity provided any goods or services in consideration for the contribution;

- The goods and/or services provided; and

- The value of the goods and services provided.

There are exceptions to this general rule for religious organizations that provide only intangible religious benefits that are not sold in commercial transactions, such as admission to religious ceremonies. The organizations are not required to value such benefits, but still must state that such benefits have been provided to the donor.

Also, if a charitable organization reports all of the information required for substantiation to the IRS, then the donor is not required to obtain substantiation from the charity.

Not-for-profit organizations may use the following letter format to fulfill the gift substantiation requirements.

Dear Mr. or Ms. Generous Contributor:

Thank you for your recent contribution of $250 in cash. [If property is contributed, include a description of the property. Example: 50 shares of ABC, Inc. Stock.]

To support your tax deductible contribution, the IRS requires the following information:

Option 1: No benefits were provided to you by [*name of organization*] in return for your contribution.

Option 2: No benefits were provided to you in return for your contribution other than intangible religious benefits.

Option 3: Membership benefits conferred upon you in return for your contribution include unlimited admission to the [*name of charity*], two invitations to our annual Spring Party, and a subscription to our quarterly magazine. The value of these benefits is $60.

Please retain this letter for your tax records, since it fulfills the substantiation requirements that must be met to deduct your contribution on your tax return.

Penalties   Organizations that knowingly provide false written substantiation to donors could be subject to penalties for aiding and abetting an understatement of tax liability.

Noncash Charitable Contributions

Form 8283 [Noncash Charitable Contributions] is used by taxpayers to disclose certain information about charitable deductions of $500 or more in noncash items (other than publicly traded securities) to charitable organizations. Form 8283, and any necessary documents (see below), should be attached to the tax return on which the deduction for the charitable contribution was reported. If the contribution is for less than $5,000, the following information is required:

- Name and address of donee organization
- Description of donated property
- Date of the contribution
- Date and method acquired by the donor
- Donor's cost or adjusted basis
- Fair market value of the donated property
- Method used to determine the fair market value

Contribution deductions greater than $5,000 also must be accompanied by a brief summary of the overall physical condition at the time of the gift. There may be a requirement for a written appraisal by a qualified appraiser. If so, the appraiser is required to sign the Form 8283. Finally, for a deduction of a work of art worth $20,000 or more, a complete copy of the signed appraisal must be attached. Failure to file a properly completed Form 8283 could result in the entire deduction being disallowed.

Sale, Exchange, or Other Disposition of Donated Property

Organizations that sell, exchange, or otherwise dispose of charitable deduction property with a value exceeding $500 within two years after the date it received the property are required to report certain information on **Form 8282** [Donee Information Return]. This reporting requirement exists even if the organization transfers the property to a successor organization. The original donee is required to provide the successor donee the following information upon the transfer of the property:

1. The organization's name, address, and employer identification number;

2. A copy of the appraisal summary (Form 8283 received from the donor); and

3. A copy of the required filing made at the time of the transfer.

The IRS provides for strict timing of the reporting. The first two items must be furnished within 15 days after the latest of:

- The date the property was transferred;

- The date the appraisal summary was signed; or

- If the organization is a successor donee, the date a copy of the appraisal summary was received from the previous donee.

The successor donee also must file the required information when it disposes of or transfers the charitable deduction property, and a copy of the required form must be furnished to the original donor. This reporting is not required for property that is used for a charitable purpose (e.g., medical supplies distributed by a disaster relief organization).

Due dates   Form 8282 must be filed with the IRS Service Center, Cincinnati, Ohio, 45944, within 125 days after the date of the disposition.

Penalties   A $50 penalty will be assessed for failure to file Form 8282 by the due date, failure to include all required information, or failure to include correct information.

Issuers of Tax-Exempt Bonds

Organizations that issue tax-exempt bonds are required to file certain information returns for IRS purposes.

Generally, interest income earned on an arbitrage bond is not exempt from tax unless the bond issuer rebates to the United States the arbitrage profits that are earned from investing the bond proceeds in higher yielding nonpurpose investments. Proceeds that are to be used to finance construction expenditures are excepted from the filing requirements if the issuer elects to pay a penalty equal to

1½ percent of the difference between the unexpended proceeds and the required expenditure amount. This election must be made before the bonds are issued.

The exception applies when bond issuers anticipate completing construction within two years, and intend to either spend or designate a specific portion of the proceeds for that purpose. Issuers must also spend 10 percent of an issue within six months of issuance, 45 percent by the end of the first year, 75 percent within 18 months, 95 percent within two years, and 100 percent within three years. An additional penalty of three percent must be paid to terminate the election to pay the penalty in lieu of the arbitrage rate.

Form 8038 [Information Return for Tax-Exempt Private Activity Bond Issues] is filed by all issuers of qualified IRC Section 501(c)(3) bonds issued after December 31, 1986. The form is to be filed with the Internal Revenue Service Center, Philadelphia, Pennsylvania, 19225, by the 15th day of the second calendar month after the close of the calendar quarter during which the bond was issued.

Form 8038-T [Arbitrage Rebate and Penalty in Lieu of Arbitrage Rebate] is used to pay the arbitrage rebate or penalty in lieu of the arbitrage rebate to the United States. The Form also is used to give notice and pay the penalty associated with the termination of the election to pay a penalty in lieu of the arbitrage rebate. The arbitrage rebate installments are due 60 days after the end of every fifth bond year during the term of issue. The installments must be 90 percent of the rebatable arbitrage as of the computation date. The payment for the penalty in lieu of arbitrage is due no later than 90 days after the end of each six-month period relating to the penalty. The three percent penalty to terminate the election to pay a penalty in lieu of arbitrage rebate must be paid no later than 90 days after the date of the termination election.

Form 8038-G [Information Return for Tax-Exempt Governmental Obligations] must be filed for each issue of tax-exempt governmental obligations issued after December 31, 1986, if the price of the issue is $100,000 or more. The form is used to provide certain information to the IRS about these bonds, such as the type of issue, descriptions of the obligations, and the uses of the proceeds. It is to be filed with the Internal Revenue Service Center, Philadelphia, Pennsylvania, 19225, by the 15th day of the second calendar month after the close of the calendar quarter during which the bond was issued.

Form 8038-GC [Information Return for Small Tax-Exempt Governmental Bond Issues, Leases, and Installment Sales] must be filed for each issue of tax-exempt governmental obligations if the price of the issue is less than $100,000. The form is used to provide certain information to the IRS about the obligations, such as descriptions of the obligations, and it must be filed with the Internal Revenue Service Center, Philadelphia, Pennsylvania, 19225, by the 15th day of the second calendar month after the close of the calendar quarter during which the bond was issued.

Due dates An extension of time in which to file Forms 8038, 8038-G, and 8038-GC can be obtained by indicating on the top of the late form, "This Statement is Submitted in Accordance with Revenue Procedure 88-10," and attaching a letter explaining why the form was not filed on time. The extension will not be granted in cases of willful neglect.

Penalties Failure to pay the proper amount of penalties on Form 8038-T may cause the bond connected with the filing to be treated as non–tax-exempt, retroactive to the issue date. If the failure is not due to willful neglect, it will be treated as if it had never occurred if, in addition to paying the proper penalty, the issuer pays a penalty of 50 percent of the amount not paid on time, plus interest.

Lobbying Disclosure and Reporting

Organizations exempt from tax, other than IRC Section 501(c)(3) organizations, must report to the IRS the total amount of lobbying expenses. The portion of dues attributable to such expenses must be disclosed to members of such organizations. Members will not be allowed a business deduction for the portion of their dues attributable to the following activities of their organizations:

- *Influencing legislation (other than local legislation)*—Any attempt to influence the introduction, amendment, enactment, defeat, or repeal of acts, bills, or resolutions by the Congress, state legislatures, or by the public in a referendum, voter initiative, constitutional amendment, or similar procedure is considered influencing legislation. Communications with any member or employee of a state or federal legislative body also are included in "influencing legislation"; however, attempts to influence any local council or governing body are excluded.

- *Grass roots lobbying*—Any attempt to influence the general public (including an organization's own members) with respect to legislation or elections is considered grass roots lobbying.

- *Political activities*—Participation in or intervention in any campaign on behalf of (or in opposition to) a candidate for public office is a political activity

- *Certain executive branch communications*—Any direct communications with the President, Vice President, Cabinet members or other White House employees in an attempt to influence the official actions or positions of such officials are considered executive branch communications.

If an organization's in-house expenditures for such activities during a taxable year do not exceed $2,000, the organization would not be required to disclose such activities on its dues statements. These "in-house" expenditures do not include overhead costs allocated to such activities, payments to others engaged in lobbying on behalf of the taxpayer, or dues and assessments allocable to such activities. Even if the organization's "in-house" expenses fall within the de minimis exception, amounts paid to lobbyists and dues paid to organizations engaged in lobbying will not be deductible.

A **proposed** Revenue Procedure automatically excepts from the reporting requirements all organizations exempt from tax under Section 501(a) other than Section 501(c)(4) social welfare organizations, Section 501(c)(5) agricultural or horticultural organizations, and Section 502(c)(6) organizations. Relief may be available to organizations not automatically excepted if certain requirements are met or if a private letter ruling is requested.

In addition, the **proposed** Revenue Procedure provides automatic relief to local associations of employees exempt under Section 501(c)(4), as well as labor unions exempt under Section 501(c)(5). Only Section 501(c)(6) organizations, Section 501(c)(4) social welfare organizations, and Section 501(c)(5) agricultural and horticultural organizations do not qualify for automatic exemption from the reporting and notice requirements. Section 501(c)(4) social welfare and 501(c)(5) agricultural and horticultural organizations are relieved of the reporting requirements if:

- The largest amount of dues and assessments paid by any member is $50 or less; or

- More than 90 percent of their members are Section 501(c)(3) organizations.

Relief is still available if an organization has some members who pay more than $50 annually, as long as the total payments by these members are less than 10 percent of the total dues and assessments paid by all members. Section 501(c)(6) organizations are relieved of the reporting requirements if more than 90 percent of their members are Section 501(c)(3) organizations. Organizations that intend to rely on the second exception should ensure that more than 90 percent of their members are recognized by the IRS as tax-exempt under Section 501(c)(3) by making certain their members are listed in the current publication of 501(c)(3) organizations or have valid documentation supporting their Section 501(c)(3) status.

A private letter ruling must be requested by a Section 501(c)(4) social welfare organization, a Section 501(c)(5) agricultural or horticultural organization, or a Section 501(c)(6) organization that does not meet any of the requirements outlined above to obtain relief. Substantially all of the organization's dues or similar amounts paid by its members must not be deductible for this exception to apply. To receive a favorable ruling from the IRS, an organization must provide evidence that at least 90 percent of its dues and assessments are not deductible to its members without regard to Section 162(e).

Proposed regulations issued to allow organizations to use any reasonable method for allocating costs of influencing legislation and communications with certain executive branch employees do not apply to the allocation of the costs of grass roots lobbying or political activities. The **proposed** regulations outline three specific methods that may be used to allocate lobbying activity costs:

1. Ratio method
2. Gross-up method
3. Section 263A inventory-capitalization method

Organizations that do not incur labor costs for persons engaged in lobbying cannot use the ratio method or the gross-up method.

Penalties   If an organization fails to provide its members with notices, or if its actual lobbying expenditures exceed the amount of estimated expenditures included in its notice to members, a proxy tax equal to the highest corporate income tax rate will be imposed on undisclosed or underreported amounts. The IRS may waive the tax if the organization agrees to adjust its estimates for the following year to correct the underreported amount. The IRS also will waive the tax if an organization can show that substantially all (90 percent) of the dues and assessments paid by members are not deductible, regardless of the IRC Section 162(e) disallowance. For example, an organization that receives 90 percent of its dues from tax-exempt organizations, or from individuals subject to the two percent floor on miscellaneous itemized deductions (which prevents them from deducting the dues), probably would be granted a waiver of the disclosure requirements.

The proxy tax is also applicable to organizations that fail to report or underreport, on Form 9900, the total amount of prohibited expenditures and the total amount of dues and assessments allocable to such expenditures. The tax can be waived if substantially all of the organization's dues are otherwise nondeductible. The proxy tax may be imposed *in addition to* any other penalties that may apply.

The penalty for filing a Form 990 with incorrect or incomplete information is $10 per day for each day the return remains incorrect or incomplete, up to a maximum of $5,000 or five percent of gross receipts.

INTERMEDIATE SANCTIONS

The Taxpayer Bill of Rights 2, which was signed into law on July 30, 1996, extended the private inurement prohibition of Internal Revenue Code section 501(c)(3) to nonprofit organizations described in section 501(c)(4). The law also provided for intermediate sanctions that may be imposed when tax-exempt organizations described in 501(c)(3) or (c)(4) engage in transactions with certain insiders that result in private inurement. These changes seek to ensure that the advantages of tax-exempt status ultimately benefit the community rather than private individuals inside these public charities and social welfare organizations.

The intermediate sanctions under this law impose a two-tiered excise tax when a section 501(c)(3) or 501(c)(4) organization engages in an "excess benefit transaction." The law imposes these excise taxes on "disqualified persons" who receive the excess benefit and on organization managers who knowingly, willfully, and without reasonable cause participate in the transaction. The intermediate sanctions are imposed directly on the participating individuals, rather than on the tax-exempt organization, and revocation of the organization's tax-exempt status now appears to be reserved for only the most extreme situations.

The punishable "excess benefit transaction" is any transaction where an economic benefit is provided directly or indirectly to any "disqualified person" if that benefit exceeds the value of the consideration (including services rendered) received by the organization in exchange. Also, the new law gives the Treasury Department the authority to promulgate regulations to include as an "excess benefit transaction" any compensation received by a "disqualified person" that is based on the revenue of the organization in a way that violates the present-law standards for the prohibition against private inurement.

Rebuttable Presumption of Reasonableness

The legislative history to the law states that existing tax-law standards will apply in determining reasonableness of compensation and fair market value. The existing tax-law standard for reasonable compensation generally means an amount that would ordinarily be paid by comparable concerns for comparable services under similar circumstances. Significantly, the House Ways and Means Committee report indicates that the parties to a transaction under the law will be entitled to rely on a rebuttable presumption of reasonableness when determining the reasonableness of compensation and fair market value. While this rebuttable presumption of reasonableness has not been codified in the statutory changes, the House Committee Report explicitly instructs the Internal Revenue Service ("IRS") to issue guidance regarding the reasonableness standard and to incorporate this rebuttable presumption.

New regulations are anticipated to codify congressional intent to allow persons subject to the new intermediate sanctions rules to rely on a rebuttable presumption of reasonableness if certain procedures are followed, and shift the burden of proof to the IRS as to the reasonableness of transactions. The procedures described in the House Committee Report establish a rebuttable presumption that a compensation arrangement is reasonable, or that a transaction is for fair market value, if the arrangement is approved in advance by a board of directors or trustees (or committee thereof) that:

1. is composed entirely of individuals unrelated to and not controlled by the disqualified person(s) involved in the transaction,

2. obtains and relies on appropriate comparability data, and

3. adequately documents the basis for its determination.

If these three criteria are satisfied, the subject transaction will have the benefit of a rebuttable presumption of reasonableness, and consequently, intermediate sanctions cannot be imposed unless the IRS can rebut the presumption by demonstrating sufficient contrary evidence to undo the independent board's determination.

Planning to Invoke the Presumption

Satisfying the criteria to invoke the rebuttable presumption of reasonableness appears to be the most significant planning opportunity for tax-exempt organizations subject to the intermediate sanctions legislation. Even if the adopted Treasury regulations do not mirror the procedures described in the legislative history, public charities and social welfare organizations should develop and implement those procedures to qualify for the presumption. Following those procedures should at the very least dissuade the IRS from reaching the conclusion that an excess benefit transaction has occurred, unless credible contrary evidence is presented.

Additionally, the second-level 200-percent excise tax is so prohibitive that it amounts to a de facto requirement that any excess benefit be repaid to the exempt organization. Therefore, an exempt organization's executives may be forced to live under the threat that their compensation may be found excessive, requiring them to return the excess to their employer. The executive's peers in the non-tax-exempt business community are not subject to this type of threat. Consequently, if circumstances warrant, compensation arrangements and transactions with "insiders" should be approved in advance by an independent board, relying on appropriate comparability data, while completely documenting the grounds for their determination. Taking such steps should reduce any potential chilling effect on executive recruitment, as well as insulate the tax-exempt organization's board members from any potential personal liability.

Conclusion

Congress expects $33 million of revenues to be raised over the next seven years as the result of taxable infractions occurring under the new intermediate sanctions legislation. Therefore, public charities and social welfare organizations should do everything possible to avoid triggering the excise taxes against their managers and "insiders." The most consequential planning opportunity appears to be taking the steps necessary to qualify for the presumption of reasonableness when establishing compensation and determining fair market value in transactions with anyone who may be considered a "disqualified person."

Public charities and social welfare organizations should consult with their tax advisors to ensure they are doing everything possible to qualify for the presumption and to attempt to make it irrebuttable.

CONTENTS

Chapter 15
OFFICE OF MANAGEMENT
AND BUDGET

CROSS-REFERENCES

2000 MILLER GAAP GUIDE: Chapter 19, "Government Contracts"

2000 MILLER GAAS GUIDE: Sections 150, 161, 201, 210, 220, 230, 311, 317, 319, 325, 339, 508, 544, 551, 801

Not-for-profit organizations may receive financial assistance from the federal government directly or indirectly in the form of grants, contracts, loans, cooperative agreements, loan guarantees, property, interest subsidies, insurance, direct appropriations, and other non-cash assistance. For example, organizations that assist new immigrants to the United States may receive grants from the Department of State; hospitals may receive research grants from the National Institutes of Health; day-care centers may receive food from the Department of Agriculture. Because of this federal assistance, such entities are subject to additional reporting and audit responsibilities.

Financial statements and other reports of entities that are recipients of *governmental financial assistance* are often subjected to greater scrutiny because of the level of public accountability, legal and regulatory requirements, and the visibility and sensitivity of government programs, activities, and functions. A not-for-profit organization that receives such assistance must comply with laws, regulations, contracts, and grant agreements and, in many instances, must retain independent auditors to report to the entity and its funding agencies on compliance with certain provisions of the laws, regulations, contracts, and grants to which it is subject.

The standards for reporting by entities receiving governmental financial assistance are contained principally in OMB Circular A-133 (now titled "Audits of States, Local Governments, and Non-Profit Organizations"). Funding agencies may require special-purpose reports to satisfy a variety of needs, including the establishment of indirect cost rates to be paid by the agencies and reimbursement rates to be paid by third-party funders.

OMB and Congress have worked together to rewrite the face of single audits. Circulars A-128 and A-133 have been combined into one new Circular A-133 (Audits of States, Local Governments, and Non-Profit Organizations) and the Single Audit Act was amended. The effects on not-for-profit organizations will be significant, and independent auditors will now assess risk to determine which federal programs to audit. Even determining the amount of federal expenditures of a particular entity to audit will be subject to risk assessments. Gone is the clear-cut monetary determinations of the original Circular. The expected guidance from OMB in the form of a final version of new Circular A-133 and a provisional *Compliance Supplement* was issued during the last week of June 1997 and the first week of July 1997. In June 1998, an expanded *Compliance Supplement* was issued to replace the one designated as "provisional." In April 1999, OMB again revised the *Compliance Supplement* providing audit guidance for over 30 additional federally funded programs. For extensive guidance on audits of not-for-profit organizations, see the 2000 *Miller Not-for-Profit Organization Audits*.

In March 1998, the AICPA issued Statement of Position 98-3 (Audits of States, Local Governments, and Not-for-Profit Organizations Receiving Federal Awards).

Following, to help put all of this in some perspective, is a summary of the Circular as it affects not-for-profit organizations, some key terms to help readers understand the Circular, and a history of federal audits of federal assistance to not-for-profit organizations. The revised Circular A-133 issued in June 1997 and a discussion of the amendments to the Single Audit Act as of July 1996 are included.

OMB CIRCULAR A-133

Background

Office of Management and Budget (OMB) Circular A-133 (Audits of Institutions of Higher Education and Other Nonprofit Organizations) was issued in 1990 by the OMB to establish audit requirements and define federal responsibilities for implementing and monitoring such requirements for institutions of higher education and other not-for-profit institutions receiving federal awards. Before its issuance, recipients of federal financial assistance were subject to Attachment F of Circular A-110 (Uniform Administrative Requirements for Grants and Agreements with Institutions of Higher Education, Hospitals, and Other Nonprofit Organizations).

The concept of one audit encompassing an entity's basic financial statements and compliance with the requirements of federally funded programs was an outgrowth of activities that took place in the 1960s and 1970s, when federal programs grew in amount and complexity. Federal funders often had different laws and regulations with which they wanted compliance. Audit requirements differed from agency to agency, as did administrative requirements. Much of these activities focused on state and local governments as recipients. For example, OMB Circular A-128 (Audits of State and Local Governments), issued in 1985, required federal funders to adopt the provisions of the Single Audit Act of 1984.

In April 1996, OMB released a revised version of Circular A-133 ("April 1996 revision"), which superseded the March 1990 version. The April 1996 revision noted that it would apply to audits of organizations covered by the March 1990 Circular, but not to non–U.S.-based entities expending federal awards received either directly as a recipient or indirectly as a subrecipient. Then, Congress approved and the President signed into law the Single Audit Act Amendments of 1996, which would (1) establish uniform requirements for audits of federal awards administered by non-federal entities and (2) reduce burdens on state and local governments, Indian tribes, and *not-for-profit organizations.*

Later, not-for-profit organizations and state and local governments were brought together in one document. (OMB activities leading up to this document are outlined in the Appendix to this chapter.) Then, in November 1996, OMB published in the *Federal Register* proposed revisions (the "November proposal") to the April 1996 revision of Circular A-133. The November proposal would incorporate the provisions of the Single Audit Act Amendments of 1996, rescind Circular A-128, and make state and local governments subject to Circular A-133. In June 1997, OMB issued its revised Circular A-133 and a provisional *Compliance Supplement*. A revised *Compliance Supplement* was issued in April 1999.

Key Sections of the Revision of OMB Circular A-133

Purpose   Circular A-133 is to "set forth standards for obtaining consistency and uniformity among federal agencies for the audit . . . of non-profit organizations expending federal awards."

Definitions   Some of the significant terms used throughout Circular A-133 are included in the this section. Among those that will receive the widest use, because auditors and auditees alike have questions about them, are the following:

> *Cluster of programs*—Federal programs with different numbers assigned by the Catalog of Federal Domestic Assistance (CFDA) that are defined as *cluster of programs* in the *Compliance Supplements* because they are closely related programs and share common compliance requirements. A cluster of programs shall be considered as one program for determining *major programs* (defined below). The provisional *Compliance Supplement* identi-

fies research and development and student financial assistance as clusters.

Federal financial assistance—Assistance received or administered to carry out a program. Such assistance may be in the form of grants, cooperative agreements, donated surplus property, food commodities, loans, loan guarantees, property, interest subsidies, insurance, direct appropriations, and other assistance. It does not include amounts received as reimbursement for services rendered to individuals for Medicare of Medicaid.

Federal program—(1) All federal awards under the same CFDA number. When no CFDA number is assigned, all federal awards from the same agency made for the same purpose should be combined and considered one program. (2) A category of federal awards that is a group of awards in one of the following categories: (a) research and development (R&D), (b) student financial aid, or (c) other cluster of programs.

Major program—A federal program **determined by the auditor** to be a major program in accordance with Section 520 [Major program determination] or a program identified as a major program **by a federal agency or pass-through entity** in accordance with Section 215(c) [Request for a program to be audited as a major program].

Nonprofit organization—Any corporation, trust, association, cooperative, or other organization that:

(a) is operated primarily for scientific, educational, service, charitable, or similar purposes in the public interest;

(b) is not organized primarily for profit; and

(c) uses net proceeds to maintain, improve, or expand the operations of the organization.

This term includes non-profit institutions of higher education and hospitals.

Oversight agency for audit—The federal awarding agency that provides the predominant amount of direct funding to a recipient not assigned a cognizant agency for audit. When there is no direct funding, the federal agency with the predominant indirect funding shall assume the oversight responsibilities.

Recipient—A non-federal entity that expends federal awards received directly from a federal agency to carry out a federal program.

Subrecipient—A non-federal entity that expends federal awards received through another non-federal entity to carry out a federal program, but does not include an individual, who receives financial assistance through such awards. A subrecipient may also be a recipient of other federal awards directly from a federal awarding agency.

Subpart B—Audits

Section 200, "Audit requirements" Notes that a single or program-specific audit is required for nonprofit organizations that expend $300,000 or more in federal awards in a year. *Program-specific audits* may be elected when the organization "expends federal awards under only one federal program (excluding R&D) and the federal program's laws, regulations, or grant agreements do not require a financial statement audit of the auditee." A program-specific audit *may be elected for R&D* if all expenditures are for federal awards received from the same federal agency, or the same federal agency and the same pass-through entity, and that federal agency, or pass-through entity in the case of a subrecipient, approves in advance a program-specific audit.

Single (organization-wide) audits are mandated for not-for-profit organizations that expend federal awards of $300,000 or more in a fiscal year. Organizations may elect program-specific audits if the conditions noted above are met.

Not-for-profit organizations with federal award expenditures of less than $300,000 are exempt from audits for the year, unless required by a federal agency. If such an audit is requested, the federal agency will pay the related costs.

Section 205, "Basis of determining federal awards expended" Will help the auditee and auditor *determine federal awards expended*, an area that has been confusing in the past. This Section includes the following:

> The determination of when an award is expended should be based on when the activity related to the award occurs. Generally, the activity pertains to events that require the [organization] to comply with laws, regulations, and the provisions of contracts or grant agreements, such as: expenditure/expense transactions associated with grants, cost-reimbursement contracts, cooperative agreements, and direct appropriations; the disbursement of funds passed through to subrecipients; the use of loan proceeds under loan and loan guarantee programs; the receipt of property; the receipt of surplus property; the receipt or use of program income; the distribution or consumption of food commodi-

ties, the disbursement of amounts entitling the [organization] to an interest subsidy; and the period when insurance is in force.

Some of the more unusual federal awards that should be considered expended include the following:

Endowment funds—The cumulative balance of federal awards for endowment funds that are federally restricted are considered *awards expended in each year* in which the funds are still restricted.

Free rent—Received by itself is *not* considered an award expended. Free rent received as part of an award to carry out a federal program should be used to determine federal awards expended.

Loan and loan guarantees—The value of federal awards expended includes:

- Value of new loans made or received during the fiscal year; plus

- Balance of loans from previous years for which the federal government imposes continuing compliance requirements; plus

- Any interest subsidy, cash, or administrative cost allowance received.

For *loans made to students of institutions of higher education* that are not made by the institution, only the value of loans made during the year are to be considered federal awards expended in that year. Prior-year loans are accounted for by the lender.

Loans received and expended in prior years are not awards expended in the current year when the only continuing compliance requirement is to repay the loan.

Medicare and Medicaid—Are not considered federal awards expended unless, in the case of Medicaid, a state requires the funds to be treated as federal awards expended because reimbursement is on a cost-reimbursement basis.

Section 210, "Subrecipient and vendor determinations"   Helps the auditee and auditor determine applicability of Circular A-133 to federal funding. It outlines characteristics that distinguish a federal award from a payment for goods and services received by a vendor, as follows.

Federal Award	*Payment for Goods and Services*
• Organization determines who is eligible to receive federal financial assistance.	• Organization provides the goods and services within normal business operations.
• Organization has its performance measured against whether the objectives of the federal program are met.	• Organization provides similar goods or services to many different purchasers.
• Organization has responsibility for programmatic decision-making.	• Organization operates in a competitive environment.
• Organization has responsibility for adherence to applicable federal program compliance requirements.	• Organization is not subject to compliance requirements of the federal program.
• Organization uses the federal funds to carry out a program of the organization, as compared to providing goods or services for a program of the pass-through entity.	• Organization provides goods or services that are ancillary to the operation of the federal program.

When the subrecipient is a for-profit entity, the requirements of Circular A-133 do not apply to that entity. Accordingly, the pass-through entity is responsible for establishing the requirements that the for-profit entity must meet to assure compliance with the federal award terms.

Section 215, "Relation to other audit requirements" Discusses the need for other audits. Generally, an audit in accordance with Circular A-133 reduces the need for additional audits required by a federal agency. However, the provisions of Circular A-133 do not preclude a federal agency from arranging for or conducting additional audits. In the latter situation, the federal agency will "arrange for funding the full cost of such additional audits." In this Section, OMB notes that a "federal agency may request an auditee to have a particular federal program audited as a major program in lieu of the federal agency conducting or arranging for the additional audits." The auditee and its auditor should inform the requesting federal agency if the program would have been selected for audit as a major program under the risk-based audit approach required by Circular A-133. If audited as a major program solely because the federal agency requests it, the federal agency must agree to pay the incremental cost of the audit.

Section 220, "Frequency of audits" The Circular A-133 organization-wide audit should be carried out annually. Program audits may be done every two years, but must cover both years.

Section 225, "Sanctions" describes when audit costs should not be charged to federal awards, i.e., when audits required by the Circular have not been made or have been made but not in accordance with A-133. Actions that may be taken by the federal agency or pass-through entities include:

- Withholding a percentage of federal awards until the audit is completed satisfactorily,
- Withholding or disallowing overhead costs,
- Suspending federal awards until the audit is conducted, or
- Terminating the federal award.

Section 230, "Audit costs" Such costs are allowable charges to federal awards—either as a direct cost or as an allocated indirect cost.

There are certain circumstances in which audit costs will not be allowable:

- When the audit is not conducted in accordance with Circular A-133,
- When the organization is exempt from the audit requirements of A-133 because it has expended less than $300,000 of federal awards.

However, a pass-through entity may charge to a federal award the cost associated with limited scope audits conducted for the purpose of monitoring its subrecipients, i.e., agreed-upon procedures addressing "one or more of the compliance requirements: activities allowed or unallowed; allowable costs/cost principles; eligibility; matching, level of effort, earmarking; and reporting."

Section 235, "Program-specific audits" Notes that "in many cases, a program-specific Audit Guide will be available to provide specific guidance to the auditor with respect to internal control, compliance requirements, suggested audit procedures, and audit reporting requirements." When a program-specific guide is not available to the auditor, the responsibilities for the federal program are the same as those for a major program. In this instance, the audit of the program's financial statements, is performed in accordance with generally accepted government auditing standards (GAGAS). The auditor will:

- Obtain an understanding of internal control and perform tests of internal control over the federal program consistent with those required for a major program.
- Perform procedures to determine if the auditee has complied with laws, regulations, and the provisions of contracts or grant agreements that could have a direct and material effect on the federal program.

- Follow up on prior audit findings; perform procedures to assess the reasonableness of the summary schedule of prior audit findings prepared by the auditee; and report, as a current year finding, when the auditor concludes that the summary schedule of prior audit findings materially misrepresents the status of any prior audit finding.

The revision of Circular A-133 allows auditors' reports to be combined or remain separate. These reports will state that the audit was conducted in accordance with Circular A-133 and will include the following:

1. An opinion (or disclaimer of opinion) as to whether the financial statement(s) of the federal program is presented fairly in all material respects in accordance with the stated accounting policies.
2. A report on internal control related to the federal program, which shall describe the scope of testing of internal control and the results of the tests.
3. A report on compliance that includes an opinion (or disclaimer of opinion) as to whether the auditee complied with laws, regulations, and the provisions of contracts or grant agreements that could have a direct and material effect on the federal program.
4. A schedule of findings and questioned costs for the federal program that is consistent with the requirements of Circular A-133 and includes a summary of the auditors' results applicable to the audit of the federal program.

This Section also provides information about the due date for reports on program-specific audits (nine months unless another period is agreed to in advance by the federal agency) and how the reports should be submitted in various circumstances. A two-year extension of the 13-month filing requirement was included in this section.

> **OBSERVATION:** Chapter 11 of SOP 98-3 (Audits of States, Local Governments, and Not-for-Profit Organizations Receiving Federal Awards) provides guidance on program-specific audits, including examples of auditor's reports.

Subpart C—Auditees

Section 300, "Auditee responsibilities" The auditee is required to identify in its accounts all federal awards received and expended—

including the program, CFDA number, award number and year, federal agency, and, if applicable, pass-through entity. The auditee must maintain internal control over federal awards to provide reasonable assurance that the federal awards are being managed in compliance with laws, regulations, and provisions of contracts or grant agreements that *could have a material effect on each of its programs.* In addition, the auditee must comply with such laws, regulations, and provisions; prepare appropriate financial statements, *including the schedule of expenditures of federal awards;* arrange for properly performed and timely audits; and follow up on and take corrective action on audit findings, *including preparation of a summary schedule of prior audit findings and a corrective action plan.*

Section 305, "Auditor selection" Refers auditees to the procurement standards addressed in Circular A-110, or to the Federal Acquisition Regulation for determining how to arrange for audit services. In evaluating each proposal for audit services, the auditee should consider such factors as the responsiveness to the request for proposal, relevant experience, availability of staff with professional qualifications and technical abilities, the results of external quality control reviews, and price.

Circular A-110 also covers recipient responsibilities in Section 41, indicating that "the recipient is the responsible authority . . . regarding the settlement and satisfaction of all contractual and administrative issues arising out of procurements entered into in support of an award or other agreement." In other Sections of Circular A-110, recipients are instructed:

- To maintain "written standards for conduct governing the performance of its employees engaged in the award and administration of contracts" (Section 42)

- That all "procurement transactions shall be conducted in a manner to provide, to the *maximum extent practical,* open and free competition. . . . Any and all bids or offers may be rejected when it is in the recipient's interest to do so" [emphasis added] (Section 43)

- To establish written procurement procedures (Section 44)

- To perform and document a cost or price analysis in the procurement files (Section 45)

- To maintain in the files for purchases in excess of the small purchase threshold (currently $25,000): (*a*) basis for contractor selection, (*b*) *justification of lack of competition when competitive bids or offers are not obtained,* and (*c*) basis for award cost or price [emphasis added] (Section 46)

- To maintain a system for contract administration "to ensure contractor conformance with the terms, conditions and specification of the contract and to ensure adequate and timely follow up of all purchases" (Section 47)

- To include certain provisions in all contracts and subcontracts (Section 48)

Section 305 of Circular A-133 sets forth the restriction on auditors preparing indirect cost proposals. For audits of fiscal years beginning on or after June 30, 1998:

> An auditor who prepares the indirect cost proposal or cost allocation plan may not also be selected to perform the audit required by [Circular A-133] when the indirect costs recovered by the auditee during the prior year exceeded $1 Million.

Section 310, "Financial statements" The auditee-prepared financial statements should, for the same organizational unit and fiscal year, "reflect its financial position, results of operations, and where appropriate, cash flows for the fiscal year audited." The auditee also will prepare a schedule of expenditures of federal awards, which will:

1. List individual programs by federal agency and major subdivision. For R&D, total federal awards expended may be shown either by individual award or by federal agency and major subdivision within the federal agency. If the entity receiving the awards is a subrecipient, the name of the pass-through entity and program identification should be included.

2. Provide total expenditures for each individual federal program and the CFDA number or other identifying number when the CFDA information is not available.

3. Include notes that identify the significant accounting policies used and the dollar threshold used.

4. When practical, require pass-through entities to identify amounts provided to subrecipients from each federal program.

5. Include in the schedule or in a note to the schedule the value of non-cash assistance expended, insurance in effect during the year, and loans or loan guarantees outstanding at year-end.

Section 315, "Audit findings follow-up" Sets out the auditee's responsibilities for follow-up and corrective action on all audit findings in prior and current years. For prior-year findings, the auditee-prepared summary schedule should report the status. When findings have been fully corrected, the summary schedule should list the findings and indicate that corrective action was taken. When findings have not been fully corrected, the summary schedule should describe the planned corrective action and partial corrective action taken, if any. An explanation should be provided in the summary schedule when corrective action taken in response to prior findings is different than that which was previously reported. If the auditee believes that the findings are no longer valid, the reasons should be explained in the summary schedule. The corrective action plan should contain the following information:

- Name of the contact person responsible for corrective action
- The corrective action planned
- The anticipated completion date
- The reasons and explanations for disagreements with findings or belief that no action is required

Section 320, "Report submission"   The organization is to submit the reporting package within nine months of the end of the fiscal year, unless a longer period is agreed to in advance by the cognizant or oversight agency. The revised Circular A-133 permits a transition period for fiscal years beginning before June 30, 1998, during which the auditee may submit the reporting package 13 months after the end of the period audited.

The auditee will submit a data collection form that contains several specific elements. The elements of the data collection form include the following:

- The type of auditors' report issued on the financial statements (unqualified, qualified, adverse, or disclaimer)
- A statement that reportable conditions in internal control were disclosed by the financial statement audit and whether any were material weaknesses
- A statement whether the audit disclosed any noncompliance that is material to the financial statements
- A statement as to whether any reportable conditions in internal control over major programs were disclosed by the audit and whether any were material weaknesses
- The type of auditors' report issued on compliance for major programs (unqualified, qualified, adverse, or disclaimer)
- A list of federal awarding agencies that will receive a copy of the reporting package
- A statement as to whether the organization qualified as a low-risk auditee
- The dollar threshold used to distinguish between Type A and Type B programs

- The CFDA number for each federal program

- The name of each federal program and identification of each major program

- The amount of expenditures in the schedule of expenditures of federal awards associated with each program

- Whether there were, for each federal program, audit findings related to compliance requirements, and the total amount of any questioned costs

- The organization's name, employer identification number, name and title of certifying official, telephone number, signature, and date

- Auditor name, name and title of contact person, address, telephone number, signature, and date

- Whether the organization has either a cognizant or an oversight agency for audit

- The name of such agency

The form also will state whether the audit was completed in accordance with Circular A-133, and it will provide "information about the auditee, its federal programs and the results of the audit." The data collection form will contain a statement—signed by a senior level representative of the organization, e.g., director of finance, CEO, or CFO—that the organization complied with A-133 and that the "information included in the form, in its entirety, is accurate and complete."

The auditor as well is responsible for specific parts of the form. The auditor is responsible for signing a statement, included as part of the form, indicating the source of the information in the form, the auditor's responsibility for the information, that the form is not a substitute for the reporting package, and that the content of the form is limited to the elements prescribed by OMB.

> **OBSERVATION:** The Federal Audit Clearinghouse has rejected filings for a number of reasons as a result of the Data Collection Form being prepared incorrectly. Among the reasons for rejection are lack of CFDA number or other identification of federal funding agency in the listing of programs of the auditee; indication that copies of the reporting package should be distributed to funding agencies even when there are no findings related to the programs of those funding agencies; listing all of the compliance requirements tested and not just the compliance requirements for which there were findings reported in the auditor-prepared summary of audit.

The reporting package will include the following:

- Financial statements and schedule of expenditures of federal awards
- Summary schedule of prior audit findings
- Auditors' report
- Corrective action plan

Copies of the reporting package will be sent to the OMB's designated central clearing house, currently the Federal Audit Clearinghouse, Bureau of the Census, 1201 E. 10th Street, Jeffersonville, IN 47312. Copies also will be sent to each federal awarding agency for which a finding or questioned cost was disclosed either in the current year or in the summary of prior audit findings.

Subrecipients also will send to each pass-through entity a copy of its certificate of audit and the reporting package, when the schedule of findings and questioned costs or the summary schedule of prior audit findings contains information relating to the federal awards provided by the pass-through entity.

Subpart D—Federal Agencies and Pass-Through Entities

Section 400, "Responsibilities"   This Section defines the term *cognizant agency.* Recipients with federal expenditures of more than $25 million in a fiscal year generally will have as a *cognizant agency for audit* the federal awarding agency that provides the predominant amount of direct funding. This designation will be for a 5-year term. The responsibilities of the cognizant agency will include, among others, technical audit advice and liaison, consideration of requests for extensions for report submission, and arranging for quality control reviews of the non-federal auditor, and informing other federal agencies of any auditee- or auditor-reported irregularities or illegal acts. In addition, the agency will:

- Advise the auditor and the auditee of any deficiencies found in the audits when the deficiencies require corrective action by the auditor
- Coordinate audits that are in addition to the A-133 audit, so that the additional audits build on the A-133 audit
- Coordinate the decisions about audit findings that affect the programs of more than one federal agency
- Work to achieve the most cost-effective audit
- Consider auditee requests to qualify as a low-risk auditee in situations that permit biennial audits

This section also includes a description of the federal awarding agency's responsibilities:

- Inform each recipient of the CFDA title and number and other identifying information
- Advise recipients of requirements imposed on them
- Ensure that audits are completed and reports are timely received
- Provide technical advice to auditees and auditors
- Issue a management decision on audit findings and monitor the recipient's corrective action
- Provide annual updates of the A-133 *Compliance Supplement*

For pass-through entities, Section 400 notes the following responsibilities:

- Inform each subrecipient of the CFDA title and number and other identifying information
- Advise subrecipients of requirements imposed on them
- Ensure that audits are completed and reports are timely received, when the subrecipients expend $300,000 or more in federal awards
- Issue a management decision on audit findings and monitor the recipient's corrective action
- Consider whether subrecipient audits necessitate adjustment of the pass-through entity's own records
- Require each subrecipient to permit the pass-through entity and auditors to have access to the records and financial statements as necessary to comply with A-133

An *oversight agency* will be appointed for those recipients not having a cognizant agency. The responsibilities of the oversight agency will be similar to those of a cognizant agency.

> **OBSERVATION:** The cost of subrecipient audits in accordance with Circular A-133 will **not** be permitted to be charged to the federal program, if the subrecipient has less than $300,000 of federal expenditures. OMB believes that there are more cost-effective methods for monitoring subrecipients in these circumstances, for example, on-site visits, review of subrecipient documentation, limited-scope audits of compliance, and financial statement audits in accordance with government auditing standards.

Section 405, "Management decision"   Discusses actions to be taken by cognizant agencies or pass-through entities relative to audit findings and corrective action plans and steps taken.

Subpart E—Auditors

This subpart of the revision of Circular A-133 is significant, because it will change the way the programs subject to audit are selected. This is one of the three most publicized changes, the others being the increased reporting responsibilities of the auditee and the reduced period in which to file the required reports.

Section 500, "Scope of audit"   The audit is to be conducted in accordance with GAGAS, and the auditor will determine whether the financial statements of the auditee are presented fairly in all material respects in conformity with generally accepted accounting principles (GAAP). The schedule of expenditures of federal awards should be presented fairly in all material respects in relation to the auditee's financial statements taken as a whole.

In relation to the auditee's *internal controls,* the auditor must obtain an understanding of internal control over federal programs "sufficient to plan the audit to achieve a low assessed level of control risk for major programs." Accordingly, except when internal control over some or all of the compliance requirements for a major program is likely to be ineffective in preventing or detecting noncompliance, the auditor will plan to achieve a low assessed level of control risk for assertions related to compliance requirements for each major program and perform testing of internal control over major programs. If controls are likely to be ineffective, the planning and testing of controls are not required, and the auditor will include this conclusion as a reportable condition or material weakness, assess the control risk at the maximum, and determine whether additional compliance tests are required because of the ineffective internal control over the major program.

GAGAS requires the auditor to evaluate the auditee's compliance with laws and regulations; noncompliance with such laws and regulations may have a material effect on the financial statements. Circular A-133 adds to the auditors' responsibility. The auditee also must comply with laws, regulations, and provisions of contracts and agreements that may have a *direct and material effect on each of its major programs.* Accordingly, the auditor is required to conduct audit procedures to provide "sufficient evidence to support an opinion on compliance for each major program." The Circular directs the auditor to determine requirements from the *Compliance Supplement.* If, after discussions with the applicable federal agency(ies), the auditor determines that a major program is *not* in the *Compliance Supplements*, the auditor will be guided by the types of requirements in the *Compliance Supplements*, e.g., cash management, federal financial reporting, allowable costs/cost principles, types of services allowed or disallowed, eligibility, and matching, as well as by the provisions of contracts and grant agreements.

The auditor also will be responsible for following up on prior audit findings, and for performing procedures (*a*) to assess the reasonableness of the auditee-prepared summary schedule of prior audit findings, and (*b*) to report as a finding disagreement with the auditee's assessment of the status of the prior findings. The auditor also must complete and sign certain sections of the data collection form.

Section 505, "Audit reporting"   The independent auditor must issue the following reports:

- An opinion (or disclaimer of opinion) as to whether the financial statements are presented fairly in all material respects in conformity with GAAP, and an opinion (or disclaimer of an opinion) as to whether the schedule of expenditures of federal awards is presented fairly in all material respects in relation to the financial statements taken as a whole

- A report on internal control related to the financial statements and major programs

- A report on compliance with laws, regulations, and the provisions of contracts or grant agreements, noncompliance with which could have a material effect on the financial statements, and an opinion (or disclaimer of opinion) as to whether the auditee complied with laws, regulations, and the provisions of contracts or grant agreements that could have a direct and material effect on each major program

    In September 1998, effective for reports issued after December 31, 1998, the AICPA's Auditing Standards Board issued Statement on Auditing Standards (SAS) No. 87 (Restricting the Use of an Auditor's Report). This new Standard clarifies when an auditor should restrict the use of a report, and as a result it changes the standard language for use in reports on audits conducted in accordance with GAS and for compliance with the requirements of OMB Circular A-133. SAS-87, relative to audits conducted in accordance with GAS, amends the sample reports on compliance and on internal control in SOP 98-3 (Audits of States, Local Governments, and Not-for-Profit Organizations Receiving Federal Awards). The last paragraph of each of the examples now reads:

This report is intended solely for the information and use of the audit committee, management, [*specify legislative or regulatory body*], and federal awarding agencies and pass-through entities and is **not intended to be and should not be used by anyone other than these specified parties**. [emphasis added]

- A schedule of findings and questioned costs that includes a summary of the auditors' results. The summary of auditors' results includes:

  — The type of report issued by the auditor on the financial statements

  — A statement, if applicable, that the reportable conditions in internal control were disclosed by the financial statement audit and whether any were material weaknesses

  — A statement about any noncompliance that is material to the financial statements

  — The type of report issued on compliance for major programs

  — A statement, if applicable, about reportable conditions in the internal control over major programs and whether the reportable conditions are major weaknesses

  — A statement as to whether the audit disclosed material non-compliance in a major program

  — A statement as to whether the audit disclosed questioned costs

  — A statement, if applicable, that the schedule of findings and questioned costs contains instances of fraud

  — A statement, if applicable, that the auditee-prepared summary schedule of prior audit findings materially misrepresents the status of prior audit findings

  — Identification of major programs

  — The dollar threshold used to distinguish between Type A programs and Type B programs

  — A statement as to whether the auditee qualified as a low-risk auditee

The summary should also include findings related to the financial statements that are required to be reported in accordance with generally accepted government auditing standards, as well as findings and questioned costs for federal awards.

Section 510, "Audit findings" The auditor should prepare a schedule of findings and questioned costs covering six major requirements:

1. Reportable conditions in internal control over major programs, in relation to a compliance requirement for a major program or

an audit objective identified in the *Compliance Supplements.* Reportable conditions that are individually or cumulatively material weaknesses will be identified.

2. Material noncompliance with the provisions of laws, regulations, contracts, or grant agreements that has occurred *or is likely to have occurred,* based on evidence obtained, in relation to a type of compliance requirement for a major program or an audit objective identified in the *Compliance Supplements.*

3. *Known* questioned costs (that is, costs that are specifically identified) in excess of $10,000 for a compliance requirement of a major program. The auditor also will determine *likely* questioned costs (that is, best estimate of total questioned costs). The auditor will report known questioned costs when likely questioned costs exceed $10,000 for a type of compliance requirement for a major program. For example, if, as a result of testing a sample, the auditor finds known questioned costs of $8,000 and likely questioned costs for the population are $13,000, the auditor will report the $8,000. If the likely questioned costs are $9,500, the auditor is not required to report the known questioned costs of $8,000.

4. If applicable, the circumstances concerning why the auditors' report on compliance for major programs is other than unqualified.

5. Known fraud affecting a federal award.

6. When follow-up procedures disclose that the auditee-prepared summary schedule of prior audit findings materially misrepresents the status of a prior audit finding.

Section 510 also specifies the information that should be included in the detail of an audit finding. A finding needs to be presented in sufficient detail for the auditee to prepare a corrective action plan and for the appropriate entities to arrive at a management decision about the effectiveness of the plan and the action taken. Specifically, the finding should include the following:

1. Identification information: CFDA title and number, award number and year, federal agency, and, if applicable, the pass-through entity

2. Criteria or specific requirement on which the finding is based

3. The condition found by the auditor

4. Identification of questioned costs

5. Information to allow management to determine if the finding is an isolated incident or a systemic problem. Also, details relating to the sample size and population in monetary terms, if applicable

6. Information to permit the auditee and other entities to determine the cause and effect to "facilitate prompt and proper corrective action"

7. Recommendations to prevent future occurrences

8. Views of auditee management when there is disagreement about the finding, if applicable

Section 515, "Audit working papers"   Auditors must maintain and make accessible working papers (a minimum of three years from the date of issuance of the auditors' reports to the auditee) to the cognizant or oversight agency for audit or its designee.

Section 520, "Major program determination"   This Section is the heart of the revised Circular A-133. It selects *major* federal programs according to a risk-based, four-step approach, which considers:

- Current and prior audit experience
- Oversight by federal agencies and pass-through entities
- Inherent risk of the federal program

Step 1   Identify the larger federal programs, which will be labeled "Type A." These are federal programs with expenditures during the audit period exceeding the larger of $300,000 or 3% of total federal expenditures for an auditee with total federal expenditures equal to or exceeding $300,000 but less than or equal to $100 million. There is a sliding scale for auditees with total federal expenditures greater than $100 million: $3 million or 3/10% of total federal expenditures if they are greater than $100 million but less than $10 billion; $30 million or 15/100% of total federal expenditures if they are in excess of $10 billion.

The Circular makes allowances for large loan or loan guarantee programs that might create an imbalance in the number of Type A programs identified: "When a federal program providing loans significantly affects the number or size of Type A programs, the auditor shall consider this federal program as a Type A program and exclude its values in determining other Type A programs."

Step 2   Identify "low-risk" Type A programs. These programs have two significant attributes:

- They have been audited as a major program in at least one of the two most recent audit periods.
- There have been no audit findings in the most recent audit period, but auditor judgment may determine that findings of questioned costs, fraud, and audit follow-up do *not* preclude the Type A program from being low-risk. (Later Sections discuss criteria for federal program risk.)

Notwithstanding the foregoing, a federal agency may request that a Type A program *not* be considered low-risk and will notify the recipient and, if known, the auditor, at least 180 days prior to the end of the fiscal year to be audited.

Step 3—The auditor will identify high-risk Type B programs using professional judgment and criteria discussed in Section 525 of Circular A-133. Those programs that are not Type A are Type B. The auditor, generally, will perform risk assessments on Type B programs that exceed the larger of:

- $100,000 or 3/10% of total federal expenditures when auditee has up to and including $100 million in total federal expenditures; or
- $300,000 or 3/100% of total federal expenditures when auditee has more than $100 million in total federal expenditures.

Step 4—At a minimum, all of the following are audited as major programs:

- All Type A programs, except those identified as low-risk that the auditor chooses to exclude
- At least one-half of the Type B programs identified as high-risk under Step 3, except the auditor is not required to audit more high-risk Type B programs than the number of Type A programs identified as low-risk under Step 2
- Such additional programs as may be necessary to ensure that the auditor audits as major programs those federal programs that in the aggregate encompass at least 50% of total federal expenditures.

As discussed below (see Section 530), under certain circumstances this last part of Step 4 may not apply to an entity. OMB will allow certain entities to be considered as low-risk auditees.

Section 520 reminds auditors to document in the working papers the risk analysis process used in determining major programs. OMB acknowledges that professional judgment plays an important part in the risk-assessment process:

> When the major program determination was performed and documented in accordance with [the Circular], the auditor's judgment in applying the risk-based approach to determine major programs shall be presumed correct. Challenges by federal agencies and pass-through entities shall only be for clearly improper use of the guidance in [the Circular]. However, federal agencies and pass-through entities may provide auditors guidance about the risk of a particular federal pro-

gram and the auditor shall consider this guidance in determining major programs in audits not yet completed.

For first-year audits, the auditor may elect to determine major
programs as all Type A programs plus any Type B programs necessary to achieve the 50% level discussed above. This would eliminate
Steps 2 through 4. The definition of a *first-year audit* includes the year
in which there is a change in auditors, but only once every three
years.

Section 525, "Criteria for federal program risk"   Helps the auditee
and auditor to determine which federal programs to audit as major
programs. The auditors' determination "should be based on an overall evaluation of the risk of noncompliance occurring which could be
material to the federal program." Often, the auditor's judgment will
be affected by discussions with auditee management and the federal
agency or pass-through entity. Section 525 expands on the considerations for the risk analysis, as follows:

- **Current and prior audit experience**—Weaknesses in internal
  control over federal programs may indicate higher risk. The
  auditor should consider management's adherence to applicable laws and regulations and the provisions of contracts and
  grant agreements, and consider the experience of personnel
  who administer the federal programs. Prior audit findings may
  indicate higher risk, as would federal programs that have not
  recently been audited.

- **Oversight exercised by federal agencies and pass-through
  entities**—The extent of oversight and the results of recent reviews conducted by these entities could disclose risk or the
  absence thereof. Federal agencies may also indicate programs
  with higher risk.

- **Inherent risk of the federal program**—Section 525 identifies
  four situations that could indicate the risk associated with a
  program, notwithstanding the nature of the auditee's internal
  control:
  - *Nature of the program*—Includes, for example, a program's
    complexity, the presence of third parties, and the type of
    costs incurred.
  - *Phase of the program's life cycle*—A newer program may not
    be as time-tested and therefore may present higher risk.
  - *Phase of the program's life cycle at the auditee*—If a program is
    new to the auditee, there may be higher risk, simply because
    a learning curve may be present.
  - *Type B programs* with larger expenditures would be of higher
    risk than programs with substantially smaller expenditures.

Section 530, "Criteria for a low-risk auditee"   OMB offers an opportunity for certain entities to reduce the programs that would otherwise be audited. In the description of how to determine major programs, Circular A-133 addresses the concept of "low-risk auditee." A low-risk auditee would be able to reduce the audit coverage from 50% of total federal expenditures to 25%. To qualify, an auditee would need to meet *all* of the following conditions for each of the preceding two years:

- The audits were performed in accordance with Circular A-133.

- The auditors' opinions on the financial statements and the schedule of expenditures of federal awards were unqualified. A federal agency may judge a qualification to be of little impact on the management of federal awards and so may waive this requirement.

- No material weaknesses were identified in internal control under the requirements of GAGAS. A federal agency may judge a qualification to be of little impact on the management of federal awards and so may waive this requirement.

- None of the programs had audit findings from any of the following: internal control deficiencies that were identified as material weaknesses; noncompliance with the provisions of laws, regulations, contracts, or grant agreements that have a material effect on the Type A program; or known or likely questioned costs that exceed 5% of the total expenditures for a Type A program during the year.

OMB CIRCULAR A-122

Recipients of federal financial assistance may charge only certain costs to federal funding agencies. OMB Circular A-122 (Cost Principles for Nonprofit Organizations) establishes the federal requirements for the determination of allowable and unallowable direct and indirect costs and the preparation of indirect cost proposals. OMB Circular A-21 (Cost Principles for Educational Institutions) serves a similar purpose for educational institutions. Appendix E of 45 CFR part 74, "Principles for Determining Costs Applicable to Research and Development Under Grants and Contracts with Hospitals," is the guide for health care entities.

Costs that may be charged to federal awards are equal to the sum of allowable direct and allocable indirect costs, less any applicable credits. The *Compliance Supplement* to Circular A-133 notes:

> A cost is allowable for Federal reimbursement only to the extent of benefits received by Federal programs, and costs

must meet the basic guidelines of allowability, reasonableness, and allocability and be the net of all applicable credits.

> **OBSERVATION:** OMB has issued final revisions to A-122 to amend the definition for *equipment*; require the breakout of indirect costs into two categories—facilities and administration—for not-for-profit organizations receiving more than $10 million in direct federal funding; modify the multiple allocation basis to be consistent with OMB Circular A-21 (organizations receiving more than $10 million are not required to use the multiple allocation basis); and clarify the treatment of certain cost items, including, for example, alcoholic beverages, advertising, automobiles, living expenses, and memberships. The implementation of the proposed ceiling on the administrative portion of indirect costs for organizations with federal funding over $10 million, which was discussed in the 1998 *Miller GAAP for Not-for-Profit Organizations*, has been deferred to allow OMB to collect "better data on indirect costs at non-profit organizations."

Circular A-122 lists the factors affecting allowability of costs:

- Costs must be reasonable and allocable.
- Costs must conform to limitations or exclusions in the cost principles or in the award.
- Costs must be consistent with policies and procedures that apply uniformly to federally financed and other activities of the entity.
- Costs must be accorded consistent treatment.
- Costs must be determined in accordance with generally accepted accounting principles.
- Costs must not be included as a cost to meet cost-sharing or matching requirements of another federally assisted program.
- Costs must be adequately documented.

Circular A-122 gives the following definitions:

Reasonable—The cost does not exceed in nature or amount that which would be incurred by a prudent person under the circumstances prevailing at the time the decision was made to incur the cost.

Allocable—The cost must be treated consistently with other costs incurred for the same purpose in like circumstances and it (1) is incurred specifically for the award, (2) benefits both the award and other work and can be distributed in reasonable or proportion to the benefits received, or (3) is necessary to the overall operation of the organization, although a direct relationship to any particular cost objective cannot be shown.

Applicable credits—Applicable credits are those receipts, or reduction of expenditures, that reduce allocable expense items (e.g., purchase discounts, rebates or allowances, and insurance refunds).

Circular A-122 notes that "it is often desirable to seek a written agreement with the cognizant or awarding agency in advance of the incurrence of special or unusual costs." This would apply to situations in which the reasonableness and allocability of certain costs may be difficult to determine. Reasonableness and allocability are not affected by the absence of such advance understanding.

Direct costs are those costs that can be identified with a particular award, project, service, or other direct activity of an organization. If another cost incurred for the same purpose, in similar circumstances, has been allocated to an award as an indirect cost, the item of cost should not be assigned to an award as a direct cost.

Certain costs are not allowable as charges to federal awards (e.g., fund-raising costs). Although these costs are unallowable, they are treated as direct costs when determining indirect cost rates and should bear their share of the organization's indirect costs if they represent activities that:

- Include personnel salaries.
- Occupy space.
- Benefit from the organization's indirect costs.

Indirect costs are those costs that have been incurred for common or joint objectives and cannot be readily identified with a particular final cost objective. If another cost incurred for the same purpose, in similar circumstances, has been allocated to an award as a direct cost, the item of cost should not be allocated to an award as an indirect cost. Circular A-122 discusses indirect costs.

There will be two broad categories of indirect costs: Facilities and Administration.

Facilities—depreciation and use allowances on buildings, equipment, and capital improvement; interest on debt associated with certain buildings, equipment, and capital improvements; and operations and maintenance expenses.

Administration—general administration and general expenses such as the director's office, accounting, personnel, library administration, and all other types of expenditures not listed specifically under one of the subcategories of Facilities.

Indirect Cost Rate Considerations

A not-for-profit entity may have only one major function, or, if it has more that one, all of its major functions may benefit from its indirect costs to the same degree. In such situations, the allocation of indirect costs and the computation of an *indirect cost rate* may be accomplished simply.

When the organization has several major functions that benefit from its indirect costs in varying degrees, cost allocation may be more complex. In such situations, costs are accumulated into separate cost groupings, and the groupings are allocated to the different functions by means of a base, which measures the relative degree of benefit. The indirect costs are then distributed to the awards and activities included in each function on the basis of an indirect cost rate.

Major functions depend on the purpose of the organization, the types of services it renders to the public, its clients, and its members, and the amount of effort it devotes to such activities as fund raising, public information, and membership. The *base period* for the allocation of indirect costs is the period in which such costs are incurred and accumulated for allocation. Circular A-122 describes several methods for allocating indirect costs and for the determination of indirect cost rates:

- Simplified allocation method
- Multiple allocation base method
- Direct allocation method
- Special indirect cost rate

Simplified allocation method   The simplified allocation method is effectively used when the organization has only one major function or when its major functions all benefit from the indirect costs to the same degree. The result of this method is an indirect cost rate that is used to distribute such costs to individual awards. The simplified method for determining an indirect cost rate involves:

1. Separating total base period costs between direct and indirect, and
2. Dividing allowable indirect costs by an "equitable" distribution base.

Capital expenditures and unallowable costs are excluded from the determination in (1) but "unallowable costs which represent activities must be included in direct costs" if they "represent activities which include the salaries of personnel, occupy space, and benefit from the organization's indirect costs."

Not-for-profit organizations have some flexibility when choosing a distribution base (e.g., total direct costs or direct salaries and wages).

Multiple allocation base method The multiple allocation base method is used when an organization's indirect costs benefit its major functions in varying degrees. According to Circular A-122:

> Indirect costs shall be accumulated into separate cost groupings. . . . Each grouping shall then be allocated individually to benefiting functions by means of a base which best measures the relative benefits.

The groupings should contain expenses that are similar in terms of the functions they benefit and in terms of the allocation base that provides the best measure of the relative benefits. Increasing the number of groupings will enhance the precision of the allocations, but it should be held to a number that is practical when considering the materiality of the amounts involved. The allocation base selected for allocating these costs should produce a result that is equitable to both the government and the organization.

The base must be one that:

- Can be readily expressed in quantitative measures (e.g., dollars, hours, square feet, number of documents, visits, population served), and
- Is common to the functions benefited during the base period.

Direct allocation method The direct allocation method is used when a not-for-profit organization treats all its costs except general and administration expenses as direct costs. Costs are separated into three categories:

1. General and administration expenses
2. Fund raising
3. Other direct functions

Those expenses that are joint in nature (e.g., depreciation, rent, and facility costs) are prorated as direct costs into each category and to each award using an appropriate base. According to Circular A-122:

> This method is acceptable provided each joint cost is prorated using a base which accurately measures the benefits provided to each award or other activity. The bases must be established in accordance with reasonable criteria and must be supported by current data.

Special indirect cost rate   The special indirect cost rate method is used when a single indirect cost rate for all activities of an organization or for each major function of the organization may not be appropriate. This situation arises when different factors exist that may substantially affect the indirect costs applicable to a single award or to a group of awards performed in a common environment. When a particular segment of work is performed in a environment that appears to generate a significantly different level of indirect costs, provisions should be made for a separate indirect cost pool applicable to such work.

Negotiation and Approval of Indirect Cost Rates

The recipient of federal awards must negotiate its indirect cost rate with its cognizant agency, described in Circular A-122 as:

> The Federal agency responsible for negotiating and approving indirect cost rates for a nonprofit organization on behalf of all Federal agencies.

As soon as possible after notification of an award, but not later than three months after such notification, the not-for-profit organization must submit its indirect cost rate proposal. Thereafter, organizations with established indirect cost rates must submit new proposals within six months after the end of each fiscal year.

Circular A-122 permits a predetermined rate or a fixed rate to be negotiated under certain circumstances. When there is reasonable assurance that the rate is not likely to exceed a rate based on the organization's actual costs, a predetermined rate may be used. When a predetermined rate is deemed to be inappropriate, a fixed rate should be used. When neither predetermined nor fixed rates are deemed appropriate, the cognizant agency and the recipient may negotiate provisional and final rates.

Unallowable Costs

Attachment B to Circular A-122 discusses selected items of cost. It describes those costs that are allowable (e.g., certain types of advertising costs) and those that are unallowable (e.g., bad debts).

Applicability

Attachment C to Circular A-122 lists not-for-profit organizations that do not fall under the terms of this Circular. Most of these are research organizations, such as Brookhaven National Laboratory and Rand

Corporation. Also included are "nonprofit insurance companies such as Blue Cross and Blue Shield Organizations." Usually, these entities have negotiated other requirements with their cognizant agencies or are applying Cost Accounting Standards (discussed in Chapter 16, "Cost Accounting Standards").

OMB CIRCULAR A-21

Circular A-21 (Cost Principles for Educational Institutions) is applicable to "all federal agencies that sponsor research and development, training, and other work" at educational institutions ("sponsored agreements"), and its principles should be used as a guide when pricing fixed-price or lump-sum agreements. Also, according to Circular A-21, "federally funded research and development centers associated with educational institutions shall be required to comply with the Cost Accounting Standards, rules and regulations issued by the Cost Accounting Standards Board."

Sponsored agreements are subject to negotiations, and Circular A-21 acknowledges that each institution should be encouraged to conduct research and educational activities in a "manner consonant with its own academic philosophies and institutional objectives." The cost principles also consider that there is a dual role of students engaged in research and this dual role will be recognized in the application of the cost principles. The cost principles also do not change generally accepted accounting principles for colleges and universities, but these institutions may be held to a higher degree of responsibility regarding the determination of adequate documentation to support costs.

Circular A-21 defines the following major functions of an educational institution:

> *Instruction*—All teaching and training activities except for research training

> *Sponsored instruction and training*—Activity established by grant, contract, or cost principles

> *Departmental research*—Research and development activities not separately budgeted and accounted for

> *Organized research*—Research and development activities that are separately budgeted and accounted for

> *Sponsored research*—Activities sponsored by federal and nonfederal agencies and organizations

University research—Activities that are separately budgeted and accounted for under an internal application of institutional funds

Other sponsored activities—Sponsored activities other than instruction and organized research

Other institutional activities—All activities except:

- Instruction
- Departmental research
- Organized research
- Other sponsored activities
- Indirect cost activities
- Specialized service facilities

Other A-21 definitions include:

Sponsored agreement—Any grant, contract, or other agreement with the federal government

Allocation—The process of assigning costs to an objective

Section C of Circular A-21 discusses basic cost considerations of a sponsored agreement, including the following:

1. *Total costs* include allowable direct costs, plus allocable indirect costs less applicable credits.
2. To be *allowable*, costs should be reasonable, allocable to sponsored agreements, consistently treated, and conform to specified limitations and exclusions.
3. *Reasonable costs* are those that reflect the action of a prudent person.
4. *Allocable costs* advance the work under the agreement, benefit the agreement and other work of the institution, or are necessary to the institution and assignable to sponsored projects. As added in the most recent revision of Circular A-21, the institution should have controls to ensure "that no one person has complete control over all aspects of a financial transaction." Costs should be documented.
5. *Applicable credits* that reduce costs are receipts or negative expenditures that offset or reduce direct or indirect cost items (e.g., purchase discounts, rebates, indemnities on losses).

6. *Costs incurred by state and local governments* on behalf of their colleges and/or universities may be allowable.

7. *Statutory requirements*, such as the cap on indirect costs, may limit allowable costs.

8. *Collection of unallowable costs* by the institution will be refunded to the resource provider with interest.

9. The sponsored agreement may include an *adjustment of a previously negotiated indirect cost rate.* This may occur if the negotiated rate is later found to have included costs that are unallowable by law, regulation, Circular A-21, or agreement, or not clearly allocable to the sponsored agreement.

Circular A-21 defines *direct costs* as those costs "that can be identified specifically with a particular sponsored project, an instructional activity, or that can be directly assigned to such activities relatively easily with a high degree of accuracy." Direct and indirect costs are distinguished from each other by the identification with the sponsored project and not by the type of cost incurred. Typical direct costs might be compensation and related fringe benefit costs for sponsored work under the agreement and materials consumed.

Circular A-21 also addresses indirect costs—costs incurred that cannot be easily identified with a sponsored project or any institutional activity. These costs are in the nature of depreciation of, and use allowances related to, fixed assets, general and administrative expenses, operation and maintenance expenses, and library and student administration expenses. Circular A-21 notes that the institution must develop a base period (normally the fiscal year of the organization) and must group costs in pools that are to be distributed to the related cost objectives using the most appropriate distribution base or method. Section E describes typical situations that may warrant the establishment of cost groupings within an indirect cost category in order to properly compute the indirect cost rate:

1. Where items or categories of expense relate to less than all functions.

2. Where expenses ordinarily treated as administration are charged as direct costs of a sponsored agreement and similar expenses are incurred for other activities, the similar costs must be separately grouped and not included as indirect costs for allocation.

3. Where costs can be identified with a service unit whose output is susceptible to measurement.

4. Where activities provide their own administration services.

5. Where fringe benefits are treated by the organization as indirect costs.

When selecting a method for distributing the indirect costs, the organization must consider the base "best suited for assigning the pool of costs to cost objectives in accordance with benefits derived" (i.e., if the cost grouping can be identified with the objective benefited, it should be so assigned).

Cost analysis studies are appropriately done when the expenses in a cost grouping are more general in nature. The studies must (1) be sufficiently documented, (2) distribute the costs relative to the benefits derived, (3) be statistically sound, (4) be performed at the institution, and (5) be reviewed periodically. If a cost analysis study is not undertaken, or if such a study does not result in an equitable distribution of indirect costs, other steps must be taken, including the simplified method for computing indirect cost rates.

The 1993 revisions to Circular A-21 added a new subsection to Section F, "Definition of Facilities and Administration." The cost category "Facilities" includes depreciation and use allowances, interest on building-related debt, equipment and capital improvements, operations and maintenance expense, and library expense. "Administration" includes general administration and general expenses, departmental administration, sponsored projects administration, student administration and services, and all other costs not specifically listed under facilities.

Section G of Circular A-21 describes the determination and application of indirect cost rate or rates. It assists the organization in its computation of the indirect cost rate for each of the major functions in Section F so that the indirect costs can be distributed to individual sponsored agreements. It informs the organization that the cost rate process must be appropriately designed to "ensure that federal sponsors do not in any way subsidize the indirect costs of other sponsors, specifically activities sponsored by industry and foreign governments.

According to Circular A-21, "A single rate basis for use across the board on all work within a major function at an institution may not be appropriate." For example, research might not take into account those environmental factors and other conditions that may affect substantially the indirect costs applicable to a particular segment of research at the institution. Where a segment of a sponsored agreement is performed in an environment that appears to generate a significantly different level of indirect costs, the organization should allow for a separate indirect cost pool for such work.

In determining the distribution basis of indirect costs, the institution must compute "modified total direct cost." This consists of all salaries and wages, fringe benefits, materials and supplies, services, travel, and subgrants and subcontracts up to the first $25,000 of each subgrant or subcontract.

In some instances (e.g., self-contained, off-campus, or primarily subcontracted activities where the benefits derived from an institution's indirect services cannot be readily determined), a negotiated fixed amount in lieu of indirect costs may be appropriate. These costs should be offset against others before allocation to instruction, organized research, other sponsored activities, and other institutional activities.

Public Law 87-638 (76 Stat. 437), in an attempt to simplify the administration of cost-type research and development contracts with educational institutions, permits the use of *predetermined rates* applicable under research agreements. Section G of Circular A-21 notes:

> Negotiation of predetermined rates for indirect costs for a period of two to four years should be the norm in those situations where the cost experience and other pertinent facts available are deemed sufficient to enable the parties involved to reach an informed judgment as to the provable level of indirect costs during the ensuing accounting periods.

Negotiated fixed rates determined in advance result in over- or under-recovery for the fiscal year. These amounts may be applied to the next subsequent rate negotiation. In determining these negotiated fixed rates, the organization will apply the expected indirect costs adjusted for the carryforward from prior periods to the forecast distribution base.

In some instances, a *provisional rate* will be established. This will occur when the cognizant agency determines that cost experience and other pertinent factors do not permit the use of either a negotiated predetermined rate or a fixed rate with a carryforward provision. Section G notes that the cognizant agency may adjust the provisional rate during the year to prevent substantial over- or underpayment. These provisional rates are destined to be replaced by a predetermined or fixed rate before the end of the organization's fiscal year.

According to A-21, only 26 percent of total direct administration costs can be charged to federal sponsored agreements awarded or amended with effective dates beginning on or after the organization's first fiscal year which begins on or after October 1, 1991.

To avoid preparing a cost proposal for the administration portion of the indirect cost rate, an institution coming under the provisions of Circular A-21 may elect to claim a fixed allowance for these costs. Under this method, a fixed allowance equal to the lower of 24 percent of modified total direct costs or 95 percent of the most recently negotiated fixed or predetermined rate for the cost pools is included under administration as defined in Section F.

Simplified Allocation Method

Institutions with total annual direct cost of work covered by Circular A-21 that is less than $10 million may use the simplified allocation method. The institution's most recent annual financial statement and supporting information with salaries and wages segregated from other cost will be used as a basis for determining the indirect cost rate applicable to all sponsored agreements.

Allowable and Unallowable Costs

Circular A-21 lists certain costs, including advertising, alcoholic beverages, bad debts, compensation for personal services, contingency provisions, defense and prosecution of litigation, donations, employee morale, housing and personal living expenses, insurance (including malpractice), interest, fund-raising, lobbying, memberships, professional services, profits and losses on disposition of property, and travel (including commercial air travel and foreign travel), and states whether they are allowable. Some unallowable costs, such as costs to purchase alcoholic beverages, are clearly not allowable. Other costs, such as travel costs, must be reviewed closely to determine if they are allowable.

DEPARTMENT OF LABOR GUIDE

In October 1993, the U.S. Department of Labor (DOL) published "A Guide for Nonprofit Organizations" as an aid "to understanding the requirements for the determination of indirect costs on grants, contracts, and other agreements awarded by the U.S. Department of Labor." This Guide includes guidelines for preparing indirect cost rate proposals, sample indirect cost rate proposals, submission of indirect cost proposals, and common problems disclosed by Office of Inspector General (OIG) audits. It describes a *cost allocation plan* as:

> A document that identifies, accumulates, and distributes allowable direct and indirect costs under grants and contracts and identifies the allocation methods used for distribution.

Indirect cost proposals are individual cost allocation plans submitted by operating departments performing under grants and contracts. The proposals allocate the costs of services incurred within the department. The DOL Guide provides examples of computations that a not-for-profit organization receiving federal awards might employ when submitting indirect cost proposals and suggested bases for cost distribution. Some of these bases are:

Type of Service	Suggested Basis for Allocation
Data processing	System usage
Occupancy costs	Square feet of space
Payroll services	Number of employees
Local telephone	Number of telephone instruments

The DOL Guide also provides guidelines for preparing indirect cost rate proposals. It directs the reader to obtain a thorough knowledge of the cost principles in Circular A-122 before beginning the preparation process. The following are some of the principal steps the Guide recommends to potential recipients of federal awards:

1. Prepare a written narrative outlining those costs believed to be direct and indirect and the rationale therefor.

2. Prepare a personnel costs worksheet that will be the basis for the provisional indirect cost proposal and the final indirect cost proposal. The latter will include actual personnel costs that will be documented in accordance with the appropriate cost principles.

3. Prepare a plan to indicate the appropriate percentage allocation of personnel costs for each cost objective or federally sponsored project or program. Each class of personnel (e.g., job title) should be allocated 100 percent to the various objectives.

The organization should establish and maintain a time-distribution system for employees whose time is charged to the various programs. This allows the appropriate audit or review procedures to take place, after the costs are allocated and reported to the federal agency.

Another element of the process is the preparation of a statement of employee benefits. It contains the costs of the items in the employee benefit pool (e.g., vacation, sick leave and holidays, FICA, pension, insurance, and state unemployment contributions). These benefits follow the individual employee's salary and are included in the determination of the reasonableness of compensation.

After establishing a time-distribution system and preparing a statement of employee benefits, the not-for-profit organization should prepare the indirect cost rate proposal. The DOL Guide provides examples of computations under the direct allocation and simplified allocation methods. The multiple allocation rate method is not demonstrated in this Guide because it is not used by not-for-profit organizations when the Department of Labor is the cognizant agency.

OMB CIRCULAR A-110

Many of the documents issued by federal agencies refer to the provisions of OMB Circular A-110 (Uniform Administrative Requirements for Grants and Agreements with Institutions of Higher Education, Hospitals, and Other Nonprofit Organizations). Circular A-110 was revised and reissued in November 1993, and its provisions affecting federal agencies were effective December 29, 1993. Provisions that affect grantees were to be adopted by agencies in codified regulations by May 30, 1994, and many, but not all, have done so. An organization receiving federal assistance should discuss the applicability of Circular A-110 with its funding agency representative. Circular A-110 was further amended in August 1997.

Circular A-110 establishes uniform administrative requirements for federal grants and agreements issued to institutions of higher education, hospitals, and other not-for-profit organizations. Its provisions also apply to subrecipients performing work under the award if the subrecipients are institutions of higher education, hospitals, or other not-for-profit organizations.

Circular A-110 gives the following definitions:

Award—Financial assistance that provides support or stimulation to accomplish a public purpose. Awards include grants and other agreements in the form of money or property in lieu of money, by the federal government to an eligible recipient. The term does not include technical assistance, which provides services instead of money; other assistance in the form of loans, loan guarantees, interest subsidies, or insurance; direct payments of any kind to individuals; and contracts that are required to be entered into and administered under procurement laws and regulations.

Federal funds authorized—The total amount of federal funds obligated by the federal government for use by the recipient. This amount may include any authorized carryover of unobligated funds from prior funding periods when permitted by agency regulations or agency implementing instructions.

Recipient—An organization receiving financial assistance directly from federal awarding agencies to carry out a project or program. The term may include commercial, foreign, or international organizations (such as agencies of the United Nations) that are recipients, subrecipients, contractors, or subcontractors of recipients or subrecipients, at the discretion of the federal awarding agency.

Subrecipient—The legal entity to which a subaward is made, which is accountable to the recipient for the use of the funds provided. The term may include foreign or international organizations (such as agencies of the United Nations), at the discretion of the federal awarding agency.

Working capital advance—A procedure whereby funds are advanced to the recipient to cover its estimated disbursement needs for a given initial period.

Circular A-110 differentiates between *grants* and *cooperative agreements*. Cooperative agreements are used when there is expected to be "substantial involvement between the executive agency and the state, local government, or other recipient when carrying out the activity contemplated in the agreement."

Post-Award Requirements

In a section on "Post-Award Requirements," Circular A-110 describes:

- Standards for financial management systems
- Methods for making payments
- Cost-sharing or matching requirements
- Program income
- Budget revisions
- Audit requirements
- Cost allowability
- Availability of funds
- Property standards
- Procurement standards
- Reports and records
- Termination
- Enforcement

Financial management systems   The not-for-profit organization's financial management systems should allow for "accurate, current, and complete" reporting of the financial results of each sponsored program. Its records should identify the source and application of funds, and it should have control over and accountability for all related funds, property, and other assets. Written procedures should be in place to minimize the time between the transfer of funds from the federal government and their use for program purposes by the recipient, and to determine the reasonableness, allocability, and allowability of costs. Also, the accounting records, including cost accounting records, should have supporting source documentation.

Methods for making payments   Payments for cash advances to the not-for-profit recipient are limited to the minimum amounts needed to carry out the purpose of the program. These payments should be made as close as possible to the disbursement by the organization for direct costs and a share of the allowable indirect costs. If the organization is a recipient of awards from several projects or programs, the advances should be consolidated. Advances may be made in the form of check or electronic fund transfers.

When the not-for-profit recipient cannot maintain the written procedures or other requirements regarding its financial management system, the agency making the award should consider reimbursement-of-cost rather than advances as the preferred method of payment. Circular A-110 provides the awarding agency latitude in arranging the method(s) for making payments to the recipient.

Circular A-110 lists the requirements for the use of banks and other institutions as depositories of funds advanced under awards. Generally, advances should be deposited in insured accounts; recipients are encouraged to use women-owned or minority-owned banks; and the advances should be deposited in interest-bearing accounts. Interest-bearing accounts need not be used if awards are less than $120,000 per year, interest would not exceed $250 per year, or the depository would require an unreasonably high average or minimum balance. Circular A-110 also lists the forms recipients will need to complete to request advances and reimbursements.

Cost-sharing or matching requirements   When an agreement calls for *cost-sharing or matching*, the criteria used to determine the acceptability of contributions are set forth in Circular A-110:

- Contributions must be verifiable from the recipient's records;
- Contributions must not be included as contributions for any other federally assisted project or program;
- Contributions must be necessary and reasonable for proper and efficient accomplishment of project or program objectives;
- Contributions must be allowable under the applicable cost principles;
- Contributions must not be paid by the federal government under another award, except when authorized to be used for cost-sharing or matching;
- Contributions must be provided for in the approved budget when required by the federal awarding agency; and
- Contributions must conform to other provisions of Circular A-110, as applicable.

The values of contributions of services and property should be in accordance with the applicable cost principles. Generally, real property donated will be valued at the lower of the "certified [by an independent appraiser] value of the remaining life... recorded in the recipient's accounting records at the time of the donation," or the current fair market value. Volunteer services will be valued at rates, including fringe benefits, consistent with those paid for similar work in the recipient's organization or paid for similar work in the labor market. Donated supplies are valued at fair market value at the time of the donation. These valuation principles may change depending on the purpose of the award.

Program income   The recipient's treatment of *program income* will vary, but in general, program income is retained by the recipient. It should be:

- Added to federal funds committed to the program;
- Used to finance the nonfederal portion of the program; or
- Deducted to determine net allowable costs of the program.

If the federal agency does not specify the use to which program income should be put, then program income should be deducted to determine the program's net costs. If the sponsored project is research and the agency has not specified a particular use, the program income should be added to the federal funds committed to the project. Program income earned after the end of the project period may be used in any fashion by the organization, unless regulations or the terms and conditions of the award state otherwise.

Gross income may be reduced by the costs incurred to generate program income when arriving at the amount to be considered under this section of Circular A-110. However, these costs should not be charged to the award. It should be noted that proceeds from the sale of property will need to be reviewed in light of the property standards in Circular A-110. These standards are discussed later in this chapter.

Budget revisions   Circular A-110 requires not-for-profit organizations to report deviations from budget and to request prior approvals for budget revisions in the following instances:

- If a change is made in program scope or objective;
- If the key person identified in documents is changed;
- If additional funding is needed;
- If the approved project director or principal investigator will be on a prolonged absence;

- If there are changes in category (e.g., indirect to direct or vice versa) of cost;
- If costs that require prior federal agency approval are included;
- If training allowances are transferred to other categories of expense; or
- If a subaward or transfer will be made or if any work will be contracted out.

For construction awards, the recipient must request written approval for budget revisions when:

- The request is caused by a change in scope or objective of the program;
- Additional federal funds are needed to complete a project; or
- A revision involves specific costs for which applicable OMB cost principles require prior written approval.

Audit requirements   Circular A-110 requires recipients and subrecipients to be subject to the audit requirements of the Single Audit Act Amendments of 1996 and Circular A-133. If the recipient is a for-profit hospital not covered by the audit provisions of Circular A-133, it will be subject to the audit requirements of the federal awarding agency(ies) from which it receives awards.

Cost allowability   Circular A-110 instructs the federal agencies that fall under its provisions about the appropriate cost principles to be used to determine *allowable costs* of recipients of federal awards. As noted above, Circular A-122 contains cost principles for not-for-profit organizations; Circular A-21 contains cost principles for institutions of higher education; and Appendix E of 45 CFR part 74 contains cost principles for hospitals.

Availability of funds   Circular A-110 notes that a recipient may charge to the award only allowable costs arising from obligations incurred during the period of availability of funds specified in the agreement.

Property standards   Property standards set forth uniform standards governing management and disposition of property furnished by the federal government whose cost was charged to a project supported by a federal award. These standards govern:

- *Insurance coverage*—Equivalent to coverage owned by the recipient

- *Real property*—Concerning the use and disposition of property acquired under awards
- *Federally owned and exempt property*—Control of property and vesting of title
- *Equipment*—Control and use of equipment and vesting of title
- *Supplies and other expendable property*—Control and use of supplies and use of proceeds of sale of excess supplies
- *Intangible property*—Control and use of work subject to copyright and the ability to obtain copyright for such work
- *Property trust relationship*—Property held by recipients for the beneficiaries of the program or project

Procurement standards Procurement standards set forth guidelines governing procedures for the procurement of supplies and other expendable property, equipment, real property, and other services with federal funds. These standards relate to:

- *Recipient responsibilities*—The recipient is the responsible authority regarding the settlement of contractual and administrative issues arising out of procurements entered into.
- *Codes of conduct*—Recipients must have written standards of conduct governing the performance of its employees engaged in the award and administration of contracts.
- *Competition*—Transactions should be conducted in a manner that provides open and free competition.
- *Procurement procedures*—Recipients must establish minimum requirements for written procedures governing the purchase of goods and services.
- *Cost and price analysis*—Recipients must document every procurement action and maintain files.
- *Procurement records*—Procurement records for purchases in excess of $25,000 (current small purchase threshold) must include the basis for selection, justification for lack of competitive bids (when none obtained), and basis for price.
- *Contract administration*—Recipients must establish contract administration systems to ensure contractor conformance with terms, conditions, and specifications.
- *Contract provisions*—Recipients must include certain mandatory provisions in all contracts for purchases.

Reports and records Reports and records standards set forth the procedures for monitoring and reporting on performance and also record retention requirements. Not-for-profit organizations receiving awards are responsible for *monitoring and reporting program per-*

formance for each project supported by the award, including the monitoring of subawards to ensure subrecipients have met audit requirements. Completion of Financial Status Report, Form SF-269 or SF-269A, is part of the *financial reporting* requirement included in Circular A-110. The awarding agency will determine whether these reports should be on the cash or accrual basis of reporting and the frequency of the reports. Completion of Report of Federal Cash Transactions, Form SF-272, is required for reporting of the use of cash advances. Generally, the provisions relating to *retention require-ments for records* state that financial records, supporting documents, statistical records, and all other records pertinent to an award should be retained for three years from the date of submission of the final expenditure report. Circular A-110 notes that the awarding agency has *right of access* to the records for the purpose of audit, examina-tion, excerpts, and copies. This right also includes access to organiza-tion personnel for interviews to discuss the documents.

Termination   According to Circular A-110, *termination* may occur under the following three conditions:

1. The federal agency may terminate the award if the recipient demonstrates a material failure to comply with the award.
2. The award may be terminated through mutual agreement of the federal agency and the recipient.
3. The recipient may terminate the award.

Enforcement   If the recipient materially fails to comply with the award, the federal agency has the following remedies under Circular A-110:

- The federal agency may temporarily withhold cash payments pending correction of the deficiencies.
- The federal agency may disallow all or part of the cost of the activity that is not in compliance.
- The federal agency may suspend or terminate the award and withhold further awards.
- The federal agency may make use of other legally available remedies.

After-the-Award Requirements

Subpart D of Circular A-110, "After-the-Award Requirements," in-cludes discussions of the following:

- Closeout procedures
- Subsequent adjustments and continuing responsibilities
- Collection of amounts due

Closeout procedures   As part of the *closeout procedures*, recipients will undertake certain reporting requirements and will liquidate all obligations incurred under the award within 90 calendar days after the date of completion of the award. The federal agency and the recipient will make prompt payment of the amounts due or the excess received. In the latter situation, the recipient may be authorized to retain the excess funds for use in other projects.

Subsequent adjustments and continuing responsibilities   Although an award may be closed out, the recipient remains subject to *subsequent adjustments and continuing responsibilities*. The federal agency may disallow costs on the basis of a subsequent audit or review.

Collection of amounts due   Excess funds received by a recipient must be repaid within a reasonable period after the agency makes a demand. The federal agency has further remedies it may pursue, and overdue amounts will bear an interest cost.

AUDITING CONSIDERATIONS

In December 1992, the AICPA, through its Not-for-Profit Organizations Committee, issued—and has subsequently reissued—SOP 92-9 (Audits of Not-for-Profit Organizations Receiving Federal Awards) to provide guidance on the independent auditor's responsibilities when conducting an audit in accordance with Circular A-133. Organization-wide audits, sometimes referred to as "single audits," performed in accordance with Circular A-133 were developed to reduce the efforts of the various federal funders that were carrying out their own audits of individual programs. A single entity that was the recipient of federal assistance from several sources may have been subjected to several audits during the year. The organization-wide audit is often conducted by the entity's independent CPA, who will ascertain the various requirements of the programs from which his or her client receives funding and design audit steps to conduct an effective and efficient audit.

Under OMB Circular A-133 before its revision, auditing requirements and the related reports to be issued by the auditor were determined by the amount of federal assistance—in total and in relation to each program. The auditor had a higher level of responsibility to report on compliance with specific requirements of major programs than for nonmajor programs.

With the issuance of the revisions to Circular A-133, much has changed. Refer to the section titled "OMB Circular A-133" above for a more complete description of the A-133 revisions and their effect on auditees and their independent auditors.

In March 1998, the AICPA issued SOP 98-3, which incorporates "auditing guidance through AICPA Statement on Auditing Standards No. 85, *Management Representations*." The new SOP supersedes SOP 92-9 effectively for "audits of fiscal years beginning after June 30, 1996, in which the related field work commences on or after March 1, 1998."

The new SOP is more comprehensive than the one that it replaced. It will make compliance with the revised OMB Circular A-133 easier for auditors and auditees, because it contains (in Chapter 3, "Planning and Other Special Audit Consideration of Circular A-133") guidance regarding initial-year audit considerations, including how to deal with an auditee that was previously audited by another auditor. It also discusses materiality differences between the financial statement audit and the "single audit" performed in accordance with Circular A-133 and materiality for purposes of reporting audit findings—gray areas under the superseded SOP 92-9 and the original version of Circular A-133.

There is discussion in SOP 98-3 about developing an efficient audit approach, joint audits, and reliance on others. As noted earlier, the SOP contains guidance on program-specific audits and their reports, and on submission of the single audit reporting package and the Data Collection Form to the Federal Clearinghouse.

Federal Financial Reports

As part of the organization-wide audit approach, the independent auditor will conduct an audit of the entity's financial statements in accordance with generally accepted auditing standards (GAAS) and the financial audit standards contained in *Government Auditing Standards* (GAS). GAAS are issued by the AICPA in Statements on Auditing Standards; GAS are contained in the Yellow Book, issued by the Comptroller General of the United States.

The independent auditor will issue several reports to satisfy the requirements of the revised Circular A-133, GAS, and GAAS. The form and content of such auditor reports will be determined in part by the programs selected for audit, the specific requirements of the programs, the extent of testing of transactions, and the results of the tests performed by the auditor. These reports include:

- Opinion (or disclaimer of opinion) on financial statements and Supplementary Schedule of Expenditures of Federal Awards
- Report on compliance and on internal control over financial reporting based on an audit of financial statements

- Report on compliance (opinion or disclaimer of opinion) and internal control over compliance applicable to each major program
- Schedule of Findings and Questioned Costs.

Appendix D of SOP 98-3 contains examples of each of the required reports.
The situations covered for not-for-profit organizations include:

- Unqualified opinion on financial statements and supplementary schedule of expenditures of federal awards
- Report on compliance and on internal control over financial reporting based on an audit of financial statements performed in accordance with *Government Auditing Standards* (No reportable instances of noncompliance and no material weaknesses [no reportable conditions identified])
- Report on compliance and on internal control over financial reporting based on an audit of financial statements performed in accordance with *Government Auditing Standards* (Reportable instances of noncompliance and reportable conditions identified)
- Report on compliance with requirements applicable to each major program and on internal control over compliance in accordance with OMB Circular A-133 (Unqualified opinion on compliance and no material weaknesses [no reportable conditions identified])
- Report on compliance with requirements applicable to each major program and on internal control over compliance in accordance with OMB Circular A-133 (Qualified opinion on compliance and reportable conditions identified)
- Report on compliance with requirements applicable to each major program and on internal control over compliance in accordance with OMB Circular A-133 (Qualified opinion on compliance—scope limitation for one major program, unqualified opinion on compliance for other major programs, reportable conditions identified)
- Report on compliance with requirements applicable to each major program and on internal control over compliance in accordance with OMB Circular A-133 (Adverse opinion on compliance for one major program, unqualified opinion on compliance for other major programs and material weaknesses identified)
- Unqualified opinion on the financial statement of a federal program in accordance with the program-specific audit option under OMB Circular A-133

- Report on compliance with requirements applicable to the federal program and on internal control over compliance in accordance with the program-specific audit option under OMB Circular A-133 (Unqualified opinion on compliance and no material weaknesses [no reportable conditions identified])

Noncompliance and Questioned Costs

To the extent they are noted during the course of the audit, and to the extent they fall within the new A-133 reporting guidelines (see the section titled "OMB Circular A-133" above), matters of noncompliance, and expenditures that may not be appropriately charged against the grant or agreement under which the item was claimed, should be reported. When such findings are included in the auditor's report, the not-for-profit organization should submit a corrective action plan that addresses the areas of noncompliance or internal control matters addressed in the auditor's reports. If, in the auditor's judgment, the instances of noncompliance are not significant, they are not required to be reported in the Schedule of Findings and Questioned Costs.

The requirements with which the entity must comply are found in the OMB's Circular A-133 *Compliance Supplement* or in the grant agreements and contracts themselves. The *Compliance Supplement* lists requirements and audit procedures for significant federal programs. A provisional *Compliance Supplement* has been issued as an Appendix to the revised A-133. In June 1998, an expanded *Compliance Supplement* was issued. These requirements may be supplemented by information in the *Catalog of Federal Domestic Assistance* (CFDA), a government-wide summary of federal programs administered by federal government departments and agencies, and in OMB Circular A-110, which lists administrative requirements. The auditor should research all of these sources to design an audit program that will allow him or her to report on compliance.

Compliance Requirements

The *Compliance Supplement* attached as an Appendix to Circular A-133 identifies the requirements with which recipients of federal awards must comply. These include:

- Activities Allowed or Unallowed
- Allowable Costs/Cost Principles
- Cash Management
- Davis–Bacon Act
- Eligibility

- Equipment and Real Property Management
- Matching, Level of Effort, Earmarking
- Period of Availability of Federal Funds
- Procurement and Suspension and Debarment
- Program Income
- Real Property Acquisition and Relocation Assistance
- Reporting
- Subrecipient Monitoring
- Special Tests and Provisions

The foregoing replace the General and Specific Requirements of the former version of Circular A-133.

COMPLIANCE SUPPLEMENT

In June 1998 and again in April 1999, OMB revised the provisional *Compliance Supplement* that it had issued in 1997. The changes include the following:

- A new subsection for certain federal programs, to provide additional information about the program's objectives, procedures, and compliance requirements.
- A new paragraph clarifying the "safe harbor" status of the *Compliance Supplement*. Ordinarily, "the auditor should not consider this Supplement to be a 'Safe Harbor' for identifying the audit procedures to apply in a particular engagement," because the suggested audit procedures are general in nature and because auditor "judgment will be necessary to determine whether the suggested audit procedures are sufficient." The added paragraph notes that "the auditor can consider this Supplement a 'safe harbor' for identification of compliance requirements to be tested for the programs included herein if . . . the auditor (1) performs reasonable procedures to ensure that the requirements in this Supplement are current and to determine whether there are any additional provisions of contract and grant agreements that should be covered by an audit under the 1996 Amendments, and (2) updates or augments the requirements contained in this Supplement as appropriate."
- Updated the Matrix of Compliance Requirements to include new programs and to report the changes for existing programs. The change also amends the guidance to the auditor for use of the Matrix. Approximately 120 programs are now included in the *Compliance Supplement*.

- Revised Part 3, "Compliance Requirements," by adding guidance to indicate that the descriptions of the compliance requirements are summaries and by supplying cross-references to the complete descriptions.

> **OBSERVATION:** This part of the *Compliance Supplement* "does not include suggested audit procedures to test internal control. The auditor must determine appropriate procedures to test internal control on a case by case basis considering factors such as the non-Federal entity's internal control, the compliance requirements, the audit objectives for compliance, the auditor's assessment of control risk, and the audit requirement to test internal control as prescribed in OMB Circular A-133." However, Chapter 8 of SOP 98-3 (Audits of States, Local Governments, and Not-for-Profit Organizations Receiving Federal Awards) does provide significant discussion and guidance.

- Revised Part 4, "Agency Program Requirements," to add a new subsection titled "Other Information," and clarified the meaning of the phrase "not applicable" to indicate "either that there are no compliance requirements or that the auditor is not required to test compliance."
- Added programs from U.S. Department of Agriculture, Department of the Interior, Department of Labor, Department of Transportation, Environmental Protection Agency, Federal Emergency Management Agency, Department of Education, Department of Health and Human Services, Corporation for National and Community Service, and Social Security Administration.

GAAS versus GAS

The differences between audits conducted in accordance with GAAS and those conducted in accordance with GAS can be found in the 1994 revision of the Yellow Book. This publication discusses auditors' responsibilities (GAS, par. 1.14):

> The comprehensive nature of auditing done in accordance with these standards places on the audit organization the responsibility for ensuring that (1) the audit is conducted by personnel who collectively have the necessary skills, (2) independence is maintained, (3) applicable standards are followed in planning and conducting audits and reporting the results, (4) the organization has an appropriate internal control system in place, and (5) the organization undergoes an external quality control review.

In Chapters 3, 4, and 5 the Yellow Book discusses audit standards—general standards, fieldwork standards for financial audits, and reporting standards for financial audits, respectively.

General standards   The GAS general standards are similar to, but not the same as, the general standards issued by the AICPA, as shown in the following table:

GAAS	GAS
1. The audit is to be performed by a person or persons having adequate technical training and proficiency as an auditor.	1. The staff assigned to conduct the audit should collectively possess adequate professional proficiency for the tasks required.
2. In all matters relating to the assignment, an independence in mental attitude is to be maintained by the auditor or auditors.	2. In all matters relating to the audit work, the audit organization and the individual auditors, whether government or public, should be free from personal and external impairments to independence, should be organizationally independent, and should maintain an independent attitude and appearance.
3. Due professional care is to be exercised in the performance of the audit and the preparation of the report.	3. Due professional care should be used in conducting the audit and in preparing related reports.
	4. Each audit organization conducting audits in accordance with these standards should have an appropriate internal quality control system in place and undergo an external quality control review.

Continuing education   The first of the GAS general standards includes continuing education requirements. It notes (GAS, par. 3.6):

> Individuals responsible for planning or directing an audit, conducting substantial portions of the field work, or reporting on the audit under these standards should complete at least 24 of the 80 hours of continuing education and training [required every two years] in subjects directly related to the government environment and to government auditing. If the audited entity operates in a specific or unique environment, auditors should receive training that is related to that environment.

The AICPA general standards do not include a specific requirement for hours of continuing education. The AICPA, however, does have a specific requirement for its members, and many states and CPA firms have their own internal requirements.

Quality control   The fourth GAS general standard includes quality control requirements. It notes (GAS, par. 3.31):

> Each audit organization conducting audits in accordance with these standards should have an appropriate internal quality control system in place and undergo an external quality control review.

Audit organizations seeking to enter into a contract to perform an audit in accordance with these standards should provide their most recent external quality control review report to the party contracting for the audit (GAS, par. 3.36).

The AICPA does not have a standard that relates to required external quality control reviews. However, the SEC Practice Section of the AICPA does have a peer review program in place and the Private Companies Practice Section also has in place a program for external quality control reviews.

Fieldwork standards   The three GAAS fieldwork standards have been incorporated into GAS. In addition, the Yellow Book adds additional standards for the following:

- *Planning*—"Auditors should follow up on known material findings and recommendations from previous audits" (GAS, par. 4.7).

- *Noncompliance other than illegal acts*—"Auditors should design the audit to provide reasonable assurance of detecting material misstatements resulting from noncompliance with provisions of contracts or grant agreements that have a direct and material effect on the determination of financial statement amounts. If specific information comes to the auditors' attention that provides evidence concerning the existence of possible noncompliance that could have a material indirect effect on the financial statements, auditors should apply audit procedures specifically directed to ascertaining whether that noncompliance has occurred" (GAS, par. 4.20).

Working papers   SAS-41 (Working Papers) is included in the AICPA standards of fieldwork and sets forth the functions and nature of working papers:

> Working papers serve mainly to provide the principal support for the auditor's report, including his representation regarding observance of the standards of field work, which is

implicit in the reference in his report to generally accepted auditing standards.

GAS adds an additional standard for working papers (GAS, par. 4.35):

> Working papers should contain sufficient information to enable an experienced auditor having no previous connection with the audit to ascertain from them the evidence that supports the auditors' significant conclusions and judgments.

Reporting standards The AICPA has established four reporting standards. GAS incorporates the AICPA standards and includes five additional reporting standards. These relate to the following (GAS, pars. 5.5–5.32):

1. *Communication with audit committees or other responsible individuals*—Auditors should communicate certain information related to the conduct and reporting of the audit to the audit committee or to the individuals with whom they have contracted for the audit.

2. *Reporting compliance with generally accepted government auditing standards*—Audit reports should state that the audit was made in accordance with generally accepted government auditing standards.

3. *Reporting on compliance with laws regulations and on internal controls*—The report on the financial statements should either (1) describe the scope of the auditors' testing of compliance with laws and regulations and internal controls and present the results of those tests or (2) refer to separate reports containing that information. In presenting the results of those tests, auditors should report irregularities, illegal acts, other material noncompliance, and reportable conditions in internal controls. In some circumstances, auditors should report irregularities and illegal acts directly to parties external to the audited entity.

4. *Privileged and confidential information*—If certain information is prohibited from general disclosure, the audit report should state the nature of the information omitted and the requirement that makes the omission necessary.

5. *Report distribution*—Written audit reports are to be submitted by the audit organization to the appropriate officials of the auditee and to the appropriate officials of the organizations requiring or arranging for the audits, including external funding organizations, unless legal restrictions prevent it. Copies of the reports also should be sent to other officials who have legal oversight authority or who may be responsible for acting on

audit findings and recommendations and to others authorized to receive such reports. Unless restricted by law or regulation, copies should be made available for public inspection.

APPENDIX: CHRONOLOGY

Early 1970s: Circular A-102 and GAO Standards

In 1971, OMB Circular A-102 (Uniform Administrative Requirements for Grants-in-Aid to State and Local Governments) became the key pronouncement in standard-setting for audits of federal awards to state and local governments. Following its issuance, federal funders were required to seek approval from OMB for any non-legislated standards not already imposed on recipients. OMB Circular A-102 called for audits to determine, at a minimum:

- The fiscal integrity of financial transactions and reports
- The compliance with laws, regulations, and administrative requirements

The grantee was advised to schedule the audits with reasonable frequency, usually annually, but not less frequently than once every two years, and to consider the nature, size, and complexity of the program for which funding was received.

Contemporaneously with the activity at OMB, the General Accounting Office (GAO) was active in establishing standards for audits. In 1972, GAO issued *Standards for Audits of Governmental Organizations, Programs, Activities, and Functions* (GAO Standards). This precursor of the *Yellow Book* acknowledged the existence of auditing standards established by the American Institute of Certified Public Accountants (AICPA) and included similar concepts for the audits of federal government agencies and recipients of federal funds, whether conducted by federal auditors or by external organizations on behalf of the federal government. Later, GAO developed and issued an Audit Guide to be tested. The expectation was that a single guide could serve the many funders that issued their own guides, which often were not kept current.

Late 1970s: Changes to Circular A-102; Circular A-110 Introduced

Additional requirements for state and local governments were introduced as federal revenue-sharing became more widespread. For years ending after January 1, 1977, these governments were now required to have all financial statements audited in accordance with generally accepted auditing standards (GAAS) at least once every three years. Then, in 1977, changes to OMB Circular A-102 clarified that audits conducted in accordance with GAAS and the GAO Standards were:

- To be carried out by qualified, independent auditors.
- Intended to ascertain the effectiveness of the financial management systems and internal procedures that have been established to meet the terms and conditions of the grant.
- Not intended to examine each grant awarded to a recipient.
- To be conducted on an organization-wide basis to test the fiscal integrity of financial transactions and compliance with the terms and conditions of the federal grants.
- To be "conducted with reasonable frequency on a continuing basis or at scheduled intervals usually annually but not less frequently than every two years."

In 1976, OMB issued Circular A-110. In accordance with Circular A-110, federal funders were required to standardize the administration of federal grants and subgrants.

Although intended to conform to Circular A-102's guidance to state and local governments, Circular A-110 differed from it in several respects. As noted above, Circular A-102 was specific in its audit requirements; Circular A-110 instructions, however, were not as specific.

For example, Circular A-110 was notably less clear about the scope of the audits, using such terms as:

- Generally, examinations should be conducted on an organization-wide basis. . . .
- Such tests would include appropriate sampling. . . .
- The frequency of these examinations shall depend upon the nature, size and complexity of the activity. . . .

The requirements of Circular A-110 *were* clear about the significant topic of independence:

> Such audits shall be made by qualified individuals who are sufficiently independent of those who authorize the expenditure of federal funds, to produce unbiased opinions, conclusions or judgments. They shall meet the independence criteria along the lines of Chapter 3, Part 3 of the [GAO Standards].

At the end of the 1970s, Congress enacted legislation that resulted in the creation of the Office of Inspectors General. Also, GAO began the process of establishing a single Audit Guide to replace a large number of agency-produced Audit Guides.

In 1979, GAO performed a study in which it concluded that of the $240 billion awarded by the federal government between 1974 and 1977, inclusive, "it is possible the government did not provide audits for nearly $192 billion." The study, which reviewed 73 major grantees, also noted that there were significant deficiencies in nearly all cases. In fact, 17 of the 73 grantees had not been audited at all. Of the 56 that had been audited, many had audits by more than one federal agency.

Early 1980s: Toward the Single Audit Act of 1984 . . . Which Did Not Cover Not-for-Profits

In 1980 and 1981, other events affected the single audit process. A new, joint Audit Guide, *Guidelines for Financial and Compliance Audits of Federally Assisted Programs,* was issued by OMB and GAO; all of the inspectors general were fired, only to be rehired after Congress complained; renewal of the general revenue-sharing program heightened the need for audits of federal programs; and an amendment to OMB Circular A-102 provided opportunities for small and minority audit firms to participate in single audits. Finally, in 1981, legislation was introduced in Congress to enact a requirement for a single audit.

In 1981, the GAO Standards were revised to clarify the differences between them and GAAS, and to segment the GAO Standards into those applicable to financial and compliance audits and those applicable to performance audits.

In 1982, two proposals were introduced in Congress to require single audits at least once every two years of recipients of more than $100,000 of federal assistance. These actions, which reflected dissatisfaction with OMB, caused the latter to again review its own policies related to audits of federal financial assistance. As a consequence, OMB issued a plan for the conduct of audits of block grant programs. The plan and guidance on the responsibilities of recipients relating to cash management were incorporated into the 1992 *Compliance Supplement for Single Audits of State and Local Governments.* Also, OMB revised its audit follow-up rules contained in Circular A-50 (Audit Follow-Up), subjecting the findings of reports from inspectors general, GAO, and other auditors to greater follow-up effort.

In 1983, however, Congress again developed concern about oversight of federal programs. Legislation was introduced that would have required entities that had received more than $25,000 of federal assistance during a year to have an independent, organization-wide audit at least once every two years. The tests to be performed would be determined by the independent auditors. Findings from the audit would relate to financial and internal-control-related matters. The versions of the proposed legislation introduced in each chamber had clear differences: The Senate bill provided for biannual single audits of all funds for state and local governments receiving more than $25,000 of federal assistance. *Major program* expenditures exceeded the greater of $500,000 or 3% of federal assistance, plus all programs over $30 million. The House bill provided for annual single audits of all funds for state and local governments receiving more than $100,000. *Major program* expenditures exceeded the greater of $100,000 or 3% of federal assistance, plus all programs over $3 million.

These differences were reconciled in the Single Audit Act of 1984. The Act provided for an *annual single audit* of state and local governments receiving *more than $100,000 in federal assistance during a fiscal year*. Governments receiving less than $100,000 but more than $25,000 could choose between submitting to an entity-wide single audit or to the audit requirements of the programs from which they received funds. For assistance less than $25,000 annually, there were *no* audit requirements—only a requirement to have records available for federal funders that may wish to audit their funds. *Major programs* were defined by a sliding scale, beginning with the greater of $300,000 or 3% of total federal expenditures if the total expenditures were between $100,000 and $100 million. At the top of the scale, for total federal expenditures greater than $7 billion, a *major program* was one with expenditures of $20 million or more.

Audits of not-for-profit organizations were not included in the Single Audit Act of 1984 because, by that time, the experience of auditing federal assistance to state and local governments was more extensive. Also, the standards for state and local government audits were more greatly developed, enabling their codification in legislation that could be supported by auditors and auditees. In contrast, similar legislative action could not be supported for audits of not-for-profits, because of the lack of clarity in Attachment F, "Standards for Financial Management Systems," of Circular A-110. Hence, OMB Circular A-110 continued to provide the leading guidance for audits of not-for-profit organizations.

Late 1980s: Circular A-128 Introduced

In 1985, OMB issued Circular A-128 (Audits of State and Local Governments). The Circular required federal funders to adopt the provisions of the Single Audit Act of 1984; as a result, the audits of federal assistance to such entities were standardized. At that time there was no movement towards revising the audit provisions of Circular A-110. OMB did not act on audits of not-for-profit organizations until the issuance of Circular A-133.

Early 1990s: Circular A-133 Introduced, Circular A-110 Revised

In 1990, OMB Circular A-133 (Audits of Institutions of Higher Education and Other Nonprofit Institutions) was published. Circular A-133 superseded the audit guidance in paragraph 2h of Attachment F of Circular A-110. It is applicable to federal agencies responsible for "administering programs that involve grants, cost-type contracts and other agreements with institutions of higher education and other non-profit recipients." It also is applicable to not-for-profit organizations, "whether they are recipients, receiving awards directly from federal agencies, or are subrecipients, receiving awards indirectly through other recipients."

OMB Circular A-110 was revised in 1993. In Section 26, "Non-Federal Audits," OMB sets out audit requirements:

> (a) Recipients and subrecipients that are institutions of higher education or other nonprofit organizations shall be subject to the audit requirements contained in OMB Circular A-133, *Audits of Institutions of Higher Education and Other Nonprofit Institutions.*
>
> (b) State and local governments shall be subject to the audit requirements contained in the Single Audit Act. . .and federal awarding agency regulations implementing OMB Circular A-128, *Audits of State and Local Governments.*
>
> (c) Hospitals not covered by the audit provisions of OMB Circular A-133 shall be subject to the audit requirements of the federal awarding agencies.
>
> (d) Commercial organizations shall be subject to the audit requirements of the federal awarding agency or the prime recipient as incorporated into the award document.

In 1996 and 1997, OMB revised the original Circular A-133 and, with the actions of Congress, abandoned its Circular A-128 covering audits of state and local government recipients of federal funding. The new A-133 is titled "Audits of States, Local Governments, and Non-Profit Organizations." In June 1998, and then again in April 1999, OMB issued a revised *Compliance Supplement* to assist auditors and auditees in fulfilling the requirements of the new Circular.

OMB has also been active in the area of cost principles, working to bring into harmony its various cost Circulars. In mid-1998, OMB issued revisions to Circular A-122, "Cost Principles for Nonprofit Organizations." Among other matters, the revisions amend the definition of *equipment*; require the breakout of indirect costs into two categories—facilities and administration; modify the multiple allocation basis to be consistent with OMB Circular A-2; and clarify the treatment of certain cost items, including, for example, alcoholic beverages, advertising, automobiles, living expenses, and memberships.

CHAPTER 16
COST ACCOUNTING STANDARDS

CONTENTS

CHAPTER 16
COST ACCOUNTING STANDARDS

Overview

The federal government requires that the method used to accumulate estimated costs in the preparation of a proposal be consistent with an entity's internal practices for recording and reporting costs.

OMB Circular A-21 (Cost Principles for Educational Institutions) is cited in the Federal Acquisition Regulation (FAR) as the source for determining the costs of research and development, training, and other work performed by educational institutions under contracts with the government. In addition, Circular A-21 notes:

> Federally Funded Research and Development Centers associated with education institutions shall be required to comply with the Cost Accounting Standards, rules and regulations issued by the Cost Accounting Standards Board . . . provided that they are subject thereto under defense related contracts.

OMB Circular A-122 (Cost Principles for Nonprofit Organizations) is cited as the source of principles for determining the costs applicable to work performed by not-for-profit organizations under contracts, grants, and other agreements with the government. A-122 states:

> It is unlikely that the type of grantees covered by this Circular would have contracts large enough to be covered by the CASB [Cost Accounting Standards Board]. In the event that they do, however, the regulations of the CASB would apply.

CROSS-REFERENCES

2000 MILLER NOT-FOR-PROFIT REPORTING: Chapter 5, "Assets"; Chapter 6, "Liabilities"

2000 MILLER GAAP GUIDE: Chapter 33, "Pension Plans—Employers"

2000 M<small>ILLER</small> GAAP I<small>MPLEMENTATION</small> M<small>ANUAL</small>: Chapter 7, "Capitalization and Expense Recognition Concepts"; Chapter 29, "Pension Plans—Employers"

2000 M<small>ILLER</small> G<small>OVERNMENTAL</small> GAAP G<small>UIDE</small>: Chapter 22, "Pension Obligation"; Chapter 29, "Pension Trust Funds"

Background

The Cost Accounting Standards Board was originally formed in 1970 to publish uniform cost accounting standards for use by government contractors. This entity was not renewed by Congress, but in 1988, a new, independent board known as the Cost Accounting Standards Board (CASB) was established to issue standards to be followed by all executive agencies and their contractors and subcontractors.

CASB has issued 20 Cost Accounting Standards—last revised in 1996, and contained in the Federal Register at 48 CFR 9904. Each is discussed in this chapter.

Cost Accounting Standard 401: Consistency in Estimating, Accumulating, and Reporting Costs

Through the issuance of Cost Accounting Standard 401, the government requires consistency in the application of cost accounting practices to:

- Enhance the likelihood that comparable transactions are treated alike.
- Facilitate the preparation of reliable cost estimates used in pricing a proposal.
- Permit cost estimates to be compared with the costs of performance of the resulting contract.
- Provide a basis for financial control over costs during contact performance.
- Aid in establishing accountability for cost in the manner agreed to by both parties at the time of entering into the contract.

Cost Accounting Standard 402: Consistency in Allocating Costs Incurred for the Same Purpose

Cost Accounting Standard 402 ensures that each type of cost is allocated on only one basis and only once to a contract or other cost objective. This will serve to:

- Guard against the overcharging of some cost objectives.
- Prevent *double counting*, which occurs when cost items are allocated directly to a cost objective but are not eliminated from indirect cost pools also allocated to that cost objective.

Cost Accounting Standard 403: Allocation of Home Office Expenses to Segments

Cost Accounting Standard 403, to limit the amount of home office expenses to the expenses of managing the organization as a whole, establishes criteria for allocation of a home office to the segments of an organization. The allocation should be based on the beneficial or causal relationship between such expenses and the receiving segments. The Standard provides for:

- Identification of expenses for direct allocation to segments to the maximum amount possible
- Accumulation of significant nondirectly allocated expenses into logical and relatively homogeneous pools
- Allocation of any remaining or residual home office expenses to all segments

Cost Accounting Standard 404: Capitalization of Tangible Assets

Contractors, for purposes of cost measurement, must establish and adhere to policies with respect to capitalization of tangible assets that satisfy criteria specified in Cost Accounting Standard 404. Major acquisitions will be capitalized so that the cost can be allocated properly to cost objectives of current and future periods.

Cost Accounting Standard 405: Accounting for Unallowable Costs

Cost Accounting Standard 405 is designed "to facilitate negotiation, audit, administration and settlement of contracts." It establishes guidelines for:

- Identification of costs specifically identified as unallowable
- The cost accounting treatment for such identified unallowable costs

Unallowable costs are those costs that, under provisions of any pertinent law, regulation, or contract, cannot be included in prices, cost reimbursements, or settlements under a government contract to which it is allocable. When an auditor identifies, in the Schedule of Findings and Questioned Costs, a cost as one not authorized by a contract, the contracting officer will issue a written decision regarding that cost, and the recipient organization will respond according to the contracting officer's decision.

Cost Accounting Standard 406: Cost Accounting Period

Cost Accounting Standard 406 provides criteria for the selection of cost accounting periods for contract cost estimating, accumulating, and reporting. It provides that the organization's fiscal year will be the cost accounting period, but lists several exceptions to this rule:

- The contractor has previously established the practice that the cost accounting period is different than the organization's fiscal year.
- A change in fiscal year has occurred.
- The organization's tax year may be used, even if differs from the cost accounting period.
- Certain interim indirect costs may be allocated to an interim portion of the cost accounting period.

Cost Accounting Standard 407: Use of Standard Costs for Direct Material and Direct Labor

Cost Accounting Standard 407 provides:

- Criteria for the use of standard costs to be used for estimating, accumulating, and reporting costs of direct material and direct labor
- Criteria relating to the establishment of standards, accumulation of standard costs, and accumulation and disposition of variances from standard costs

To use standard costs for estimating, accumulating, and reporting costs of direct material and direct labor, the organization must meet all three of the following criteria:

1. Standard costs are entered in the books.

2. Standard costs and variances are accounted for at the level of the production unit.

3. Practices with respect to the setting and revising of standards, use of standard costs, and disposition of variances are stated in writing and are consistently followed.

Cost Accounting Standard 408: Accounting for Costs of Compensated Personal Absence

Cost Accounting Standard 408 promotes uniformity in the measurement of costs related to compensated absences. These include vacation, sick leave, holiday, illness, jury duty, or military training, or paid personal activities for which compensation is paid by an employer under the terms of a plan or custom.

These costs will be reported in the cost accounting period in which they were earned, and the total of such costs will be allocated among the final cost objectives associated with that period.

Cost Accounting Standard 409: Depreciation of Tangible Capital Assets

Cost Accounting Standard 409 provides criteria and guidance for assigning costs of tangible capital assets to cost accounting periods and for allocating them consistently to cost objectives. The Standard does not apply to "nonwasting" assets or natural resources subject to depletion.

Depreciation costs should be a reasonable measure of the expiration of service potential. The Standard does not mandate a specific method of depreciation, and the organization should select the method that best reflects the pattern of consumption of the asset. The chosen method should be used for financial accounting unless:

- The selected method does not reflect the expected consumption of the asset.

- The selected method is not acceptable for federal income tax purposes.

This Standard also addresses the amount of cost—capitalized cost less estimated residual value—that may be depreciable, and the accounting for gains and losses on disposition of the capitalized tangible asset. The gain or loss should be assigned to the cost accounting period in which the disposition occurs.

Standard 409 provides an exemption for situations in which compensation for use of these assets is based on use rates or allowances by other federal regulations such as those governing educational institutions.

Cost Accounting Standard 410: Allocation of Business Unit General and Ad3ministrative Expenses to Final Cost Objectives

Cost Accounting Standard 410 provides criteria for the allocation of the general and administrative expenses of a business unit based on beneficial or causal relationships and for the allocation of home office expenses received by a segment to the cost objectives of that segment.

The expenses covered by this Standard include management, financial, and other expenses that are for the general management and administration of the business unit as a whole, including allocated home office expenses received by the business unit.

The costs discussed in this standard must be grouped in a separate indirect cost pool and allocated only to the final cost objectives through the use of an appropriate allocation base. The allocation may be based on total cost input, value-added cost input, or single element cost input, depending on which base best represents the total activity in a typical cost accounting period.

Cost Accounting Standard 411: Accounting for Acquisition Costs of Material

Cost Accounting Standard 411 establishes criteria to determine acquisition costs of material. It does not cover the costs of tangible capital assets (see Cost Accounting Standard 404) or government-furnished assets. Costing of inventory may be done in a manner similar to that used for financial reporting (i.e., FIFO, average cost, LIFO, standard cost). The cost of materials should include extra charges but also should reflect discounts and credits received.

The organization must keep records for each category of inventory material. It also must maintain written policies concerning accumulation and allocation of costs of material.

Cost Accounting Standard 412: Composition and Measurement of Pension Cost

Cost Accounting Standard 412 provides guidance for determining and measuring the components of pension cost and the basis on which such costs are assigned to cost accounting periods. The Standard does not deal with specific cost allocations or the effect of actuarial gains and losses on pension costs. Using the Employee Retirement Income Security Act (ERISA) and APB Opinion No. 8 (Accounting for the Cost of Pension Plans) as guides, the CASB noted that ERISA is less restrictive than is desirable and that some of the provisions of APB Opinion No. 8 are inappropriate for contract costing purposes.

In recognizing two basic types of pension plans, defined benefit plans and defined contribution plans, the Standard allows for the determination of cost in the following manner:

Defined Benefit Plans

- The sum of the following:
    - — Normal cost for the cost accounting period;
    - — Amortization of unfunded actuarial liability;
    - — Interest equivalent on the unamortized portion of any un-funded actuarial liability; and
    - — Adjustment for actuarial gains and losses

Defined Contribution Plans

- The net contribution for the cost accounting period

The appropriate base for measuring the pension cost for the cost accounting period is the accrued benefit cost method or a projected benefit cost method if the method is used to measure pension costs for financial accounting purposes.

Cost Accounting Standard 413: Adjustment and Allocation of Pension Cost

Cost Accounting Standard 413 addresses the methodology used to adjust pension cost for actuarial gains and losses assigned to a cost accounting period. The appropriate bases used to allocate pension cost to segments of the organization also are addressed.

Cost Accounting Standard 414: Cost of Money as an Element of the Cost of Facilities Capital

Under Cost Accounting Standard 414, the cost of money that can be identified with the facilities used in a business unit may be recognized as an element of contract cost. The amount of facilities capital associated with each indirect cost pool is identified, an imputed interest cost—determined by reference to interest rates specified by the Secretary of the Treasury—is computed, and then, the imputed interest cost is allocated to contracts on the basis of the same measure used to allocate other costs. The standard notes:

> Facilities capital cost of money factor for an indirect cost pool shall be determined in accordance with Form CASB CMF, and its instructions. . . . One form will serve for all of the indirect cost pools of a business unit.

The standard does not apply in situations where the use of tangible capital assets is compensated for based on other federal regulations, such as those for educational institutions.

Cost Accounting Standard 415: Accounting for the Cost of Deferred Compensation

Except for deferred compensated pension absence and pension plan costs, Cost Accounting Standard 415 provides measurement criteria for deferred compensation and criteria for the assignment of such costs to cost accounting periods.

The costs should be included in the cost accounting period during which the employer incurs an obligation to compensate the employee. The cost to be recognized will be the present value of the deferred compensation using a discount rate equal to the interest rate determined by the Secretary of the Treasury at the time the cost is assignable.

Standard 415 provides guidance for various types of deferred compensation, including those that will be satisfied by payment of moneys or other assets or shares of stock of the employer. Also discussed in this Standard are those awards that require future service, those that are to be paid with interest, and those that require funding or have provisions that relate to forfeitures.

Cost Accounting Standard 416: Accounting for Insurance Costs

Cost Accounting Standard 416 provides criteria for the measurement of insurance costs and assignment to cost accounting periods. The amount of cost is the sum of "projected average loss for the period" plus related administration expenses of the period. The term *projected average loss* is defined as the "estimated long-term average loss per period for periods of comparable exposure to risk of loss." Insurance administration expenses are the costs of administering an insurance program including risk management, processing of claims, and actuarial and service fees.

Cost Accounting Standard 417: Cost of Money as an Element of the Cost of Capital Assets under Construction

Cost Accounting Standard 417 requires that the "cost of money applicable to the investment in tangible and intangible capital assets being constructed, fabricated, or developed" be included as part of the capitalized acquisition costs of these assets. The rate to be used should be based on interest rates determined by the Secretary of the Treasury, and an amount should be determined for each cost accounting period. Methods used for financial accounting purposes are appropriate if the result is not materially different from the amount determined in accordance with the method prescribed by the standard.

Cost Accounting Standard 418: Allocation of Direct and Indirect Costs

The CASB issued Cost Accounting Standard 418 to provide consistent determination of direct and indirect costs and to provide guidance for the accumulation of indirect costs and for the selection of allocation measures "based on the beneficial or causal relationship between an indirect cost pool and cost objectives."

The Standard requires a business unit to have a written statement of accounting policies and practices for classifying costs. Also, pooled indirect costs will be allocated to cost objectives in "reasonable proportion to the beneficial or causal relationship of the pooled costs to the cost objectives." The Standard does not cover accounting for costs of special facilities if they are included in separate indirect cost pools.

Cost Accounting Standard 419

Cost Accounting Standard 419 has been withdrawn.

Cost Accounting Standard 420: Accounting for Independent Research and Development Costs and Bid and Proposal Costs

Standard 420 provides criteria for the accumulation of research and development costs and bid and proposal costs and the allocation of such costs to cost objectives. These costs exclude general and administrative expenses of the business unit. The costs of research and development generally will be included in the cost accounting period in which they were incurred. Exceptions to this general rule relate to costs that may be deferred pursuant to law, regulation, or other factors. However, bid and proposal costs will always be assigned to the cost accounting period in which they were incurred.

PROPOSED RULES FOR COST ACCOUNTING STANDARDS OF EDUCATIONAL INSTITUTIONS

In June 1992, the CASB published an "advance notice of proposed rulemaking" following up on a Staff Discussion Paper that was issued to solicit public views about the pricing and administration of contracts to educational institutions. The Discussion Paper was published in response to information received that some colleges and universities were improperly allocating indirect costs to federal programs.

The Board stated that the application of selected Cost Accounting Standards would improve the cost accounting practices by colleges and universities when "estimating, accumulating, and reporting costs deemed allocable to federal contracts, and that the costs of implementation will be minimal." The Board also indicated that ensuring compliance with Cost Accounting Standards would reduce the institutions' costs to respond to federal auditors' inquiries, and the amount of testing deemed necessary by auditors—thereby reducing the cost again.

The CASB's advance notice proposed to incorporate four new standards to be applicable to educational institutions:

1. Requiring consistency in estimating, accumulating, and reporting costs.

2. Requiring consistency in allocating costs.

3. Requiring contractor identification of specific unallowable costs.

4. Requiring consistency in the selection and use of a cost accounting period.

The proposed amendments would require the inclusion of a Cost Accounting Standard clause in contracts or subcontracts in excess of $500,000, awarded to educational institutions. The institutions would be required to follow established cost accounting practices. Additionally, certain institutions would be required to disclose in writing their cost accounting policies; identify costs that are not reimbursable as allowable costs; and use consistently the same accounting period for purposes of estimating, accumulating, and reporting costs. These requirements apply to those institutions that:

- Received more than $10,000,000 of such contracts in a prior fiscal year;
- Received such contracts that comprised 10 percent or more of the institution's or segment's revenues in a prior fiscal year;
- Receive a contract of $10,000,000 or more in the current year; or
- Receive a contract of $500,000 or more and are listed in Exhibit A of OMB Circular A-21.

CASB Disclosure Statement for Educational Institutions

The proposed CASB Disclosure Statement for Educational Institutions would help provide the information required with proposals for educational institutions. It contains eight parts:

1. General information
2. Direct costs
3. Direct versus indirect
4. Indirect costs
5. Deprecation and capitalization practices
6. Other costs and credits
7. Deferred compensation and insurance costs
8. Central system or group expenses

The disclosure statement would be applicable to educational institutions with segments or business units that have costs included in a covered contract exceeding $500,000. A separate disclosure statement is not needed for each segment if the cost accounting practices under such contracts are identical for the segments.

APPENDIX A

SAMPLE FINANCIAL STATEMENTS—
NET ASSET CLASS MODEL

NOT-FOR-PROFIT ORGANIZATION

**Financial Statements for the
Year Ended June 30, 19X1
and Independent Auditor's Report**

NOT-FOR-PROFIT ORGANIZATION

Table of Contents

INDEPENDENT AUDITOR'S REPORT

To the Board of Directors of Not-for-Profit Organization:

We have audited the accompanying statement of financial position of Not-for-Profit Organization (the "Organization") as of June 30, 19X1, and the related statements of activities and cash flows for the year then ended. These financial statements are the responsibility of the Organization's management. Our responsibility is to express an opinion on these financial statements based on our audit.

We conducted our audit in accordance with generally accepted auditing standards. Those standards require that we plan and perform the audit to obtain reasonable assurance about whether the financial statements are free of material misstatement. An audit includes examining, on a test basis, evidence supporting the amounts and disclosures in the financial statements. An audit also includes assessing the accounting principles used and significant estimates made by management, as well as evaluating the overall financial statement presentation. We believe that our audit provides a reasonable basis for our opinion.

In our opinion, the financial statements referred to above present fairly, in all material respects, the financial position of Not-for-Profit Organization as of June 30, 19X1, and the results of its activities and its cash flows for the year then ended in conformity with generally accepted accounting principles.

February 10, 19X2

NOT-FOR-PROFIT ORGANIZATION

Statement of Financial Position
June 30, 19X1
(in thousands)

ASSETS

CASH AND CASH EQUIVALENTS (Note 2)	$	75
ACCOUNTS AND INTEREST RECEIVABLE— Less allowance for doubtful accounts of $500 in 19X1		2,130
INVENTORIES AND PREPAID EXPENSES		610
CONTRIBUTIONS RECEIVABLE (Note 2)		2,025
SHORT-TERM INVESTMENTS (Notes 2 and 4)		1,400
ASSETS RESTRICTED TO INVESTMENT IN LAND, BUILDINGS, AND EQUIPMENT (Notes 2 and 6)		5,210
PREPAID PENSION COST (Note 10)		1,000
LAND, BUILDINGS, AND EQUIPMENT—Net (Notes 2 and 3)		61,700
LONG-TERM INVESTMENTS (Notes 2 and 4)		218,070
TOTAL ASSETS	$	292,220

LIABILITIES AND NET ASSETS

LIABILITIES:

Accounts payable and accrued expenses (Note 11)	$	1,220
Refundable advance		650
Grants payable		875
Notes payable		700
Annuity obligations (Note 2)		1,685
Long-term debt (Note 5)		5,500
Total Liabilities		10,630

Statement of Financial Position (continued)

NET ASSETS:

Unrestricted	115,228
Temporarily restricted (Note 6)	24,342
Permanently restricted (Note 7)	142,020
Total net assets	281,590
TOTAL LIABILITIES AND NET ASSETS	$ 292,220

See notes to financial statements.

NOT-FOR-PROFIT ORGANIZATION

Statement of Activities
Year Ended June 30, 19X1
(in thousands)

	Unrestricted	Temporarily Restricted	Permanently Restricted	Total
REVENUES, GAINS, AND OTHER SUPPORT:				
Contributions	$ 8,640	$ 8,110	$ 280	$ 17,030
Fees	5,400	—	—	5,400
Income on long-term investments (Note 4)	5,600	2,580	120	8,300
Other investment income (Note 4)	850	—	—	850
Net realized and unrealized gains on long-term investments (Note 4)	8,228	2,952	4,620	15,800
Other	150	—	—	150
Net assets released from restrictions (Note 8):				
Satisfaction of program restrictions	11,990	(11,990)	—	—
Satisfaction of equipment acquisition restrictions	1,500	(1,500)	—	—
Expiration of time restrictions	1,250	(1,250)	—	—
Total revenues, gains, and other support	43,608	(1,098)	5,020	47,530
EXPENSES AND LOSSES:				
Program A	13,100	—	—	13,100
Program B	8,540	—	—	8,540
Program C	5,760	—	—	5,760
Management and general	2,420	—	—	2,420
Fund raising	2,150	—	—	2,150

Statement of Activities (continued)

Total expenses (Note 9)	31,970	—	—	31,970
Fire loss	80	—	—	80
Actuarial loss on annuity obligations	—	30	—	30
Total expenses and losses	32,050	30	—	32,080
CHANGE IN NET ASSETS	11,558	(1,128)	5,020	15,450
NET ASSETS, BEGINNING OF YEAR	103,670	25,470	137,000	266,140
NET ASSETS, END OF YEAR	$ 115,228	$ 24,342	$ 142,020	$ 281,590

See notes to financial statements.

NOT-FOR-PROFIT ORGANIZATION

Statement of Cash Flows
Year Ended June 30, 19X1
(in thousands)

CASH FLOWS FROM OPERATING ACTIVITIES:

Change in net assets	$ 15,450
Adjustments to reconcile change in net assets to net cash used in operating activities:	
Depreciation	3,200
Fire loss	80
Actuarial loss on annuity obligations	30
Increase in accounts and interest receivable	(460)
Decrease in inventories and prepaid expenses	390
Increase in contributions receivable	(192)
Increase in prepaid pension cost	(133)
Increase in accounts payable and accrued expenses	170
Decrease in grants payable	(425)
Contributions restricted for long-term investment	(2,740)
Interest and dividends restricted for long-term investment	(300)
Net unrealized and realized gains on long-term investments	(15,800)
Net cash used in operating activities	(730)

Statement of Cash Flows (continued)

CASH FLOWS FROM INVESTING ACTIVITIES:

Insurance proceeds from fire loss on building	250
Purchase of equipment	(1,500)
Proceeds from sale of investments	76,100
Purchase of investments	(74,900)
Net cash used in investing activities	(50)

CASH FLOWS FROM FINANCING ACTIVITIES:

Proceeds from contributions restricted for:

Investment in endowment	200
Investment in term endowment	70
Investment in plant	1,210
Investment subject to annuity agreements	200
	1,680

Other financing activities:

Interest and dividends restricted for reinvestment	300
Payments of annuity obligations	(145)
Payments on notes payable	(440)
Payments on long-term debt	(1,000)
	(1,285)
Net cash used in financing activities	395

NET DECREASE IN CASH AND CASH
  EQUIVALENTS $ (385)

CASH AND CASH EQUIVALENTS,
  BEGINNING OF YEAR   460

CASH AND CASH EQUIVALENTS,
  END OF YEAR $ 75

SUPPLEMENTAL DATA:

  Noncash investing and financing activities:

  Gifts of equipment $ 140

  Gift of paid-up life insurance, cash
    surrender value   80

  Interest paid   382

NOT-FOR-PROFIT ORGANIZATION

Notes to Financial Statements
Year Ended June 30, 19X1

1. ORGANIZATION AND PURPOSE

Not-for-Profit Organization (the "Organization") is a not-for-profit organization devoted to the prevention of cruelty to animals. A major portion of its funding is from individual contributions and fees collected from member groups and services rendered.

2. SUMMARY OF SIGNIFICANT ACCOUNTING POLICIES

a. *Basis of Presentation*—The financial statements are presented on the basis of unrestricted, temporarily restricted, and permanently restricted net assets.

b. *Cash and Cash Equivalents*—For financial statement purposes, the Organization considers all highly liquid investments with a maturity of three months or less when purchased to be cash equivalents.

c. *Investments*—Investments are carried at market value or appraised value, and realized and unrealized gains and losses are reflected in the statement of activities.

d. *Life Annuities*—The Organization has entered into Life Annuity Trusts whereby donors receive payments for the remainder of their life with any remainder at death reverting to the Organization unless specifically restricted by the donor. The liability is determined based on actuarial assumptions and is included in the liability section of the accompanying financial statements. The amount of the contribution recorded by the Organization is the fair value of the trust assets received less the present value of the estimated annuity payments.

e. *Capital Assets*—Land, buildings, and equipment are stated at cost less accumulated depreciation and amortization.

Depreciation is provided using the straight-line method over the estimated useful lives of the assets.

f. *Revenue Recognition*—Contributions are recognized as revenue when they are received or unconditionally pledged.

The Organization reports gifts of cash and other assets as restricted support if they are received with donor stipulations that limit the use of the donated assets. When a donor restriction expires, that is, when a stipulated time restriction ends or purpose restriction is accomplished, temporarily restricted net assets are reclassified to unrestricted net assets and reported in the statement of activities as net assets released from restrictions.

The Organization reports gifts of land, buildings, and equipment as unrestricted support unless explicit donor stipulations specify how the donated assets must be used. Gifts of long-lived assets with explicit restrictions that specify how the assets are to be used and gifts of cash or other assets that must be used to acquire long-lived assets are reported as restricted support. Absent explicit donor stipulations about how these long-lived assets must be maintained, the Organization reports expirations of donor restrictions when the donated or acquired long-lived assets are placed in service.

Contributions receivable represent amounts committed by donors that have not been received by the Organization. Allowance for estimated uncollectible contributions amounted to $275 as of June 30, 19X1.

Contributions of services shall be recognized if the services received (a) create or enhance nonfinancial assets or (b) require specialized skills, are provided by individuals possessing those skills, and would typically need to be purchased if not provided by donation.

g. *Income Taxes*—The Organization is a not-for-profit organization and is exempt from federal income taxes under Section 501(c)(3) of the Internal Revenue Code.

3. LAND, BUILDINGS, AND EQUIPMENT

Land, buildings, and equipment consisted of the following at June 30, 19X1:

Land	$	10,300
Buildings		48,500

Equipment:	
Computer	2,950
Office	15,310
	77,060
Less accumulated depreciation	(15,360)
	$ 61,700

4. INVESTMENTS

The Organization invests cash in excess of daily requirements in short-term investments. At June 30, 19X1, $1,400 was invested in short-term investments, and during the year earned $850. Most long-term investments are held in two investment pools. Pool A is for permanent endowments and the unappropriated net appreciation of those endowments. Pool B is for amounts designated by the board of trustees for long-term investment.

Annuity trusts, term endowments, and certain permanent endowments are separately invested. Long-term investment activity is reflected in the following table:

	Pool A	Pool B	Other	Total
Investments at beginning of year	$ 164,000	$ 32,800	$ 6,700	$ 203,500
Gifts available for investment:				
Gifts creating permanent endowment	200	—	80	280
Gifts creating term endowments	—	—	70	70
Gifts creating annuity trusts	—	—	(200)	(200)
Amount withdrawn at death of annuitant	—	—	(400)	(400)
Investment returns (net of expenses of $375):				
Dividends, interest, and rents	6,000	2,000	300	8,300
Realized and unrealized gains	12,000	3,800	—	15,800

Amounts appropriated for current operations	(7,500)	(2,000)	—	(9,500)
Annuity trust income for current and future payments	—	—	(180)	(180)
Investments at end of year	$ 174,700	$ 36,600	$ 6,770	$ 218,070

The participation in the pools and ownership of the other invest-ments at June 30, 19X1, is shown in the table below:

	Pool A	Pool B	Other	Total
Permanently restricted net assets	$ 136,820	—	$ 2,200	$ 139,020
Temporarily restricted net assets	10,752	—	4,570	15,322
Unrestricted net assets	27,128	$ 36,600	—	63,728
Investments at end of year	$ 174,700	$ 36,600	$ 6,770	$ 218,070

The board of trustees has interpreted state law as requiring the preservation of the purchasing power (real value) of the perma-nent endowment funds unless explicit donor stipulations specify how net appreciation must be used. To meet that objective, the Organization's endowment management policies require that net appreciation be retained permanently in an amount neces-sary to adjust the historic dollar value of original endowment gifts by the change in the Consumer Price Index. After main-taining the real value of the permanent endowment funds, any remainder of total return is available for appropriation. In 19X1, the total return on Pool A was $18,000 (10.6 percent), of which $4,620 was retained permanently to preserve the real value of the original gifts. The remaining $13,380 was available for appropriation by the board of trustees. State law allows the board to appropriate so much of net appreciation as is prudent considering the Organization's long- and short-term needs, present and anticipated financial requirements, expected total return on its investments, price level trends, and general eco-nomic conditions. Under the Organization's endowment spend-ing policy, 5 percent of the average market value at the end of the previous 3 years is appropriated, which was $7,500 for the year ended June 30, 19X1.

5. LONG-TERM DEBT

Long-term debt at June 30, 19X1, was as follows:

Term loan payable (a)	$ 1,500
Mortgage payable (b)	4,000
	$ 5,500

(a) This term loan, which is secured by the Organization's accounts receivable, is payable to a bank and bears interest at the bank's prime rate plus .50 percent. Monthly principal payments of $21 are required through January 19X6.

(b) The mortgage obligation bears interest at a rate of 12 percent per annum and is secured by land and a residence. The mortgage is payable over a 20-year period with monthly principal payments of $62, with interest through July 19X7.

The maturities schedule of all long-term debt is as follows:

Year Ending June 30	Amount
19X2	$ 1,000
19X3	1,200
19X4	1,100
19X5	1,000
19X6	700
Thereafter	500
	$ 5,500

6. TEMPORARILY RESTRICTED NET ASSETS

Temporarily restricted net assets are available for the following purposes or periods:

Program A activities:	
Purchase of equipment	$ 3,060
Research	4,256
Educational seminars and publications	1,520
Program B activities:	
Disaster relief	2,240
Educational seminars and publications	2,158
Program C activities:	2,968
Total program activities	16,202

Buildings and equipment	2,150
Annuity trust agreements	2,850
For periods after June 30, 19X1	3,140
	$ 24,342

7. PERMANENTLY RESTRICTED NET ASSETS

Permanently restricted net assets are restricted to:

Investment in perpetuity, the income from which is expendable to support:		
Program A activities	$	27,524
Program B activities		13,662
Program C activities		13,662
Any activities of the organization		81,972
		136,820
Endowment requiring income to be added to original gift until fund's value is $2,500		2,120
Paid-up life insurance policy that will provide proceeds upon death of insured for an endowment to support general activities		80
Land required to be used as a recreation area		3,000
	$	142,020

8. NET ASSETS RELEASED FROM DONOR RESTRICTIONS

Net assets were released from donor restrictions during the year ended June 30, 19X1, by incurring expenses satisfying the restricted purposes or by occurrence of other events specified by donors.

Purpose restrictions accomplished:		
Program A expenses	$	5,800
Program B expenses		4,600
Program C expenses		1,590
		11,990
Program A equipment acquired and placed in service		1,500

Time restrictions expired:

Passage of specified time	850
Death of annuity beneficiary	400
	1,250
Total restrictions released	$ 14,740

9. FUNCTIONAL EXPENSES

	Total	A	B	C	Management and General	Fund Raising
Salaries, wages, and benefits	$ 15,115	$ 7,400	$ 3,900	$ 1,725	$ 1,130	$ 960
Grants to other organizations	4,750	2,075	750	1,925	—	—
Supplies	3,155	865	1,000	490	240	560
Services and professional fees	2,840	160	1,490	600	200	390
Office and occupancy	2,528	1,160	600	450	218	100
Depreciation	3,200	1,440	800	570	250	140
Interest	382	—	—	—	382	—
Total expenses	$ 31,970	$ 13,100	$ 8,540	$ 5,760	$ 2,420	$ 2,150

10. PENSION PLAN

The Organization provides certain pension benefits, which cover substantially all of its full-time employees under a defined benefit pension plan (the "Plan"). The Plan is administered by a trustee and has all of its past service costs funded. Benefits are based on years of service and compensation during the last 10 years of employment.

	June 30, 19X1
Actuarial present value of benefit obligations:	
Vested benefits	$ 17,428
Nonvested benefits	983
Total accumulated benefit obligations	$ 18,411

Projected benefit obligations for services rendered to date	$ 21,665
Plan net assets at fair value	29,382
Plan assets in excess of projected benefit obligations	7,717
Unrecognized net gain	(5,263)
Unrecognized net assets	(2,432)
Unrecognized prior service cost	978
Prepaid pension cost	$ 1,000

Net pension credit includes the following components:

	June 30, 19X1
Service cost	$ 592
Interest cost on projected benefit obligations	1,183
	1,775
Actual return on assets	(2,538)
Net amortization and deferral	290
Net pension credit	$ (473)

The weighted-average discount rate and average rate of increase in future compensation levels used in determining the unrecognized net obligations and the net pension credit for 19X1 was as follows:

Discount rate	8.0%
Rate of increase in future compensation levels	6.2%

The corresponding rates for determining the actuarial present value of the accumulated and projected benefit obligations as of June 30, 19X1, were as follows:

Accumulated benefit obligations	8.0%
Projected benefit obligations	8.0%

The expected long-term rate of return on assets was 8% as of June 30, 19X1.

Plan assets are stated at fair value and are composed primarily of corporate equity securities, debt securities, government securities, and cash equivalents. Unrecognized net excess plan assets are being amortized against net pension costs over 15 years. Prepaid pension cost is included in the Organizations' statements of financial position.

11. POSTRETIREMENT BENEFIT PLANS OTHER THAN PENSIONS

The Organization has a plan that provides for post-retirement benefits other than pensions (the "Plan"). The Plan provides certain medical and life insurance benefits for retired Executive and Supervisory employees. Such employees of the Organization may become eligible for these benefits if they remain employed until normal retirement age and fulfill other eligibility requirements as specified by the Plan. All retirees are covered by the Plan until death. Retirees who were employed January 1, 19X0, or later would be required to pay 15 percent of the cost of premiums for dependent coverage. Benefits are continued for dependents of eligible retired participants for a maximum period of the earlier of (a) 24 months after the death of the retiree or (b) providing the dependent is under age 65 (Medicare eligible). If the dependent of the retiree is age 65 or older and Medicare eligible, the cost to the retiree would be 15% of the senior care rate.

The Organization is currently evaluating a funding policy for future contributions to the Plan.

Reconciliation of funding status as of:

	June 30, 19X1
Accumulated postretirement benefit obligation:	
Current retirees and dependents	$ (1,893)
Active employees currently eligible for benefits	(1,319)
Other active employees	(942)
Total	(4,154)
Fair value of plan assets	—
Unrecognized transition obligation	3,752
Unrecognized prior service cost	(982)
Unrecognized net loss	994
(Accrued) postretirement benefit cost	$ (390)

The components of net periodic postretirement benefit cost are as follows:

Service cost	$	32
Interest cost		56
Unrecognized transition obligation		46
Amortization of other components		(20)
Net periodic postretirement benefit cost	$	114

The discount and weighted-average rate of increase in future compensation levels used in determining the net periodic postretirement benefit cost for 19X1 were 8.0% and 5.8%, respectively. The same rates were used for determining the actuarial present value of the accumulated postretirement benefit obligation.

A one-percentage point increase in the assumed health care cost trend rates increases the total of the service and interest cost components of the net periodic postretirement benefit costs and the end-of-year accumulated postretirement benefit obligation by $64 and $72, respectively.

The health care cost trend rate begins in 19XX at a maximum of 15% and decreases over 11 years to 6.5%.

The Organization has accounted for postretirement benefits on an accrual basis in 19X1 whereas, in all prior years, costs were determined by the pay-as-you-go basis. The effects of recognizing the change in accounting principle prospectively is $425 for fiscal 19X1.

OBSERVATION: FAS-132 (Employers' Disclosures about Pensions and Other Postretirement Benefits) revises the disclosures mandated by FAS-87 (Employers' Accounting for Pensions), FAS-88 (Employers' Accounting for Settlements and Curtailments of Defined Benefit Pension Plans and for Termination Benefits), and FAS-106 (Employers' Accounting for Postretirement Benefits Other Than Pensions). FAS-132 suggests combined formats for presentation of required information relating to pension and other postretirement benefits, and, for nonpublic entities, the Statement permits reduced disclosures. The following presents such combined and reduced disclosures that would replace notes 10 and 11 to the financial statements:

Pension Plan   The Organization provides certain pension benefits, which cover substantially all of its full-time employees under a defined benefit pension plan (the "Pension Plan"). The Pension Plan is administered by a trustee and has all of its past service costs funded. Benefits are based on years of service and compensation during the last 10 years of employment.

Other Postretirement Benefits   The Organization has a plan that provides for postretirement benefits other than pensions (the "Postretirement Plan"). The Postretirement Plan provides certain medical and life insurance benefits for retired executive and supervisory employees. Such employees of the Organization may become eligible for these benefits if they remain employed until normal retirement age and fulfill other eligibility requirements as specified by the Postretirement Plan. All retirees are covered by the Postretirement Plan until death. Retirees who were employed January 1, 19X0, or later would be required to pay 15% of the cost of premiums for dependent coverage. Benefits are continued for dependents of eligible retired participants for a maximum period of the earlier of (a) 24 months after the death of the retiree or (b) until the dependent becomes Medicare-eligible. If the dependent of the retiree is both age 65 or older and Medicare-eligible, the cost to the retiree would be 15% of the senior care rate.

The Organization is currently evaluating a funding policy for future contributions to the Postretirement Plan.

	Pension Benefits	Other Benefits
Benefit obligation—June 30	$21,665	$4,154
Fair value of plan assets— June 30	29,382	—
Funded status	$7,717	$(4,154)
Prepaid (accrued) benefit cost recognized in the statement of financial position	$1,000	$(390)

	Pension Benefits	Other Benefits
Weighted-average assumptions as of June 30		
Discount rate	8.0%	8.0%
Expected return on plan assets	8.0%	—
Rate of compensation increase	6.2%	5.8%

For measurement purposes, a 15% annual rate of increase in the per capita cost of covered healthcare benefits was assumed for 19X2. The rate was assumed to decrease gradually to 6.5% for 19Y3 and remain at that level thereafter.

	Pension Benefits	Other Benefits
Benefit cost (credit)— Year ended June 30	$(473)	$114
Employer contribution— Year ended June 30	325	—
Plan participants' contributions— Year ended June 30	—	96
Benefits paid—Year ended June 30	400	210

12. CONTINGENCIES

The Organization is involved in several lawsuits in the normal course of business. Management believes that the outcome of such lawsuits will not have a material adverse effect on the Organization's financial statements.

APPENDIX B

SAMPLE FINANCIAL STATEMENTS—
FUND ACCOUNTING MODEL

EDUCATIONAL INSTITUTION

**Financial Statements for the
Year Ended June 30, 1995**

EDUCATIONAL INSTITUTION

Balance Sheet
June 30, 1995

ASSETS			LIABILITIES AND FUND BALANCES		
CURRENT FUNDS:			CURRENT FUNDS:		
Unrestricted:			Unrestricted:		
Cash	$	210,000	Accounts payable	$	125,000
Investments		450,000	Accrued liabilities		20,000
Accounts receivable, less allowance			Students' deposits		30,000
of $18,000		228,000	Due to other funds		158,000
Inventories, at lower of cost (first-in,			Deferred credits		30,000
first-out basis) or market		90,000	Fund balance		643,000
Prepaid expenses and deferred charges		28,000			
Total unrestricted		1,006,000	Total unrestricted		1,006,000
Restricted:			Restricted:		
Cash		145,000	Accounts payable		14,000
Investments		175,000	Fund balances		446,000
Accounts receivable, less allowance					
of $8,000		68,000			
Unbilled charges		72,000			
Total restricted		460,000	Total restricted		460,000
TOTAL CURRENT FUNDS	$	1,466,000	TOTAL CURRENT FUNDS	$	1,466,000

Balance Sheet (continued)

ASSETS

LOAN FUNDS:

Cash	$ 30,000
Investments	100,000
Loans to students, faculty, and staff, less allowance of $10,000	550,000
Due from unrestricted funds	3,000
TOTAL LOAN FUNDS	$ 683,000

ENDOWMENT AND SIMILAR FUNDS:

Cash	$ 100,000
Investments	13,900,000
TOTAL ENDOWMENT AND SIMILAR FUNDS	$ 14,000,000

ANNUITY AND LIFE INCOME FUNDS:

Annuity funds:	
Cash	$ 55,000
Investments	3,260,000
Total annuity funds	3,315,000
Life income funds:	
Cash	15,000
Investments	2,045,000
Total life income funds	2,060,000
TOTAL ANNUITY AND LIFE INCOME FUNDS	$ 5,375,000

LIABILITIES AND FUND BALANCES

LOAN FUNDS:

Fund balances:	
U.S. government grants refundable	$ 50,000
University funds:	
Restricted	483,000
Unrestricted	150,000
TOTAL LOAN FUNDS	$ 683,000

ENDOWMENT AND SIMILAR FUNDS:

Fund balances:	
Endowment	$ 7,800,000
Term endowment	3,840,000
Quasi-endowment—unrestricted	1,000,000
Quasi-endowment—restricted	1,360,000
TOTAL ENDOWMENT AND SIMILAR FUNDS	$ 14,000,000

ANNUITY AND LIFE INCOME FUNDS:

Annuity funds:	
Annuities payable	$ 55,000
Fund balances	3,260,000
Total annuity funds	3,315,000
Life income funds:	
Income payable	5,000
Fund balances	2,055,000
Total life income funds	2,060,000
TOTAL ANNUITY AND LIFE INCOME FUNDS	$ 5,375,000

Balance Sheet (continued)

PLANT FUNDS:			PLANT FUNDS:	
Unexpended:			Unexpended:	
Cash	$ 275,000		Accounts payable	$ 10,000
Investments	1,285,000		Notes payable	100,000
Due from unrestricted current funds	150,000		Bonds payable	400,000
			Fund balances:	
			Restricted	1,000,000
			Unrestricted	200,000
Total unexpended	1,710,000		Total unexpended	1,710,000
Renewals and replacements:			Renewals and replacements:	
Cash	5,000		Fund balances:	
Investments	150,000		Restricted	25,000
Deposits with trustees	100,000		Unrestricted	235,000
Due from unrestricted current funds	5,000			
Total renewals and replacements	260,000		Total renewals and replacements	260,000
Retirement of indebtedness:			Retirement of indebtedness:	
Cash	50,000		Fund balances:	
Deposits with trustees	250,000		Restricted	185,000
			Unrestricted	115,000
Total retirement of indebtedness	300,000		Total retirement of indebtedness	300,000

Balance Sheet (continued)

ASSETS

PLANT FUNDS (continued)

Investment in plant:

Land	500,000
Land improvements	1,000,000
Buildings	29,000,000
Equipment	19,000,000
Library books	400,000
Less accumulated depreciation	(8,300,000)
Investment in plant	41,600,000

TOTAL PLANT FUNDS	$ 43,870,000

AGENCY FUNDS:

Cash	50,000
Investments	60,000
TOTAL AGENCY FUNDS	$ 110,000

LIABILITIES AND FUND BALANCES

PLANT FUNDS (continued)

Investment in plant:

Notes payable	790,000
Bonds payable	2,200,000
Mortgages payable	400,000
Net investment in plant	38,210,000
Investment in plant	41,600,000

TOTAL PLANT FUNDS	$ 43,870,000

AGENCY FUNDS:

Deposits held in custody for others	$ 110,000
TOTAL AGENCY FUNDS	$ 110,000

See notes to financial statements.

EDUCATIONAL INSTITUTION

Statement of Changes in Fund Balances
Year Ended June 30, 1995

	Current Funds		Loan Funds	Endowment and Similar Funds	Annuity and Life Income Funds	Plant Funds			
	Unrestricted	Restricted				Unexpended	Renewal and Replacements	Retirement of Indebtedness	Investment in Plant
REVENUES AND OTHER ADDITIONS:									
Unrestricted current fund revenues	$ 7,540,000	—	—	—	—	—	—	—	—
Expired term endowment—restricted	—	—	—	—	—	$ 50,000	—	—	—
State appropriations—restricted	—	—	—	—	—	50,000	—	—	—
Federal grants and contracts—restricted	—	$ 500,000	—	—	—	—	—	—	—
Private gifts, grants, and contracts—restricted	—	370,000	$ 100,000	$ 1,500,000	$ 800,000	115,000	—	$ 65,000	875,000
Investment income—restricted	—	224,000	12,000	10,000	—	5,000	$ 5,000	5,000	—
Realized gains on investments—unrestricted	—	—	—	109,000	—	—	—	—	—
Realized gains on investments—restricted	—	—	4,000	50,000	—	10,000	5,000	5,000	—
Interest on loans receivable	—	—	7,000	—	—	—	—	—	—

Statement of Changes in Fund Balances (continued)

| | Current Funds | | Loan Funds | Endowment and Similar Funds | Annuity and Life Income Funds | Plant Funds | | | |
	Unrestricted	Restricted				Unexpended	Renewal and Replacements	Retirement of Indebtedness	Investment in Plant
U.S. government advances	—	—	18,000	—	—	—	—	—	—
Expended for plant facilities (including $100,000 charged to current funds expenditures)	—	—	—	—	—	—	—	—	1,550,000
Retirement of indebtedness	—	—	—	—	—	—	—	—	220,000
Accrued interest on sale of bonds	—	—	—	—	—	—	—	3,000	—
Matured annuity and life income restricted to endowment	—	—	—	10,000	—	—	—	—	—
Total revenues and other additions	7,540,000	1,094,000	141,000	1,679,000	800,000	230,000	10,000	78,000	2,645,000

Statement of Changes in Fund Balances (continued)

EXPENDITURES AND OTHER DEDUCTIONS:									
Educational and general expenditures	4,400,000	1,014,000	—	—	—	—	—	—	—
Auxiliary enterprises expenditures	1,830,000	—	—	—	—	—	—	—	—
Indirect costs recovered	—	35,000	—	—	—	—	—	—	—
Refunded to grantors	—	20,000	10,000	—	—	—	—	—	—
Loan cancellations and write-offs	—	—	1,000	—	—	—	—	—	—
Administrative and collection costs	—	—	1,000	—	—	—	—	1,000	—
Adjustment of actuarial liability for annuities payable	—	—	—	—	75,000	—	—	—	—
Expended for plant facilities (including noncapitalized expenditures of $50,000)	—	—	—	—	—	1,200,000	300,000	—	—
Retirement of indebtedness	—	—	—	—	—	—	—	220,000	—
Interest on indebtedness	—	—	—	—	—	—	—	190,000	—
Depreciation of plant and equipment	—	—	—	—	—	—	—	—	860,000
Disposal of plant facilities	—	—	—	—	—	—	—	—	115,000
Expired term endowments ($40,000 unrestricted, $50,000 restricted to plant)	—	—	—	90,000	—	—	—	—	—
Matured annuity and life income funds restricted to endowment	—	—	—	—	10,000	—	—	—	—
Total expenditures and other deductions	6,230,000	1,069,000	12,000	90,000	85,000	1,200,000	300,000	411,000	975,000

Statement of Changes in Fund Balances (continued)

	Current Funds		Loan Funds	Endowment and Similar Funds	Annuity and Life Income Funds	Plant Funds			
	Unrestricted	Restricted				Unexpended	Renewal and Replacements	Retirement of Indebtedness	Investment in Plant
TRANSFERS AMONG FUNDS— ADDITIONS (DEDUCTIONS):									
Mandatory:									
Principal and interest	(340,000)	—	—	—	—	—	—	340,000	—
Renewals and replacements	(170,000)	—	—	—	—	—	170,000	—	—
Loan fund matching grant	(2,000)	—	2,000	—	—	—	—	—	—
Unrestricted gifts allocated	(650,000)	—	50,000	550,000	—	50,000	—	—	—
Portion of unrestricted quasi-endowment funds investment gains appropriated	40,000	—	—	(40,000)	—	—	—	—	—
Total transfers	(1,122,000)	—	52,000	510,000	—	50,000	170,000	340,000	—
NET INCREASE (DECREASE) FOR THE YEAR	188,000	25,000	181,000	2,099,000	715,000	(920,000)	(120,000)	7,000	1,670,000
FUND BALANCE, BEGINNING OF YEAR	455,000	421,000	502,000	11,901,000	2,505,000	2,120,000	380,000	293,000	36,540,000
FUND BALANCE, END OF YEAR	$ 643,000	$ 446,000	$ 683,000	$ 14,000,000	$ 3,220,000	$ 1,200,000	$ 260,000	$ 300,000	$ 38,210,000

See notes to financial statements.

EDUCATIONAL INSTITUTION

Statement of Current Funds Revenues, Expenditures, and Other Changes
Year Ended June 30, 1995

	Current Year		Total
	Unrestricted	Restricted	
REVENUES:			
Tuition and fees	$ 2,600,000		$ 2,600,000
Federal appropriations	500,000	—	500,000
State appropriations	700,000	—	700,000
Local appropriations	100,000	—	100,000
Federal grants and contracts	20,000	$ 375,000	395,000
State grants and contracts	10,000	25,000	35,000
Local grants and contracts	5,000	25,000	30,000
Private gifts, grants, and contracts	850,000	380,000	1,230,000
Endowment income	325,000	209,000	534,000
Sales and services of educational departments	190,000	—	190,000
Sales and services of auxiliary enterprises	2,200,000	—	2,200,000
Expired term endowment	40,000	—	40,000
Other sources (if any)	—	—	—
Total current revenues	7,540,000	1,014,000	8,554,000
EXPENDITURES AND MANDATORY TRANSFERS:			
Educational and general:			
Instruction	2,960,000	489,000	3,449,000
Research	100,000	400,000	500,000
Public service	130,000	25,000	155,000
Academic support	250,000	—	250,000
Student services	200,000	—	200,000
Institutional support	450,000	—	450,000
Operation and maintenance of plant	220,000	—	220,000
Scholarships and fellowships	90,000	100,000	190,000
Educational and general expenditures	4,400,000	1,014,000	5,414,000
Mandatory transfers for:			
Principal and interest	90,000	—	90,000
Renewals and replacements	100,000	—	100,000
Loan fund matching grant	2,000	—	2,000
Total educational and general	4,592,000	1,014,000	5,606,000

Statement of Current Funds Revenues, Expenditures and Other Changes (continued)

Auxiliary enterprises:			
Expenditures	1,830,000	—	1,830,000
Mandatory transfers for:			
Principal and interest	250,000	—	250,000
Renewals and replacements	70,000	—	70,000
Total auxiliary enterprises	2,150,000	—	2,150,000
Total expenditures and mandatory transfers	6,742,000	1,014,000	7,756,000
OTHER TRANSFERS AND ADDITIONS (DEDUCTIONS):			
Excess of restricted receipts over transfers to revenues	—	45,000	45,000
Refunded to grantors	—	(20,000)	(20,000)
Unrestricted gifts allocated to other funds	(650,000)	—	(650,000)
Portion of quasi-endowment gains appropriated	40,000	—	40,000
NET INCREASE IN FUND BALANCES	$188,000	$ 25,000	$ 213,000

See notes to financial statements.

EDUCATIONAL INSTITUTION

Summary of Significant Accounting Policies
Year Ended June 30, 1995

The significant accounting policies followed by Sample Educational Institution are described below to enhance the usefulness of the financial statements to the reader.

Accrual Basis—The financial statements of Sample Educational Institution have been prepared on the accrual basis. The statement of current funds revenues, expenditures, and other changes is a statement of financial activities of current funds related to the current reporting period. It does not purport to present the results of operations or the net income or loss for the period as would a statement of income or a statement of revenues and expenses.

To the extent that current funds are used to finance plant assets, the amounts so provided are accounted for as (1) expenditures, in the case of normal replacement of movable equipment and library books; (2) mandatory transfers, in the case of required provisions for debt amortization and interest, and equipment renewal and replacement; and (3) transfers of a nonmandatory nature for all other cases.

Fund Accounting—In order to ensure observance of limitations and restrictions placed on the use of the resources available to the Institution, the accounts of the Institution are maintained in accordance with the principles of "fund accounting." This is the procedure by which resources for various purposes are classified for accounting and reporting purposes into funds that are in accordance with activities or objectives specified. Separate accounts are maintained for each fund; however, in the accompanying financial statements, funds that have similar characteristics have been combined into fund groups. Accordingly, all financial transactions have been recorded and reported by fund group.

Within each fund group, fund balances restricted by outside sources are so indicated and are distinguished from unrestricted funds allocated to specific purposes by action of the governing board. Externally restricted funds may only be utilized in accordance with the purposes established by the source of such funds and are in contrast with unrestricted funds over which the governing board retains full control to use in achieving any of its institutional purposes.

Endowment funds are subject to the restrictions of gift instruments requiring in perpetuity that the principal be invested and the income only be utilized. Term endowment funds are similar to endowment funds except that upon the passage of a stated period of time or the occurrence of a particular event, all or part of the principal may be expended. While quasi-endowment funds have been established by the governing board for the same purposes as endowment funds, any portion of quasi-endowment funds may be expended.

All gains and losses arising from the sale, collection, or other disposition of investments and other noncash assets are accounted for in the fund which owned such assets. Ordinary income derived from investments, receivables, and the like is accounted for in the fund owning such assets, except for income derived from investments of endowment and similar funds, which income is accounted for in the fund to which it is restricted or, if unrestricted, as revenues in unrestricted current funds.

All other unrestricted revenue is accounted for in the unrestricted current fund. Restricted gifts, grants, appropriations, endowment income, and other restricted resources are accounted for in the appropriate restricted funds. Restricted current funds are reported as revenues and expenditures when expended for current operating purposes.

Other Significant Accounting Policies—Other significant accounting policies are set forth in the financial statements and the notes thereto.

1. Investments are recorded at cost; investments received by gift are carried at market value at the date of acquisition. Quoted market values of investments (all marketable securities) of the funds indicated were as follows:

Unrestricted current funds	$ 510,000
Restricted current funds	180,000
Loan funds	105,000
Unexpended plant funds	1,287,000
Renewal and replacement funds	145,000
Agency funds	60,000

Investments of endowment and similar funds and annuity and life income funds are composed of the following:

	Carrying Value
Endowment and similar funds:	
Corporate stocks and bonds (approximate market, $15,000,000)	$13,000,000
Rental properties—less accumulated depreciations, $500,000	900,000
	$13,900,000
Annuity funds:	
U.S. bonds (approximate market, $200,000)	$ 200,000
Corporate stocks and bonds (approximate market, $3,070,000)	3,060,000
	$ 3,260,000
Life income funds:	
Municipal bonds (approximate market, $1,400,000)	$ 1,500,000
Corporate stocks and bonds (approximate market, $650,000)	545,000
	$ 2,045,000

Assets of endowment funds, except nonmarketable investments of term endowment having a book value of $200,000 and quasi-endowment having a book value of $800,000, are pooled on a market value basis, with each individual fund subscribing to or disposing of units on the basis of the value per unit at market value at the beginning of the calendar quarter within which the transaction takes place. Of the total units, each having a market value of $15.00, 600,000 units were owned by endowment, 280,000 units by term endowment, and 120,000 units by quasi-endowment at June 30, 1995.

The following tabulation summarizes changes in relationships between cost and market values of the pooled assets:

	Market	Cost	Net Gains (Losses)	Market Value Per Unit
End of year	$ 15,000,000	$ 13,000,000	$ 2,000,000	$ 15.00
Beginning of year	10,900,000	10,901,000	(1,000)	12.70
Unrealized net gains for year			2,001,000	
Realized net gains for year			159,000	
Total net gains for year			$ 2,160,000	$ 2.30

The average annual earnings per unit, exclusive of net gains, were $.56 for the year.

2. Physical plant and equipment are stated at cost at date of acquisition or fair value at date of donation in the case of gifts, except land acquired prior to 1940, which is valued at appraisal value in 1940 at $300,000. Depreciation on physical plant and equipment is provided on a straight-line basis over the estimated useful lives of the respective assets.

3. Long-term debt includes: bonds payable due in annual installments varying from $45,000 to $55,000 with interest at 5 7/8%, the final installment being due in 2007, collateralized by trust indenture covering land, buildings, and equipment known as Smith dormitory carried in the accounts at $2,500,000, and pledged net revenue from the operations of said dormitory; and mortgages payable due in varying amounts to 2005 with interest at 6%, collateralized by property carried in the accounts at $800,000 and pledged revenue of the Student Union amounting to approximately $65,000 per year.

Aggregate maturities of long-term debt are summarized as follows.

1996	$	230,000
1997		240,000
1998		250,000
1999		260,000
2000		270,000
Thereafter		1,750,000
	$	3,000,000

4. The Institution participates in a defined contribution multiemployer pension plan covering substantially all of its employees. Contributions and cost are determined as 1 percent of each covered employee's salary and totaled $ 30,000 for the year ended June 30, 1995.

The Institution also sponsors a noncontributory defined benefit postretirement health care plan covering substantially all its employees. The plan is funded by contributing an amount equal to a level percentage of the employees' salaries annually. For the year ended June 30, 1995, that amount was 4.25, and the contribution for the plan was $34,000.

The following table sets forth the plans funded status reconciled with the amount included in the Institution's balance sheet at June 30, 1995.

Accumulated postretirement benefit obligation:

Retirees	$	(187,000)
Fully eligible active plan participants		(100,000)
Other active plan participants		(297,400)
		(584,400)
Plan assets at fair value, primarily listed U.S. stocks and bonds		120,960
Accumulated postretirement benefit obligation in excess of plan assets		(463,440)
Unrecognized net gain from past experience different from that assumed and from changes in assumptions		(40,000)
Prior service cost not yet recognized in net periodic postretirement benefit cost		19,000
Unrecognized transition obligation		470,250
Accrued postretirement benefit cost	$	(14,190)

Net periodic postretirement benefit cost for 1995 included the following components:

Service cost–benefits attributed to service during the period	$	15,000
Interest cost on accumulated postretirement benefit obligation		44,400
Actual return on plan assets		(3,960)
Amortization of transition obligation over 20 years		24,750
Net amortization and deferral		1,000
Net periodic postretirement benefit cost	$	81,190

For measurement purposes, a 16 percent annual rate of increase in the per capita cost of covered health care benefits was assumed for 19XI; the rate was assumed to decrease gradually to 6 percent for 2020 and remain at that level thereafter. The health care cost trend rate assumption has a significant effect on the amounts reported. To illustrate, increasing the assumed health care cost trend rates by 1 percentage point in each year would increase the accumulated postretirement benefit obligation as of June 30, 19XI by $73,000 and the aggregate of the service and interest cost components of net periodic postretirement benefit cost for the year then ended by $13,000.

The weighted-average discount rate used in determining the accumulated postretirement benefit obligation was 8 percent. The expected long-term rate of return on plan assets after estimated taxes was 6.6 percent.

5. Contracts have been let for the construction of additional classroom buildings in the amount of $3,000,000. Construction and equipment are estimated to aggregate $5,000,000, which will be financed by available resources and an issue of bonds payable over a period of 40 years amounting to $4,000,000.

6. All interfund borrowings have been made from unrestricted funds. The amounts due to plant funds from current unrestricted funds are payable within one year without interest. The amount due to loan funds from current unrestricted funds is payable currently.

7. Pledges totaling $260,000, restricted to plant fund uses, are due to be collected over the next three fiscal years in the amounts of $120,000, $80,000, and $60,000, respectively. It is not practicable to estimate the net realizable value of such pledges.

8. The following methods and assumptions were used to estimate the fair value of each class of financial instruments, other than investments, for which it is practicable to estimate that value:

    Accounts and Loans Receivable—Included in accounts and loans receivable are long-term receivables of $500,000 which are non-interest bearing and will not be realized for periods of up to five years. Their fair values are estimated based on an imputed interest rate of __ percent.

    Notes, Bonds, and Mortgages Payable—The fair value of notes and mortgages payable is estimated based on rates currently available to the Institution for loans with similar terms and average maturities. The fair value of bonds payable is based on quoted market prices for the same or similar issues or on the current rates offered to the Institution for debt of the same remaining maturities.

Student Bank Loans Payable—The fair value of student bank loan guarantees is based on the estimated cost to terminate them or otherwise settle the obligations with the counterparties at the reporting date.

The estimated fair values of the Institution's financial instruments are as follows:

	Carrying Amount	Fair Value
Loans receivable	$ 500,000	$ 465,000
Notes, bonds, and mortgages payable	(3,890,000)	(3,900,000)
Student bank loan guarantees	—	(75,000)

9. At June 30, 1995, the Institution has guaranteed bank loans to some of its students totaling $250,000.

APPENDIX C
SAMPLE FINANCIAL STATEMENTS— SPECIALIZED ORGANIZATIONS

CONTENTS

> **OBSERVATION:** The AICPA's Not-for-Profit Organizations Committee announced recently that it was amending the guidance to independent auditors relative to reporting on financial statements containing comparative prior-year information. If the prior-year information is less than a full presentation—e.g., the statement of activities includes amounts in total rather than by net asset class, as required by generally accepted accounting principles (GAAP)—the auditor's report should be modified to disclose this circumstance and a note to the financial statements should disclose that the prior-year information is not a complete presentation (see Note 1, *1995 Financial Information*). Sample Public Broadcasting Corporation provides an example of a financial presentation that does not include full prior-year financial statements. Accordingly, the scope paragraph has been modified to disclose the limitations of the presentation.

SAMPLE COLLEGE

**Financial Statements for the
Year Ended June 30, 1996, and
Independent Auditors' Report**

INDEPENDENT AUDITORS' REPORT

The Board of Trustees of
Sample College

We have audited the accompanying statement of financial position of Sample College (the "College") as of June 30, 1996 and the related statements of activities and of cash flows for the year then ended. These financial statements are the responsibility of the management of the College. Our responsibility is to express an opinion on these financial statements based on our audit.

We conducted our audit in accordance with generally accepted auditing standards. Those standards require that we plan and perform the audit to obtain reasonable assurance about whether the financial statements are free of material misstatement. An audit includes examining, on a test basis, evidence supporting the amounts and disclosures in the financial statements. An audit also includes assessing the accounting principles used and significant estimates made by management, as well as evaluating the overall financial statement presentation. We believe that our audit provides a reasonable basis for our opinion.

In our opinion, such financial statements present fairly, in all material respects, the financial position of Sample College as of June 30, 1996, and the changes in its net assets and its cash flows for the year then ended in conformity with generally accepted accounting principles.

September 5, 1996

SAMPLE COLLEGE

STATEMENT OF FINANCIAL POSITION
JUNE 30, 1996

ASSETS

Cash and cash equivalents	$ 734,905
Short-term investments	1,942,797
Student accounts receivable (less allowance for doubtful accounts $198,000)	226,190
Notes receivable (less allowance for doubtful notes $575,862)	1,179,346
Other accounts receivable	715,844
Interest receivable	217,483
Pledges receivable (Note 1)	1,937,067
Other assets	331,271
Investments - long-term (Note 2)	43,558,364
Receivable from investment transactions	544,301
Bond reserve funds	2,409,368
Property, plant and equipment - net (Notes 3, 5 and 6)	16,791,109
TOTAL ASSETS	$ 70,588,045

LIABILITIES

Accounts payable and accrued expenses	$ 2,794,398
Deferred revenues	962,690
Interest payable	57,096
Liability under split interest agreements	93,906
Payable on investment transactions	2,313,730
Refundable government loan program	832,277
Postretirement benefits payable (Note 4)	1,180,237
Notes and bonds payable (Notes 5 and 6)	7,434,504
Total liabilities	15,668,838

NET ASSETS (Note 9):

Unrestricted	19,317,904
Temporarily restricted	8,827,400
Permanently restricted	26,773,903
Total net assets	54,919,207
TOTAL LIABILITIES AND NET ASSETS	$ 70,588,045

See notes to financial statements.

SAMPLE COLLEGE

STATEMENT OF ACTIVITIES
YEAR ENDED JUNE 30, 1996

	Unrestricted	Temporarily Restricted	Permanently Restricted	Total
REVENUE GAINS AND OTHER SUPPORT:				
Tuition and fees	$18,705,381			$ 18,705,381
State appropriations	116,219			116,219
Investment return designated for current operations (Note 2)	733,282	$ 1,322,668		2,055,950
Other investment income	348,282	239,358		587,640
Federal grants and contracts	333,920	102,960		436,880
State grants		211,166		211,166
Private gifts and grants	1,254,379	3,005,370		4,259,749
Auxiliary enterprises	7,213,042			7,213,042
Other sources	246,754	26,247		273,001
Total revenue	28,951,259	4,907,769		33,859,028
NET ASSETS RELEASED FROM RESTRICTIONS (Note 10)	3,268,436	(3,268,436)		
EXPENSES:				
Program expenses:				
Instruction	8,559,400			8,559,400
Research	640,904			640,904
Public services	238,190			238,190
Academic support	1,286,037			1,286,037
Student services	2,521,314			2,521,314
Financial aid	6,227,239			6,227,239
Auxiliary enterprises	7,963,124			7,963,124
Total program expenses	27,436,208			27,436,208
Institutional support	4,469,541			4,469,541
Total expenses	31,905,749			31,905,749
RESULTS FROM OPERATIONS	313,946	1,639,333		1,953,279
OTHER CHANGES				
Investment return in excess of amounts designated for current operations (Note 2)	419,357	717,199	$ 13,121	1,149,677
Contributions for endowments			1,654,699	1,654,699
Reclassifications (Note 9)		(715,384)	715,384	-
Changes in value of split interest agreements	6,394	13,318		19,712
Change in net assets	739,697	1,654,466	2,383,204	4,777,367
NET ASSETS, BEGINNING OF YEAR (Note 1)	18,578,207	7,172,934	24,390,699	50,141,840
NET ASSETS, END OF YEAR	$19,317,904	$ 8,827,400	$26,773,903	$ 54,919,207

See notes to financial statements.

SAMPLE COLLEGE

STATEMENT OF CASH FLOWS
YEAR ENDED JUNE 30, 1996

CASH FLOWS FROM OPERATING ACTIVITIES:	
Increase in net assets	$ 4,777,367
Adjustments to reconcile change in net assets to	
to net cash provided by operating activities:	
Nonoperating items:	
Contributions for long-term endowments	(1,654,699)
Net gains on endowment investments	(1,149,677)
Noncash items:	
Depreciation and amortization	1,380,628
Changes in assets and liabilities:	
Decrease in student accounts receivable	5,987
Decrease in other receivables	22,665
Increase in pledges receivable	(805,200)
Decrease in other current assets	6,562
Increase in accounts payable and accrued expenses	780,932
Net cash provided by operating activities	3,364,565
CASH FLOWS FROM INVESTING ACTIVITIES:	
Purchase of investments	(54,819,372)
Proceeds from the sale of investments	51,430,205
Building renovations and purchase of equipment	(462,299)
Student loans granted	(143,445)
Student loans repaid	120,738
Net cash used by investing activities	(3,874,173)
CASH FLOWS FROM FINANCING ACTIVITIES:	
Payment of notes and bonds payable	(852,243)
Contributions for endowments	1,654,699
Net cash from financing activities	802,456
NET CHANGE IN CASH AND CASH EQUIVALENTS	292,848
CASH AND CASH EQUIVALENTS AT BEGINNING OF YEAR	442,057
CASH AND CASH EQUIVALENTS AT END OF YEAR	$ 734,905
SUPPLEMENTAL DISCLOSURE OF CASH FLOW INFORMATION:	
Cash paid during the year for interest	$ 619,941

See notes to financial statements.

SAMPLE COLLEGE

NOTES TO FINANCIAL STATEMENTS
YEAR ENDED JUNE 30, 1996

1. SUMMARY OF SIGNIFICANT ACCOUNTING POLICIES

Organization - Sample College (the "College") is a not-for-profit independent liberal arts college for women. The College is exempt from Federal income taxes under the provisions of Section 501(a) of the Internal Revenue Code as an organization described in Section 501(c)(3).

a. *Basis of Presentation* - The financial statements are presented on the basis of unrestricted, temporarily restricted, and permanently restricted net assets.

b. *Cash and Cash Equivalents* - For financial statement purposes, the Organization considers all highly liquid investments with a maturity of three months or less when purchased to be cash equivalents.

c. *Investments* - Investments are carried at market value or appraised value, and realized and unrealized gains and losses are reflected in the statement of activities.

d. *Life Annuities* - The Organization has entered into Life Annuity Trusts whereby donors receive payments for the remainder of their life with any remainder at death reverting to the Organization unless specifically restricted by the donor. The liability is determined based on actuarial assumptions and is included in the liability section of the accompanying financial statements. The amount of the contribution recorded by the Organization is the fair value of the trust assets received less the present value of the estimated annuity payments.

e. *Capital Assets* - Land, buildings, and equipment are stated at cost less accumulated depreciation and amortization. Depreciation is provided using the straight-line method over the estimated useful lives of the assets.

f. *Revenue Recognition* - Contributions are recognized as revenue when they are received or unconditionally pledged.

The Organization reports gifts of cash and other assets as restricted support if they are received with donor stipulations that limit the use of the donated assets. When a donor restriction expires, that is, when a stipulated time restriction ends or purpose restriction is accomplished, temporarily restricted net assets are reclassified to unrestricted net assets and reported in the statement of activities as net assets released from restrictions.

The Organization reports gifts of land, buildings, and equipment as unrestricted support unless explicit donor stipulations specify how the donated assets must be used. Gifts of long-lived assets with explicit restrictions that specify how the assets are to be used and gifts of cash or other assets that must be used to acquire long-lived assets are reported as restricted support. Absent explicit donor stipulations about how these long-lived assets must be maintained, the Organization reports expirations of donor restrictions when the donated or acquired long-lived assets are placed in service.

Contributions receivable represent amounts committed by donors that have not been received by the Organization. Allowance for estimated uncollectible contributions amounted to $275 as of June 30, 19X1.

Contributions of services shall be recognized if the services received (a) create or enhance nonfinancial assets or (b) require specialized skills, are provided by individuals possessing those skills, and would typically need to be purchased if not provided by donation.

g. *Income Taxes* - Organization is a not-for-profit organization and is exempt from federal income taxes under Section 501(c)(3) of the Internal Revenue Code.

Use of Estimates - The preparation of financial statements in conformity with generally accepted accounting principles requires management to make estimates and assumptions that affect the reported amounts of assets and liabilities and disclosure of contingent assets and liabilities at the date of the financial statements. Estimates also affect the reported amounts of revenues and expenses during the reporting period. The reserves for student accounts, pledges receivable, the present value of multi-year pledges, actuarial calculations used for postretirement benefits and the recognition of restricted revenues require the significant use of estimates. Actual results could differ from those estimates.

Cash and cash equivalents - The College considers all liquid debt instruments purchased with temporary cash that have an original maturity of three months or less to be cash equivalents.

Marketable Securities - Marketable securities are carried at market value at the balance sheet date. Realized and unrealized gains and losses on investments (determined based upon average cost) and investment income are included in the statement of activities.

Student Accounts Receivable - Student accounts receivable are reported at the estimated net realizable amount from students.

Temporarily and Permanently Restricted Net Assets - Temporarily restricted net assets are restricted by donors for designed purposes. When they are used they are recorded in the statement of activities as assets released from restrictions - operations if designated by the donor to support College activities or as assets released from restrictions - capital acquisitions if designated by the donor to acquire or improve, property, plant and equipment.

Temporarily restricted net assets include annuity and life income funds subject to the restrictions of gift instruments requiring that the College periodically pay stipulated amounts of annuity funds or the income earned on the assets of life income funds to designated beneficiaries. Such payments terminate at the time specified by the donor, which is usually upon the death of the beneficiary. At such time, the assets of life income funds become available to the College for its unrestricted use or for use as restricted by the donor.

Permanently restricted net assets include endowment funds received by the College for which only the income can be expended for scholarships and other programs. Gains on permanently restricted net assets are available for the designated purpose as specified by the donor.

Property Plant and Equipment - Property, plant and equipment is stated at cost or, in the case of gifts, at fair market value at the date of the gift, less accumulated depreciation and amortization. Depreciation and amortization is computed by the straight-line method based upon the estimated useful lives of the assets.

Donor-Restricted Gifts - Gifts of cash and other assets are reported as restricted contributions if they are received with donor stipulations that limit the use of the donated assets. When a donor restriction expires, that is, when a stipulated time restriction ends or purpose restriction is accomplished, temporarily restricted net assets are reclassified to unrestricted net assets and reported in the statement of activities as net assets released from restrictions. Donor-restricted contributions whose restrictions are met within the same year as received are classified as unrestricted contributions in the accompanying financial statements.

Split Interest Agreements - The College is the beneficiary of trusts, annuities and pooled income funds. The College's interest in these split interest agreements is reported as a contribution in the year received at its net present value based upon actuarially determined rates.

Allocation of Certain Expenses - The College allocates operation and maintenance of plant and depreciation based upon building square footage in the statement of activities.

Fund Raising Expense - The College recognized fund raising expenses of $838,090 and is included as part of institutional support in the statement of activities.

Pledges - Pledges, less an allowance for uncollectible amounts, are recorded at the net present value, determined using a discount rate commensurate with the rate on U.S. Treasury bills whose maturities correspond to the maturities of the pledges (at 7.5%) , as receivables in the year made. Restricted pledges are reported as additions to the appropriate restricted net assets.

The pledges from various corporations, foundations, and individuals were as follows:

In less than one year	$ 123,129
In one to five years	1,668,717
In more than five years	466,412
Gross pledges receivable	2,258,258
Allowance for uncollectible pledges	68,811
Allowance for net present value	252,380
Net pledges receivable	$ 1,937,067

2. INVESTMENTS

Short-term investments of unrestricted net assets (at cost, which approximates market) are composed of the following:

U.S. Government securities	1,505,370
Bonds	144,519
Common stocks	132,235
Total	$ 1,942,797

Long-term investments are composed of the following:

Short-term investments	$ 5,460,679
U.S. Government obligations	10,187,941
Corporate bonds	4,679,976
Common and preferred stocks	23,229,768
Total	$43,558,364

The College has a total return policy of utilizing its endowment resources. To the extent that the total return requirement for the current year is not achieved by income from investments, the College utilizes appreciation of its pooled investment funds.

The following schedule summarizes the investment return and its classification in the statement of activities:

	Unrestricted	Temporarily Restricted	Permanently Restricted	Total
Interest and dividend (net of expenses of $268,823)	$ 359,609	$ 836,258	$ -	$1,195,867
Net gains	793,030	1,203,610	13,121	2,009,761
Return of long-term investments	1,152,639	2,039,868	13,121	3,205,628
Investment return designated for current operations	(733,282)	(1,322,669)	-	(2,055,951)
Investment return in excess of amounts designated for current operations	$ 419,357	$ 717,199	$ 13,121	$1,149,677

3. PROPERTY, PLANT, AND EQUIPMENT

Property, plant and equipment, at cost, and accumulated depreciation are summarized as follows:

Land	$ 561,186
Buildings	32,297,890
Furniture, fixtures, and equipment	4,139,157
	36,998,233
Less accumulated depreciation	20,207,124
Total	$16,791,109

4. **POSTRETIREMENT BENEFITS OTHER THAN PENSION**

The College sponsors a defined benefit postretirement medical plan. For non-union employees to be eligible for the medical benefits, the employee must be at least 62 years old and employed by the College from the age of 52 to 62 or a total of age and years of service equal to 80 with a minimum of 15 years of service. To be eligible, union employees, must be 62 years old and employed by the College for at least 10 years. The plan is unfunded and the College sponsors no other postretirement benefit plan.

The following table sets forth the amounts recognized in the College's balance sheet at June 30, 1996:

Accumulated postretirement benefits obligation:	
Retirees	51
Fully eligible active plan participants	239
Accumulated postretirement benefit obligation	$1,180,237
Accrued retirement benefits payable	
Net periodic postretirement benefit cost includes the following components:	
Service cost	$ 31,950
Interest cost	102,150
Net periodic postretirement benefit cost	$ 134,100

The assumed healthcare cost trend rate used in measuring the accumulated postretirement benefit obligation ranged from 8%, gradually decreasing to 3% by the year 2001 and thereafter in determining HMO costs, and from 10%, gradually decreasing to 5% by the year 2001 and thereafter for noncommunity rated plans. Increasing the assumed health care trend rates by 1% in each year would increase the accumulated postretirement benefit obligation by approximately $39,000, and increase the aggregate of the service and interest cost components of net periodic postretirement benefit cost by approximately $4,500. The weighted average discount rate used in determining the accumulated postretirement benefit obligation was 9%.

5. NOTES AND BONDS PAYABLE

Notes and bonds payable consisted of the following:

Noninterest-bearing note payable to food service vendor, due in quarterly installments of approximately $13,000 through June 1998 (payable on demand if annual food service contract is not renewed)	$ 99,720
Note payable to the U.S. Department of Housing and Urban Development, due in semi-annual installments of approximately $11,000 including interest at 3% per annum to 1999, secured by a mortgage on certain dormitory facilities and a first lien on the net revenues derived from those facilities	73,584
Notes payable	173,304
Sample College Dormitory bonds of 1960, due serially to 1999, interest at 3-1/8% per annum	40,950
Sample College Academic Building bonds of 1967, due serially to 1997, interest at 3% per annum	96,300
Dormitory Authority of the State of New York College and University Variable/Fixed Rate Insured Revenue Bonds (1985 Pooled Capital Program), Sample College Series A & B Bonds, interest currently at 7.8%, due serially to 2002 (Note 6)	6,902,460
Dormitory Authority of the State of New York College and University Variable/Fixed Rate Insured Revenue Bonds (1985 Pooled Capital Program), Sample College Series B Bonds, interest currently at 7.8%, due serially to 2002 (Note 6)	221,490
Bonds payable	7,261,200
Total	$ 7,434,504

Annual aggregate principal payments applicable to notes and bonds payable for years subsequent to June 30, 1996 are:

	Payable	Payable	Total
1997	$ 841,050	$ 70,287	$ 911,337
1998	904,050	70,540	974,590
1999	914,400	21,490	935,890
2000	975,150	10,987	986,137
2001	1,051,200	-	1,051,200
Thereafter	2,575,350	-	2,575,350
	$ 7,261,200	$ 173,304	$ 7,434,504

In accordance with the provisions of certain of the bond agreements the College is required to deposit reserve funds with trustees. These funds, which totaled $2,409,368 at June 30, 1992 was invested in U.S. Government securities.

6. DORMITORY FINANCING

The College and the N.Y. State Dormitory Authority executed a loan agreement for $11,192,000 and $355,000 under the Authority's $90,000,000 College and University Variable/Fixed Rate Insured Revenue Bonds (1985 Pooled Capital Program) in connection with the construction of a dormitory to house approximately 180 students.

As security for the loan, the College has pledged tuition revenues in the amount of $1,127,520 annually, granted a security interest in all fixtures, furnishings and equipment of the new dormitory and executed a fee mortgage and leasehold mortgage on certain buildings and properties. The loan agreement also contains covenants which restrict the College's ability to incur additional debt.

7. INTERCORPORATE AGREEMENT

An intercorporate agreement between the College and Intercorporate University provides for payment for the exchange of certain services between the two institutions. These services include cross-registration for students, library services, faculty exchange and certain special services and support costs.

During the year ended June 30, 1996, Sample paid Intercorporate $337,000, for services provided under the terms of the agreement.

8. PENSION PLANS

Substantially all employees of the College are covered under two defined contribution pension plans established with Teachers Insurance and Annuity Association. The College's contributions to the pension plans are based on specified percentages, ranging from 5% to 12%, of each employee's annual salary. Total pension expense for the year ended June 30, 1996 was approximately $1,071,405.

9. NET ASSETS

Unrestricted net assets are designated as follows:

Designated for endowments	$ 9,991,106
Invested in property, plant and equipment	8,983,744
Other	343,054
	$19,317,904

Temporarily restricted net assets are available for the following purposes:

Program services:	
Instruction, research and library	$ 4,525,035
Financial aid	1,709,675
Debt service	768,562
Plant improvements	860,577
Gifts to be designated	963,551
	$ 8,827,400

During the year ended June 30, 1996, donors designated $715,397 of previously recognized contributions resulting in a reclassification from temporarily restricted to permanently restricted net assets.

Permanently restricted net assets are restricted to:

Investments to be held in perpetuity, the income from which is expendable to support:	
Financial aid	$ 10,521,340
Instruction and other programs	9,851,311
	$20,372,651

10. RELEASED FROM RESTRICTIONS

Net assets were released from donor restrictions by incurring expenses satisfying the restricted purposes or by the occurrence of other events specified by donors.

Purpose restrictions accomplished were as follows:

Instruction	$ 1,226,510
Research	37,572
Public service	142,846
Academic support	42,877
Student Services	164,538
Institutional support	264,191
Financial aid	1,364,584
Auxiliary enterprises	25,318
	$3,268,436

* * * * * *

SAMPLE PUBLIC BROADCASTING CORPORATION

**Financial Statements as of and for the
Year Ended September 30, 1996 with
Comparative Totals for 1995 and
Independent Auditors' Report**

INDEPENDENT AUDITORS' REPORT

Board of Directors
Sample Public Broadcasting Corporation:

We have audited the accompanying statement of financial position of Sample Public Broadcasting Corporation (the "Corporation") as of September 30, 1996, and the related statements of activities and changes in net assets and of cash flows for the year then ended. These financial statements are the responsibility of the Corporation's management. Our responsibility is to express an opinion on these financial statements based on our audit. The prior year summarized comparative information has been derived from the Corporation's 1995 financial statements; and in our report dated November 21, 1995, we expressed an unqualified opinion on those financial statements.

We conducted our audit in accordance with generally accepted auditing standards. Those standards require that we plan and perform the audit to obtain reasonable assurance about whether the financial statements are free of material misstatement. An audit includes examining, on a test basis, evidence supporting the amounts and disclosures in the financial statements. An audit also includes assessing the accounting principles used and significant estimates made by management, as well as evaluating the overall financial statement presentation. We believe that our audit provides a reasonable basis for our opinion.

In our opinion, such financial statements present fairly, in all material respects, the financial position of Sample Public Broadcasting Corporation as of September 30, 1996, and the results of its activities and changes in net assets and its cash flows for the year then ended in conformity with generally accepted accounting principles.

November 20, 1996

SAMPLE PUBLIC BROADCASTING CORPORATION

STATEMENT OF FINANCIAL POSITION
SEPTEMBER 30, 1996 WITH COMPARATIVE TOTALS FOR 1995

	1996	1995
ASSETS		
CURRENT ASSETS:		
Cash and cash equivalents	$ 369,304	
Restricted cash (Note 4)	1,069,920	$ 3,506,668
Accounts and pledges receivable, less allowance for doubtful		
accounts of $136,600 in 1996 and $50,606 in 1995	2,454,618	2,744,158
Grants receivable	6,407,086	6,573,398
Broadcast rights	4,589,096	4,310,826
Other current assets	3,222,232	1,581,932
Total current assets	18,112,256	18,716,982
PREPAID PRODUCTION COSTS (Note 8)	2,491,200	-
BOND FINANCING COSTS	1,185,622	-
PROPERTY AND EQUIPMENT, Net (Note 2)	57,391,316	58,837,922
INVESTMENTS	2,822,024	2,486,420
TOTAL	$ 82,002,418	$ 80,041,324
LIABILITIES AND NET ASSETS		
CURRENT LIABILITIES:		
Accounts payable	$ 2,037,892	$ 5,547,958
Accrued broadcast rights	4,818,418	4,991,304
Other accrued expenses	3,451,578	5,705,604
Current portion of notes payable (Note 3)	1,074,516	1,490,080
Current portion of bonds payable (Note 4)	1,660,000	1,800,000
Deferred production and underwriting revenues	2,607,332	6,057,290
Net liabilities (assets) of discontinued operations, (Note 8)	696,766	(3,246,640)
Total current liabilities	16,346,502	22,345,596
BONDS PAYABLE (Note 4)	23,940,000	25,600,000
NOTES PAYABLE (Note 3)		3,785,628
Total liabilities	40,286,502	51,731,224
NET ASSETS:		
Unrestricted	32,792,162	24,583,144
Temporarily restricted (Note 5)	6,101,730	1,240,536
Permanently restricted (Note 1)	2,822,024	2,486,420
Total net assets	41,715,916	28,310,100
TOTAL	$ 82,002,418	$ 80,041,324

See notes to financial statements.

SAMPLE PUBLIC BROADCASTING CORPORATION

STATEMENT OF ACTIVITIES AND CHANGES IN NET ASSETS
YEAR ENDED SEPTEMBER 30, 1996 WITH COMPARATIVE TOTALS FOR 1995

	1996				1995
	Unrestricted	Temporarily Restricted	Permanently Restricted	Total	Total
REVENUES, SUPPORT AND OTHER CHANGES:					
Contributions and membership fees	$ 28,597,202	$ 5,956,752	$ 335,604	$ 34,889,558	$ 29,966,512
Development	2,484,710			2,484,710	2,734,458
Development production grants	3,503,300			3,503,300	2,550,238
Programming and production	10,647,340			10,647,340	8,891,450
Community service grants	4,184,384			4,184,384	5,100,620
Instructional television	1,457,430			1,457,430	2,147,088
Special events	503,618			503,618	1,279,406
Other	2,019,036			2,019,036	2,051,518
Other grants	202,594			202,594	699,762
Net assets released from restrictions due to expiration of time restrictions	1,095,558	(1,095,558)			
Total revenues, support and other changes	54,695,172	4,861,194	335,604	59,891,970	55,421,052
EXPENSES:					
Program services:					
Programming and production:					
Television:					
Local	12,802,080			12,802,080	13,706,648
For distribution to public broadcasting entities	4,419,992			4,419,992	4,699,970
Broadcasting	6,139,202			6,139,202	6,818,814
FM production and broadcasting	5,918,750			5,918,750	6,321,696
Program information	533,264			533,264	909,946
Total program services	29,813,288			29,813,288	32,457,074
Supporting services:					
Fund-raising and membership development:					
Membership and pledges	10,272,744			10,272,744	10,982,130
Program underwriting and grant solicitation	1,582,690			1,582,690	1,704,050
Development	1,389,560			1,389,560	1,242,782
Special events	422,170			422,170	1,196,946
Total fund-raising and membership development	13,667,164			13,667,164	15,125,908
Interest	1,958,234			1,958,234	2,080,762
Management and general	6,903,754			6,903,754	5,908,708
Capital expenses	54,530			54,530	156,422
Total supporting services	22,583,682			22,583,682	23,271,800
Total continuing expenses	52,396,970	-	-	52,396,970	55,728,874
INCREASE (DECREASE) IN NET ASSETS BEFORE DISCONTINUED OPERATIONS	2,298,202	4,861,194	335,604	7,495,000	(307,822)
INCREASE (DECREASE) IN NET ASSETS FROM DISCONTINUED OPERATIONS	5,910,816			5,910,816	(145,740)
INCREASE (DECREASE) IN NET ASSETS	8,209,018	4,861,194	335,604	13,405,816	(453,562)
NET ASSETS:					
Beginning of year	24,583,144	1,240,536	2,486,420	28,310,100	28,763,662
End of year	$ 32,792,162	$ 6,101,730	$ 2,822,024	$ 41,715,916	$ 28,310,100

See notes to financial statements.

SAMPLE PUBLIC BROADCASTING CORPORATION

STATEMENT OF CASH FLOWS
YEAR ENDED SEPTEMBER 30, 1996 WITH COMPARATIVE TOTALS FOR 1995

	1996	1995
OPERATING ACTIVITIES:		
Increase (decrease) in net assets	$ 13,405,816	$ (453,562)
Adjustments to reconcile increase (decrease) in net assets to net cash provided by (used in) operating activities:		
Cash flows from discontinued operations	(5,910,814)	145,740
Depreciation and amortization	2,036,218	2,040,000
Receipt of permanently restricted contribution	(335,604)	
Contributed property and equipment	(5,430)	(20,800)
Public Broadcasting System dues financed by note payable		2,365,434
Net effect of changes in:		
Accounts and pledges receivable	289,540	(348,316)
Grants receivable	166,312	(140,372)
Broadcast rights	(278,270)	1,306,642
Other current assets	(282,500)	144,110
Accounts payable	(3,510,066)	211,908
Accrued broadcast rights	(172,886)	(1,483,462)
Other accrued expenses	(2,254,026)	1,527,908
Deferred production and underwriting revenues	(3,449,958)	(807,094)
Net cash provided by (used in) continuing operating activities	(301,668)	4,488,136
Net cash used in discontinued operations	(2,293,952)	(2,250,056)
Net cash provided by (used in) operating activities	(2,595,620)	2,238,080
INVESTING ACTIVITIES:		
Purchases of equipment	(559,752)	(886,000)
Purchases of investments	(335,604)	
Proceeds from sale of discontinued operations	8,305,144	
Net cash provided by (used in) investing activities	7,409,788	(886,000)
FINANCING ACTIVITIES:		
Proceeds from issuance of the 1996 Series Bonds	26,800,000	
Repayment of the 1990 Series Bonds	(27,400,000)	
Payment on the 1996 Series Bonds	(1,200,000)	
Long term borrowings from Wells Fargo Bank		3,236,112
Payments on borrowings from Wells Fargo Bank	(3,011,112)	(3,351,520)
Payments on note payable to Public Broadcasting System	(1,190,080)	
Payment of deferred financing costs	(1,216,024)	
Receipt of permanently restricted contribution	335,604	
Net cash used in financing activities	(6,881,612)	(115,408)
NET INCREASE (DECREASE) IN CASH, CASH EQUIVALENTS AND RESTRICTED CASH	(2,067,444)	1,236,672
CASH, CASH EQUIVALENTS AND RESTRICTED CASH:		
Beginning of year	3,506,668	2,269,996
End of year	$ 1,439,224	$ 3,506,668
SUPPLEMENTAL DATA:		
Interest paid	$ 1,958,234	$ 2,080,762
Noncash investing and financing activities:		
Contributed property and equipment	$ 5,430	$ 20,800
Public Broadcasting Service dues financed by note payable	$ -	$ 2,365,434

See notes to financial statements.

SAMPLE PUBLIC BROADCASTING CORPORATION

NOTES TO FINANCIAL STATEMENTS
YEAR ENDED SEPTEMBER 30, 1996 WITH COMPARATIVE TOTALS FOR 1995

1. **SUMMARY OF SIGNIFICANT ACCOUNTING POLICIES**

   Corporation - Sample Public Broadcasting Corporation (the "Corporation") is a nonprofit corporation which operates a noncommercial public television station ("SPBC-TV") and a noncommercial public radio station ("SPBC-FM") in Long Beach, California.

   Basis of Presentation - The Corporation's financial statements are presented on the basis of unrestricted, temporarily restricted, and permanently restricted net assets.

   Cash and Cash Equivalents - The Corporation considers all highly liquid debt instruments with original maturities of three months or less to be cash equivalents.

   Pledges receivable represent amounts committed by donors that have not been received by the Corporation. As of September 30, 1996 and 1995, pledges receivable were approximately $1,266,000, and $1,016,000, respectively.

   Broadcast Rights - The Corporation purchases broadcast rights for certain programs from the Public Broadcasting Service ("PBS") and other sources, and expenses these costs over the period of expected telecasts or the term of the agreement, whichever is shorter. Broadcast rights purchased during the years ended September 30, 1996 and 1995, approximated $7,238,000 and $7,340,000, respectively. The associated expense recognized during the years ended September 30, 1996 and 1995 amounted to $6,960,000 and $8,647,000, respectively.

   Prepaid publication costs represent future copies of Long Beach Focus Magazine which will be supplied to the Corporation's members for the three years following the sale of Long Beach Focus Magazine (see Note 8).

   Property and equipment are stated at cost. Donated assets are recorded at the estimated fair value at the date of donation. Depreciation and amortization are computed using the straight-line method based upon estimated useful lives of the assets ranging from 3 to 50 years.

   Investments - Investments are carried at estimated fair value based on quoted market prices. Investments received through gifts are recorded at estimated fair market value at the date of donation. As of September 30, 1996 and 1995, investments consisted of money market accounts with estimated fair values of $2,822,024 and $2,486,420, respectively.

   Bond financing costs represent expenses incurred in connection with the issuance of bonds payable during the year ended September 30, 1996 (see Note 4), which are being amortized on a straight-line basis over the life of the Series 1996 Bonds.

   Temporarily restricted net assets represent contributions and other inflows of assets whose use by the Corporation is limited by donor-imposed stipulations that either expire by passage of time or can be fulfilled and removed by actions of the Corporation pursuant to those stipulations (see Note 5).

Permanently restricted net assets are restricted by the donor for investment in perpetuity, the income from which is available to support any activity of the Corporation, but which has been designated by the Corporation's Board of Directors to support the production of art and current affairs programs.

Revenue Recognition - Contributions are recognized as revenue when they are received or unconditionally pledged.

The Corporation reports gifts of cash and other assets as restricted support if they are received with donor stipulations that limit the use of the donated assets. When a donor restriction expires, that is, when a stipulated time restriction ends or purpose restriction is accomplished, temporarily restricted net assets are reclassified to unrestricted net assets and reported as net assets released from restriction.

Contributions of services are recognized when received if the services (a) create or enhance nonfinancial assets or (b) require specialized skills, are provided by individuals possessing those skills, and would typically need to be purchased if not provided by donation.

In-kind contributions consist of donated legal, accounting and other professional services and donated goods and facilities. The estimated fair value of these donations approximated $334,800 and $912,000 for the years ended September 30, 1996 and 1995, respectively, and are reflected in the accompanying Statements of Activities and Changes in Net Assets. Donated personal services of volunteers are not reflected in the accompanying financial statements, because such services do not require specialized skills. The estimated fair value of such donated volunteer services is based upon standard valuation rates and job classifications developed by the Corporation for Public Broadcasting ("CPB"), and amounted to approximately $664,000 for each of the years ended September 30, 1996 and 1995.

Functional Expense Allocations - Certain expenses, such as depreciation and amortization, design, building services and personnel, are allocated among program services and supporting services based primarily on direct payroll charges, equipment usage or space occupied and on estimates made by the Corporation's management. Management of the Corporation has chosen not to allocate interest and capital expenses, amounting to $2,012,764, on a functional basis.

Use of Estimates - The preparation of financial statements in conformity with generally accepted accounting principles requires management to make estimates and assumptions. These estimates and assumptions affect the reported amounts of assets and liabilities and disclosure of contingent assets and liabilities at the date of the financial statements and the reported amounts of revenue and expenses during the reporting period. Actual results could differ from those estimates.

Income Taxes - The Corporation's principal activities are exempt from federal and state income taxes under Section 501(c)(3) of the U.S. Internal Revenue Code and Section 23701(d) of the California Tax Code.

1995 Financial Information - The financial statements include certain prior-year summarized comparative information in total but not by net asset class. Such information does not include sufficient detail to constitute a presentation in conformity with generally accepted accounting principles. Accordingly, such information should be read in conjunction with the Corporation's financial statements for the year ended September 30, 1995, from which the summarized financial information was derived. Certain reclassifications have been made to the 1995 amounts to conform to the 1996 presentation.

2. PROPERTY AND EQUIPMENT

Property and equipment at September 30, 1996 and 1995 consisted of the following:

	1996	1995
Land	$ 2,539,382	$ 2,539,382
Building and improvements	54,374,032	54,374,032
Furniture, fixtures, office equipment and vehicles	7,776,122	7,874,882
Production equipment	13,102,634	13,020,096
Broadcast equipment	3,477,588	4,016,644
Radio station equipment	1,760,074	1,660,486
Total	83,029,832	83,485,522
Less accumulated depreciation and amortization	(25,638,516)	(24,647,600)
Property and equipment, net	$57,391,316	$58,837,922

3. NOTES PAYABLE

	1996	1995
Note payable to the Public Broadcasting Service, interest at 6.5% commencing July 1996, monthly payments of $100,880 through August 1997, unsecured	$ 1,074,516	$2,264,596
Note payable to Cargo Bank under term loan		1,275,000
Note payable to Cargo Bank under line-of-credit		1,736,112
Subtotal	1,074,516	5,275,708
Less current portion	(1,074,516)	(1,490,080)
Total	$ 0	$3,785,628

During 1996, the corporation repaid both the term loan to Cargo Bank and the note payable under the Cargo Bank line of credit agreement. Proceeds for the repayment of debt came from the sale of discontinued operations (see Note 8).

The Corporation has a revolving line of credit in the amount of $3,000,000 which expires on April 1, 1997. The line of credit contains certain covenants and is secured by the Corporation's real and personal property (see Note 4). Interest rates are based upon Debt Service Coverage Ratio, as defined, however, the maximum interest rate is Prime Rate plus .75% per annum. The Corporation had no outstanding balances on this line of credit at September 30, 1996.

4. **BONDS PAYABLE**

In April 1996, the Corporation entered into a loan agreement with the California Economic Development Financing Authority for $26,800,000 of Variable Rate Demand Refund Revenue Bonds, Series 1996 (the "Series 1996 Bonds"). The Series 1996 Bonds mature on April 1, 2020. The proceeds of the Series 1996 Bonds were used to repay the 1990 tax-exempt bonds issued by the City of Oceanside (the "Series 1990 Bonds"). The Corporation makes monthly deposits to a special fund, in amounts which are sufficient to pay Bond principal and interest as the bond payments become due and payable. The $1,069,920 balance of the special fund as of September 30, 1996 has been reflected as restricted cash on the accompanying 1996 Statement of Financial Position. The bonds bear interest at a Weekly Interest Rate during a Weekly Interest Rate Period or a Term Interest Rate during a Term Interest Rate Period. A Term Interest Rate Period can have a duration of one year or any multiple of one year, or the period of time remaining to the final maturity of the Series 1996 Bonds. The rate is set by the remarketing agent and cannot exceed 11% per annum. Interest on the Series 1996 Bonds was based on a Weekly Interest Rate and averaged 3.75% during 1996. The interest rate was 6.3% for the Series 1990 Bonds in 1995.

The terms of the loan agreement require that a letter of credit be maintained as long as the Series 1996 Bonds are outstanding. Accordingly, the Corporation has an irrevocable letter of credit with Wells Fargo Bank for $26,800,000 as of September 30, 1996, which expires on April 23, 2003 and is collateralized by a deed of trust on all the real and personal property of the Corporation. The nonrefundable letter of credit fee as of September 30, 1996 was 1.75% on $14,396,000 (real estate portion) and 1.3% on $11,600,000. The letter of credit fee can increase to 2.75% on the real estate portion and 2% on the other letter of credit portion if the Corporation falls below a specified Debt Service Coverage ratio. The agreement contains certain covenants which, among other things, require the Corporation to maintain certain financial ratios and places limitations on capital expenditures, other indebtedness, pledge of assets, lease expenditures and guaranties. The Corporation was in compliance with the covenants at September 30, 1996.

In connection with the Series 1996 Bonds and letter of credit, the Corporation paid $1,216,024 of issuance costs.

The Series 1996 Bonds mature on April 1, 2020, are subject to mandatory redemption at a redemption price equal to the Bond principal amount, and are payable in installments as follows as of September 30, 1996:

Year ending September 30:	
1997	$ 1,660,000
1998	1,830,000
1999	2,010,000
2000	2,200,000
2001	2,390,000
Thereafter	15,510,000
Total	$25,600,000

During the variable interest rate period, the bonds are subject to a demand purchase option, whereby any bond must be purchased upon the demand of the bond holder. Additionally, the bonds will be purchased at the beginning of the fixed interest rate period and remarketed by the agent. In the event that the remarketing agent cannot place all or part of the purchased bonds, a drawing will be made on the letter of credit.

The terms of the Series 1990 Bonds required the Corporation to maintain a bond reserve fund equal to 10% of the principal amount of the bonds outstanding, to be used solely to reimburse the Bank for drawings on the letter of credit. The bond reserve fund balance was $3,506,668 as of September 30, 1995, which is reflected on the accompanying 1995 Statement of Financial Position as restricted cash.

5. TEMPORARILY RESTRICTED NET ASSETS

Temporarily restricted net assets were available for the following purposes as of September 30, 1996 and 1995:

	1996	1995
To underwrite specific productions or areas of programming	$4,293,284	
To be used in the Corporation's unrestricted operations in future periods	1,808,446	$ 1,240,536
Total	$6,101,730	$ 1,240,536

6. COMMITMENTS AND CONTINGENCIES

The following is a schedule of future minimum lease payments required under noncancelable operating leases through February 28, 2005, as of September 30, 1996:

Year ending September 30:	
1997	$ 540,000
1998	530,000
1999	320,000
2000	312,000
2001	308,000
Thereafter	994,000
Total minimum rental payments	$3,004,000

The minimum lease payments do not include future cost of living escalations and pro rata property tax allocations, which are required for certain of the leases.

Total rent expense, including month-to-month leases, was $380,000 and $500,000 for the years ended September 30, 1996 and 1995, respectively.

The Corporation is involved in various claims and legal actions arising in the ordinary course of business. In the opinion of management, the ultimate disposition of these matters will not have a material adverse effect on the Corporation's financial position or results of activities.

7. **RETIREMENT PLAN**

The Corporation has a contributory trusteed defined contribution pension plan covering substantially all employees. Pension costs, funded currently, were $819,200 and $998,800 for the years ended September 30, 1996 and 1995, respectively.

8. **DISCONTINUED OPERATIONS**

In 1996, the Corporation made a decision to concentrate on its core services of public television and public radio. As a result of this decision, the Corporation sold Long Beach Focus Magazine on May 23, 1996 and sold the SPBC Books & Tapes Division on June 14, 1996.

The assets and liabilities have been classified in the accompanying Statements of Financial Position as net assets (liabilities) of discontinued operations as follows:

	1996	1995
Cash and cash equivalents	$ 526,494	
Accounts and pledges receivable, net		$2,217,370
Other current assets		2,737,894
Property and equipment, net		122,284
Accounts payable		(1,283,476)
Other accrued liabilities	(1,223,260)	(547,432)
Assets (liabilities) of discontinued operations, net	$ (696,766)	$3,246,640

The results of activities of Long Beach Focus Magazine and SPBC Books and Tapes Division have been classified as discontinued operations for all periods presented in the accompanying Statements of Activities and Change in Net Assets as follows:

	1996	1995
Sales	$ 10,441,146	$ 16,413,342
Expenses	12,901,840	16,559,082
Loss from continuing operations	(2,460,694)	(145,740)
Gain on disposal of operations	8,371,510	
Increase (decrease) in net assets from discontinued operations	$ 5,910,816	$ (145,740)

The net cash received from the transactions was used to pay past due payables and other debt, including a required $1,200,000 reduction in bond debt. Additionally, as part of the agreement with the purchaser of Long Beach Focus Magazine, the purchaser will supply up to 200,000 copies (subject to adjustment) of the magazine to the Corporations' members on an annual basis over three years following the sales transaction. The estimated fair value of this part of the agreement is $3,850,000 and is reflected in the gain on disposal of operations. The current position of this asset ($1,358,800) is included in other current assets and the noncurrent portion ($2,491,200) is reflected as prepaid publication costs on the accompanying 1996 Statement of Financial Position.

* * * * * *

SAMPLE FOUNDATION

**Financial Statements for the Year Ended
June 30, 1996 and Independent Auditors' Report**

INDEPENDENT AUDITORS' REPORT

Board of Trustees of
 SAMPLE Foundation:

We have audited the accompanying statement of financial position of SAMPLE Foundation (the "Foundation") as of June 30, 1996 and the related statements of activities and cash flows for the year then ended. These financial statements are the responsibility of the Foundation's management. Our responsibility is to express an opinion on these financial statements based on our audit.

We conducted our audit in accordance with generally accepted auditing standards. Those standards require that we plan and perform the audit to obtain reasonable assurance about whether the financial statements are free of material misstatement. An audit includes examining, on a test basis, evidence supporting the amounts and disclosures in the financial statements. An audit also includes assessing the accounting principles used and significant estimates made by management, as well as evaluating the overall financial statement presentation. We believe that our audit provides a reasonable basis for our opinion.

In our opinion, the financial statements referred to above present fairly, in all material respects, the financial position of the Foundation at June 30, 1996, and the changes in its net assets, and its cash flows for the year then ended in conformity with generally accepted accounting principles.

September 5, 1996

SAMPLE FOUNDATION

STATEMENT OF FINANCIAL POSITION
JUNE 30, 1996

ASSETS

Cash and cash equivalents	$ 204,501
Unrestricted investments	196,986
Accounts receivable	92,294
Inventory	70,793
Prepaid expenses	64,818
Joint ventures	82,346
Pledges receivable	250,772
Property and equipment - net	1,275,679
Restricted investments	512,804
TOTAL	$2,750,993

LIABILITIES AND NET ASSETS

Accounts payable and accrued expenses	$ 136,701
Deferred revenue	19,570
Total liabilities	156,271

CONTINGENCIES (Note 11)

NET ASSETS:	
Unrestricted	1,679,053
Temporarily restricted	854,053
Permanently restricted	61,616
Total net assets	2,594,722
TOTAL	$2,750,993

See notes to financial statements.

SAMPLE FOUNDATION

STATEMENT OF ACTIVITIES
YEAR ENDED JUNE 30, 1996

	Unrestricted	Temporarily Restricted	Permanently Restricted	Total
CHANGES IN NET ASSETS:				
Contributions	$ 494,761	$ 557,163		$ 1,051,924
Net assets released from restrictions	273,970	(273,970)		
Total contributions	768,731	283,193		1,051,924
Revenues:				
Museum admissions	1,280,876			1,280,876
Retail operations	538,515			538,515
Membership dues	91,565			91,565
Education program fees	58,980			58,980
Exhibition lease fees	31,933			31,933
Net equity increase in joint ventures	17,126			17,126
Interest and dividends	5,486	16,365		21,851
Other	40,608	157		40,765
Total revenues	2,065,089	16,522		2,081,611
Total contributions and revenues	2,833,820	299,715		3,133,535
EXPENSES:				
Program service	1,981,466			1,981,466
Management and general	289,912			289,912
Fund raising	49,771			49,771
Total expenses	2,321,149			2,321,149
CHANGE IN NET ASSETS	512,671	299,715		812,386
NET ASSETS, BEGINNING OF YEAR	1,166,382	554,338	$ 61,616	1,782,336
NET ASSETS, END OF YEAR	$ 1,679,053	$ 854,053	$ 61,616	$ 2,594,722

See notes to financial statements.

SAMPLE FOUNDATION

STATEMENT OF CASH FLOWS
YEAR ENDED JUNE 30, 1996

CASH FLOWS FROM OPERATING ACTIVITIES:		
Change in net assets		$ 812,386
Adjustments to reconcile change in net assets to net cash		
provided by operating activities:		
Depreciation and amortization	$ 99,025	
Income temporarily restricted	(16,522)	
Change in assets and liabilities:		
Accounts receivable	64,557	
Pledges receivable	(104,222)	
Inventory	(3,839)	
Prepaid expenses	(18,279)	
Accounts payable and accrued expenses	(125,757)	
Joint ventures	26,208	
Deferred revenues	(144,473)	(223,302)
Net cash provided by operating activities		589,084
CASH FLOWS FROM INVESTING ACTIVITIES:		
Change in unrestricted investments - net		(196,986)
Change in restricted investments - net		(169,970)
Purchase of property		(246,014)
Net cash used by investing activities		(612,970)
CASH FLOWS FROM FINANCING ACTIVITIES		
Income temporarily restricted		16,522
Net cash provided by financing activities		16,522
NET DECREASE IN CASH AND CASH EQUIVALENTS		(7,364)
CASH AND CASH EQUIVALENTS AT BEGINNING OF YEAR		211,865
CASH AND CASH EQUIVALENTS AT END OF YEAR		$ 204,501
SUPPLEMENTAL DISCLOSURE OF NONCASH INVESTING		
ACTIVITIES:		
Gifts of equipment		$ 3,100

See notes to consolidated financial statements.

SAMPLE FOUNDATION

NOTES TO FINANCIAL STATEMENTS
JUNE 30, 1996

1.   ORGANIZATION AND PURPOSE

The SAMPLE Foundation ("Foundation") is a California nonprofit public benefit corporation dedicated to furthering the public's understanding of science and technology. SAMPLE operates the Museum ("Armada District" or "Operations") where it produces, licenses, and presents state-of-the-art media productions (films and multi-media productions); produces and displays interactive exhibits; offers science education for students, teachers, and the general public; and operates a retail science store and food service ("retail operations").

2.   SUMMARY OF SIGNIFICANT ACCOUNTING POLICIES

Basis of Presentation - The financial statements are presented on the basis of unrestricted, temporarily restricted, and permanently restricted net assets.

Cash and Cash Equivalents - For financial statement purposes, the Foundation considers all highly liquid investments with a maturity of less than three months when purchased to be cash equivalents.

Property - Exhibits, equipment and buildings are stated at cost less accumulated depreciation and amortization. Depreciation is provided using the straight-line method over the estimated useful lives of the assets.

Revenue Recognition - Contributions are recognized as revenue when they are received or unconditionally pledged.

The Foundation reports gifts of cash and other assets as restricted support if they are received with donor stipulations that limit the use of the donated assets. When a donor restriction expires, that is, when a stipulated time restriction ends or purpose restriction is accomplished, temporarily restricted net assets are reclassified to unrestricted net assets and reported in the statement of activities as net assets released from restrictions.

The Foundation reports gifts of land, buildings, and equipment as unrestricted support unless explicit donor stipulations specify how the donated assets must be used. Gifts of long-lived assets with explicit restrictions that specify how the assets are to be used and gifts of cash or other assets that must be used to acquire long-lived assets are reported as restricted support. Absent explicit donor stipulations about how these long-lived assets must be maintained, the Foundation reports expirations of donor restrictions when the donated or acquired long-lived assets are placed in service.

Contributions of services are recognized if the services received (a) create or enhance nonfinancial assets or (b) require specialized skills, are provided by individuals possessing those skills, and would typically need to be purchased if not provided by donation. The Foundation reports such contributions at their estimated fair value when received. Included in contributions are $186,264 which consist primarily of donated advertising.

Income Taxes - The Foundation is a not-for-profit organization and is exempt from federal income taxes under Section 501(c)(3) of the Internal Revenue Code.

Inventory - Inventory is carried at the lower of average cost or market.

Use of Estimates in the Preparation of Financial Statements - In preparing financial statements in conformity with generally accepted accounting principles, management is required to make estimates and assumptions that affect the reported amounts of assets and liabilities and the disclosure of contingent assets and liabilities at the date of the financial statements and revenues and expenses during the reporting period. Actual results could differ from those estimates.

3. **INVESTMENTS**

Investments are carried at fair value, which is based on quoted market prices at June 30, 1996.

Unrestricted	
Treasury Bills	$ 196,986
Restricted	
Temporarily restricted:	
Bond Fund	$ 416,379
Cash	30,825
Permanently restricted:	
Certificates of deposit	65,600
Total	$ 512,804

The Foundation's investment activities for the year ended June 30, 1996 resulted in income of $28,111; and a net unrealized loss on investments and a decrease in temporarily restricted net assets of $6,261.

4. **JOINT VENTURES**

General - It has been the normal business practice of SAMPLE to enter into joint venture agreements for production and licensing of films; these joint ventures are carried on the equity basis of accounting. The most significant of the agreements currently in effect are as follows:

Joint Venture - SAMPLE is the managing partner, whose principal purpose is to distribute the film "Chronometer". Under the terms of the joint venture agreement, SAMPLE received an exhibition quality print and sound track of such film, the right to exhibit the film in the Armada District, and participation in future profits and losses of the joint venture.

The agreement provides for a five-stage recoupment schedule for the distribution of film rental proceeds and profits and losses to the joint venture partners. This recoupment schedule first contemplates the recovery of each joint venture partner's contribution to the film, and second, the pro rata distribution of film rental profits. Distribution of profit is recognized as a return of the capital investment. As of June 30, 1996, the net unrecovered investment is $24,000.

Film Partnership - SAMPLE is a general partner in a partnership whose principal purpose is to distribute the film "Eruption". SAMPLE shares in the profits and losses at the rate of its partnership interest, 15%. For the year ended June 30, 1996, SAMPLE received $33,500 in distributions from the partnership, of which $12,842 is recognized as a reduction of the capital investment. As of June 30, 1996, the net unrecovered investment is $25,550.

Central Park Participation Agreement - In April 1993, SAMPLE entered into a prelicense and participation agreement with an unrelated company. The principal purpose of the agreement is for the company to produce and distribute a film, "Central Park". Under the terms of the agreement, SAMPLE received non-exclusive exhibition rights in the Armada District for a term of 25 years from the date the film is delivered, the right to receive an exhibition quality print and soundtrack of the film, and participation in future profits derived from the agreement.

The agreement provides for a five-stage recoupment schedule for the distribution of the film's gross proceeds. This recoupment schedule first contemplates the recovery of the company's production, distribution and debt service costs, and second, the agreed upon participation percentages provided for in the agreement. Distribution of profit is recognized as a return of the capital investment. As of June 30, 1996, the net unrecovered investment is $29,500.

5. CONTRIBUTIONS

As of June 30, 1996, the Foundation has unconditional pledges receivable as follows:

Due within one year	$235,981
Due within 1 to 5 years	18,000
	253,981
Less unamortized discount	3,209
Pledges receivable	$250,772

At June 30, 1996, the Foundation had also received conditional promises to give totaling $360,000. These conditional promises to give are not recognized as assets and, if they are received, they will be restricted for specific purposes stipulated by the donors.

6. PROPERTY AND EQUIPMENT - NET

Included in property are exhibits, equipment, furniture and buildings which consisted of the following at June 30, 1996:

Less accumulated depreciation and amortization	(631,414)
Property - net	$1,275,679

7. AGREEMENT WITH THE CITY

Master Agreement - The building and land in which the Armada District ("District") is located, is owned by the City and leased to SAMPLE. Thus the building and underlying land are not assets of SAMPLE and are not reflected in the financial statements. SAMPLE operates the District under a 30-year lease with the City. As part of this agreement, SAMPLE is to make available to the City, without charge, the premises up to three times per calendar year for civic events and special programs.

Under the agreement, in place of cash rent for the use of the premises, the consideration to the City from SAMPLE will be the continuous operation, development and maintenance of the premises. The only additional consideration is the one time payment to the City of the difference between amount remaining in order to retire the original construction bonds and the amount in the Planetarium Authority Reserve of $23,296. This amount, which was included in accrued expenses at June 30, 1996, was paid in July 1996.

8. ENTERPRISE LEARNING CENTER AGREEMENT

In 1991, SAMPLE entered into the Enterprise Learning Center Agreement. In connection with the agreement, SAMPLE purchased a learning center simulator fabricated by the Enterprise Center for Science Education for $177,000 and is required to pay an annual license fee. SAMPLE's cost is being amortized over the estimated useful life of the simulator (15 years). $122,843 is included in property at June 30, 1996 and $5,000 was paid as a license fee in 1996.

9. FEDERAL GRANT AWARDS

In May 1992, the Foundation was awarded a grant, with funding through October 31, 1997, of approximately $493,000 by the National Science Foundation ("NSF") in support of the Signals exhibition project. Through June 30, 1996, SAMPLE had incurred expenditures of $328,000 and received reimbursements from NSF totaling $305,500.

In August 1994, the Foundation was awarded a General Operating Support grant of $56,500 by Institute of Museum Services for general operating expenses. The grant will be administered over a two-year period beginning October 1, 1994 and funds will be received in equal quarterly payments. Through June 30, 1996, SAMPLE has incurred expenditures of $49,200 and received $49,200 under this grant.

10. PENSION PLAN

SAMPLE has a pension plan in which all employees meeting service and age requirements and not covered by a collective bargaining agreement may participate. Benefits under the plan are funded by annuities purchased for employees then becoming eligible to participate. The purchases of annuities under the plan in fiscal 1996 were $47,100. The plan may be terminated by SAMPLE at any time.

11. CONTINGENCIES

Temporarily Restricted - Included in the fund is the annual payments of a $1,000,000 pledge, part of which is restricted for equipment purchases. The payment schedule provides for ten annual payments of $100,000 in principal and $10,000 in interest through fiscal 1997. Pursuant to the terms of such pledge, $810,000 has been received through June 30, 1996, and is to be used primarily for construction of a planned theater. In the event that the planned theater is not built, $480,000 of contributions received through June 30, 1996 must be returned to the pledgor.

In October 1992, the City Council approved the Rocky Garden Abstract Plan which includes SAMPLE's master plan for expansion of its facility. As part of its master plan, SAMPLE intends to construct a theater and expand its science center and education facilities. As of June 30, 1996, construction had not commenced.

*   *   *   *   *   *

SAMPLE PERFORMING ARTS ORGANIZATION

**Financial Statements for the
Year Ended June 30, 1996 and
Independent Auditors' Report**

INDEPENDENT AUDITORS' REPORT

To the Board of Directors of
Sample Performing Arts Association:

We have audited the accompanying statement of financial position of the Sample Performing Arts Association (the "Association") as of June 30, 1996 and the related statements of activities and cash flows for the year then ended. These financial statements are the responsibility of the Association's management. Our responsibility is to express an opinion on these financial statements based on our audit.

We conducted our audit in accordance with generally accepted auditing standards. Those standards require that we plan and perform the audit to obtain reasonable assurance about whether the financial statements are free of material misstatement. An audit includes examining, on a test basis, evidence supporting the amounts and disclosures in the financial statements. An audit also includes assessing the accounting principles used and significant estimates made by management, as well as evaluating the overall financial statement presentation. We believe that our audit provides a reasonable basis for our opinion.

In our opinion, the financial statements referred to above present fairly, in all material respects, the financial position of Sample Performing Arts Association as of June 30, 1996, and the changes in its net assets and its cash flows for the year then ended in conformity with generally accepted accounting principles.

September 5, 1996

Sample Performing Arts Association

STATEMENTS OF FINANCIAL POSITION
JUNE 30, 1996

ASSETS		1996
CURRENT ASSETS:		
Cash	$	851,692
Short-term investments		5,400,120
		6,251,812
Receivables:		
Ticket sales		920,544
Grants and contributions		517,510
Other		264,340
		1,702,394
Prepaid and deferred expenses		490,170
Total current assets		8,444,376
NON-CURRENT ASSETS:		
Land, building and equipment		1,179,496
Long-term investments		1,452,432
Pooled income fund		458,906
Endowment assets		4,830,404
TOTAL	$	16,365,614

LIABILITIES AND NET ASSETS

CURRENT LIABILITIES:		
Accounts payable and accrued expenses	$	263,736
Deferred ticket sales		5,563,520
Total current liabilities		5,827,256
COMMITMENTS (Note 7)		
Net assets:		
Unrestricted		2,715,444
Temporarily restricted		2,542,558
Permanently restricted		5,280,356
Total net assets		10,538,358
TOTAL	$	16,365,614

See notes to financial statements.

SAMPLE PERFORMING ARTS ASSOCIATION

STATEMENT OF ACTIVITIES
YEAR ENDED JUNE 30, 1996

	Unrestricted	Temporarily Restricted	Permanently Restricted	Total
REVENUES AND GAINS:				
International season ticket sales	$ 6,846,474			$ 6,846,474
Production, rental and other revenues	1,367,650			1,367,650
Special events	401,604			401,604
Interest income	291,112			291,112
Educational programs	128,640			128,640
Endowment income	131,336		$ 18,180	149,516
Total	9,166,816		18,180	9,184,996
EXPENSES:				
International season	8,561,904			8,561,904
Production overhead and shop expenses	1,970,416			1,970,416
Administrative overhead	1,774,860			1,774,860
Marketing overhead	1,177,716			1,177,716
Development overhead	1,221,742			1,221,742
Special events	121,328			121,328
Educational programs	886,410			886,410
Total	15,714,376		0	15,714,376
REVENUES AND GAINS LESS EXPENSES	(6,547,560)		18,180	(6,529,380)
CONTRIBUTIONS AND PUBLIC SUPPORT:				
Contributions	3,750,276	$ 2,096,304	185,104	6,031,684
Contributions-release of restrictions	1,159,370	(1,159,370)		0
Government grants	1,245,100			1,245,100
Other activities	471,144			471,144
Total	6,625,890	936,934	185,104	7,747,928
Total revenues, gains, contributions and public support over expenses	78,330	936,934	203,284	1,218,548
CHANGES IN RESTRICTED ASSETS:				
Endowment gains			238,584	238,584
SDCF endowment gains			292,236	292,236
Pooled income fund		22	490	512
Transfer to endowment	(100,000)		100,000	0
Total	(100,000)	22	631,310	531,332
CHANGES IN NET ASSETS	(21,670)	936,956	834,594	1,749,880
NET ASSETS AT BEGINNING OF YEAR	2,737,114	1,605,602	4,445,762	8,788,478
NET ASSETS AT END OF YEAR	$ 2,715,444	$ 2,542,558	$ 5,280,356	$ 10,538,358

See notes to financial statements.

SAMPLE PERFORMING ARTS ASSOCIATION

STATEMENT OF CASH FLOWS
YEAR ENDED JUNE 30, 1996

CASH FLOWS FROM OPERATING ACTIVITIES:

Changes in net assets	$ 1,749,880
Adjustments to reconcile change in net assets to net cash provided by operating activities:	
Depreciation	310,632
Contributions restricted for long-term investments	(285,104)
Interest and dividends restricted for long-term investments	(18,180)
Net gains on long-term investments	(531,310)
Changes in assets and liabilities:	
Receivables	(513,248)
Prepaid and deferred expenses	(181,836)
Accounts payable and accrued expenses	48,236
Deferred ticket sales	1,012,546
Net cash provided by operating activities	1,591,616

CASH FLOWS USED IN INVESTING ACTIVITIES:

Purchases of property	(398,986)
Purchases of investments	(4,462,800)
Sale of investments	2,890,310
Net cash used in investing activities	(1,971,476)

CASH FLOWS USED IN FINANCING ACTIVITIES:

Proceeds from contributions restricted for:	
Investment in endowment	276,464
Investment in pooled income fund	9,130
Other financing activities:	
Gains restricted for reinvestment	459,976
Endowment gains reinvested	84,144
Net cash used in financing activities	829,714

NET INCREASE IN CASH	449,854
CASH AT BEGINNING OF YEAR	401,838
CASH AT END OF YEAR	$ 851,692

See notes to financial statements.

SAMPLE PERFORMING ARTS ORGANIZATION

NOTES TO FINANCIAL STATEMENTS
YEAR ENDED JUNE 30, 1996

1. **SUMMARY OF SIGNIFICANT ACCOUNTING POLICIES**

Description of Business - The Sample Performing Arts Association (the "Association") currently produces and presents fifteen performances of three Operas in their mainstage international season at The City Center in downtown City. The Association also produces recitals, concerts and musical presentations including a wide variety of educational and community outreach programs. The Association's live audience was in excess of 276,000 for the year ended June 30, 1996. The Association is the successor corporation of a July 1, 1974 merger between City Opera Inc. and The City Opera Guild and is exempt under Section 501(c)(3) of the Internal Revenue Code and Section 23701d of the State Franchise Tax Board Revenue and Taxation Code.

General - The financial statements of the Sample Performing Arts Association (the "Association") have been prepared on the accrual basis. The significant accounting policies followed are described below to enhance the usefulness of the financial statements to the reader.

Financial Statement Presentation - For presentation of financial statements, net assets and revenue, gains, expenses and losses are classified as unrestricted, temporarily restricted and permanently restricted based upon the following criteria:

- Unrestricted net assets represent expendable funds available for operations which are not otherwise limited by donor restrictions.

- Temporarily restricted net assets consist of contributed funds subject to specific donor-imposed restrictions contingent upon specific performance of a future event or a specific passage of time before the Association may spend the funds.

- Permanently restricted net assets are subject to irrevocable donor restrictions requiring that the assets be maintained in perpetuity usually for the purpose of generating investment income to fund current operations. Included in permanently restricted net assets are funds transferred by the Board to permanently restricted endowment trust assets from which the corpus may never be withdrawn.

Contributions - Contributions received as well as collectible unconditional promises to give are recognized in the period received. Contributions with donor-imposed restrictions are reported as temporarily or permanently restricted revenues. Temporarily restricted net assets are reclassified to unrestricted net assets when the donor restrictions are satisfied.

Investments - The Association reports certain investments at fair value.

Revenue and Expense Recognition - Costs (constructed sets and properties, production and advertising) applicable to operas to be presented in subsequent fiscal years are deferred and subsequently expensed in the fiscal year in which the production occurs. Although sets and properties may be used again by the Association in future productions or rented to others, there is no certainty that there will be any future recovery of these costs; therefore, they are expensed during the fiscal year in which they are first used. Revenues from season ticket sales and special events which are received in advance of the related opera season are deferred.

Land, Building and Equipment - Land, building and equipment are stated at cost when purchased or at fair market value when contributed. Depreciation and amortization are computed by the straight-line method over estimated useful lives of 3 - 8 years, except buildings which use 30 years.

Functional Allocation of Expenses - The costs of providing the various programs and other activities have been summarized on a functional basis in the statement of activities. Accordingly, certain costs have been allocated among the programs and supporting services benefited.

Accounting Estimates - The preparation of financial statements in conformity with generally accepted accounting principles requires management to make estimates and assumptions that affect the reported amounts of assets and liabilities and disclosure of contingent assets and liabilities at the date of the financial statements and the reported amounts of revenues and expenses during the reporting period. Actual results may differ from those estimates.

2.   **LAND, BUILDING AND EQUIPMENT**

Land, building and equipment at June 30 consists of:

	1996
Land	$ 156,050
Building and improvements	923,074
Production equipment	1,016,552
Office equipment and computers	933,616
Motor vehicles	343,144
	3,372,436
Less accumulated depreciation	2,192,940
Total	$1,179,496

3. **INVESTMENTS**

Investments are presented at fair value based on market quotes; those with maturities greater than one year are classified as long-term. Investments are comprised of the following:

Short-Term	1996
Money Market Funds	$ 3,687,888
Certificate of Deposits	822,620
Treasury Notes	889,612
Corporate Bonds	
Total	$ 5,400,120

Long-Term	
Certificate of Deposit	$ 210,000
Treasury Notes	1,142,432
Israel Bond	100,000
Total	$ 1,452,432

4. **ENDOWMENT ASSETS**

Sample Performing Arts Association Endowment Trust (Scripps Bank) - On June 21, 1990, the Association established the "City Opera Endowment Fund", an irrevocable charitable endowment trust to receive and invest funds for the benefit of the Association. The investments are administered and held by Bank (the trustee) as directed by a fund director as pursuant to the trust document. All income from the trust is unrestricted, however, all income has been reinvested in the trust since it's inception. On November 1, 1995, the Association's Board of Directors approved the transfer of $100,000 of unrestricted funds into this endowment. This transfer is listed as permanently restricted because it is an irrevocable gift to a permanent endowment.

City Community Foundation (City Opera Trust) - On April 18, 1983, the Association established a charitable endowment fund, the "City Opera Permanent Endowment Fund," with the City Community Foundation ("SACF"), a not-for-profit California corporation. By contract, the Association receives at least the current income less related expenses; currently SACF is distributing an average of 4% from the total return of the fund. The Association received distributions of $126,142 in 1996.

The following table reflects the endowment assets at fair value:

	Endowment	Endowment	Endowment Assets
Balance on June 30, 1995	$ 2,821,650	$ 1,183,290	$4,004,940
Additions to fund	2,000	363,488	365,488
Increase in fair value	292,236	167,740	459,976
Balance on June 30, 1996	$ 3,115,886	$ 1,714,518	$4,830,404

5. POOLED INCOME FUND

Sample Performing Arts Association's Pooled Income Fund was established in May 1992 and is administered by Amalgamated Bank as the Trustee. Assets donated to the trust by a donor provide income to the donor for the remainder of the donor's life and upon the death of the donor, the asset is transferred to the Association subject to donor restrictions. The amounts recorded reflect the fair value of the trust asset net of the present value of the estimated future payments based upon the donor's life expectancy.

6. PENSION PLANS

The Association sponsors a 403(b) pension plan covering substantially all of its non-union employees. Under the 403(b) plan, employees may contribute from 3% to 10% of eligible compensation. The total employee contribution may not exceed $10,000. The Association will match the first 3% of eligible compensation contributed by the employee. The Association also pays all administrative costs of this plan. Matching contributions under this plan totaled $42,500 in 1996.

The Association also participates in three pension plans administered subject to collectively bargained agreements. Amounts charged to pension cost and contributed to these plans totalled $457,168 in 1996.

7. COMMITMENTS

On December 1, 1992, the Association moved its principal offices and entered into a three-year sublease agreement with the employer of a member of the Board of Directors. The current amendment to the sublease calls for annual payments of $109,632 and terminates on June 30, 1997. Office rent expense for the year ended June 30, 1996 was $107,852.

The Association has entered into various contracts for services with employees and independent contractors for future productions and services.

At June 30, 1996 the annual requirements to fulfill these commitments and leases are as follows:

1997	$3,115,340
1998	1,753,508
1999	571,008
2000	1,668
	$5,441,524

8. **GOVERNMENT GRANTS**

During the year ended June 30, 1996 the following grants were received from domestic governmental agencies:

	1996
City	$ 931,488
County	20,100
State Arts Council	207,512
National Endowment for the Arts	86,000
Total government grants	$ 1,245,100

Direct and indirect costs incurred by the Association and reimbursed by the above governmental agencies are subject to audit by such agencies.

On June 1, 1994, the Association was awarded a $500,000 Challenge Grant from the National Endowment for the Arts. This grant requires matching contributions totalling $1,500,000 during the grant term of June 1, 1994 to September 30, 1997. The purpose of this grant is to establish a $2,000,000 cash reserve fund. Included in the temporarily restricted net assets is $166,800 received under this grant.

9. **RESTRICTED NET ASSETS**

The Association's temporarily restricted net assets are available for the following purposes and generally available subject to the passage of time:

	1996
International Season	$ 1,620,098
Special events	600,000
Education Programs	146,704
Operations	175,756
Total temporarily restricted	$2,542,558

The Association's permanently restricted net assets are restricted to investment in perpetuity, although the income from these permanently restricted assets is available to support the operations of the Association.

* * * * * *

SAMPLE VOLUNTARY HEALTH AND WELFARE ORGANIZATION

Financial Statements
for the Year Ended
June 30, 1996
and Independent Auditors' Report

INDEPENDENT AUDITORS' REPORT

Board of Trustees
Sample Voluntary Health and Welfare Organization

We have audited the accompanying statement of financial position of Sample Voluntary Health and Welfare Organization as of June 30, 1996, and the related statements of activities, functional expenses, and cash flows for the year then ended. These financial statements are the responsibility of Sample Voluntary Health and Welfare Organization's management. Our responsibility is to express an opinion on these financial statements based on our audit.

We conducted our audit in accordance with generally accepted auditing standards. Those standards require that we plan and perform the audit to obtain reasonable assurance about whether the financial statements are free of material misstatement. An audit includes examining, on a test basis, evidence supporting the amounts and disclosures in the financial statements. An audit also includes assessing the accounting principles used and significant estimates made by management, as well as evaluating the overall financial statement presentation. We believe that our audit provides a reasonable basis for our opinion.

In our opinion, the financial statements referred to above present fairly, in all material respects, the financial position of Sample Voluntary Health and Welfare Organization at June 30, 1996, and the changes in its net assets and cash flows for the year then ended in conformity with generally accepted accounting principles.

September 5, 1996

SAMPLE VOLUNTARY HEALTH AND WELFARE ORGANIZATION

STATEMENT OF FINANCIAL POSITION
JUNE 30, 1996

ASSETS

Cash and cash equivalents	$	2,320,866
Investments (Note 2)		8,622,756
Accounts receivable, less allowance for doubtful accounts of $300,400		4,845,276
Accounts receivable from affiliated organizations (Note 6)		1,437,212
Pledges receivable, less allowance for doubtful accounts of $92,800		439,154
Property and equipment, net (Note 3)		23,955,858
Deferred compensation plan deposits		1,002,022
Other assets		57,570
TOTAL	$	42,680,714

LIABILITIES AND NET ASSETS

LIABILITIES:

Payable to Catholic Federation (Note 6)	$	142,580
Accounts payable and accrued expenses		1,337,534
Estimated payable to third-party payors (Note 4)		528,166
Deferred compensation		1,002,022
Other liabilities		85,830
Total liabilities		3,096,132

NET ASSETS:

Unrestricted		34,878,302
Temporarily restricted (Note 7)		2,722,506
Permanently restricted (Note 7)		1,983,774
Total net assets		39,584,582
TOTAL	$	42,680,714

See accompanying notes to financial statements.

SAMPLE VOLUNTARY HEALTH AND WELFARE ORGANIZATION

STATEMENT OF ACTIVITIES
YEAR ENDED JUNE 30, 1996

	Unrestricted					Temporarily Restricted	Permanently Restricted	Total
		Board Designated						
	Operating	Land, Buildings and Equipment	Capital	Non-operating	Total			
EXPENSES:								
Program services:								
Food services	$ 78,678				$ 78,678			$ 78,678
School	1,191,052				1,191,052			1,191,052
Residential treatment	1,585,730				1,585,730			1,585,730
Residential group counseling	2,296,506				2,296,506			2,296,506
Intensive group counseling	2,114,188				2,114,188			2,114,188
Intensive group short-term	1,377,244				1,377,244			1,377,244
Counseling and casework	925,900				925,900			925,900
Group therapeutic activities	651,990				651,990			651,990
Health service	558,760				558,760			558,760
Day treatment	1,229,284				1,229,284			1,229,284
Therapeutic foster care	2,005,832				2,005,832			2,005,832
Intensive in-home treatment	1,385,826				1,385,826			1,385,826
Adoptee counseling	123,870				123,870			123,870
Total program services	15,524,860				15,524,860			15,524,860
Support services:								
Administrative and general	2,393,478				2,393,478			2,393,478
Building operations	660,044				660,044			660,044
Depreciation		$ 1,834,340			1,834,340			1,834,340
Loss on sale of fixed assets		8,774			8,774			8,774
Other		1,012	$ 52,690	$ 22,398	76,100			76,100
Total support services	3,053,522	1,844,126	52,690	22,398	4,972,736			4,972,736
Total expenses	18,578,382	1,844,126	52,690	22,398	20,497,596			20,497,596
CHANGES IN NET ASSETS	(1,479,888)	(1,115,496)	271,834	161,858	(2,161,692)	$ 122,384		(2,039,308)
NET ASSETS (DEFICIT), BEGINNING OF YEAR	(1,727,820)	29,761,994	6,407,162	2,598,658	37,039,994	2,600,122	$ 1,983,774	41,623,890
TRANSFERS TO LAND, BUILDING AND EQUIPMENT FUND	(77,370)	77,370						
TRANSFERS FROM CAPITAL FUND	254,000		(254,000)					
NET ASSETS (DEFICIT), END OF YEAR	$ (3,031,078)	$ 28,723,868	$ 6,424,996	$ 2,760,516	$ 34,878,302	$ 2,722,506	$ 1,983,774	$ 39,584,582

See accompanying notes to financial statements.

(Concluded)

SAMPLE VOLUNTARY HEALTH AND WELFARE ORGANIZATION

STATEMENT OF ACTIVITIES
YEAR ENDED JUNE 30, 1996

	Unrestricted (Board Designated)					Temporarily Restricted	Permanently Restricted	Total
	Operating	Land, Buildings and Equipment	Capital	Non-operating	Total			
SUPPORT AND REVENUE:								
Support:								
Appropriations from affiliated organizations (Note 6)	$ 985,936	$ 106,322			$ 1,092,258			$ 1,092,258
Donations and grants - individuals organizations, government, and bequests	667,358	524,582	$ 177,686	$ 200	1,369,826	$ 145,180		1,515,006
Total support	1,653,294	630,904	177,686	200	2,462,084	145,180		2,607,264
Revenue:								
Program services:								
Public agencies - local	7,497,654				7,497,654			7,497,654
Ohio public agencies - nonlocal	2,980,642				2,980,642			2,980,642
Non-Ohio public agencies and individuals	3,798,058				3,798,058			3,798,058
Individual fees - local	330,914				330,914			330,914
Education	626,822				626,822			626,822
Government food program	50,564				50,564			50,564
	15,284,654				15,284,654			15,284,654
Rental income	32,214				32,214			32,214
Investment and other interest income	27,832	97,726	146,838	155,796	428,192	105,964		534,156
Total revenue	15,344,700	97,726	146,838	155,796	15,745,060	105,964		15,851,024
NET ASSETS RELEASED FROM RESTRICTIONS:								
Satisfaction of program restrictions (Note 8)	100,950			14,130	64,380	(64,380)		
TOTAL SUPPORT AND REVENUE	17,098,944	728,630	324,524	170,126	18,271,524	186,764		18,458,288

See accompanying notes to financial statements.

(Continued)

SAMPLE VOLUNTARY HEALTH AND WELFARE ORGANIZATION

STATEMENT OF FUNCTIONAL EXPENSES
YEAR ENDED JUNE 30, 1996

	Food Services	School	Residential Treatment	Residential Group Counseling	Intensive Group Counseling	Intensive Group Short-Term	Counseling & Casework	Group Therapeutic Activities	Health Services	Day Treatment
Salaries	$ 12,480	$ 331,244	$ 1,039,154	$ 1,439,378	$ 1,318,264	$ 913,568	$ 684,304	$ 351,796	$ 324,936	$ 776,454
Employee benefits	2,186	38,620	134,764	175,544	182,052	95,558	84,224	40,014	37,712	79,574
Payroll taxes	2,164	39,118	136,960	178,124	184,754	96,936	85,978	40,536	38,262	80,866
Medical and professional fees			91,382	104,868	94,812	60,790	840		49,008	2,566
Food and supplies	47,388	12,632	4,886	180,500	136,496	96,558	34,954	52,116	92,146	167,520
Telephone	438	5,356	11,550	6,988	8,240	3,336	554	2,996	234	4,902
Occupancy	5,248	88,642	59,052	97,098	97,742	66,320	29,114	115,446	5,940	80,116
Transportation	8,524	2,528	12,638	41,244	30,662	11,058	1,250	15,944		26,130
Assistance to individuals		672,420	1,434	70,642	60,150	32,680	508	33,034	1,952	9,820
Staff development and conferences	250	402	92,914	1,990	552	440	3,674	108	7,860	924
Printing, dues, postage and subscriptions		90	996	130	464		500		710	412
TOTAL	$ 78,678	$ 1,191,052	$ 1,585,730	$ 2,296,506	$ 2,114,188	$ 1,377,244	$ 925,900	$ 651,990	$ 558,760	$ 1,229,284

See accompanying notes to financial statements.

SAMPLE VOLUNTARY HEALTH AND WELFARE ORGANIZATION

STATEMENT OF FUNCTIONAL EXPENSES
YEAR ENDED JUNE 30, 1996

	Intensive In-Home Treatment	Adoption Service	Plate Grant	Total	Administrative and General	Building Operations	Total	Combined Total
Salaries	$ 1,012,300	$	$ 83,130	$ 8,862,348	$ 973,968	$ 112,068	$ 1,086,036	$ 9,948,384
Employee benefits	106,458			1,043,360	129,940	25,748	155,688	1,199,048
Payroll taxes	103,090			1,054,416	63,392	26,212	89,604	1,144,020
Medical and professional fees	8,446		25,514	1,584,986	332,958		332,958	1,917,944
Food and supplies	21,440	108	7,168	870,250	182,504	3,758	186,262	1,056,512
Telephone	9,380		24	56,426	73,560	5,196	78,756	135,182
Occupancy	7,496			668,996	64,218	468,112	532,330	1,201,326
Transportation	86,324		2,034	293,684	24,678	15,390	40,068	333,752
Assistance to individuals	11,042		1,308	939,862				939,862
Staff development and conferences	18,328		3,612	144,546	114,448	3,496	117,944	262,490
Printing, dues, postage and subscriptions	776	32	940	5,240	149,914	64	149,978	155,218
Equipment purchases and repairs	746			746	83,898		83,898	84,644
Bad debt expense					200,000		200,000	200,000
TOTAL	$ 1,385,826	$ 140	$ 123,730	$ 15,524,860	$ 2,393,478	$ 660,044	$ 3,053,522	$ 18,578,382

See accompanying notes to financial statements.

(Concluded)

SAMPLE VOLUNTARY HEALTH AND WELFARE ORGANIZATION

STATEMENT OF CASH FLOWS
YEAR ENDED JUNE 30, 1996

OPERATING ACTIVITIES:	
Changes in net assets	$ (2,039,308)
Adjustments to reconcile changes in net assets to	
net cash provided by operating activities:	
Depreciation	1,834,340
Loss on disposal of fixed assets	8,774
Changes in operating assets and liabilities:	
Decrease in accounts receivable	888,906
Decrease in pledges receivable	1,220,010
Increase in other assets	(12,546)
Decrease in accounts payable and accrued expenses	(6,106)
Net cash provided by operating activities	1,894,070
INVESTMENT ACTIVITIES:	
Purchases of property and equipment	(498,586)
Increase in investments	(262,654)
Increase in accounts receivable from affiliated organizations	(104,032)
Proceeds from sale of automobile	14,000
Net cash used in investing activities	(851,272)
INCREASE IN CASH AND CASH EQUIVALENTS	1,042,798
CASH AND CASH EQUIVALENTS, BEGINNING OF YEAR	1,278,068
CASH AND CASH EQUIVALENTS, END OF YEAR	$ 2,320,866

See accompanying notes to financial statements.

SAMPLE VOLUNTARY HEALTH AND WELFARE ORGANIZATION

NOTES TO FINANCIAL STATEMENTS
YEAR ENDED JUNE 30, 1996

1. SUMMARY OF SIGNIFICANT ACCOUNTING POLICIES

Organization - Sample Voluntary Health and Welfare Organization provides services for adolescents with mental health problems or other behavioral disorders. These services include residential treatment, therapeutic foster care, intensive in-home services, and counseling. Sample Voluntary Health and Welfare Organization is tax-exempt under Section 501(c)(3) of the Internal Revenue Code.

Basis of Presentation - The financial statements are presented in accordance with Statement of Financial Accounting Standards No. 116, "Accounting for Contributions Received and Contributions Made" ("SFAS No. 116") and Statement of Financial Accounting Standards No. 117, "Financial Statements of Not-for-Profit Organizations." Contributions are recognized as revenue when they are received or unconditionally pledged. SFAS No. 117, which eliminates the utilization of fund accounting for financial reporting purposes, requires net assets to be classified as either 1) unrestricted, 2) temporarily restricted, or 3) permanently restricted depending on limitations placed on the net assets.

Use of Estimates - The preparation of financial statements in conformity with generally accepted accounting principles requires management to make estimates and assumptions that affect the reported amounts of assets and liabilities and disclosures of contingent assets and liabilities at the date of the financial statements and the reported amounts of revenues and expenses during the reporting period. Actual results could differ from those estimates.

Concentration of Credit Risk - Concentration of credit risk relating to accounts receivable is limited to some extent by the diversity and number of Sample Voluntary Health and Welfare Organization's clients and payors. Accounts receivable consist of amounts due from government programs including Cleveland Heights/University Heights school districts, commercial insurance companies and private pay clients. Sample Voluntary Health and Welfare Organization maintains an allowance for losses based on the expected collectibility of accounts receivable.

Cash Equivalents - Sample Voluntary Health and Welfare Organization considers all highly liquid investments with an initial maturity of three months or less to be cash equivalents.

Investments - Investments in equity securities with readily determinable fair values and all investments in debt securities are reported at fair value with gains and losses included in the statement of activities.

Property - Land, buildings and equipment are recorded at cost. Depreciation of buildings and equipment is provided on the straight-line basis over the estimated useful lives of the assets.

Donated Services - Amounts have not been reported in the statements for donated services because they did not meet the criteria for recognition under SFAS No. 116, "Accounting for Contributions Received and Contributions Made". A substantial number of volunteers have donated significant amounts of their time to Sample Voluntary Health and Welfare Organization's services.

Contributions of services shall be recognized if the services received (a) create or enhance nonfinancial assets or (b) require specialized skills, are provided by individuals possessing those skills, and would typically need to be purchased if not provided by donation.

Revenue Recognition - Contributions are recognized as revenue when they are received or unconditionally pledged.

Contributions - Contributions received are recorded as unrestricted, temporarily restricted, or permanently restricted support, depending on the existence and/or nature of any donor restrictions.

Support that is restricted by the donor is reported as an increase in unrestricted net assets if the restriction expires in the reporting period in which the support is recognized. All other donor-restricted support is reported as an increase in temporarily or permanently restricted net assets, depending on the nature of the restriction. When a restriction expires (that is, when a stipulated time restriction ends or purpose restriction is accomplished), temporarily restricted net assets are reclassified to unrestricted net assets and reported in the Statement of Activities as net assets released from restrictions.

The Organization reports gifts of land, buildings, and equipment as unrestricted support unless explicit donor stipulations specify how the donated assets must be used. Gifts of long-lived assets with explicit restrictions that specify how the assets are to be used and gifts of cash or other assets that must be used to acquire long-lived assets are reported as restricted support. Absent explicit donor stipulations about how these long-lived assets must be maintained, the Organization reports expirations of donor restrictions when the donated or acquired long-lived assets are placed in service.

Contributions receivable represent amounts committed by donors that have not been received by the Organization.

2. **INVESTMENTS**

Sample Voluntary Health and Welfare Organization invests principally in equity and fixed income securities.

The cost of investments and market values are as follows:

Description	June 30, 1996	
	Cost	Market
Unrestricted	$ 5,138,022	$ 5,900,978
Temporarily restricted	1,544,886	1,864,256
Permanently restricted	710,618	857,522
Total	$ 7,393,526	$ 8,622,756

3. PROPERTY AND EQUIPMENT

Property and equipment consist of the following:

Description	June 30, 1996
Land	$ 613,138
Building	33,434,412
Machinery and equipment	3,458,578
Automobiles	413,858
	37,919,986
Accumulated depreciation	(13,964,128)
Total	$23,955,858

4. THIRD-PARTY RATE ADJUSTMENTS AND REVENUE

Substantially all program service revenue was derived under federal, state and local third-party reimbursement programs. These revenues are based, in part, on cost reimbursement of third party payors and are subject to audit and retroactive adjustment by the respective third-party fiscal intermediaries. Retroactive adjustments are accrued on an estimated basis in the period the related services are rendered and adjusted in future periods as final settlements are determined.

5. PENSION PLAN

All eligible employees of Sample Voluntary Health and Welfare Organization, who elect to participate, are included in the Catholic Federation Employees' Retirement Plan (the "Plan") a multi-employer contributory defined benefit pension plan. Pension cost, as well as long-term disability and life insurance costs are allocated among the Federation and its agencies, including Sample Voluntary Health and Welfare Organization, and is based principally on relative salary levels of all active participants in the Plan. Sample Voluntary Health and Welfare Organization's policy is to expense and fund its share of these allocated costs annually which was $415,712 in 1996. Sample Voluntary Health and Welfare Organization's respective share of the accumulated plan benefits and net assets available for plan benefits has not been determined.

6. TRANSACTIONS WITH AFFILIATES

For the year ended June 30, 1996, Sample Voluntary Health and Welfare Organization received appropriations from CF of $985,936. At June 30, 1996 Sample Voluntary Health and Welfare Organization had a net receivable from CCB, payable on demand, of $1,323,900 and a net payable to CF of $28,548. Sample Voluntary Health and Welfare Organization recorded interest income of $110,000 related to the receivable from CB in 1996.

7.   **TEMPORARILY AND PERMANENTLY RESTRICTED NET ASSETS**

Temporarily restricted net assets are available for the following purposes:

Client activities	$ 771,480
Staff related activities	145,444
Scholarship and program support	573,960
Research related activities	1,231,622
	$ 2,722,506
Assets:	
Cash	$ 48,072
Investments	1,544,886
Receivable from operations	686,368
Receivable from affiliated organization	443,180
	$ 2,722,506

Permanently restricted net assets are restricted to:

Investment in perpetuity, the income from which is expendable to support:	
Research activities	$ 140,000
Student loan activities	50,000
Any activities of the organization	1,793,774
	$ 1,983,774
Assets:	
Cash	$ 43,926
Investments	1,939,848
	$ 1,983,774

8.   **NET ASSETS RELEASED FROM DONOR RESTRICTIONS**

Net assets were released from donor restrictions during the year ended June 30, 1996 by incurring expenses satisfying the restricted purposes or by occurrence of other events specified by donors.

Research expenses	100,000
Total restrictions released	$ 128,760

9.   **SUBSEQUENT EVENT**

The executive committee of the board approved submitting for vote by the board and general membership of Bellefaire and Catholic Children's Bureau the merger of Catholic Children's Bureau into Bellefaire, with Bellefaire as the surviving entity. This merger would occur on January 1, 1997.

* * * * * *

INDEX